D1159831

THE ORIGINS OF THE RUMANIANS

THE EARLY HISTORY OF THE RUMANIAN LANGUAGE

BY

ANDRÉ DU NAY

1996

MATTHIAS CORVINUS PUBLISHING
Toronto-Buffalo

Acknowledgements

An earlier version of this book appeared in 1977 as

Edward Sapir Monograph No. 3,

published by Jupiter Press, Lake Bluff, IL,

(ISBN 0-933-104-03-0, Library of Congress No. 79-115770)

Special thanks to Professors Adam Makkai and Valerie Becker Makkai

of Jupiter Press for permission to reprint portions of the erlier version.

ISBN 1-882785-08-8

Library of Congress No. 96-76316

Printed in the United States of America

To the memory of my Grandfather

CONTENTS

Chapter I: HISTORY

Chapter II: FROM LATIN TO RUMANIAN

Chapter III: THE THEORY OF THE DEVELOPMENT OF RUMANIAN NORTH OF THE DANUBE

Chapter IV: A CRITICAL ANALYSIS OF THE THEORY OF CONTINUITY

Chapter V: CONCLUSONS

Chapter VI: THE POPULATIONS NORTH OF THE LOWER DANUBE IN THE 4th TO THE 13th CENTURIES

LIST OF MAPS

Chapter I

Chapter II

Chapter III

Chapter IV

Chapter VI

LIST OF TABLES

Chapter I

Chapter II

Chapter III

LIST OF FIGURES

Chapter II

Chapter IV

Notes:

Quotations from Rumanian, Italian, and Hungarian texts are given in English translation. Quotations in German and French appear in the original language. The English translations of these are found on pp. 299–307. All translations were made by the present author.

The full title of each reference is given when first mentioned. Subsequently, abbreviations are used. The key to these is given in the Bibliography.

FOREWORD

to *The Early History of the Rumanian Language,* 1977

Is Rumanian an indigenous development out of the Latin of the Roman colonists in the area of Dacia to the north of the Danube, and has it been spoken in the territory of present day Rumania ever since the times of the Roman Empire? – or is it a more recent importation from elsewhere, presumably south or west of the Danube? There has been a long debate over this point, not unrelated to nationalist territorial claims. The "official" view is that the former of these two hypotheses is valid, despite absence of concrete evidence to support it. The later hypothesis has been, in general, rejected.

The merit of the present book is that it marshals and presents the evidence on behalf of the second, or "non-Dacian" hypothesis. In the absence of detailed historical records for the post-Imperial period in the non-Byzantine regions of the Balkans, we must rely on the indirect evidence furnished by linguistic and other cultural relaitonships. Dr. Du Nay has sifted and weighed the relevant material with thorough and objective scholarship, making it evident that the "non-Dacian" hypothesis must be taken seriously and reckoned with.

We shall of course never know what actually happened in those centuries when Proto-Rumanian was being formed; nor exactly where it took shape, unless by some chance we come into possession of more detailed historical accounts than are at present known. In the meanwhile, it is good to have Dr. Du Nay´s reasoned presentation of the "non-Dacian" side of the argument, to set over against the dominant official view.

Ithaca, N.Y., March, 1977.

ROBERT A. HALL, Jr.
Professor Emeritus of Linguistics
and Italian; Cornell University

PREFACE

by **Adam Makkai,** Professor of Linguistics, University of Illinois at Chicago:

A Note on the Importance of Phonemic Change and Etymology: Language as an Eco-System

I feel honored to have been asked by André Du Nay to write a brief Preface to the new edition of his book *The Origins of the Rumanians – The Early History of the Rumanian language.*

The point I will try to make in this preface is one which is becoming more and more recognized in Linguistics both in Europe and in the USA – the fact that the planet´s natural languages are living eco-systems. What this means is that there are no isolated or random events in the history of a language and that, therefore, everything that happens in the course of a language´s development **organically interdepends with every other part.** Thus, phonemic change affects the morphology; the loss of morphological endings, in turn, affects the syntax and the semantics of a language. **That this is so is a language universal** regardless to where one does one´s research.

Think of English, for example. Between the arrival of the Angles, the Saxons and the Jutes and the Norman Conquest in 1066, the British Isles developed a number of versions of Anglo-Saxon, or Old English. Whatever the differences between these OE dialects were, they were all Germanic, even if one adds the Scandinavian loan words that were added by the several Viking raids on Britain. But in 1066 all of this changed – the conquering Normans brought Old French with them and since they were the dominant nobility, an overwhelming amount of French vocabulary entered the English language changing its character forever.

The Middle English Period lasted for a relatively short time – from the Norman Conquest till the beginning of the 16th century; a mere three hundred years. This was also the period that saw the "Great Vowel Shift" take place between 1400 and 1500, one of the most mysterious and least understood events in the history of a major Indo-European language. The greatest poetic genius of this Middle English period was, of course, Geoffrey Chaucer.

It is interesting to compare the original Old English *Beowulf* with the *Canterbury Tales* by Chaucer, and say, Shakespears´s *Hamlet.* With the latter we are in the New English period. Although some of Shakespeare´s words are no longer in use, almost everyone who speaks fluent English can enjoy a performance of *Hamlet* and follow the language.

Nobody is seriously questioning in Linguistics today whether English is a Germanic or a Romance language. The answer is obvious to all: English is, basically, a Germanic language with a heavy overlay of Romance vocabulary. Yet if some extraterrestrial visitors were to scan the printed output of the English speaking world with some megacomputer for a month and send a report to their mother ship, they would probably come to the conclusion that English is one of the Romance languages. How wrong would such a report be? Not very – on the surface, at least. Words such as *international, situation, atomic, bomb, revolution, abandon, masses, report* – the kind of ´intellectual language´ newspapers and magazines are full of – is not of Anglo-Saxon provenance. Our extraterrestrials simply would have made the mistake of going by the printed media only and not listening to the conversations of families at home, where they would have heard words such as *brother, mother, father, sister, son, daughter, foot, arm, hand, fire, water,* etc.

Someone exposed to this kind of home-spun, basic English only, could understandably miss the Romance elements in English and say "English is a purely Germanic language."

Obviously the truth is that English is **both** Germanic and Romance with a very large number of additional loan vocabulary from Greek, Italian, Spanish, Swedish, Norwegian, Arabic, Hebrew, Chinese and Japanese – to mention just the few most obvious sources.

Yet English is the world language. Esperanto will never overtake it. Now that the computer rules mass communications and ´virtual reality´ and ´cyberspace´ have become household words, the English language has once again gained an advantage over all other tongues on earth. We can all wonder, of course, whether this is good or bad for mankind and opinions will differ widely.

The United States is a complex culture of immigrants – including the 10 American Indian Phyla with the many languages therein that are no longer mutually intelligible, since they span from the Arctic to Tierra del Fuego and cover anywhere between 10.000 and 35.000 years of linguistic separation. Yet the Indian presence is tangibly there in state names (*Delaware, Illinois, Iowa, Massachusetts, Oklahoma, Wisconsin*) and in city names (*Chicago, Wichita, Kansas,* etc.). Our Black population speaks Black English and creates enchanting music and poetry in this particular version of English. Our public and private schools and universities cater to our Hispanic population in a wide variety of programs known as ´bilingual education´.

It is well known that almost every place-name in America is either of English, French, Spanish, Italian, or Amerindian origin – with a few of the minor languages of the world also having contributed interesting data for toponymic research. *Ypsilanti,* Michigan is, for instance, named after the Greek word *upsilon,* the ancestor of the Latin letter [y], and the city of *Philadelphia,* where the Declarararation of Independence was read on July 4, 1776, means ´City of Brotherly Love´ also from the Greek.

If, therefore, some natural catastrophe were to wipe out the population of the United States but somehow the place-names survived in a library some place else, scholars in that imaginary, distant future would be able to reconstruct with a fair amount of precision the **settlement history of America.**

It would emerge with reasonable clarity that the states and cities that begin with the word *new* and are followed by an English toponym (*New York, New Hampshire, New England* [as an entire region]) indicate English settlements. The old name of *New York* was, of course, *New Amsterdam,* and in that we see the name of a Dutch city being introduced by an English prefix. The place, then, was a Dutch colony which was later taken over by the English. (Originally it belonged to the Indians, of course.)

The English word *new* also occurs before French and Spanish place-names – consider *New Orleans* and *New Mexico.*

Straightforward French place-names on the North American Continent are so many that entire volumes have been written about them. I will just mention some of the best known examples. The city of *Des Moines,* Iowa, pronounced /diy móyn/, derives from the French *des moines,* [de: moan] ´those monks´. It was obviously the place of a French monastery where people went to pray and to do business much as the German city of *München* which derives from German *zu den Mönchen* ´to the monks´. A place of pilgrimage or of Sunday market is one that draws travellers. The same happened in Byzantium. The Greeks said ´we are going to that city´ *eis tan polín*, and this phrase, spoken rapidly, contracted to today´s ´Turkish´ city name *Istanbul.*

Etymology is truly fascinating and can reveal many popular misconceptions. Here is a famous example, again from the USA. The State of *Connecticut,* according to mistaken folk belief, derives from English and indicates that this state is a ´connecting cut´ between Massachusetts and New York. Nothing could be farther from the truth. *Connecticut* is an Indian word, *kwinnahtahqut,* and means ´the fast river´. But let us return to more French examples:

The city of *Detroit,* MI. pronounced /ditróyt/ derives from the French for ´straights´, ´narrow sea or fresh water passage´, *D´étroites*. One look at the map of the Great Lakes, and one can see why the French named it that. In the State of Wisconsin, a famous town is called Fondulac, pronounced /fá:ndžulaek/. It is also a French toponym, *fond du lac* [fõ dü lak], meaning ´bottom of the lake´.

Many people mistakenly believe that *Chicago* and *Michigan* are also French – the reason for this belief is the pronunciation of *ch* as /š/, obviously a French habit. It turns out that both words are of Algonquian Indian origin. It was simply that the Indian words were first heard and recorded by French explorers who applied French orthography to the Indian words. *Chicago* means ´wild onion leaves´ or ´skunk weed´, and the morpheme spelled *[-chi-]* is the same in both *Chi*cago and Mi*chi*gan, referring to the sharp smell. Out of the five Great Lakes only *Lake Superior* has an English name (curiously following the French word order from an earlier *Lac Supérieur,*) the rest, *Erie, Ontario, Huron* and *Michigan* are all of Amerindian origin.

The Spanish language has contributed a tremendous number of Hispanic toponyms to the USA. Consider *Colorado, Florida, San Francisco, San Antonio, Las Vegas, Palos Verdes, San Juan Capistrano* – the list is a huge one. ´The colorful one´, the ´flowery one´, Saint Francis, Saint Anthony, ´The brushes´, 'green branches/sticks', 'Saint John of Capistrano' – these would be the awkward English translations of these Spanish place-names.

Russian has left a mark on North America as well. In Alaska the place-names were left in the original – *Sitka,* Alaska, was settled by Russians. But the capital of the State of Idaho is *Moscow,* not *Moskva* or *Muscovy;* i.e., the original Russian city's name shows up in its anglicized version.

It should be reasonably clear from the foregoing that a scientific and objective study of the toponyms of the USA casts light on the immigration and settlement patterns of this huge continent.

As I said above, a language can be seen as a gigantic and complex ecosystem where the fate of phonology affects the morphology which, in turn, affects the syntax and the semantics. Let me illustrate from the history of English once more.

In Old English the paradigm for the noun *dog* went as follows:

SINGULAR		PLURAL	
Nominative	*hund*	Nominative	*hundas*
Accusative	*hund*	Accusative	*hundas*
Genitive	*hundes*	Genitive	*hunda*
Dative	*hunde*	Dative	*hundum*

It is interesting to compare this paradigm to modern German, where one gets *Hund, Hund, Hundes, Hunde* in the singular paralleling the OE exactly; the plural has been levelled out as *die Hunde.* OE *hund* got respelled under French influence as *hound,* since [ou] stood for /u/, whereas [u] would have stood for /ü/. The word, together with most monosyllables containing stressed /u/ has diphthongized into [au] – thus today we have *hound,* /hawnd/, 'a kind of dog' ('greyhound', 'bloodhound'). The phenomenon is commonly known as **semantic narrowing**. The paradigm itself shrank and almost disappeared. The stress having settled down on the first syllable of English words, the second syllable vowels became a murmured "schwa" sound, and eventually dropped. The genitive singular survives as *hound's* as in *the hound's leash broke;* the nominative and the accusative plural, which already coincided in OE, survive as *hounds,* as in *the police used the bloodhounds to track the criminal,* (accusative usage), and *the hounds are howling* (nominative usage). All the other cases have disappeared. This, in turn, has caused English to change its typological character from an inflectional into an isolating language. Whereas in OE one could still distinguish the nominative and the accusative singular by the definite article *sē* and *þone*, (*sē hund waes gōd* 'the dog was good' vs. *wē wyllad cweljan þone hund* 'we wanted to kill the dog'), this is no longer the case in modern English. Thus *the hound/dog chased the man* and *the man chased the hound/dog* have identical forms for 'dog[nom]'and 'dog[acc]', and it is strictly by the word order that one can tell which occurrence of *hound/dog* is nominative (subject) and which one is accusative (direct object).

This example illustrates the immense power of phonemic change over the morphology which, then, affects the entire syntactic structure of the language.

Let us consider semantic change for a moment.

Once upon a time the word *queen* simply meant 'woman'as it still does in Swedish *kvinna.* (The word is, of course, a well attested cognate of *gyne-* as in *gynecology,* the women's name *Gwen* and *Gwendolyn.*) In the Middle Ages the word underwent 'semantic depression or pejoration' and came to mean 'tavern wench' – a girl who sells beer, or may even be a prostitute. Centuries later, *queen,* spelled with a capital letter as *Queen,* means 'ruling monarch'or 'ruling monarch's wife.' It has, therefore, obviously undergone 'semantic amelioration'or 'upward shift'.

What this example illustrates is that in the world's most influential language, English, in which 90% of all the world scholarly and scientific research is being carried out, has an extremely complex, **ecological history,** in which everything interdepends with everything else.

The orthographic or spelling history of a language is equally important.

Once upon a time the Germanic languages were written in **runes.** Runic script gave way to Latinization which shows the advent of Christianity, Western style. Older styles of English writing that resemble older German, still use the Gothic script, which is a Germanicized variety of Latin.

Russian writing, known today as 'Cyrillic' after the Byzantine monks Cyrill and Method, has also undergone many phases of development from 'Glagolitic' to the Old Church Slavic through Old Russian and Bulgarian to modern Russian. Several countries neighboring the Slavs where Orthodox Christianity was practiced, started to write in Cyrillic and only changed to Romanized script later. Rumanian is a case in point.

All natural human languages are living eco-systems.

"Etymologies are fossil poetry," as already Ralph Waldo Emerson observed in *The Poet*. What does this mean? All languages are full of idioms. Consider the saying *fly off the handle* 'become angry' and *kick the bucket* 'die'. *The first of these* comes from falconry – the medieval habit of hunting with a falcon. When the falcon, sitting on T-shaped piece of wood, sees the rabbit, it becomes excited and literally 'flies off the handle', i.e., becomes airborne. Hence when someone becomes overly excited or angry, he is comparable to a hunting falcon that just saw a rabbit.

People still argue where the frequent idiom *kick the bucket* comes from. Some think it derived from Western style hanging (criminal stands on a bucket with the rope around his neck attached to a tree's branch; the sheriff comes and kicks the bucket out from under him; he becomes hanged or 'rope borne'. Others believe it comes from 16th century English farms where pigs were tied to beams, called *bucqet* (from French), and when the farmer slit their throats, their feet, that were tied to these beams, ´kicked´ in protest. Whatever the actual origin, the saying survives and conjures up live cultural images.

In a functional eco-system – and natural languages are just such eco-systems – everything has a role. In Africa the tiniest insect counts as much as a large elephant. In an area covered by a language, phonetic change may seem like a small thing, yet it is of considerable importance – it may reveal the actual origin of a word. The same goes for etymologies.

This insight has important implications for World History.

It is common knowledge that whereas North America is geologically the oldest continent with the "newest humanity" inhabiting its soil, Europe, on the other hand, is laid out the other way around: It is the youngest continent geologically, with the "oldest humanity" inhabiting it. One would think that the older the humanity, the better known its history would be but, unfortunately, it doesn´t quite work that way. Whereas the history of Canada and the USA is reasonably well documented, in Europe, and especially in the Southeastern part of the Continent, history can be extremely complex and shrouded in the mystery of unrecorded migration patterns. In such cases the **history of the language** – replete with phonemic change, etymologies and toponyms – is almost the only tool that scholarship can use in an attempt at reconstructing the lost portions of history. This is one of the major contributions of the present volume: It fills a number of historic gaps through objective linguistic means.

INTRODUCTION

Ethnic Continuity in the Carpatho-Danubian Area, written by Elemér Illyés, in which the problem of the origins of the Rumanians is discussed, was published in 1988.[1] This did not, however, make the present book unnecessary, because the two works complement each other. The latter is a thoroughly revised version of *The Early History of the Rumanian Language,*[2] published more than 18 years ago. The organization of the text has been improved, the vast and complicated material more clearly arranged, and relevant new material added. Of course, every effort has also been made to correct a number of errors, many of which were also pointed out by critics. The new title expresses the topic: although the evolution of the language is in the centre of discussion, it is placed into a context of written records and archaeological material. The result is that obscure periods in the history of the only Romance language to survive in Southeastern Europe, Rumanian, can be explained, and basic circumstances regarding the origins and the early history of the speakers of this language are described.

There are two main reasons why historical research has not yet arrived at a general consensus about these problems : (1) methodological and (2) political.

1. The methodological difficulties.

The history of the Romance languages, such as Portuguese, Spanish, Catalan, French, Provençal, Italian, is remarkably well documented. The first written Romance texts are quite early: there are short texts on maps from the 8th century and the *Glosas de Silos* from the beginning of the eleventh century in Spanish, the *Cancioneiro* of Alphonse le Saga from the end of the 13th century in Portuguese, the *Serments de Strasbourg* from 842 AD in French, two short formulas in Latin maps from 960 and 964 in Italian. The oldest Rhaeto-Romance text is from the beginning of the 12th century. The study of the Romance languages, with the possibility of comparing different stages of development with each other and of relating existing forms to their Latin counterparts has contributed considerably to the solution of many general linguistic prolems, especially in the field of language change. The territories in which these languages developed are well known; in general, they continue the speech of the original Latin-speaking population of the respective areas.

In contrast, no records are known concerning the early history of Rumanian, a Romance language, spoken by about 22 million people in south-eastern Europe, predominantly north of the lower Danube. In that area, a Roman province, Dacia

[1] Illyés, E., *Ethnic Continuity in the Carpatho–Danubian Area*, Boulder, East European Monographs, No. CCXLIX, Columbia University Press, New York, 1988; second, revised edition: Hunyadi Öcs. Mk., Hamilton, ON., Canada, Struktura Press, 1992.

[2] Published by Jupiter Press, Lake Bluff, Illinois, USA, Edward Sapir Monograph Series in Language, Culture, and Cognition, No. 3, 1977.

Traiana, existed between 106 and 275 AD. The extent to which this province became Romanized is not clear, and there is no historical mention of any Roman population there after the province was abandoned by the Roman Empire. It was about 800 years later, in the second half of the 11th century that Vlachs (Rumanians) were reported north of the lower Danube. Towards the mid-thirteenth century, Vlach political organizations (small principalities) appeared in present day Muntenia. The first known written Rumanian text is a letter written in 1521 to the judge of Brassó (Kronstadt, Braşov), Hans Benkner.

Dacia Traiana was a part – less than 40% – of the territory in which Northern Rumanian ("Daco-Roman") is spoken today; it was one of the most distant provinces of the Roman Empire over which Roman domination lasted at most 169 years. In spite of this, the hypothesis that Latin continued to be spoken in Dacia Traiana after 275 AD and that it developed into present day Rumanian **there** was presented long ago: In the mid-fifteenth century, Italian humanists travelling in eastern Europe discovered a people whose language contained many Latin words also existing in Italian. Knowing that the Roman Empire once dominated Dacia Traiana, these humanists assumed that the Vlachs were the descendants of the Romans, who once subdued the Dacians.

Particularly during the last four decades, Rumanian archaeologists and historians have made great efforts to find remains in present day Rumania of a Roman population between the end of the 3rd and the end of the 11th centuries. Reports of such a population were based on material remains of Roman style. However, some Rumanian scholars (A. Philippide, I. Iordan, I.I. Russu) expressed the opinion that the material finds from earlier periods are not sufficiently specific for such conclusions. This is because of the powerful influence of Roman culture and civilization on the material culture of all European peoples outside the Roman Empire. Thus, there is no historical or archaeological evidence of the ancestors of the Rumanians in the territory of present day Rumania before the 11th century. One may claim that this is not decisive, the "Daco-Romans" were humble people, not important for the chroniclers. However, the question is inevitable: **if** the Rumanians are not the descendants of Traian´s Romans, where did they come from?

Large territories in the Balkan peninsula were Roman provinces for six centuries and were strongly Romanized. Records and finds such as ruins of churches show that Christianity was propagated in that part of the Roman Empire as early as the 3rd century. There are numerous descriptions of incursions of Goths, Huns, Avars, Slavs, and other "barbarian" peoples in the Balkan provinces. Many Roman towns were destroyed, and their inhabitants killed or forced to leave their homes. However, records end in the 6th century; by the mid-seventh century, almost the entire peninsula was taken over by the Slavs. Roman and Byzantine chroniclers no longer had access to these territories, and there are no records of the destinies of the Roman population in these times. It is probable that most of the remaining Romans were in a short time assimilated to the Slavs. From the 8th century, there is a mention of a Romance population (Vlachs) living in the valley of the Rhinos, and towards the end of the 10th century, beginning with 976 AD, Vlachs are repeatedly recorded in different places of the Balkan peninsula.

While the surrounding populations designated them by the equivalents of the name Vlach, they called themselves *rumîn*, Arumanian *ar(u)mân, arrămănu,* which is an inherited Latin word (from Latin *romanus*). In English, it corresponds to *Rumanian,* in French, to *roumain,* in German, to *rumänisch,* and in Serbo-Croatian, to *rymyn.* The etymological form, *rumîn*, is still used today; it appears in the texts of Coresi (16th century), as well as in the *Palia de la Orăștie* (1581–1582), in which also the form *român* appears for the first time. This is not a popular form, but one constructed for the purpose of making it more like Latin *romanus.*[1] Since the mid-nineteenth century, the Rumanian literary language has used this form exclusively.

Where did this population live before it was mentioned in the chronicles? What were their socio-economic and ethnic characteristics? Were they the descendants of Roman colonists or of an indigenous population which became Romanized during those six centuries of Roman rule in the Balkan peninsula? In the latter case, were their ancestors Thracians, Illyrians, Dacians or other? Who were their neighbours? When was their contact with the speakers of Italian and other Romance languages severed?

There are no written records to answer these questions.

This means that it is not possible to detect anything about the early history of the Rumanians using the historical method: analyses and comparisons of different texts, – not even by the study of the material remains revealed by archaeology. The historian who sticks to these methods can only state: *ignoramus et ignorabimus*. As a reviewer of E. Illyés′ book argued:

> ...the only lesson to be drawn by a historian from this study is that artifacts and phonetic changes may confirm attested historical facts but will not substitute for a lack of them.[2]

However, modern historical science uses complementary disciplines: in addition to archaeology and numismatics, physics, chemistry, sociology, etc. In the case of early Rumanian history, the most important – in fact, decisive – complementary field of research is linguistics. **Language is unconsciously transmitted historical evidence** as is human remains, written business or military records, customs and institutions, etc.[3] The Rumanian language contains

---

[1] Rosetti, A., *Istoria limbii române,* București, 1986, pp. 332 and 448. Matilda Caragiu-Marioțeanu, *Compendiu de dialectologie română,* București, 1975, p. 93.

[2] Boba, I., in *American Historical Review*, Vol. 95, 1990, pp. 1580–1581.

[3] Dymond, D.P., *Archaeology and History. A plea for reconciliation.* 1974, p. 79, table after R.T. Shafer and John Vincent. Significant results in the study of the ancient history of the Hungarians were produced by the analysis of lexical elements, phonetic traits, etc. of the Hungarian language (cf. E. Moór, *A nyelvtudomány mint az ős- és néptörténet forrástudománya*, Akad. kiadó, Budapest, 1963).– As a complex, living, and continually changing system, language

elements of great significance regarding its early history. **The present book displays and summarizes this vast corpus** compiled to a large extent from Rumanian sources. These are facts, which must be explained in some way or other. Not all historians may be willing to do this, or to deal with these problems at all, allegedly because of the lack of written sources. For linguists, of course, it is easier to notice the historical significance of the facts of language (cf., for example, Herbert Izzo, 1984[1]; in Rumania, cf. the works of O.Densusianu, A. Philippide and, more recently, I.I. Russu).

The problem is: **how to inerpret linguistic facts?** I. Coteanu, in his introduction to *Istoria limbii române,* II, 1969, pp. 16-17, has stated clearly that linguistic research alone is unable to solve problems beyond the scope of linguistics and that it should only occupy itself with its own field, i.e., language. To be able to reach conclusions about historical problems, the scholar must use other methods than linguistics:

> Linguistic research must not concern itself with what is not linguistics. The conclusions concerning the language surely may be of service to other philological investigation but this extrapolation requires a method different from that used in linguistics. Because of this, the authors of the present volume aim only to describe, with methods specific to their own science, one of the aspects of the past of the Rumanian language. Under these circumstances, the determination of some socio-historical frontiers in the large territory in the east of the Roman Empire, within which the Latin language was spoken, is not possible by exclusively linguistic methods.

Many examples will be found in this book of the necessity of using known, well-established historical circumstances as a framework in the interpretation of facts revealed by linguistics. **In this way, these facts receive the status of historical evidence,** giving indications about the "socio-historical frontiers [...] within which the Latin language [which forms the basis of Rumanian] was spoken". Thus, for example, the pre-Latin substratum of the Rumanian language is to a significant part identical with Albanian: about one hundred lexical elements, of which more than half pertain to the life of shepherds living in high

---

is comparable to other complex systems, for example those of living organisms. Biologists have pointed out the parallelisms between the different stages of development of animals and of languages. Thus, for example, where other mammals have their hind legs, the whale has certain rudimentary bones. The English word *calf* is pronounced with the *l* silent. These small bones as well as the *l* in *calf* are vestiges of an earlier stage of development as shown by other mammals and German *Kalb,* in which *l* is pronounced, respectively (cf. Hesse-Doflein: *Tierbau und Tierleben*, 2nd edition, vol. I, *Der Tierkörper;* Gustav Fischer, Jena, 1935, pp. 80-81).

[1] Izzo, H., "On the history of Rumanian", in *The Twelfth Lacus Forum,* 1985, pp. 139–47; ed. M.C. Marino and L.A. Pérez, Lake Bluff, Illinois. Writing about *The Early History of the Rumanian Language*, 1977, Izzo states among other things : ..."the mass of information he [A. Du Nay] has assembled destroys the hypothesis that Rumanian descends from the Latin of Dacia Traiana."

mountains, and there also are correspondences regarding the Latin elements of these languages. This suggests that the ancestors of the Rumanians spoke the same language as those of the Albanians. One must infer that the ancient areas of the Rumanians were the same as (or close to) those of the Albanians. If it would not been known where the latter were living before the Roman occupation of the Balkans, these facts would only have relevance for linguistic research. Fortunately, the ancient areas of the early Albanians are quite well known. Similarly, the presence in Rumanian of the innovations of Late Latin indicates that the ancestors of the Rumanians lived, during the Late Latin period, in close contact with other areas where Latin was spoken (particularly with Italy). However, in order to determine the territory in which they were living, the study of the Roman domination in that period in southeastern Europe, the shifting frontiers of the Empire, etc. is also necessary. The significance of the very powerful South Slavic influence upon the Rumanian language can only be appreciated if one takes into account historical data from a large part of southeastern Europe after the fall of the Roman Empire; namely, the Slavic colonization of large areas of the Balkans starting in the 6th century, the emergence of differences between Bulgarian and Serbo-Croatian towards the end of the first millennium A.D., Bulgarian dialects being also spoken in Macedonia; the Christianization of the Bulgarians in the second half of the 9th century, etc.

2. The political circumstances.

Another obstacle in the way of arriving at a generally accepted conclusion about the origins of the Rumanian people and language is that the subject has great political significance.

This historical problem became at an early stage the subject of political consideration and struggle. The *Supplex libellus Valachorum,* written in 1791 by Rumanian intellectuals living in Transylvania to King Leopold II in Vienna, was a petition for more rights. To strengthen their demands, the authors affirmed that the Vlachs were the most ancient population in the country, since they originated from the Roman veterans who were brought to Dacia by Emperor Trajan in the 2nd century AD. The affirmation of autochthoneity was here a means in a political struggle. The theory was developed in detail by Petru Maior, one of the members of the *"Transylvanian School"* (*Şcoala ardeleană*).

During and after the First World War, the political situation in South-East Europe once again made the question of the origin of the Rumanian people a topic of political debates. This did not contribute to the objectivity of the publications on the subject. Although the problem is in reality a strictly scientific one, considerations alien to objective investigation are still prevailing in this field. This has been pointed out by Georg Stadtmüller, among others:

> Diese Kinderkrankheit der Autochthonomanie ist für die Frühzeit der modernen Geschichtsforschung in dem Vielvölkerraum des östlichen Europa durchaus charakteristisch und wirkt in mancherlei, wenn auch

abgeschwächten Formen bei der Erörterung frühgeschichtlicher Fragen auch heute noch fort.[1]

While the writings of the *Transylvanian School* may scarcely be regarded as scientific studies, later, extremely valuable work was done by many eminent Rumanian linguists, such as Alexandru Philippide (1859–1933), Ovid Densusianu (1873–1938), and Sextil Puşcariu (1877–1948), to mention only the most brilliant ones among them. Their extensive study of all dialects of the Rumanian language has thrown light upon most of the problems of the early history of this language, showing its intimate relations with several Balkan languages. Mostly on the basis of these interrelationships, Philippide concluded that the Rumanian language developed, at least until the 7th century AD in the Balkan peninsula, south of the Danube. This view was also expressed by several scholars outside Rumania, of whom we here only mention R.Rösler (*Romanische Studien. Untersuchungen zur älteren Geschichte Rumäniens,* Leipzig, 1871) and L. Tamás ("Romains, Romans et Roumains dans l'histoire de Dacie Trajane", *Études sur l'Europe Centre-Orientale* I, Budapest, 1936).

However, in spite of the above-mentioned results of exhaustive linguistic research, the theory that the Rumanian language developed (mainly) from Latin spoken in Dacia Traiana (the theory of continuity) was the official thesis of the Rumanian Communist Party. Thus, this theory has been adopted in all publications from Rumania during the last four decades; for example, in the following works: Daicoviciu, C. (red.), *Istoria Romîniei* [The History of Rumania], Bucharest, 1960; Daicoviciu, C., Petrovici, E., & Ştefan, G., *Istoria României. Compendiu,* Bucharest; 1969 (first edition), 1974 (2nd edition, red. Ş. Pascu); Condurachi, E. & Daicoviciu, C., *The Ancient Civilization of Romania,* London, 1971. Constantin Daicoviciu (1898–1973) has conducted extensive research into the period of the Dacian states, the Roman colonization north of the lower Danube, as well as the Migration Period in south-eastern Europe. His most important articles were published in one volume in 1969 *(Dacica,* Cluj). Dumitru Protase (born in 1926), published in one volume the more important archaeological material found in the territory of the former Roman province of Dacia Traiana that was known up to the mid 1960s, trying to find arguments for Daco-Roman continuity (*Problema continuităţii în Dacia în lumina arheologiei şi numismaticii* [The Problem of Continuity in Dacia in the Light of Archaeology and Numismatics], Bucharest, 1966). Also the articles published in *Dacoromania I, Jahrbuch für östilche Latinität,* edited by P. Miron, Freiburg-München, 1973, argued for the theory of continuity. (These are only some of the more important examples, because the literature pertaining to the problem of continuity, especially of archaeological material found in Rumania published during the last decades is enormous.)

This interpretation of Rumanian history did not change significantly after the

[1] Stadtmüller, G., *Forschungen zur albanischen Frühgeschichte,* 1966, p. 34.

political change in Rumania in 1989; the theory of Daco-Roman continuity is still considered axiomatic. It continues to be part of Rumanian national consciousness. Its message implies that the Rumanians are the only indigenous people in all the territory of present day Rumania. Consequently, all other populations living in the country are considered foreign intruders, without the right to live there and keep their own identity, distinct from the Rumanians.

The sensitivities of many Rumanian historians, intellectuals, – and also of the general populace – do not permit an objective discussion of the theory. A recent example will throw some light upon this: a Hungarian archaeologist said recently in an interview that the excavations started in central Cluj (Hungarian Kolozsvár, German Klausenburg) in the summer of 1994 will not yield any evidence of Daco-Roman continuity. It has been stated long ago by Rumanian archaeologists that on the site of Roman Napoca, there are no signs of life after the end of the 4th century AD until the appearance of the earliest Hungarian remains, from the 10th century. However, in a major Rumanian newspaper, an indignant article retorted with the question: "how far should our tolerance go?" [The Hungarians are now] "questioning the historical rights of Rumanians in Rumania."[1]

This is not an isolated opinion of a single journalist, but a typical example of the intellectual atmosphere today in Rumania. The Hungarian archaeologist did not question the thesis of Daco-Roman continuity, he only said that **there, in Cluj,** there are no signs of it. If this statement evokes such a fierce response, one can imagine what the reaction would be if the archaeologist would declare that there are no signs of continuity at all! The situation is thus similar to that before 1989, when continuity was the official thesis of the Communist Party and the government. Rumanian critics of *The Early History of the Rumanian language*[2] referred mainly to details or to material not taken into consideration, but without going into a real, comprehensive debate. Their conclusion was nonetheless that the text was biased and tendentious. The hope expressed by Blair A. Rudes,[3] that *"Du Nay's work will, by bringing the 'theory of discontinuity' back into discussion"* stimulate research, was not fullfilled. Glanville Price[4] stated: [Du Nay demonstrates] *"the difficulties raised by the theory of continuity whose supporters will now have to present an equally well documented and argued answer."* To the best of my knowledge, such an answer has not appeared in the

[1] "Până unde merge toleranţa?" [How far should our tolerance go?] by Adrian Bucurescu, in *România Liberă,*, (Bucharest) p. 2, September 2nd, 1994.

[2] Ligia Bârzu, "Un nou 'Anonymus'. Comentarii pe marginea lucrării lui André Du Nay, The Early History of the Rumanian Language", in *Revista de istorie,* 33, 1980, 5, pp. 953—973. Niculescu, A., "Une histoire tendancieuse de la langue roumaine", in *Rev. Roum. d'Hist.*, XIX, 2–3, pp. 555–583, Bucharest, 1980. Brezeanu, S., "Die historischen Quellen und die 'Theorien' André Du Nays."

[3] B. A. Rudes, (book review) in *Southeastern Europe/L'Europe du sud-est,* 7, Pt. 1 (1980), pp. 114–117.

[4] Glanville Price, *The Year's Work in Modern Language Studies,* Vol. 40, 1979. Published by Modern Humanities Reasearch Association, ("Rumanian Studies, 2. History of the Language", pp. 528–529).

18 years that have passed since the publication of that book.

It is absurd to claim that anyone denying or questioning this thesis, such as R. Rösler, G. Weigand, A. Philippide,[1] would do so because of political reasons. Also senseless is the accusation that Hungarians in Transylvania, who are unwilling to accept this concept, "question the historical rights of the Rumanians in Rumania". All three main nationalities now living in Transylvania have been there for many centuries, – a sufficiently long time to establish the historical right to live there also in the future.

When preparing this book, I have conducted research in an objective way, without prejudice. The problem is primarily scientific and has nothing to do with considerations outside science: it is about the development of the Rumanian language from Latin. I mention the political side of the question reluctantly, and only because I consider that the reader should be informed about a reality which impedes a free, unprejudiced discussion of the problem in the country which it concerns most, – Rumania. Even if national consciousness is often based upon some measure of myth, the enormous gap between the theory of autochthoneity in Rumania and the result of a thorough analysis is much too large. It amounts to a serious deformation of the history of the Rumanians, who should have the right to be offered as objective an account as possible about their past.

* * *

In spite of extensive polemics going on for more than a century about the problem of the origins of the Rumanians, there are facts about which there is more or less general consensus.This book starts with a survey of these: in *chapter one,* a short summary of the relevant historical circumstances is given; *chapter two* surveys the old elements of the Rumanian language: the pre-Roman vestiges, elements from Late Latin, the relationships with a number of Italian dialects and with the Balkan languages, the strong South Slavic influence, and the dialects. *Chapter six* contains a short description of the populations that lived north of the lower Danube between the end of the third and the 12th –13th centuries, based mainly on archaeological finds.

The organisation of the text is complicated (the same topic may be discussed at two or more different occasions) by the necessity of giving an objective presentation of the theory of continuity. This is done in the *third chapter.* An attempt is made to give an objective description of all the major hypotheses and arguments on which the theory is based. For this purpose, extensive use of quotations is appropriate. The arguments put forward in favour of continuity are analysed in the *fourth chapter.* Largely the same issues as in the third chapter are taken up, but now with comments and with the purpose of reaching a reasonable interpretation of the facts.The conclusions are summarized in the *fifth chapter.*

---

[1] A. Dami, K. Sandfeld-Jensen, L. Tamás, G. Schramm, D. McKay, H. Izzo, E. Illyés, G. Vékony, Á. Kosztin, etc.

Chapter I

HISTORY

A. The populations of South-East Europe before the Roman colonization

One of the most ancient populations of the Balkan peninsula are the Greeks, living in the south. Many Greek and Roman historians have occupied themselves with the peoples living north of the Greek territory before and during the Roman colonization of the Balkan peninsula, having presented considerable amounts of data about them. However, no systematic description is known and our knowledge of these peoples is therefore quite fragmentary.

In the northwest of the Balkan peninsula, approximately in the territory limited by Epiros, the Istrian peninsula, the rivers Drava and Danube and, in the east, by a line drawn between present day Belgrade and Skopje (see map 6, p. 50), a large number of different tribes were living (between 80 and 100). These were designated by the name *Illyrian* by Greek and Roman authors. This may at an early age have been the name of one tribe with which the Greeks had contact, having later been extended to all populations living in the above mentioned area. "Illyrian" is not a well-defined term, not even territorially and even less ethnically or linguistically. [1] The Illyrian language is attested with certainty to have been spoken only along the coasts of the Adriatic Sea from northwestern Greece to the Istrian peninsula.[2] No large political units existed among these tribes; they were, in fact, constantly at war with each other. They lived in villages and their main occupation was the raising of animals, especially of sheep. The cheese they produced was well known in antiquity: *caseus Dalmaticus, Docleas, Dardanicus*. A primitive agriculture contributed to their economy. Certain tribes along the coasts were fisherfolk, and the Illyrian pirates on the Adriatic Sea were

---

[1] "Der Begriff ´Illyrier´ ist von Haus aus ganz unbestimmt..." (*Real-encyklopädie der classischen Altertumswissenschaft* [Pauly, Wissova, Kroll, etc.], Stuttgart, Supplementband V, col. 312; quoted by I.I. Russu, *Illirii*, 1969, p. 27.

[2] Popović, I., *Geschichte der Serbokroatischen Sprache,* 1960, p. 68.

feared by the Greeks.

East of the Illyrian territory, from the Aegean Sea to the peaks of the Haemus mountains, lived about 100 barbarian tribes called Θρηιξ, Θραιξ, or Θραικες by the Greeks. This name was Latinized as *Thrax, Thraex,* and the above-mentioned territory became known as *Thracia.* Thracians are, however, reported to have been living also in the western parts of Asia Minor (in Bitinia, Misia, etc.) as well as north of the lower Danube and of the Black Sea. Like the Illyrians, the Thracians were also mainly shepherds, but they did pursue some agriculture. They too, were living in villages; the building of houses of stone and of towns appeared later under Greek and Roman influence.

North of the lower Danube, on what is today known as the Valachian plain, lived a population called the *Getae*. The territory within the arch of the Carpathian mountains (Transylvania) was inhabited mainly by the *Dacians.* Around 80 BC, a Dacian leader, Burebista, extended his reign after warring against the Celts and occupying the Greek towns on the northern and western coast of the Black Sea. Dacia had now common frontiers with the Roman Empire and a series of battles with the Roman army followed. The centre of the Dacian empire was in the mountainous area south of present day Orăştie (Hungarian Szászváros), at Sarmizegetusa, near present day *Grădiştea Muncelului.* Fortifications of stone built on Greek patterns, dwelling places, store rooms, workshops; vessels, pieces of pottery, tools used in agriculture, smithwork, woodwork, etc. have been unearthed there. Another strong Dacian leader, Decebal, was temporarily successful in fighting the Romans, but finally, in 106 AD, he was defeated by Emperor Trajan, and Dacia was made a Roman province. Unfortunately, very little has been preserved from the languages spoken by the groups of population designated by the names Illyrian, Thracian, Getian and Dacian (cf. below, p. 55).[1]

Besides these large groups, in parts of the Balkan peninsula there lived several other populations: Celts, Scythians, as well as the ancestors of present day Albanians and others. Of these, the Albanians are of utmost importance for the early history of the Rumanian language (see below).

B. The Roman colonization

The first intervention of the Romans in the Balkan peninsula dates back to around 230 BC. They were invited by the Greeks who needed help against

---

[1]The pertinent literature is very rich. Some of the principal works are given by I. Popović, *Geschichte der Serbokroatischen Sprache*, 1960, pp. 70 – 71 and I.I. Russu, *Illirii*, 1969 (about the Illyrians) and I. Popović, op. cit., p. 77 and I.I. Russu, *Limba traco-dacilor*, 1967, pp. 17–18 (about the Thracians). About the Dacian kingdom in English, cf. G. Vékony, *Dacians, Romans and Rumanians*, forthcoming. Of a large number of publications from Rumania, we mention here only *Istoria Romîniei*, vol. I, Bucureşti, 1960, ed. C. Daicoviciu et al., pp. 216–341.

operations, the protracted process of Roman colonization in southeastern Europe had started. The first colonies were organized on the isles and on the coasts of Dalmatia, and in 168 BC, Macedonia was conquered.

The Greek town-states, which never succeeded in uniting to resist the Romans, were successively defeated; their ultimate subjugation is marked by the dissolution of the Achaian Alliance and the destruction of its centre, Korinthos, in 146 BC.

Along the frontiers, many fierce battles were fought against different barbarian tribes. The resistance of the Illyrians and the Moesians was broken during the first century BC; by the end of this century, the Roman army reached the lower Danube. At that time, all the territory conquered was called the province of *Illyricum* but at the beginning of the first century AD it was divided into Dalmatia, Pannonia, and Moesia; Moesia was soon thereafter divided into Moesia Superior and Moesia Inferior. In 106 AD, the Dacian kingdom was defeated and part of Dacia (present day Oltenia, part of the Banat and of Transylvania) was occupied (*Dacia Traiana*). During the following 165 (or 169) years, the frontiers of the Empire reached to the north of the lower Danube, as far as to the northern part of Transylvania. After the abandonment of this province, two new provinces of Dacia were founded south of the Danube (*Dacia Ripensis* and *Dacia Mediterranea*). Emperor Diocletian (284–305) introduced a major reform in the organization of the Empire, dividing it into 4 Prefectures, 13 Dioceses and 116 provinces.

Around the camps of the Roman army divisions, *canabae* (marketplaces) were built. Giving an example of the long time span a legion may have remained in the same place, Jireček[1] mentions the Legio VII Claudia, which stayed in the area of Viminacium for about 400 years. The settlements of the veterans of this legion extended as far to the south as the region of Skopje and Prizren. The veterans received, after 20–25 years of service, ground plots, draught animals, slaves and seeds, and settled down on the land as farmers.[2]

Besides the legions, there were auxiliary contingents, composed of soldiers from many different nations living in the Empire. At the beginning of the 4th century, the organization of the army was reformed and the cavalry was strengthened. To the Roman army in this period belonged also *"foederati"*, army units formed by different barbarian peoples, led by their own chiefs.

During the first centuries of Roman rule, the Romans were more or less separated from the population they dominated. Along the coasts of Dalmatia, as well as in Thracia and in Macedonia, there were old Roman and Greek towns. In the course of time, new towns emerged through the development of the canabae.

---

[1] Jireček, G., *Geschichte der Serben,* 1911, p . 35.

[2] "Die Glanzperiode der Illyrischen Truppen war das 3. Jahrhundert. Zahlreiche Kaiser stammten aus diesem militärischen Grenzgebiete" (Jireček, 1911, p. 34). In the 3rd century, eight Roman emperors originated from Illyricum, in the 4th century, Jovianus and the Valens family, in th 5th, four emperors were from Illyricum. Justinus I and Justinian I, emperors in the 6th century, originated from Roman colonists in Dardania.

These were given municipal rights by Trajan and Hadrian at the beginning of the 2nd century AD.

The villages of the Thracians and of the Illyrians were organized in communities called *civitas*. The chiefs of these were civil clerks or soldiers, chosen from the native population as well as from the Roman colonists. These communities evolved successively from the period of Vespasian on (69–79 AD) into towns.

In 212, Caracalla made all free men Roman citizens. With this, the difference between the Roman colonists and the subjugated populations was erased.
In the northern provinces of the Balkan peninsula, Roman domination led to an economic boom. For strategic reasons, a rich network of roads was built. The large army units marching on the roads increased economic activity of all kinds. The Danube, which was the northern frontier of the Empire for several centuries, was fortified by a series of castles. A fleet of warships contributed to the defence of the frontier and to the security of the merchant navy. Along the lower Danube, from Singidunum downwards, there were six or seven legion stations. Many towns were founded on the southern shore of the river and at some distance from it towards the south: Nikopolis, Marianopolis, etc.

The most important economic activities were agriculture, the raising of animals (sheep, horses, cattle; mostly practised by the Thracians and the Illyrians), fishing and mining.

The Latin language was introduced in a comparatively short time in the coastal low-lands and in the valleys, along the Roman roads; especially in the military zone of the Danube. In the region of Naissus and Remesiana, many names of towns of military origin are preserved from this period and the Latin names also of small communities are still in use.[1] Roman veterans settled down in the lower part of the Drina-valley and in the lower Narenta region as well. The Romanization of the mountainous districts took a much longer time. Two or three centuries had to pass until most areas became Romanized : "In der Hauptsache war die sprachliche Umwälzung zu Ende des 3. Jahrhunderts abgeschlossen."[2]

In certain regions, the Illyrian population survived at least until the 4th century and the Thracian, until the 6th: *lingua bessica* (probably a Thracian dialect) was still spoken in the 6th century. Thus, Thracian was probably still spoken in the time of the Slavic colonization.

Christianity was introduced first in the southern provinces (Apostle Paul taught in Macedonia, Philippi, Thesssaloniki, and Berrhöa). It spread successively northward; there are records about persecution of Christians in the Danubian regions in the late third century. The persecution of Christians was ended by Emperor Constantine the Great in 313. There are records of rivalry between Orthodox and Arian members of the Church in Serdica, Sirmium, and Singidunum in the 4th century. "Im 5. bis 6. Jahrhundert hielten es die lateinisch

---

[1] Jireček GS 1911, p. 38.

[2] Stadtmüller, G., *Geschichte Südosteuropas*, 1950, p. 48.

redenden Provinzialen des Donaugebietes oft mit der Kirche von Rom gegen die Konstantinopler Kaiser, vor allem gegen Anastas und Justinian." Illyricum was, until 731 AD, subordinated to the Pope.[1]

Vestiges of the Christian culture in the Roman age of the Balkan peninsula are old-Christian cemeteries found at Niš and at Sofia, a funerary monument in Belgrade with sculptures showing scenes from the life of Prophet Jonas, a Latin inscription found at Remesiana which invokes the Apostles Peter and Paul in favour of a local church, as well as ruins of FORTY FIVE CHURCHES.

In the schools of the Balkan provinces, bricks were used on which the Latin alphabet and, for the higher classes, poems of Homer were carved. Although a specific literature of the Roman provincial type, as in Gaul and Africa, did not develop in the Balkan peninsula, poems written by Dalmatian and Moesian authors are known. Most of the writers in the Balkans were representatives of the Church.

In 325 AD, Constantine the Great made Byzantium the residence of the emperor. In 395, the Roman Empire was definitively divided into two halves. Moesia, Dardania, and Praevalis belonged thereafter to the Eastern Empire. The Latin language, however, maintained its influence until the early 7th century. It was used by the army (Latin commands: *cede, sta, move, transforma, torna, largiter ambula,* etc.), by the administration, the tribunals and by the Church.[2] In 397 it was ordered that all judgments of the courts be written in Latin or in Greek. At the high school of Constantinople, founded in 425, half of the professors lectured in the Latin language. It is recorded that Ioannes, the *praefectus praeterio,* tried to introduce Greek into the European parts of the Empire but his efforts were without success because the inhabitants of the Balkan provinces spoke Latin and did not understand Greek.[3] It was as late as during the reign of Emperor Heraklios (610–641) that Latin was replaced by Greek as the official language of the Eastern Empire. On the basis of a careful study of the Roman inscriptions found in the territory of the former province of Moesia Superior, the Hungarian historian A. Mócsy concluded that "...es im spätantiken Obermösien eine soziale Schicht gab die das Latein – das Spätlatein freilich – als Muttersprache sprach."[4]

During the 2nd century, the number of incursions of barbarian peoples across the Danube increased and in the subsequent centuries, the Balkan provinces were increasingly devastated. The countryside became more and more depopulated and people moved to the towns which could provide better protection from the enemy.

---

[1] Jireček GS 1911, p. 45.

[2] Cf., for example, Mihăescu, H., *Limba latină în provinciile dunărene ale imperiului roman*, Bucureşti, 1960, pp. 38; Jireček GS 1911, pp. 49.

[3] Mihăescu, 1960, p. 38.

[4] Mócsy, A., *Gesellschaft und Romanisation in der römischen Provinz Moesia Superior,* Budapest, 1970, pp. 234.

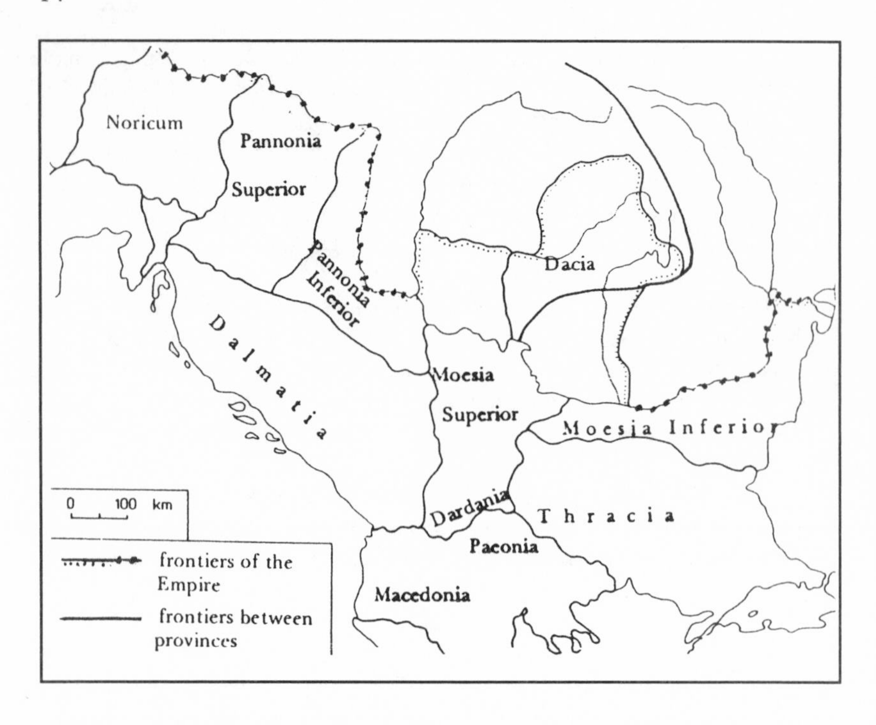

Map 1. The Roman provinces in southeastern Europe between 106–275 AD, according to general consensus (cf., for example, IR Compendiu 1974, p. 45).

In reality, the area of Roman domination north of the lower Danube was smaller. It is not quite certain that the entire area was occupied in 106 AD. The organization of *Dacia Superior* and *Inferior* in 119 and the further division of the province into *Dacia Porolissensis, Apulensis*, and *Malvensis* in 158–168 may suggest a gradual extension of the frontiers during several decades. The *limes Trans-alutanus* was built as late as about 200 AD and the area between the *limes* and the Olt was dominated by the Empire only from that year to 245 AD (cf., for example, D. Tudor, "Romanizarea Munteniei", *Apulum,* XII, 1974, p. 114). Eastern Transylvania was evacuated several years before the abandonment of the entire province in 275 AD. Only part of the Banat belonged to the Empire: the Roman military stations and civil settlements end along the border between the mountainous region and the plains (cf. Tudor, D., *Oraşe, tîrguri şi sate în Dacia română,* 1968, p. 55). On the basis of frequent finds of epigraphic material with the name *Legio IV Flavia* in the mountainous area, it is assumed that this part of the Banat was connected to Moesia Superior (Tudor Oraşe 1968, p. 55).

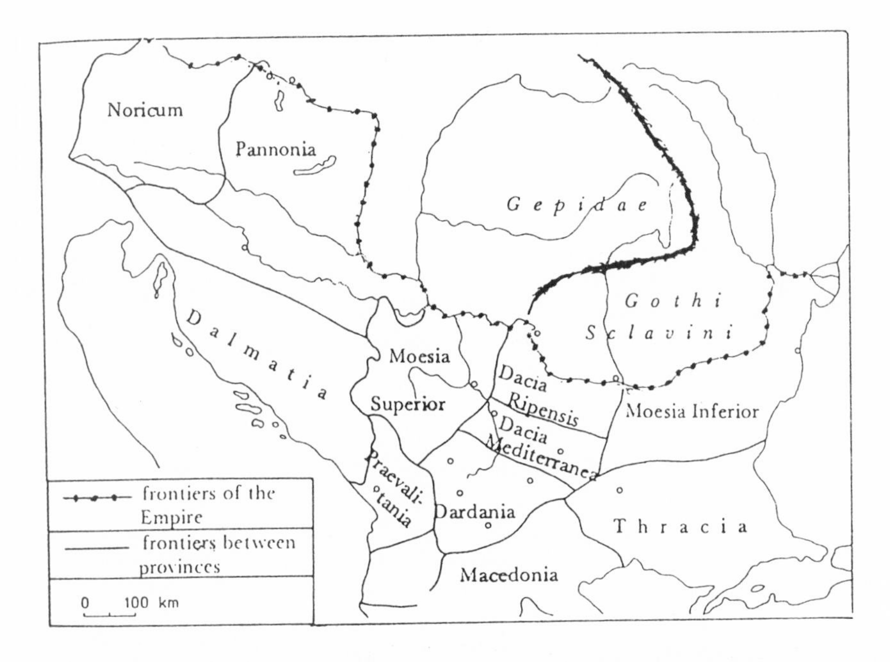

Map 2. The Roman provinces in Southeastern Europe in the 4th – 6th centuries AD. – The northeastern frontiers of the Empire were the same (the Danubian *limes*) also in the first century AD but the organization of the provinces was different. (After a map by J. Zeiler, reproduced in IR 1960.)

Province	Occupied	Abandoned AD	Roman era (years)	Number of towns	inscr.	bishops
Dalmatia	1st cent BC	c. 600	>600	24	7500	17
Noricum	"	476-493	>500	10	2000	3
Moesia Sup.	"	c. 600	>600	13	>1300	14
Moesia Inf.	"	"	"	28	>1500	15
Pannonia Sup.	1st cent AD	380-395	<400	15	3500	7
" *Inf.*	"	"	"	16	1500	4
Dacia Traiana	106 AD	271-275	165-169	11	c. 3000	0

Table 1. Some data about the Roman provinces in Southeastern Europe.

The Goths, pushed westward by the expansion of the Huns, attacked the Empire towards the end of the 4th century; in 382, they were permitted to settle down as "foederati" in the provinces south of the Danube. In 471, the East Gothic prince Theodorich conquered Singidunum (present day Belgrade). From there, the Goths conducted several incursions into the Roman provinces and also occupied Dyrrhachion; at last (in 483), Emperor Zeno settled them in Dacia Ripensis and Moesia Inferior. Some years later, Zeno succeeded in inciting Theodorich against Odovacar, the emperor of Italy. The Goths conquered Italy and founded the Eastern Gothic Empire, which comprised Italy, Dalmatia, Pannonia, and the Alp countries. This empire, in which the Goths were the dominating military class who subjugated the Roman population, was annihilated by Justinian in the middle of the 6th century.

Although of little importance because of their small number (about 3000 living in Sirmium and Singidunum around 550 AD), another Old Germanic tribe, the Herules, probably from Denmark, may be mentioned here. They were in 512 settled along the Danubian limes.

Thus, the Old Germanic populations lived only for short periods in the Balkan peninsula and did not, in contrast to what was the case in Italy, exercise any significant influence upon the ethnic situation of the areas in question:

> Die geringe "Germanreste" – Reste gotischen Volkstums, – die in einigen Berglandschaften zurückgeblieben waren, nahmen in den folgenden Menschenaltern die lateinische oder griechische Sprache an und gingen so in dem einheimischen Volkstum unter.[1]

In the middle of the 5th century, the Huns devastated about 70 towns of the Balkan peninsula, from the Danube towards the south, as far as to Serdica and Philippopolis. As a result of the frequent wars waged with the attacking barbarian peoples, as well as of the smaller skirmishes, in which the barbarians collected slaves, the population of the Balkan provinces decreased considerably during the 5th–6th centuries. To defend the empire, Emperor Justinian organized the building of fortifications. Procopius recorded about 80 fortified places along the Danube and 370 castles in other parts of the Balkans. However, as Jireček remarked:

> Alle diese Defensievbauten hatten weing Erfolg. Es fehlte an Mann- schaften zur Verteidigung. Die Grenztruppen gerieten bei finanziellen Schwierigkeiten stark in Verfall, und die Mobilarmee, nach Agathias 150.000 Mann stark, war zerstreut in Garnisonen von Südspanien bis nach Armenien und Oberägypten. Die verfallenden Stadtbevölkerungen hatten mehr Sinn für kirchliche Fragen, als für den Schutz des Vaterlandes.[2]

The line of the Danube was definitively abandoned at the end of the 6th

---

[1] Stadtmüller GS 1950, p. 21.

[2] Jireček GS 1911, p. 56.

century.

Of course, devastation and decline were not uniform in all provinces. Dacia Mediterranea and Dardania had a somewhat protected position and a Romance population was probably preserved longest in these provinces:

> Hier in diesem Raume war auch noch im Laufe der nächsten Jahr- hunderte, während welcher die Stürme der Völkerwanderung im Osten stärker wüteten, wegen der gebirgigen Lage und der mehr nach Konstantinopel zielenden Barbarenzüge noch im 6. Jh. römisches Leben möglich. Es wurde durch weitere Zuwanderung aus dem Norden und Osten *verstärkt*. Dardanien mag den grossen Kaisern Konstantin (aus Naissus – Nisch) und Justinian (aus der Gegend von Scupi – Skopje, türkisch früher Üsküb) als Heimat besonders lieb gewesen sein und so wurde letztere Stadt nich weit von der zerstörten neu aufgebaut und im Jahre 535 zum Sitze des Metropolitan-Bischofes Catellianus erhoben. Von hier ging nun die ganze vereinigte Kirchenprovinz (Dacia ripensis und mediterranea, Moesia superior, Praevalis und Macedonia secunda sowie der östliche Teil von Unterpannonien) ab.[1]

This was a very powerful Roman diocese and it possessed, through the new prefecture, also political power. Friedwagner concluded that in the above mentioned provinces, especially in Dardania, "the starting point for the development of a specific Romance language was created."[2]

C. The Albanians

G. Stadtmüller showed that the district of Mati and the region of the high mountains in northern Albania are the only areas in the western parts of the Balkan peninsula where Latin placenames are absent.[3] Stadtmüller considered this district a "*Reliktgebiet*", comparable to the mountains of Wales in Great Britain and the region of the Basque population in the Pyreneans. There, and in some adjacent areas, as Dukagjin and Merdita, as well as in the mountainous region of the Drin, lived the ancestors of the Albanians during the Roman age in the Balkans. The shepherds living in these areas during the summer used adjacent, mostly Romanized areas of lowland as grazing places during the winter season: the lowlands of western Albania, the valley of the Black Drin and some

---

[1] Friedwagner, M., "Über die Sprache un Heimat der Rumänen in ihrer Frühzeit," *Ztschr. f. romanische Philologie,* LIV, Halle, 1934, pp. 641–715.

[2] Ibid., p. 663.

[3] Stadtmüller FAF 1966, pp. 95–96.

parts of Old Serbia. In these areas, they were exposed to Romanization.[1]

The oldest elements of Greek origin in the Albanian language show the sound pattern of Old Greek, for example Albanian (Tosc) *mokërë* 'millstone', from Greek μήχανη. Greek χ corresponds in this word to Alb. *k* which shows that the word was borrowed by Albanian in an ancient period; in the Byzantine period, this sound was pronounced as a fricative. Another example of Alb. *k* (not *h*) for Greek χ is Alb. *bretëkë* 'frog', from Greek βρώταχος 'frog'.[2] This indicates that the ancestors of the Albanians lived in contact with the Greeks, in the southern parts of the Balkan peninsula.

The development of the sound pattern of certain placenames in the province of Dardania, in Old Serbia, and in western Bulgaria, seems to indicate an Albanian influence. Thus, there are in Macedonia: Oxrid, from Greek Ανχις, showing the *n* > *r* change after a velar consonant, typical of Albanian, Štip, from Greek 'Αστίβος, showing the *s* > *sh* change as well as the deletion of initial *a.* In eastern Serbia, there is Niš, from Latin Naissus, Greek Ναϊσσός, which shows *ai* > *ei* > *i* and *s* > *sh;* in western Bulgaria, Štiponje, from Greek Στοπόνιον with the *s* > *sh* change, and several others. The name of Dardania is, most probably, also of Albanian origin, connected with Alb. *dardhë* 'pear-tree'. It is not impossible that *Shqipëtar,* the name of the Albanians in their own language, derives from *Scupi,* Alb. *Shkup,* Macedonian *Skopje.*[3]

The Latin influence on Albanian started as early as in the 1st century BC, as indicated by Latin words showing the sound pattern of classical Latin. Albanian *qingëlë* < Lat. *cingula,* Alb. *vjetër* < Lat. *vetus, veteris,* etc. The Romance languages have instead forms based on Vulgar Latin, e.g., **cingla* > Rumanian *chingă,* *veteran* > Rum. *bătrân,* etc.[4]

An analysis of the Slavic loanwords in Albanian shows that the Albanian shepherds lived essentially in the same areas as shown above also in the period of their first contacts with the Slavs in the 7th century. Slavic loanwords started to be tranferred to Albanian already in that age. However, such elements became numerous only in the 11th century, when the Albanians expanded from their

---

[1] Ibid., p. 120.

[2] Popović GSKS 1960, p. 80.

[3] Popović GSKS 1960, pp. 83 - 84.

[4]The hypothesis that the Albanians were the descendants of the Carps, who were settled in the Roman Empire AT THE END OF THE 3RD CENTURY AD was put forward long ago, among others by V. Pârvan. There are river names north of the Danube: Mureş, Someş, Timiş, whose end-consonant *(ş)* was assumed to have developed in Albanian (from recorded *s[i]).* Also the name of the Carpathians may derive from Albanian *karpë* 'rock'. The different writings of the river name *Siret (Tiarantos, Hierasos, Gerasus, Seretos,* etc) were explained by Albanian. None of these arguments is, however, decisive. The Albanians are an ancient Balkan people, as shown among other things by the large number of placenames and geographical names of Albanian sound pattern in Dardania, and the early, classical Latin influence, etc. Sandfeld stated in *Linguistique balkanique*, 1930, p. 143: "Cette théorie est tout à fait inadmissible et laisse trop de choses inexpliquées." Also modern Rumanian linguists have abandoned this theory; cf. Rosetti ILR 1986, pp. 195–197 (below, p. 186, note 1).

original areas towards the plains along the coasts, where Slavs were living. The Slavic loanwords from this period show that the Albanians learned many details of agriculture, names of plants, fishing, building of dwelling places, social, political organization, etc., from the Slavs. The sound pattern of these words is Bulgarian, and the oldest of them show features of the Bulgarian dialect of Dibra, on the southeastern frontier of the Mati district.

D. The Slavs

1. THE MIGRATION OF THE SLAVS TO THE BALKANS

The first historical accounts about invasions of Slavic tribes across the Danube are given by Procopius. These invasions started during the first half of the 6th century. The Roman emperors from Justinian (527–565) to Heraklios (610–641) have the title *"Anticus."* In the second half of the 6th century, the number of incursions of the Slavs in the Balkan provinces increased and Slavs reached the Mediterranean coast at Rhodope. Slavic soldiers are mentioned in the Roman army as early as in 538. After the devastations by the Slavs and the Avars, large areas of the Balkans became depopulated.[1]

The migrations of the Slavs were frequently led by nomadic Turks. This is shown by archaeological finds (the oldest pieces of Slavis pottery and art objects of metal were borrowed from Turk peoples) as well as by numerous loanwords of Turk origin concerning state organization and cultural life.[2] The area adjacent to the lower Danube was probably the first to be occupied by the Slavs. Theophanes and Nikephoros mention that in 679, seven Slavic tribes (γενεαι)) were living between the Danube and the highest peaks of the Haemus mountains; these tribes came from what is today Valachia.[3] One of the main streams of Slavis colonization went through Moesia Superior and Dacia Ripensis to the interior of Macedonia and Lakonia. Dalmatia was heavily colonized, as well as the region of the eastern Alps along the valleys of the Sava and the Drava. It is generally considered that most of the Balkan peninsula north of Greece was already inhabited by Slavs in the mid-seventh century .

---

[1] Jireček GS 1911, p. 79.

[2] Stadtmüller GS 1950, p. 88.

[3] Jireček GS 1911, p. 100.

2. THE PLACENAMES AND THE NAMES OF RIVERS AND STREAMS IN THE FORMER BALKAN PROVINCES

A total of 654 placenames and names of rivers and streams used in the Balkan peninsula in the late 6th century were recorded by Procopios.[1] The sources of this writer were the books of the imperial administration in Constantinople. The names in question may be divided into two groups: (a) names of Thracian or (in a minor part) Illyrian origin and (b) names of Roman type, with Latin, Greek, Gothic and other elements.

A certain continuity of life from the pre-Roman age through the Roman occupation to the Slavic invasions in the 6th century may be stated in several places on the basis of finds on the same site of prehistoric tumuli, Roman stones with inscriptions and medieval churches and cemeteries.[2]

Many ancient towns were destroyed and remained uninhabited. In other places, the invading Slavs raised towers within the walls.

> Wenn dies gleich bei der Okkupation des Landes geschah, hat sich der alte Stadtname mit einer kleinen Umformung erhalten. Deshalb erscheinen bei der Errichtung von Bistümen zahlreiche ehemalige Römerstädte wieder als Zentrum ihrer Landschaft. Die Umformung der antiken Namen geschah entweder nach bestimmten Lautregeln oder mit Unterschiebung eines Sinnes durch ein anklingendes slawisches Wort. In dem Falle, wo die Städte römischen Ursprungs in der slawischen Periode einen ganz neuen Namen erhielten, wie die "weisse Burg" Belgrad (Singidunum) oder die Burg des "Verteidigers" (*branič*) Braničevo (Viminacium), war zwischen dem Untergang der antiken Stadt und ihrer Neubesiedlung jedenfalls eine längere Zeit verflossen.[3]

Of course, alongside the borrowing of old placenames and geographical names, the Slavs created names of their own, ... "mit hunderten von neuen Fluss- und Bach-namen und Tausenden von Dorf- und Flurnamen."[4]

The intensity of the Slavic colonization and the degree of the mixing of the Slavs with the local populations in the different areas are to some extent discernible from the study of the placenames. Most of the ancient names were preserved along the coasts. The smallest number of Slavic names were created in northern Albania and eastern Thracia. On the other hand, change of placenames was frequent in Moesia Superior and in the interior of Macedonia and Dalmatia. Examples of Latin names of towns preserved in Dacia Mediterranea and in Dardania are Niš (<Latin *Naissus*), *Sredec* (<Lat. *Serdica*;

---

[1]Cf. *Fontes Historiae Dacoromanae II,* Bucharest, 1970, pp. 458.

[2]Jireček GS 1911, p. 144.

[3]Jireček GS 1911, pp. 144–145.

[4]Ibid., p. 145.

today *Sofia*), *Skopje* (<Lat. *Scupi, Lipljan* (<Lat. *Ulpiana*).

Among Thracian names preserved, names of rivers and streams prevail: Ergine (<Agrianes), Lom (<Almus), Morava (<Margus), Iskar (<Oiscos), Timok (<Timacus), etc. Examples of preserved Thracian placenames are: Dristra (<Durostorum), Plovdiv (<Pulpudeva), etc.[1]

Of great interest are the traditions concerning circumstances during the Roman period which were preserved until modern times by the Slavs. Thus, the Roman roads, still present at many places, are often called "Trajan's road" (*Trojanov Put* or *Trojanski Put*), old ruins of towers are called "Trajan's tower" (*Trojanj Grad*), certain canyons "Trajan's door" (*Trojanova Vrata*). Moreover, the legend of Emperor Trajan was absorbed into the Slavic popular mythology: in medieval apocryphal texts, God Trajan is mentioned.[2]

Thus, the historical records about the Slavic incursions and migrations in the Balkan peninsula, essentially in accordance with the testimony of the placenames as well as the popular tradition of the South Slavic peoples, give a fairly good picture about the events in those times. It is well documented that when they migrated to the Balkan peninsula, the Slavs found in a large number of places Latin-speaking populations from whom they borrowed many placenames, lexical elements and also elements of popular culture.

3. BULGARIA FROM THE FOUNDATION OF THE BULGARIAN STATE TO THE 13th CENTURY

The first Bulgarian Empire

The Bulgarian state was founded in 679 AD, when the Bulgars, a Turk people, under the leadership of Isperich, conquered the area limited by the lower Danube, the Black Sea, the Haemus mountains and the river Isker. Seven Slavic tribes were living there, with whom the Bulgars entered into alliance.

The new state of Bulgaria soon emerged as a unifier of the Slavic tribes in the eastern part of the Balkan peninsula.Thus in 688 it subjugated most Slavic tribes in Macedonia and at the beginning of the 8th century it annexed Sagorie. Khan Telerig (772–777) had plans to conquer Bersitia, in northern Macedonia, but the Byzantine Emperor Konstantin Kopronimos attacked and defeated him. In 789, Bulgaria extended as far as to the valley of the river Struma.

During the period of Khan Krum (802–814), Bulgaria started a still more offensive policy. Krum subjugated those Avars who some years earlier, after the defeat of the Avar empire at the end of the 8th century, sought refuge east of the river Tisza (German *Theiss*). He occupied what are today the Banat and southern Transylvania. The Slavic tribes living there recognized the sovereignty of Krum.

[1] Ibid.,p. 101.

[2] Ibid., p. 58.

After these successes, Bulgaria had common frontiers with the Frankish Empire. In 808, Krum attacked the region of Struma and in 809, he occupied Serdica (present day *Sofia*) which until then belonged to Byzantium. The way to Macedonia was open. The Byzantine emperor Nikiphoros attacked the Bulgars but was defeated and killed in a battle (811 AD). Krum led several attacks into Thracia and Macedonia and transferred many Greeks from the occupied regions. Thus, in 813, 10.000 Greeks were settled in what is today southern Moldavia or northeastern Muntenia, north of the lower Danube. The cause of these resettlements was that Krum wanted to weaken the Greek population of Macedonia, because he planned to occupy it. In 813, Krum led a large army of Slavs and Avars against Byzantium and besieged Constantinople without success. He died in the following year.

One of the consequences of the transfer of Greeks into Bulgaria was the spread of Christianity among the population already in the early 9th century.

The Slavic tribes who lived along the river Timok under Bulgarian rule (the *Timocians*), recognized in 818 the hegemony of the Franks. Their example was soon followed by other Slavic tribes living in what is now the Banat. The successor of Krum, Omurtag (814–831) attacked these territories and in 827 succeeded in disposing the Slavic princes (*voivodes*) in the Banat who were on the side of the Franks. This success of the Bulgarians was, however, shortlived; they were driven away by the Franks in 829 and could only keep Sirmium with the city of Singidunum, which from that time on was called Belgrade.

During the reign of Omurtag, the number of Christians in Bulgaria increased and there are, from that time on, reports of persecution of the Christians.

Khan Pressian (836 - 853) took advantage of the weakness of Byzantium, at war with the Arabs. THE BULGARIAN FRONTIERS WERE NOW EXTENDED TO THE REGION OF THE VARDAR, THE BLACK DRIN, PRILEP, OCHRIDA, AND PART OF THE STRUMZI REGION. This expansion brought the Bulgarians into contact with the Serbs, who in that period used to live in small principalities. In face of the increasing power of the Bulgarians they now united and defended their territories.

Boris (853–888) also waged wars against the Serbs. It was during his reign that the Bulgarians adopted Christianity (the Greek Church of Byzantium). Boris was baptized in 865 and tok the name of *Michael* and the title of "*Czar*" instead of the heathen "*Khan*". Bulgaria came for centuries under the cultural influence of Byzantium. The new Church, using the Slavic language, contributed effectively to the Slavization of the Bulgarian ruling class.

Czar Simon the Great (893–927) waged wars with the Hungarians and with Byzantium. As a consequence of these wars, Bulgaria was forced to leave the territories north of the lower Danube. Most of these were then occupied by the Patzinaks and the Hungarians. Simeon seems to have had little interest in these territories, as his aim was to expand towards the southwest. During his reign, Bulgaria reached its largest territorial expansion, dominating the Serbs and including part of the Adriatic coast within its frontiers.

Simeon´s successor, Peter (927–969) was a weak ruler. During his reign, the

Byzantine influence increased, the representatives of the Church became increasingly corrupt and the population was discontented. Several uprisings are recorded from this period, for example that led by the prince of the Bersites in Macedonia in 963. In 968, the Russians invaded Bulgaria, the Byzantine emperor drove them away but Byzantium occupied somewhat later (during the reign of Boris II, 969–972) the eastern part of Bulgaria.

In the west, prince Nikola proclaimed himself the new emperor. This territory preserved its autonomy for another 50 years. It comprised Macedonia, southern Albania and western Moesia. Its capital was changed several times, among other towns it was Prespa, and, lastly, Ochrida. About 1020 AD, Ochrida became also the centre of the Church.

The successor of Nikola, his son David, ruled only for a short time; he was killed in 976 by some Vlach wayfarers between Prespa and Kastoria.

Another son of Nikola, Samuil, reigned between 980 and 1014. His aim was to unite all Slavs in the Balkan peninsula. He occupied Larisa, the capital of Thessaly, and reached as far as to the Peloponnesos, from which he removed a large number of people and settled them in Macedonia. At that time, Byzantium was weakened by civil wars, and Samuil succeeded to occupy Dyrrachium (Durrës, Durazzo) and extended his power to the Adriatic coast as far as to the estuary of the Drin. He devastated Dalmatia and subjugated the Serbs. In 996, he appeared in the Peloponnesos but was defeated by the Byzantine army. This started the decline of western Bulgaria. In 1014, Samuil was defeated again; in the following year, he was succeeded by his nephew, Johannes Wladislaff (1015–1018). The year 1019 marks the total subjugation of Bulgaria by Byzantium, celebrated in Constantinople by Emperor Basileos II with great triumph.

Basileos divided Bulgaria into four autonomous provinces. He removed all princes of some importance and settled them mostly in Asia Minor.The Byzantine army exercised a strong control over the population. However, Bulgaria was considered a separate country and retained its unity, its own laws and customs. The Church also preserved full autonomy. The chief of the Bulgarian Church was called the "autokephal archbishop of entire Bulgaria". The emperor ordered in 1020 that "all [Christian] believers living in the territories recently subdued by Byzantium in the Balkan peninsula, including ′the Vlachs from entire Bulgaria′ be subordinated to the archbishop of Ochrida."[1] The *Annals of Bari* recorded that in 1027 Vlachs were fighting in the Byzantine army in Sicily against the Arabs.[2]

During the reign of Basileos′ successors the situation of the people of Bulgaria deteriorated and already in the time of Konstantin VIII (1025–1028), revolts started. The Bulgarian population was exposed to the frequent incursions of the Petchenegs from the plains north of the Danube and the Vlachs conducted,

---

[1]Giurescu, C.C. (editor), *Istoria României în date*, 1971, p.59.

[2]Ibid., p. 60.

from their dwelling places in the mountains, expeditions of ravage among them.[1] In 1040, an uprising conducted by Peter Deljan started in Belgrade and soon spread over large parts of the peninsula. Finally, however, it was subdued by Byzantium.

A very important historical event is the schism of the Christian Church in 1054. Thereafter, Rome was the centre of the Roman Catholic confession and Constantinople that of the Greek Orthodox Church.

> The Rumanians remain in the group of peoples who belong to the Orthodox confession, under the canonical authority of the Patriarch of Constantinople.[2]

In the subsequent years, Byzantium waged fierce battles against the Petchenegs, mostly on Bulgarian territory. Finally, the emperor settled the Petchenegs in northeastern Bulgaria, from where they conducted incursions into other parts of the country. In 1059, the Hungarians attacked Byzantium and reached Sredetz (Sofia). Later in the same century, the Uzes, another Turk population, ravaged Bulgaria. In 1066, the Vlachs living in the region of Larisa revolted against Byzantium. In 1072, a new revolt started in Bulgaria, led by George Woitech, a Bulgarian nobleman. In this revolt, the Petchenegs helped the Bulgarians against Byzantium. However, even this revolt was subdued.

Towards the end of the 11th century, Bulgaria successively lost its separate status and was no longer considered an autonomous country but a part of Byzantium. The social situation of the population deteriorated; taxes were high and many peasants lost their property to the owners of big farms. The Byzantine Empire collected soldiers from Bulgaria, who were needed in the wars against the Petchenegs and the Cumans in the north and against the Turk-Seldjuks in the southeast. Many people fled to the forests especially when soldiers were sought. The situation worsened further in the first half of the 12th century, with the incursions of the Cumans (1124 AD), and the ravages of the Crusaders. A large part of the population of Bulgaria was forced into serfdom on the estates of rich noblemen or moved into the towns, where the masses of poor people increased. In Byzantine documents from this period, Bulgaria is called "Moesia"or "Sagori" and the Bulgarians are referred to as "Moesians"or "Vlachs". This indicates that there must have been a considerable number of Vlachs living among the Bulgarian population. Writing about the war between Byzantium and Hungary in 1161–1168, Kinnamos mentions Vlachs in the Byzantine army, "of whom it is said that they are former colonists from Italy."[3]

---

[1] Slatarski, W.N., *Geschichte der Bulgaren*, Leipzig, 1918, p. 82.

[2] Giurescu IRD 1971, p. 60.

[3] Ibid., p. 62.

The Vlacho-Bulgarian Empire

During the reign of Emperor *Andronikus I Komnenus* (118–1185), the power of Byzantium started to decline. In northern Bulgaria, where this power always was weakest, and where many people were accumulated as a result of the northward flight of the population in the preceding years, a revolt started led by two Vlach noblemen, Peter and Assan. It was probably provoked by new taxes imposed by the Byzantine emperor, which increased the burden of those who were making their living by the raising of animals, i.e., of the shepherds. This probably explains why the revolt started among the Vlachs, who were mainly shepherds.[1] Peter and Assan made a declaration of independence in the church of St Demetrius (1185 AD). It began as follows (in German translation): "Gott habe geruht, die Freiheit der Bulgaren und Walachen zurückzuerstatten und beschlossen, das langjährige Joch ihnen abzunehmen..."[2] Although Peter and Assan were defeated by the Byzantine army and forced to flee to the Cumans, north of the Danube, they came back already in the following year, helped this time by the Cumans. They succeeded in a short time in establishing the second Bulgarian empire, the *Vlacho-Bulgarian Empire* (1187 AD). At the beginning, it comprised only the territory in the northeast, between the Danube and the Haemus mountains. Its capital was Tîrnovo.

The brothers Assan and Peter were murdered by some noblemen (*boljars*), who considered that they were too despotic (1196 and 1197, respectively). Their younger brother, Ioaniţa (also called Kaloian) became the Czar (1197–1207). He received the title KING OF THE BULGARIANS AND OF THE VLACHS (*rex Bulgarorum et Blachorum*) from the Pope in 1204. During the first years of the 13th century, Constantinople was besieged by the crusaders. Kaloian succeeded in re-conquering the Bulgarian territories in western Macedonia, around the towns Prizren, Skopje, and Ochrida. In 1205, in alliance with the Cumans, Kaloian defeated the crusaders. He waged many wars against the Greeks and was killed in 1207 by the Cuman leader Manaster at the siege of Saloniki. The legal successor of Kaloian, Ivan Assan, was at that time in Cumania, the present day Valachian plain. He was sent there by Kaloian with the purpose of trying to seize power there together with his brother, Alexander.

Kaloian's nephew, Boril, used the absence of the legal successor to seize power (1207–1218). During his reign, the country declined. In 1217, Ivan Assan II came back with an army strengthened by Russian soldiers and in the following year defeated Boril and became the Czar of Bulgaria (1218–1241). During his reign, the power of the Vlacho-Bulgarian Empire increased again. In the battle at Klokotnitza (1230 AD), Ivan Assan II defeated Theodor, the king of Saloniki. This success made the expansion of the Bulgarian state possible and soon, all Bulgarians were united in the Vlacho-Bulgarian Empire.

---

[1]Giurescu, C.C., and Giurescu, D.C., *Istoria românilor din cele mai vechi timpuri pînă astăzi,* 1975 (2nd edition), p. 183.

[2]Slatarski Gesch Bulg 1918, p. 95.

To summarize: in the 11th and 12th centuries large numbers of Vlachs were living in the Bulgarian state. They are mentioned as equals to the Bulgarian population, they have played a leading role in the popular revolt against Byzantium. Since this period was after the separation of the two main dialects of Rumanian (which occurred around 1000 AD, cf. chapter II), the Vlachs we meet here must have been Northern Rumanians. Their number in Bulgaria started to decrease already at the beginning of the 13th century and the country became thereafter increasingly Bulgarian.[1]

The other main group of the Vlachs, the *Arumanians*, established themselves in the central and southern parts of the Balkan peninsula. They too succeeded in creating states of their own in the 11th and 12th centuries. In the mountainous parts of Thessaly, there was Great Valachia (Μεγάλη Βλαχία), in Doris, the western parts of Locris, in Etolia and Acarnania, Little Valachia (Μικρά Βλαχία) and in Dolopia, Upper Valachia (΄Ανω–Βλαχία).

E. The Vlachs

1. RECORDS IN DEEDS OF GIFT FROM SERBIAN MONASTERIES

The documents about this numerous Vlach population living in the Balkan peninsula, south of the Danube, during the Middle Ages, were presented and analysed by Silviu Dragomir, in his valuable work: *Vlahii din nordul peninsulei Balcanice în evul mediu* ('The Vlachs in the North of the Balkan Peninsula in the Middle Ages') published in 1959 in Bucharest. According to Dragomir, many things are still poorly known in this field:

> In the past, Rumanian historians have dealt with this problem only to a very limited degree. Lack of knowledge of the Slavic languages, as well as very deeply rooted prejudice, hindered the Rumanian historians from expressing the problem clearly and recognizing its significance in the study of the beginnings of the Rumanian people.[2]

This population, whom their neighbours called by the equivalents of the name Vlach (Serbian and Bulgarian *vlah,* Greek Βλάχος, German *Walach*, Hungarian *oláh*), called themselves *rumîni* (sing. *rumîn*). The use of this word with an ethnic meaning is attested from the mid-sixteenth century on, beginning with the

---

[1]Giurescu IRD 1971, p. 64.

[2]Dragomir, S., *Vlahii din nordul peninsulei Balcanice în evul mediu,* 1959, in the Preface.

writings of deacon Coresi. (As regards its sound pattern, cf. above, p. 5).

In the Middle Ages, the equivalents of "Vlach" were used exclusively by all authors who wrote about the ancestors of the population called today Rumanian. Sometimes the word was used to designate shepherds in general, a phenomenon caused obviously by the fact that the early Vlachs were *par excellence* shepherds. In this monograph, the designation *Vlach* is used, since this is historically correct; but it is employed exclusively to define the specific Romance population who were the ancestors of the present day Rumanians. ′Vlach′ and ′Rumanian′ are thus interchangeable.

The first known record on Vlachs is contained in a note from the 8th century, found in the monastery of Kastamunitu; it mentions Vlachs living in the valley of the Rhinos.[1] The following record is not earlier than from 976 AD. It was written by the Byzantine historian Ioan Skylitzes and relates that David, the son of prince Nikola, had been murdered by some Vlach wayfarers in the region between lake Prispa and Kastoria, near a place called "Beautiful Oaks" in northern Greece.[2]

In Serbia, 40 documents (deeds of gift, "*hrišovs*") are known which mention Vlachs living in different parts of the country, but the deeds of gift of the largest monasteries which had Vlachs in their territories have not yet been found.[3] These documents were written by Serbian kings and noblemen. From the 12th century, one is known, from the 13th, six, from the 14th, 27, and from the first half of the 15th, six. The oldest *hrişov* dates from 1198–1199 AD and mentions, among other things, that the Vlachs who belonged to the monastery of Hilander were organized in jurisdictions (*sudstvo*). They lived in the region of Prizren.[4]

A deed of gift from about 1220 AD, written by the first crowned king of Serbia, Štefan, was preserved on the walls of the monastery of Žiča, founded by Štefan. This document mentions the names of 200 Vlachs who were living west of Kosovo Polje along the upper course of the river Lim. Dragomir states that "not one of these names has an Arumanian character, on the contrary, the pattern of ′*Mic*′ compells us to think of the dialects in the north."[5] Many names found in this deed of gift are Slavic but only a few are Greek. Of the placenames in this document, three survived to this day: Batina, Bukorovac, and Bun.

The Northern Rumanian character of the language of these Vlachs is generally recognized:

[the ancestors of the Arumanians] must be distinguished from the Rumanians

---

[1]Capidan, T., *Romanitatea balcanică*, pp. 57–58; quoted by Coteanu, I., *Morfologia numelui în protoromână (română comună)*, 1969, p. 21.

[2]Giurescu IRD 1971, pp. 58–59.

[3]Dragomir Vlahii 1959, p. 30.

[4]Ibid., p. 17.

[5]Ibid., p. 19.

in Serbia, recorded during the entire course of the Middle Ages in the Serbian kingdom. The language of the Rumanians in Serbia, as well as Istrorumanian, presents characteristic features of Daco-Rumanian and belongs to the northern group of the Rumanian language while Arumanian constitutes its southern group.[1]

A deed of gift given by king Štefan Milutin about 1230 AD to the monastery of Banjska in Kosovo Polje describes the "law of the Vlachs". From the text of this law it is apparent that the Vlachs were shepherds and occupied themselves with agriculture to a limited extent. Some of them also followed the trade of wayfarers (*kjelatori*). In the same document, the frontiers of a territory in Kijevo, called *zemlja vlaška* ('Vlach territory') are described in detail.[2]

Three of the deeds of gift written by Štefan Dušan distinguish between Vlachs and Serbs. The two populations are named separately: "Vlachs as well as Serbs." Several documents mention Vlachs together with Albanians, as two distinct populations, but living in the vicinity of each other.

Concerning the Vlachs in Montenegro and Hercegovina, Dragomir gives the following account:

> They were exclusively shepherds and carters. The names they have left behind call to mind the life of shepherds: the mountains Durmitor, Visator (so called when first mentioned, the later form being Visitor) and Ţipitor; Murgule, an elevated plain below Durmitor; Palator, a ford across the Drina, where wool was washed.
>
> The tribes have sometimes characteristic Romance names: *Alunovići, Visulovići, Bukurovići, Piperi,* a family from the Dalmatian isles is called *Mrljani* (i.e., *mîrlani*), a village in Montenegro has the name *Mačuga* (cf. Rumanian *măciucă*), and a place in *Visoki* (Bosnia) *Mačugani.* According to professor Erdeljanović, it would be foolish to believe that the Serbs waited for the Vlach colonization, say, until the 9th or the 10th centuries, to find out from them that the Durmitor and the Visitor are called by these names. The deserving anthro-geographer adds that it is unreasonable to assume that these regions were deserted, without any remains of the ancient population, since it is known that they were densely inhabited. Thus, the Serbian scholar confirms that these Vlach settlements are very old: we must to go back to the period of the Slavic occupation of these areas in the 8th century, if we would accept his reasoning.[3]

The earliest mention of the Vlachs living in the region between the rivers

---

[1]Rosetti, A., *Istoria limbii române*, 1986, p. 324.

[2]Dragomir Vlahii 1959, p. 23.

[3]Ibid., p. 164. Durmitor, from Northern Rumanian *a dormi* 'to sleep', Visator, fr. *a visa* 'to dream', Ţipitor, fr. *a aţipi* 'to fall asleep' , Murgule, fr. *murg* 'brown, brown horse; the brown one', Palator, fr. *a spăla* 'to wash', *mîrlan* 'clown', *măciucă* 'club, bludgeon'.

Timok and Morava is from 1198 AD, in a report written by Ansbertus on the journey of Fredrik Barbarossa. This region was annexed by the Serbians in 1292, by King Milutin. In Serbian documents, it is not often mentioned. There are also records of Vlachs living northwest of Niš from the year 1382 and in the district of Kučevo from 1428.

The most recent Serbian deeds of gift are from the mid-fifteenth century. In that period, the Turks conquered more and more of the country, no more monasteries were built and the Serbian state declined.

About 1521, the Turkish Sultan Soliman made a law (*Canun name*) in which the rights of the Vlachs living between Braničevo and Vidin were defined. These Vlachs were enrolled in the Turkish army and, consequently, enjoyed special privileges.

2. PLACENAMES AND PERSONAL NAMES OF VLACH ORIGIN

The Vlach population recorded in the Serbian deeds of gift from the 12th to the 15th centuries left behind a large number of placenames and personal names which are still in use by the Serbians. Of these names we list those mentioned by Dragomir (table 2, pp. 30–31).

Although not complete, this list, as well as the map with several other names, showing the geographical distribution of the villages in question (see map 3, p. 32) gives a good idea about the nature and the importance of these vestiges of the Vlachs in the Balkan peninsula. They are names of mountains and of (usually small) villages, reflecting the living conditions of the Vlachs in the Middle Ages. As is also known from historical records, they were shepherds, living predominantly in the high mountains, in *cătun*-s, and they pursued some agriculture. (This applies to the great majority, but it did not exclude rising socially for several members of this population to the status of noblemen, and reaching high posts as functionaries etc.).

Besides these names of Northern Rumanian origin, many of which certainly existed before the Slavic colonization of the areas in question, there is another group of geographical names connected with the presence of Vlachs: the names of mountains and placenames given by the Slavs and based on the Slavic name of the Vlachs. These are found all over the territories in which also names of Rumanian origin were preserved. Of such names of mountains, we mention Vlasić, Vlaško Brdo, Stari Vlah, Vlasina, Vlaninja, Vlahinja Planina; and of placenames Vlahov Katun, Valakonje, Vlahoni, Vlaškido, Vlaški Do, Vlasić, Vlase, Vlasi, Vlasotinće, Novovlase, Vlaška Draca, (of the following villages, there are more than one with the same name:) Vlaška, Vlahi, Vlahinja.

Serbian	**from N. Rumanian**	meaning:
Butur-Polje	buture	stump of tree
Cape	ţap	he-goat
Carina	ţarină	dust; earth, ground
Cipitor	a aţipi	to drowse off
Gura	gură	mouth
Kalja	calea	the way, the road
Klonšor	clonţişor	beak (dimin. of clonţ)
Korbulicka Rjeka	corb	raven
Kornet	cornet	horn
Kornišor	coarnă	cornel
Krucica	cruciţă	little cross
Kampuri	câmpuri	fields (plur. of câmp)
Lagator	legător	sheafer
Lakustovo	lăcustă	locust
Lavarda	vardă	watch, guard
Ljepurov-Do	iepure	hare
Mačkat	măciucat	protruding
Maluri	maluri	shores, coasts, banks (plur. of mal)
Miel	miel	lamb
Mutulovci	mutul	the dumb one
Negrišor	negrişor	blackish
Palator	(s)pălător	washing
Pirlitor	pârlitor	burning, drying

Piskulje	piscul	the peak
Riori	râuri	small streams (plur. of râu)
Sač	saci	bags (plur. of sac)
Sakulica	sacul	the bag
Sora, Sore	soare	sun
Surdulica	surdul	the deaf one
Taor, Taure	taur	bull
Trokujev Do	troc	barter, truck
Ursule	ursul	the bear
Valje	valea	the valley
Vatoljevci	vătui	to wad

Table 2. Placenames and geographical names of Vlach (Northern Rumanian) origin in Serbia. (Compiled on the basis of data given by Dragomir, S., *Vlahii din nordul peninsulei Balcanice în evul mediu*, 1959.)

Many Rumanian placenames were preserved also in the mountainous regions of Bulgaria, particularly in the surroundings of Serdica (Sofia); smaller numbers also in Sredna Gora and in the Rhodope mountains. Such names are: Cerecel, Bukorovci, Vlasi, Banišor (villages), Ursulica (a field), Krecul (part of a mountain), Merul (a small stream) etc., (see map No 3).

Of Serbian personal names based on Rumanian ones the following may be mentioned:[1]

Alunović, Barbat, Drakulovići, Durmići, Merulići, Merulja, Mican, Serbul, Surduljani, Valnise.

[1]Dragomir Vlahii 1959, p. 154.

Map 3. Serbo-Croatian and Bulgarian placenames and geographical names of Northern Rumanian origin or containing the equivalent of the ethnic name *Vlach* (*Vlas, Vlase, Vlasovo*, etc.). Such names, not all of which are shown on this map, are the vestiges of the Northern Rumanian population living in the Balkan peninsula, south of the Danube, in the Middle Ages. All these names exist today, but many others, no more extant, are mentioned in historical documents. (After a map published by S. Dragomir in *Vlahii din nordul peninsulei Balcanice în evul mediu,* 1959.)

3. THE NORTHERN RUMANIAN INFLUENCE ON SERBIAN DIALECTS

The Serbian and Bulgarian populations in the above mentioned territories have, as shown above, borrowed geographical names and placenames from the Vlachs who once lived there, they also named a considerable number of villages and mountains after their Vlach inhabitants, and borrowed a number of personal names of them. To all this must be added a Northern Rumanian influence upon several Slavic dialects. Dragomir (p. 154) summarizes this as follows:

> We add the Romance words which were borrowed by the Serbian vocabulary in some regions, where the Serbian–Vlach symbiosis lasted longer: *brinza, bač, dos, deal, fičor, gropa, porta, urda, urdenik, strunga, strungač, faša, pasaran, muscur.* They are limited to certain local dialects, which indicates tha the Vlachs there spoke their own language until a late period.
> The Romance language was spoken in the Serbian regions also in the western part of the peninsula, while it is probable that in Bulgaria, it disappeared soon after the organization of the second empire. The silence of the historical sources concerning Vlachs after the extinction of the first Asăneşti can only be explained in this way. In the region of Strumiţa and in southwestern Bulgaria, Vlachs continued to live until the end of the Middle Ages.

In most of the areas where Vlachs have been living for some time, the word stock that the surrounding populations borrowed from them consists to a large extent of the shepherd terminology. This was the case also in Serbia; at least eight of those 14 words in Serbian dialects mentioned above are terms of shepherding, as shown in the following table:

baci	′shepherd in charge of a sheepfold′	groapă	′cavity′
brânză	′cheese′	muscur	′(sheep) with black spots on a light mouth′
deal	′hill′	pasăre	′bird′
dos	′back, bottom′	poartă	′gate′
faşă	′bandage, dressing′	strungă	′sheepfold′
fecior	′boy′ (*′Sennerknabe′*)	urdă	′soft cow cheese′

Macrea summarized the significance of the Rumanian influence on the South Slavic languages as follows:

> The influence of the Rumanian language on the word stock of the South Slavic languages is explained by the prolonged historical community of the Rumanian people with the South Slavic populations, by common political and administrative institutions, by the same religion, by the similar social structure

and by ancient occupations in common.[1]

4. THE AGES OF THE VLACH SETTLEMENTS IN THE BALKAN PENINSULA

The exact ages of the placenames presented above have not yet been determined. Although part of them (for example Banişor) can probably be explained by a migration from the Danube valley in the 14th or 15th century, most of them are much older. Rosetti (referring to Weigand, Duridanov, and Zaimov) mentions 35 placenames in central Bulgaria and in the region of Sofia which must be considered of Northern Rumanian origin, the Arumanian names having been eliminated. All these date back to the period between the 10th and 14th centuries.

The deeds of gift preserved in Serbian monasteries give us very valuable, detailed accounts from the end of the 12th century on, concerning the Vlachs who then lived in Serbia. Their way of life, their social organization, relationships to other peoples living in the same areas may be discerned quite clearly from these documents. To a certain extent, even estimates concerning the numbers of the Vlachs are possible. Although the first of these deeds of gift dates from the end of the 12th century, it is obvious tha the Vlach population they describe had been living there long before:

> The most reliable conclusion to be drawn from these accounts is that the geographic distribution of the Vlachs in the Balkans, as seen in the 12th to the 15th centuries, is very old and DATES BACK MUCH BEFORE THE 10TH CENTURY.[2]

The circumstances in Montenegro make a more exact conclusion possible: Montenegro belonged to the Roman-Byzantine Empire until about 600 AD. Its colonization by the Serbs started in the 8th century. The Serbs found there a Vlach population from whom they borrowed many geographic names: *Durmitor, Visitor*, etc. It is obvious that these Vlachs were the descendants of the Romanized shepherds of these or adjacent areas of the East Latin territory. Explaining the survival of this population, Dragomir stresses the importance of the social circumstances, i.e., the fact that while the town-dwellers and the farmers were dispersed, killed or assimilated to the Slavs, the shepherds were exsposed to these perils in a much lesser degree.

Our knowledge of the early Vlachs is, unfortunately, quite fragmentary. It must be emphasized that the placenames of Northern Rumanian origin in the Balkan peninsula, as we know them, (including those which no longer exist but

---

[1]Macrea, D., *Studii de lingvistică română,* 1970, p. 11.

[2]Dragomir Vlahii 1959, p. 165 (emphasis added).

are mentioned in historical records[1]) can only be a part of all names of this type which had existed earlier. Placenames tend to be exposed to changes of many different causes. Many Vlach names may have been translated by the Slavs, even more may have disappeared in the course of time, when the Vlach population was successively replaced by the Slavs. In the Balkan peninsula, the Slavic domination was not only temporary but definitive, which cannot have been favourable for the preservation of non-Slavic placenames.

The toponymy of Northern Rumanian origin in the Balkan peninsula is of very great significance in the study of the early history of the Rumanian language. Especially the question of the ages of the different names and their possible relationships to each other would be worth detailed and systematic investigation.

5. THE MIGRATIONS OF THE EARLY VLACHS

Mobility has always been a characteristic trait of the populations of the Balkan peninsula. There are villages in which as many as three dialects of the same language are spoken.[2]

Relevant for the problem discussed here are the wanderings of the Vlachs. As shepherds, the Vlachs were used to a high degree of mobility. Part of them practised what in Rumanian is called *transhumanţă* i.e., they had a certain sommer grazing place in the mountains and moved with their animals each autumn to a winter grazing place in the lowlands.[3]

The protracted wanderings of the Vlachs can be reconstructed from the following sources:

(a) Documents. — King Uroš Milutin (1282–1298) disposed in a deed of gift given to the monastery of Hilander that everybody coming to the kingdom, "be he *parikoi*[4], Vlach, or any foreigner, must belong to the holy Church." [5] Also documents from Ragusa tell us about the migrations of the Vlachs in the 14th and 15th centuries. "In 1332, a monk promised to the inhabitants of Ragusa to induce the Vlachs from fifty villages *(cătun*-s) to settle in their territory. In Stagno, the Vlachs came not only in order to spend the winter with their flocks there, but

---

[1]The map by Dragomir shows a number of such names, missing from map 3.

[2]"M. Malecki, Osservazioni sull'unione linguistica balcanica, Atti del III. Congresso internazionale dei linguisti, Firenze, 1935, p. 75. 'Il est ainsi dans toutes les régions de la Serbie, le long de la Morava, autour de Valjevo et le long de la Drina. Les habitants en sont, dans la proportion de 80 p. 100, des immigrés venus principalement au cours des trois derniers siècles... Les documents d'archives... ne donnent aucune idée de la grande importance des migrations' (J. Cvijić, R. ét. sl., III 6)" (quoted by Rosetti 1986 p. 195).

[3]"Ursprünglich lagen beide oft beieinander, z.B. in der Urkunde von Žiča (um 1220) die Sommerweide am Berge Kotlenik, die Winterweide im nahen Tale des Ibar" (Jireček GS 1911, p. 156).

[4]Dependent peasant.

[5]Dragomir Vlahii 1959, p. 166.

some of them also settled in the area (in the 14th century)."[1]

(b) The Jireček line (see map 6, p. 50). — All Vlach settlements south of the frontier between the Latin and Greek languages (in Rhodope, in the valley of the Marica, on the coasts of the Black Sea, etc.) must be the result of migratory movements.

(c) The placenames. — Vladimir Skarić showed that "there existed, in fact, also before the Turkish invasion, a permanent migration from the east to the northwest, of not only of Serbs but also of Vlachs."[2]

This is evidenced by placenames in Montenegro and Bosnia which have their counterpart in Kosovo or in the vicinity of Prizren. For example, the name *Drobnjaci* in Montenegro corresponds to the name of a hill in Kosovo; not far from Gacko, there is a village named *Nadinići,* a name probably derived from *Nadih-nin-Laz*, mentioned in a deed of gift by Štefan Dušan as a placename in the vicinity of the Vlach *cătun* Golubovac, near Prizren.

Thus, the settlements of the Vlach population in the western parts of the Balkan peninsula are "the result of a long historical process, the contours of which, however, may be deciphered."[3] The paths of the shepherds also served as paths of migration, which explains this slow and protracted expansion.[4]

> The Morlachs and the Istrorumanians must be considered the extreme point of the movement which started in the region of the Morava and at first headed westwards, later towards the north.[5]

The study of the placenames also suggests migration of Vlachs from the Balkan peninsula to Pannonia. On the basis of Northern Rumanian placenames in Pannonia, mentioned in medieval documents, Drăganu assumed that these Vlachs came from Moesia Superior, in an age from which no historical records exist. Thus, for example, documents mention a "*villa Vlach*" near Sirmium in 1295 and a river *Valachyza* in 1292. In 1406, *Radulfalva* is mentioned, and in 1395, in the same area, *Ušurinc.* This name calls to mind Ušur, the son of Ivan Borojević (Rumanian *uşure* = *uşor* 'light weight'). The placename Uşurei, for example, is found in Vîlcea and in Mehedinţi.[6] The name *Zemena* in Pannonia is not rhotacized (the *n* is preserved rather than changed to *r*), which indicates that its inhabitants cannot have come from the region of Rudnik–Drinjaca, but came probably from the area of the rivers Timok and Morava, where the dialect of the Vlachs is not rhotacized.

---

[1] Ibid., p. 167.

[2] V. Skarić, "Porijeklo pravoslavnoga naroda u sjeverozapadnoj Bosni" (The origin of the Orthodox population in northwestern Bosnia), in *Glasnik zem. Muzeja u Bosni i Herceg.* XXX, 1918, pp. 219–266; quoted by Dragomir Vlahii 1959, p. 167.

[3] Dragomir Vlahii 1959, p. 167.

[4] Ibid., p. 168.

[5] Ibid., p. 169.

[6] Ibid., p. 171.

The causes of this prolonged and universal migration of the Vlach population are to be sought in their way of life and social situation: they were shepherds and belonged in Bulgaria as well as in Serbia to the lower classes, being mostly dependent on their landlords or the church. "Because of this, they try to flee from one landlord to the other, using shepherds′ routes which they know very well. Good pastures and more favourable living conditions were always decisive." [1]

The Turkish invasion of the Balkan peninsula pushed all Christian populations northwards and hastened the migrations.[2]

6. DOCUMENTS ON THE SYMBIOSIS BETWEEN VLACHS AND ALBANIANS

Many documents in Serbia, written in the 13th to 15th centuries, mention Albanians, Vlachs, and often also Serbians living in the same areas. Although no written record is known from earlier periods, certain cirumstances indicate that the Vlacho–Albanian symbiosis is of an ancient date:

> The territory in which both Vlach and Albanian *cătun*-s exist side by side extends from Scutari to Ragusa and in the east to Prizren. There, the symbiosis between Albanians and Vlachs can be proved by documents, although the Serbian deeds of gift do not show this symbiosis to have been too close as the villages of the Vlachs are always presented apart from those of the Albanians. Obviously, both populations were shepherds. In Old Serbia, the Albanian settlements are rare, as well as in the northwest of Ragusa, where only the names of some Vlachs such as Burmazi and possibly Bolami, preserved their memory. In spite of this, the Vlacho–Albanian symbiosis here must have been quite ancient. This is shown by the spread of the *cătun* among the Albanians and by the development of the Vlach *frăţii* into tribes. The *cătun* is not general among the Albanians and the organization in tribes remained, also among the Serbs who survived the Turkish occupation, restricted to a small zone. The Albanian influence is also seen in the names of Vlachs in Serbia *(Cepimati, Ginovik, Tus, Hotul)* although we must point out that there are very few Albanian names among the Vlachs.
>
> All these considerations enable us to state with sufficient certainty that the settlements of the Vlachs in the regions in which they came into contact with the Albanians are very old. They may originate from the period preceding the spread of the Serbian element in the region between Scutari, Prizren, and

---

[1] Ibid., p. 172.

[2] After the end of the Common Rumanian period, Vlach shepherds migrated also *outside the Balkans*. Besides most of present day Rumania, where they have been living since the 11th–13th centuries, traces of compact masses of Vlach shepherds have been left in Slovakia, Bohemia, Poland, the Ukraine, and southern Russia. This problem willbe discussed below, pp. 122–127.

Ragusa (8th–9th centuries). This view is supported also by Erdeljanović, who considers that it was the Vlachs who handed down the indigenous, pre-Slavic (Illyrian and Roman) placenames to the Serbian population of ancient Montenegro.[1]

Besides toponyms and personal names, some lexical elements were also transferred from the language of the Vlachs to the Albanian population living in the region mentioned above. Jokl[2] described this Rumanian influence on the Albanian dialects spoken along the Drina. There are, for example: Albanian *lemnj* ′reel′, cf. Rumanian *lemne*, the plural of *lemn* ′wood′; Alb. *me trase* ′to draw up′, cf. Rum. *tras*, the past participle of *trag* ′I draw′; Alb. *fičor* ′boy who helps the shepherd making cheese′, cf. N. Rum. (dialectal) *ficior* ′boy, lad′; Alb. *gjëndërë* ′glandule′, cf. Rum. *ghindură* ′tonsil, ganglion, glandule′ (this Rumanian word was also transferred to Serbo-Croatian: *glindura*).

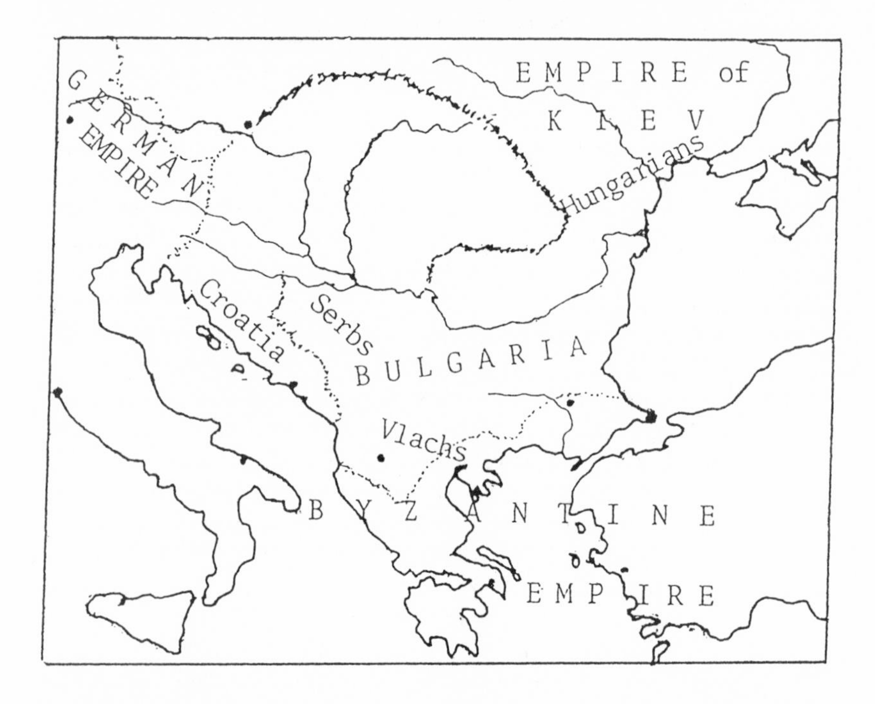

Map 4. Southeastern Europe in the 9th century AD (after *Atlas zur Weltgeschichte,* Georg Westermann, Braunschweig.) – In the Carpathian Basin, Avars, Danubian Slovenes, Bavarian-Franks, Moravians, Bulgarians, and Gepidae were living.

[1] Dragomir Vlahii 1959, p. 173.

[2] Jokl, N., "Rumänisches im Albanischen", *Revista filologică* II, pp. 246–267; quoted by Dragomir Vlahii 1959, p. 39.

Map 5. Central and Southeastern Europe in the early 13th century AD (after *Atlas zur Weltgeschichte,* Georg Westermann, Braunschweig). To the north-west of Bosnia, Croatia was situated. Bulgaria extended much more to the southwest (over Macedonia and other areas) than is the case today.

Chapter II

FROM LATIN TO RUMANIAN

A. The innovations of Latin in the 1st–3rd centuries AD

As shown by the inscriptions, Latin preserved a considerable unity for many centuries. This may probably be explained by the great mobility of the Roman army and administration. These levelling factors weakened and finally disappeared with the decline of the Empire; beginning with the 3rd century AD, dialectal differences increased.

Rumanian is, as all Neolatin (Romance) languages, the continuation of Latin. The changes during the course of time were gradual and the periods which may be distinguished from Latin to present day Rumanian are more or less arbitrary. S. Stati (*Dacoromania* I, 1973, p. 213) distinguished the following periods in the history or the Rumanian language:

2nd — 4th centuries:	Latin
5th — 7th "	East Latin or Thraco-Roman
8th — 11th "	Common Rumanian (*roumain commun*)
12th — 15th "	Ancient Dacorumanian
16th — 20th "	Rumanian

Innovations in the Latin language usually started in the capital of the Roman Empire and radiated successively to most provinces. The innovations of the second and the third centuries AD had the possibility of naturally penetrating also into Dacia Traiana, which was a Roman province between 106 and 275AD. The most important innovations of this period are the following:

Phonetics

i > *e* : *magister* > *maester* (Northern Rumanian *măestru* 'master').
v > *b* : *alveus* > *albeus* (N. Rum. *albie* 'river bed').
-tl- > *-cl-* : *vetulus* > *vechlus* (N. Rum. *vechi* 'ancient, old').
-pt- > *t* : *septembris* > *setembre* (cf. Latin *baptizare* > N. Rum. *a boteza* 'to baptize, to name').
Disappearance of the final consonants (*-r*, *-s*, *-t*): *frater* > N. Rum. *frate* 'brother'.

Conditioned sound changes

e > *a*, by assimilation: *passere* > *passar* (N. Rum. *pasăre*).
i > *a*, by assimilation: *silvaticus* > *salvaticus* (N. Rum. *sălbatic* 'wild').
o > *e*: *rotundus* > *retundus* (N. Rum. *rătund*, Old Italian *ritondo*, Provençal *redon*, Spanish and Portuguese *redondo*).
The confusion between *u* and *o* appears often in inscriptions: *marmuris* instead of *marmoris*, etc.[1]
-*v*- between vowels disappeared: *avunculus* > *aunculo* (N. Rum. *unchi* 'uncle').

B. THE INNOVATIONS OF LATE LATIN (4th – 7th CENTURIES)

The innovations of the following period, that of Late Latin, from the 4th to the 6th or 7th centuries, are numerous. They affected of course the Latin speakers of the Balkan peninsula, wich was part of the Empire until the Slavic occupation of the peninsula in the 7th century. The territories north of the lower Danube no longer belonged to the Empire in this period.

Phonetics

Stressed short *e* > *ye* is mentioned in grammars from the 5th century AD.[2]
The assibilation of Latin *t* + *e*, *i*, as well as that of Latin *d* + *i* followed by a vowel appeared, according to grammars, in the 5th century.[3] (For more details about these changes see below: Common Rumanian, pp. 106–111).

Examples of the assibilation of Latin *k´* + *i* followed by a vowel are found in inscriptions from the 2nd century. The palatalization of *k´* + *e*, *i*, appeared as late as in the 5th century.[4] When the first Latin lexical elements were transferred into German, *k* was not yet changed:

Latin	**Old Germanic**	meaning
cellarium	kelari	cellar
cista	kista	coffin
vicia	wicka	vetch

---

[1]Rosetti ILR 1986, p. 105.
[2]Ibid., p. 328.
[3]Ibid., p. 335.
[4]Ibid., p. 340.

In Bavaria, the Latin placename *Celio monte* is known from 470 AD. It was transferred to Germanic with an initial *k* : *Kellmünz,* and the same was the case of Latin *Celeusum* > Germanic *Kelsbach* (6th century.)

The late date of this change may explain its absence in certain dialects spoken in remote areas, such as Logudorian in central Sardinia and the same is the case of the Latin elements of German and Basque. In the northern dialect of Dalmatian, *k* was assibilated in front of *i* but not in front of *e.*[1] In Arumanian, *ts* stands on the place of Latin *k (+ e, i*), in Northern Rumanian, *č*. (For further discussion of this problem, see below: Common Rumanian, p.115).

The accent of intensity

In Latin, the quantitative differences between vowels were of decisive importance during the classical period and also afterwards, until the 5th century. With the disappearance of these, the accent of intensity became of primary importance.

Syntax

The verb

In classical Latin, action completed prior to some past point of time was expressed by the pluperfect, e.g., *dixi* 'I had said'. In Vulgar Latin, *after the 4th century,* the construction *habeo factum* acquired the value of the perfect: *ecce episcopum cum duce et civibus invitatum habes* 'you have invited ... the bishop'. This construction is used by all Romance languages, thus N. Rum.: *ai invitat pe episcop* 'you have invited the bishop'. (Arumanian and a small part of the population in Oltenia use the original Latin perfect.)[2]

The nominal system

The use of the genitive for the dative can be found occasionally already in classical Latin. This trendency spread continually and became "exceedingly widespread during the period of transition from Latin to Romance." The documents of later periods (the Merovingian period and Medieval Latin) show "the use of the genitive of the pronouns – sing. *illius, ipsius,* plur. *illorum, eorum,* etc., – to supply the function of the dative."[3] The process has been of great significance for the Romance languages:

> It is only against the background of the late Latin material that we can understand how *loro* in Italian, *leur* in French, etc., (from Lat. *illorum*) came to serve both as the genitive and the dative.[4]

---

[1]Ibid., p. 114.

[2]Ibid., p. 162.

[3]Löfstedt, E., *Late Latin,* 1959, p. 127.

[4]Ibid., p. 128.

Italian *loro* and French *leur* corresponds to Rumanian *lor*.

The definite article

Latin had no definite article. The Greek article was, in translations made at the end of the 3rd and the early 4th century, rendered by *ille, ipse, hic, iste,* or *idem.*[1] The Rumanian definite atricle represents *ille*. The change demonstrative pronoun > definite article was protracted; in the texts, a definite article in its present day form appeared IN THE 7TH CENTURY, in everyday speech probably somewhat earlier.The phases of this process were essentially the same in Rumanian as in the entire territory of the Neolatin languages.[2] (Regarding the postposition of the article cf. below, p. 64).

Vocabulary
New words and expressions

The Latin name of the Slavs (originally, only of the Slovenes), *Sclavus* or *Sclavinus* is found in texts from the 6th century on. The Northern Rumanian form of this word is *şchiau*, in the plural, *şchei*; the Arumanian form is *şcl'eau.*[3]

In late Vulgar Latin, periphrastic contructions appeared for *hieme* 'during the winter', *vere* 'during the spring', and *estate* 'during the summer': *tempore hiemis, hiberno tempore, verno tempore, primo vere, aestivo tempore.* This development finally resulted in the Romance terms for the seasons of the year, e.g. Italian *inverno,* French *hiver*, Rumanian *iarnă*; Italian *primavera*, Rumanian *primăvară*. (Lat. *aestas* survived in Italian *estate*, French *été*, etc.).[4]

In Late Latin texts, very often the derivations of *aeramen* and *aeramentum* are found instead of classical Latin *aes*. As judged by the texts, for example, *Peregrinatio Aethereae*, both variants were equally popular; however, in the Romance dialects, only *aeramen* survived: Italian *rame*, Rumanian *aramă*, etc.[5]

A specific East Latin feature is the preservation of Latin *imperator* 'emperor'. It is explained "by the continued existence, in Byzantium, of the Roman Empire; the Occidental forms are of learned origin"[6] (cf. N. Rum. *împărat,* Albanian *mbret*).

---

[1]Rosetti ILR 1986, p. 159.

[2]Coteanu Morfologia 1969, p. 99: "Istoria limbii române arată că articolul românesc a evoluat în mod asemănător cu cel romanic, trecerea de la valoarea de pronume propriu-zis a lui *ille* la aceea de articol prezentînd aproximativ aceleaşi faze ca în toată Romania."

[3]Mihăilă, G., *Studii de lexicologie şi istorie a lingvisticii româneşti*, 1973, p. 16.

[4]Löfstedt, E., *Syntactica*, vol. II, Lund, 1933, p. 42.

[5]Ibid., p. 44.

[6]Rosetti, A, Cazacu, B., Coteanu, I., (red.), *Istroria limbii române*, vol. II, 1969, p. 169.

Changes of meaning

Classical Latin *hostis* ′enemy′ changed its meaning to ′army′ – "an eloquent testimony, be it said in passing, to the general attitude towards armed forces at that time." [1] Some of the earliest proofs of this change are given by Löfstedt; all are from the 6th century. From *hostis* with this meaning developed Portuguese *hoste*, Spanish *hueste*, and Rumanian *oaste*, ′army′.

Clasical Latin *necare* ′to kill′ became more specialized, i.e., it received the meaning ′to drown′. This was, of course, a gradual process, perhaps through the intermediate stages of "ersticken, erwürgen." In *Greg. Tur. Hist. Franc.* VI 35, *necare* is used in both the old general meaning and the new, more narrow one. "Die endgültige Einengung und Spezialisierung des Sinnes ist also erst spät und ganz allmählich vor sich gegangen"...[2] The Latin word *necare* exists in Rumanian in the form *îneca*, with the meaning ′to drown′ (cf. French *noyer* ′to drown′).

C. FEATURES SHARED BY ITALIAN DIALECTS AND RUMANIAN

During the first five centuries AD, the populations living in Italy and in the Balkan peninsula belonged to the same state, the highly organized Roman Empire. Close contact existed between the Romans living in Italy and those in adjacent areas of the Balkans. The vestiges of this long period of community are found in the languages which carry on the Latin from those centuries spoken in Italy and in the Balkan peninsula: in Friulian, Venetian, and other Italian dialects, in Rhetoromance, in Dalmatian (until the end of the 19th century), in the Latin elements of Albanian – and in Rumanian. These are phonetical peculiarities, special expressions, and unusual meanings of certain words (changes of meaning only found in these idioms).

Phonetics

An important phonetical similarity was described by Bourciez as follows:

> La Rhétie parait avoir pris part au contraire à la diphtongaison initiale en *ie, uo*, qui de là, par le Frioul et l′Istrie, s′ ést propagée le long de la côte de Dalmatie, même dans le cas d′ entrave (istr. *mierlo, kuorno, puorta,* vegl. *fiasta, puarta*). Dans la péninsule proprement dite des Balkans, où ę seul entre en ligne de compte (pour ǫ, voir § 153), la diphtongaison se produit également devant l′entrave latine: on a non seulement roum. *ierĭ* (hĕri), mais

[1] Löfstedt Late Latin 1959, p. 17.

[2] Löfstedt Synt 1933, 380.

aussi *piept (pĕctus)* [1]

Vocabulary, loan translations

Venetian, Friulian, and Rumanian have a common expression for ´adoptive child´: Ven., *fio d'anema,* Friul., *fi d'anime*, N. Rumanian *copil de suflet* (*anema, anime*, *suflet* ´soul´ thus, literally: ´child of the soul´.)

In a moral poem written in the 13th century in the Venetian dialect an interesting word is found:

Un mat om qe redise la mateça doi ora
Fai como l can qe mança ço c'a gitadho fora.

(´A fool who says the same stupidity twice
Does as a dog which eats what it has vomited´.)

Of all Romance languages, only Rumanian has a counterpart to the use of *ora* in this sense (*doi ora* ´twice´): N. Rumanian *de două ori* ´twice´.

> Il serait difficile d´admettre que *hora* est devenue synonyme de *vices* en roumain indépendamment du vénétien. C´est une transformation trop subtile, trop surprenante, pour qu´elle ait pu s´effectuer dans deux langues sans qu´il y ait eu le moindre contact entre elle. C´est pour ces raisons que nous n´hésiterons pas à y voir un reste des plus précieux de l´époque où le roumain ne s´était pas encore isolé de l´Italien. Il y a encore une autre circonstance qui vient donner une importance particulière au mot en question. C´est que *hora* apparaît avec le même sens aussi en albanais, herɛ, qui signifie aussi ´temps´. L´alb. *herɛ,* le roum. *oară* et le vén. *ora* forment donc une famille inséparable et viennent jeter un peu de lumière sur un des chapitres les plus obscurs de l´histoire du latin balquanique.[2]

Densusianu[3] gives some examples of expressions shared by Rumanian with Italian dialects:

Latin	**N. Ital dialects**	**N. Rumanian**	meaning
* expanticare	spantegar Ven. and Mil.	spînteca	´pour out, shed´

[1]Bourciez, E., *Éléments de linguistique romane,* 1967, pp. 146–147.
– *entrave* = the position of a stressed vowel in a syllable ending in a consonant.

[2]Densusianu, O., *Histoire de la langue roumaine,* (edit. V. Russu), 1975, pp. 218 – 219.

[3]Ibid., pp. 211–226.

*impetrire	impetrir Ven. impetri Friul.	împietri	´turn into stone be dumbfounded´
*implenire	impinir Ven. impleni Friul and Tyrol. impenar Dalm	împlini	´to fill, to carry out´
*erraticare	aradegar la via Ven.	a rătăci drumul	´to go astray´
(palatum)	ol cel della bocha	cerul gurei	´palate´ (lit. ´the sky of the mouth´)
convenire ´to gather´	zurar no se covem	nu se cuvine să juri	´it is not fitting to swear´
reus ´guilty´	ri Dalm. re Campobasso	rău	´bad´

Greek κοττιζω was transferred to ancient Venetian (*scotezar*), to Istria (*kutisa*), to Albanian (*kudzon*), and to Rumanian (*cuteza* ´to dare´) during the Middle Ages. This word, among many others,

> ...confirme d´une manière éclatante ce que nous avons admis au sujet de développement du latin balkanique; elle montre, par son origine et sa diffusion, que ce latin n´a pas cessé d´être en contact avec celui d´Italie jusqu´assez tard dans le moyen âge.[1]

In the Northern Italian dialects, as well as in Rumanian, *fieri* is used in the sense of ´*esse*´ (cf. Rumanian *a fi* ´to be´).

Lexical elements shared by Rumanian and Friulian

Friulian	**Rumanian**	meaning:
brumajo ´December´	brumar	´November´ (fr. Latin brumarius)
discanta	descînta	´to cast a spell over´

[1]Densusianu HLR (1975), p. 219.

distrama	destrăma	´to unweave, unravel, break up´
dlongia	lîngă	´beneath´ (fr. Lat. de-longe)
ferbint	fierbinte	´hot, burning´
g´alinar	găinar	´stealer of poultry, roost robber´
imbina	îmbina	´to join, to connect´
imbranca	îmbrânci	´to push´
innejar (Muggia)	îneca	´to drown´
inquaglier (Engadin)	închega	´to curdle, to coagulate´ (fr. Latin incoagulare)
invernadik (Muggia)	iernatic	´wintry, winter-like´ (fr Latin hibernaticus)
legnarie	lemnărie	´wood yard´
puschmaun	poimâine	´the day after tomorrow´ (fr. Latin post mane)
sesela	secera	´to cut, to harvest´ (Lat. sicilare)

Latin *levare* ´to lighten, to alleviate´ has, in Friulian, Rumanian, and Albanian, among other senses, received also that of ´to buy´: Friul. *jeva*, N. Rumanian *lua*, Albanian *bl´ën*, (from. Latin **ablevare*) ´to buy´. Friul. *no puess jevalu, no ai vonde bez,* N. Rumanian *nu-l pot lua pentru că n-am destui bani* ´I cannot buy it because I don´t have enough money´.[1]

Latin *albus* ´white´is preserved in Rhetoromance: *alf*, in Dalmatian: *jualb*, and in Rumanian: *alb*. In all other Romance languages, this Latin word was replaced by Germanic *blank*.

Latin *intelligere* is preserved in the Rhetoromance dialect of Engadin: *incler*, and in Rumanian: *înțelege* ´to understand´. In the other Romance languages, this word was replacd by *capere, comprendere*, or *intendere*.

An expression existing in the Tyrol dialect of Rhetoromance and in N. Rumanian is *soredle da*, respectively *soarele dă* ´the sun appears´.

Rumanian shows a number of correspondences also with different southern

[1]Densusianu HLR (1975), p. 224.

Italian dialects: there are, for example, *nzurare* (Napoli), *nzurar* (Abruzzes), and N. Rum. *(a se) însura* 'to get married' (from Latin *inuxorare*) *ammessarum* (southern Italy, in the Codex Cavensis) and N. Rum. *armăsar* 'stallion' (from Lat. *admissarius*); *ammisteka* (Abruzzes) and N. Rum. *amesteca* 'to mix'; *ceppe* (Abruzzes) and N. Rum. *cep* 'bung, plug, spigot; tap' (from Lat. *cippus* 'rectangular pillar; fortification made of pointed sticks').

Some of these correspondences may represent preserved archaic elements, others are innovations, many of them of a highly specific nature. In their entirety, they indicate that the ancestors of the Rumanians were, from the 2nd–3rd centuries AD until the Slavic occupation of the Balkan peninsula, i.e., until about 600 AD, in close, everyday contact with the speakers of Latin dialects in Italy. As many circumstances pertaining to the problem of Rumanian ethnogenesis, this is not something new, – in fact, Gaston Paris arrived at the same conclusion more than one hundred years ago[1].

D. East Latin

1. THE PERIOD AND THE FRONTIERS

The division of the Romance languages can only be more or less schematic. In the west, *-s* was preserved and *-p-*, *-t-*, *-k-* were voiced, while in the east, *-s* disappeared and the intervocalic stops preserved. The first group may be called West-Romance or Pyreneo-Alpine Romance and the last, East-Romance or Appennino-Balkan Romance. The Italian dialects south of Ancona are considered to belong to the eastern group. There are, however, many exceptions. Sardinian belongs to the western group, but has preserved not only *-s,* but also *-p-*, *-t-*, *-k-*. There are southern Italian dialects which have voiced these consonants, as is the case in the west. The people living today on the Istrian peninsula speak a western Romance idiom, but as shown by ancient placenames, the peninsula belonged earlier to Eastern Romance.[2] Dalmatian had elements in common with southern Italian dialects. It is considered the link between Italo-Romance and Balkan-Romance.[3]

According to Rosetti[4], East Latin ("*grupul oriental al limbii latine*") was

---

[1]Densusianu HLR (1975), p. 228: "La conclusion à laquelle nous sommes arrivé ici est semblable à celle qu'exprimait, il y a une trentaine d'années, Gaston Paris dans l'article publié en tête du premier volume de la Romania, 11: 'le roumain ... a été en contact avec le reste du domaine roman jusqu'à l'invasion slave et a pu par conséquent subir encore au Ve et même au VIe siècle les influences qui se faisaient sentir dans le reste de ce domaine."

[2]Vidos, B.E., *Handbuch der romanischen Sprachwissenschaft,* 1975, p. 325.

[3]Ibid., p. 355.

[4]Rosetti ILR 1986, p. 75 and p. 563.

spoken in the Danubian provinces and along the shores of Dalmatia, as well as, until the 2nd half of the 3rd century AD, in Italy. Rumanian belongs to this, Appennino–Balcanic linguistic group, together with Dalmatian, the Latin elements of Albanian, and the central and southern Italian dialects (Abruzzian, Sicilian, and Puglian). However, there are concordances between Rumanian and northern Italian dialects, and also Calabrian[1], Sardinian,[2] and southern Apulian. Thirty words pertaining to shepherding are shared by Rumanian and several southern Italian dialects.

Theoretically, the division of the Romance languages may be made according to the substratum: Gallic, Iberic, Italian, etc.; the ancient political and geographical division: Gallia, Italy, Raetia; or only on the basis of geography: *Balkan Romance* or *Balkan Latin.* This Romance idiom has neither an ethnic basis (the substratum is Thracian and Illyrian), nor a political one. However, it reflects a geographic and cultural unity within a well-defined territory, distinct from the Western Romance languages.[3] Rosetti considers that Balkan Latin was spoken in the Balkan peninsula from the 5th century AD onwards, after the Roman Empire was divided (395 AD). This idiom is on the basis of Rumanian, and of the Latin elements of Albanian and Serbo–Croatian. Dalmatia belonged after the division of the Empire to the western empire, and received from that time on mostly influences from the west. But even Albanian shows some innovations from the west (for example Latin *u* > *ü*). Although Balkan Romance does not contain Italian, there are, as shown above, influences from Italian dialects in the Balkan idioms, thus also in Rumanian.

The frontiers of Balkan Latin may be drawn with considerable accuracy. Towards the west, Latin spoken in the Balkan peninsula was connected through Istria with the region of Friuli and other parts of northern Italy and by sea, with other regions of Italy. The intermediary area towards the west was thus Istria. The southern and southeastern frontiers were, on the basis of inscriptions, milestones, and coins made by the towns, determined by Jireček as follows:

> Sie verliess das Adriatische Meer bei Lissus, ging durch die Berge der Mirediten und der Dibra in das nördliche Makedonien zwischen Scupi and Stobi durch, umging Naissus und Remesiana mit ihren lateinischen Bürgern, während Pautalia (Küstendil) und Serdica (Sofia) samt die Landschaft von Pirot in das griechische Gebiet gehörten; zuletzt wendete sie sich längs des Nordabhanges des Hämus zur Pontusküste.[4]

---

[1]Rosetti ILR 1986, p. 78: N. Rum. *unde* instead of *ubi*, loan translations, such as *cerul gurii* for 'palatum', the replacement of the infinitive with the conjunctive, etc.

[2]Ibid.: Rumanian, southern Italian dialects and Sardinian share for example the following: the preservation of *ŭ*, and of the diphthong *au*, as well as of the intervocalic consonants *-s-*, *-p-*, *-t-*, *-k-*. Concordances in the vocabulary of Rumanian and Sardinian: *frig, pătrunde, rouă, şti.*

[3]Vidos Handbuch 1975, p. 298.

[4]Jirećek G 1911, pp. 38–39.

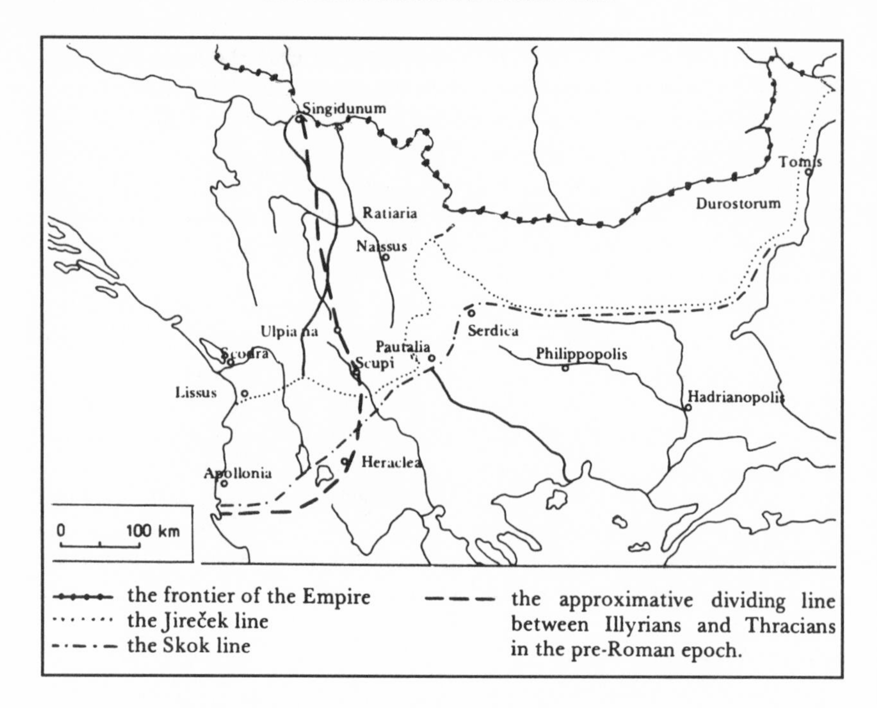

Map 6. The Roman Empire in southeastern Europe in the period of East Latin (the 4th–6th centuries AD). The dividing line between the area of Greek and that in which mostly Latin was spoken is shown by the Jireček- and the Skok-line.

This is called the "*Jireček line*" (see map 6). Skok considered that the western part of this line should be drawn somewhat more to the south. Of course, the frontier between Latin and Greek was probably not as clear-cut; bilingual areas certainly existed both north and south of the Jireček line.

In the north, a Roman population probably still lived in the former province of Pannonia at least in the 5th century. The question whether the dialect spoken there belonged to East Latin or to the Occidental dialects has been discussed[1] but is of no major significance for the problem of Rumanian. The Great Hungarian plain was never occupied by the Roman Empire.

The eastern part of the northern frontiers of Balkan Latin: Roman colonization reached the lower Danube during the 1st century BC; until 106 AD, the Danube was the northeastern frontier. Between 106 and 271–275 AD, the territories of present day Oltenia, part of the Banat and part of Transylvania were a Roman province: *Dacia Traiana.* Thus, during 169 years, the frontiers of the Empire were pushed northward as far as to northern Transylvania. However, from

[1] According to Rosetti ILR 1986, p. 81, it probably belonged to eastern Romance.

275 AD until the withdrawal of the Byzantine army at the beginning of the 7th century, i.e., for more than three centuries which roughly correspond to the period of Balkan Latin (and in entire Romania, to Late Latin), the Danubian *limes* was the northeastern frontier of the Empire, thus also of Balkan Latin.

2. THE FEATURES OF EAST LATIN

Phonetics

(a) *ŭ* was preserved in Rumanian, Albanian, and Sardinian: Latin *gula* > Rumanian *gură, lupus* > *lup, numerus* > *număr.*[1]

(b) The pronunciation *o* of the diphthong *au* is found in inscriptions: *Olii* instead of *Aulii* in Pompei, *oricla* in Gallia; it is criticized in *Appenix Probi* (written after the 3rd–4th centuries): "*a colore auri quod rustici orum dicebant.*"[2] This pronunciation was introduced in Rome by Umbrians and other groups after the war in 89 BC. The diphthong *au* was, however, preserved in Rumanian, Dalmatian, Friulian, Sicilian, Provencale, and Catalan, in a stressed position: Latin *aur* > N. Rumanian *aur*, Vegliotic *yaur*, Old Provençal *aur*; Lat. *laudare* > N. Rum. *lăuda*, Friulian *lauda*, Prov. *lauzur*. In Albanian, Lat. *au* > *a* : *aurum* > *ar, paucum* > *pak.*

(c) Examples of the change of voiceless *-p-, -t-, -k-* to voiced consonants are found already in inscriptions from Pompei (*pagatus, megum* [instead of *mecum*]). In the west, this became general after the end of the 5th century, with the exception of a number of dialects (Mozarabic, Upper Bearnese, Upper Aragonese).[3] In Balkan Latin, the voiceless stops were conserved "*avec une remarquable fidélité*":[4] Latin *pacare* > N. Rum. *împăca, ripa* > *rîpă,* Vegliotic *raipa*; and also Sicilian *ripa.*

(d) The *kw* > *p* change in front of all vowels except *a* (a phenomenon of delabialization) in Vulgar Latin is seen in inscriptions and mentioned by grammars: *conda* instead of *quondam*; *'coquens non cocens'*, etc. In front of *a* this phenomenon occurred in Sardinian and in East Latin only in the following words:[5]

Latin	Sard.	Vegl.	Old Ital.	Friul.	N.Rum.
qualis	kale	kal			care

[1]Rosetti ILR 1986 p. 105.

[2]Ibid., pp. 108–109.

[3]Rudes, B.A., in *Southeastern Europe/L'Europe de sud-est,* 7, Pt. 1 (1980), p. 115 (book review).

[4]Bourciez, É., *Éléments de linguistique romane,* 5th edition, 1967, p. 165.

[5]Rosetti ILR 1986, p. 116.

quam	ca		ca		ca
quando	kando	kand		kand	când
quantus	kantu	kont			cât

In other cases, *kw* was not delabialized and developed in the same direction in Sardinian and Rumanian: [1]

Latin	**Sardinian**	**Rumanian**
aqua	abba	apă
equa	ebba	iapă
quadragesima	—	păresimi
quadraginta	baranta	—
quadricornus	battigoru	—
*quadrone	bardone	—
quattuor	báttoro	patru

This phenomenon is not found in Albanian: Latin *quattuor* > Alb. *katrë*, *quadragesima* > *kreshmë.*
gw changed in the same way in Sardinian and Rumanian: Lat. *lingua* > Sard. *limba*, Rum. *limbă*, (Lat. *sanguine* > Sard. *sambiene*, Rum. *sânge* is an exception.)[2]

(e) Latin *cl* corresponds to Northern Rumanian *ch*: Lat. *clavis* > N.Rum. *cheie*. Istrorumanian and Arumanian have the intermediary consonant group *kl'*: e.g., Arumanian *k'lem.* According to Densusianu, this seems to have been the case in Balkan Romance when it was separated from Italian.[3] Italian has *chiave*, French *clé.*

(f) The loss of final *s* and its replacement by *i* in Italian in nouns of the third declension: N.Rum. *munţi*, Ital. *monti*, (but French *monts).*

Vocabulary

Also regarding vocabulary, there are similarities between East Latin

---

[1]Ibid.

[2]Ibid., p. 117.

[3]Densusianu HLR (1975), p. 212.

(including southern Italy) as opposed to the west. But even here, the situation is complicated. A detailed study of the East Latin vocabulary is found in *Istoria limbii române* (edit. by A. Rosetti, B. Cazacu & I. Coteanu), 1969, vol. II, pp. 110–173; written by I. Fischer. The criterion for deciding whether a word belonged to the East Latin vocabulary was its existence in at least one of the Rumanian dialects.

The PAN-ROMANIC STOCK comprises 488 words. Among these, only seven changed their meaning in Rumanian.

A total of 107 words were PRESERVED BY RUMANIAN ONLY. New formations, unknown or unusual in Latin, as well as semantic changes are numerous in this group.

A total of 214 Pan-Romanic words do NOT EXIST IN RUMANIAN. This is a very high number, "considerably higher than the number of those absent in any other Romance language, including the Iberian languages, in the extreme west of the Romance territory."[1] Many of these words belong to certain well-defined semantic spheres, which indicates that they are not lacking from Rumanian by chance. A large part of them are technical terms, marine, military, or commercial, and also agricultural. Also many Latin words pertaining to general civilization, such as *balneum* 'bath', *lanterna* 'lamp', *lectus* 'bed', *littera* 'letter', *regula* 'rule', are lacking in Rumanian. The process of simplification and impoverishment, characteristic of Popular (Vulgar) Latin, was here more pronounced than in any other Romance idiom. Many synonyms disappeared, leaving one expression where earlier several existed. Thus, *fleo, lacrimo, lamento,* and *ploro* were all replaced by *plango*: N. Rum. *plînge*, Istrorum. *plănze*, Arum. *plîngu,* Meglenorum. *plǫng,* 'to weep, to cry'.

Also the number of inherited Latin terms pertaining to art and science, administration and religion, as well as some complex activities, such as iron manufacture and wooden handicraft is very low. THE LATIN WORDS CONCERNING URBAN LIFE ARE ENTIRELY ABSENT IN THE RUMANIAN LANGUAGE.[2]

Of course, the Latin spoken by the Roman inhabitants of the numerous towns in the Balkan peninsula must have contained these and many other lexical elements which do not exist in Rumanian. Their absence in the language of the Vlachs is in accordance with information from other sources indicating that they were not town-dwellers.

Word formation

The following prefixes are frequently used:

(a) *ex (de ex-)*: Italian, N. Rum. *scurta* 'to shorten', Ital. *scapeta*, N. Rum. *scăpăta* 'to set down; tro decline'.

(b) *extra-* : Ital. *strabello* 'very beautiful', *stravecchio* 'old', N. Rum.

---

[1] ILR 1969, p. 123.

[2] Puşcariu, S., *Limba română*, vol. I, pp. 354–355.

străvechi ′ancient′, *străluci* ′to shine′.

(c) *in-* : Sicilian *intiniriri*, N. Rum. *întineri* ′to rejuvenate, to grow young again′.

Semantic change

Besides changes of meaning which occur in all languages in the course of time, there is in Rumanian a group of Latin words which changed their meaning in such a way that they now belong to the shepherd terminology.

The mechanism of this process is concisely explained by S. Ullmann:

> When a word passes from ordinary language into a specialized nomenclature – the terminology of a trade, a craft, a profession or some other limited group – it tends to acquire a more restricted sense.[...]
> *Specialization* of meaning in a restricted social group is an extremely common process; [...] In some cases, the specialized sense has completely superseded the more general one, and the range of the word has been considerably narrowed. This happened in French to a number of ordinary verbs when they passed into the language of the farm-yard:
> Latin *cubare* ′to recline, to lie down′ > French *couver* ′to hatch′
> *mutare* ′to change′ > *muer* ′to moult′
> *ponere* ′to place′ > *pondre* ′to lay eggs′
> *trahere* ′to draw′ > *traire* ′to milk′.[1]

On the basis of this process a SPECIALIZED GROUP OF PEOPLE DOES EXIST. The nature of this group (in the above example, farmers) determines the direction of the change. Other factors are also at work; for instance, in the case of *trahere* ′to draw′ > *traire* ′to milk′, a homonymic clash between *moudre* ′to milk′ and *moudre* ′to grind′ (from Latin *mulgere* and *molere*, respectively), made the elimination of one of the homonyms neccessary.

In the process of Romanization, the sense of a number of Latin words not pertaining to the life of shepherds was changed by the ancestors of the Rumanians to denote shepherding terms, obviously an indication of the main occupation of this people:

Latin	meaning	**N. Rum.**	meaning
meridies	midday, middle day	meriză	′the place where the cattle rest at midday′
animalia	′animals′	nămaie	′small cattle′

[1]Ullmann, S., *Semantics*, 1970, pp. 199–200.

coccineus	′scarlet red′	coasin	(dialectal):′sheep with reddsih spots on its head′
turma	′unit of the Roman cavalry; 30 men; (fig.): group	turmă	′flock′
*stimular(ia) (stimulus)	′pointed stake′ (used in battles)	strămurare	goad
minor	′to rise, to menace′	mâna	′to drive, urge on; to carry, push, goad′

Remarks: *turmă* is an example of a word with a special sense (military) being used in a different special sense (shepherd). Latin *stimulus* had a similar, but broader sense: pointed stake used in battle; and driving stake, with an iron point, used to drive oxen; as well as figuratively ′stimulus, irritation′.
Another Latin word, *mixticius* ′mixed, crossed, hybrid′ may be added, probably > N. Rum. *mistreț* ′wild boar, (*Sus scrofa*)′; in French, Provençal, Spanish, and Portuguese with the original Latin sense (ILR 1969, p. 150). Althoug this is not a specific shepherd term, it belongs to the life of shepherds.

E. The question of the substratum

It is often said that the substratum of Rumanian is "Thraco-Dacian", "Daco-Moesian"[1] or "Illyrian". Very little of these languages is known, however, and, moreover, nothing of what is known (mostly placenames without a known sense) can with certainty be shown to correspond to elements in the Rumanian language. Those who assume that Rumanian developed from Latin spoken in Dacia Traiana between 106 and 275 AD assume also that its substratum was Dacian. C. Poghirc[2] proposes the following principles for the study of this problem:

(a) The elements from the substratum are to be sought among Rumanian words and other elements of speech of unknown or uncertain etymology.

(b) Comparison must at first be made "with the rests, no matter how precarious and uncertain, of Daco–Moesian."

(c) Because of the paucity of the material, any of the old Balkan languages may be used when no Daco–Moesian equivalents are known: "If no sure phonetic feature which excludes a Daco-Moesian origin exists in a word, we must not

[1]Cf., for instance, Russu, I.I., *Limba traco-dacilor*, 1967, and Poghirc, C., in Rosetti, A., Cazacu, B., & Coteanu I., (red.), *Istoria limbii române*, vol. II,1969, p. 319 and in *Dacoromania*, 1973, p. 197.

[2]Poghirc, C., in ILR 1969 vol. II, pp. 319 ff.

conclude that it was borrowed from another old Balkan language, but assume that it once also belonged to Daco–Moesian, even if it at persent is only attested in Thracian, Macedonian, or Illyrian."[1]

(d) Correspondences with Albanian (or with loans from Albanian or from the substratum of other modern Balkan languages) must be considered to originate from the substratum. "But the comparison must be made between the Common Rumanian (*româna comună*) and Common Albanian (*albaneza comună*) forms and it must be extended to other Indo-European languages, with the aim to find possible relations between the respective forms and sounds."

(e) If a non-Latin word does not exist in the ancient Balkan languages or in Albanian, it may be useful to compare it with the Baltic languages or with Armenian.

(f) Besides the languages mentioned above, comparisons nay be made with words from all Indo-European languages from which Rumanian cannot have borrowed.

(g) It is not sufficient to refer to Indo-European roots; words really existing in Indo-European languages must be found and all elements of the word must be explained.

(h) A structural correspondence, without a material and functional one, permits only the possibility but not the certainty of relationship.

Using these principles, Poghirc reached the following conclusions about the substratum of Rumanian:

Phonetics

ă also found in Albanian and Bulgarian, may originate from the substratum.

h present in the substratum, although a reinforcment by numerous Slavic loanwords is admitted.

Rhotacism is considered to be the consequence of the weakening of Latin intervocalic *n* and it is stated that "the only fact to bear in mind is that also in Albanian, the simple *n* has had the same evolution as in Rumanian, i.e., that the distinction between strong and weak *n* existed."

-l- > *-r-* The transformation of weak intervocalic *-l-* into *-r-* (absent in Albanian) has been explained by the substratum but may, according to Poghirc, as well be a consequence of Romance evolution. The same applies to:

kw, gw > *k, g; p, b* – the non-uniform treatment of these Latin consonant groups.

ks > *ps* in Rumanian and *ks* > *fs* in Albanian is explained by the fact that this consonant group was weak also in Latin (cf. *coxim* > *cossim*). "Only in a few cases is this group treated as *ps* in Rumanian and as *fs* in Albanian (Latin *coxa* > Rum. *coapsă*, Alb. *kofshë*; Lat. *fraxinus* > Rum. dialectally *frapsin*; Lat. *toxico* > *toapsec*; Lat. *laxa* > Alb. *lafshë*)."

kt > Rum. *pt,* Alb. *ft* or *jt* is considered an effect of the substratum. (The

[1]ILR 1969 vol. I, p. 319.

pre-Latin populations in certain parts of the Balkan peninsula seem to have eliminated *kt* , as shown by Alb. *nate*, cf. Lat. *nocte*, Lithuanian *naktis*.)

The diphthongs *ea, oa, ie,* the change of unstressed *o* to *u* and some other phenomena are by certain authors assumed to have originated from the substratum. Poghirc does not accept these assumptions.

Morphology and syntax.

The definite article, which is enclitic in both Albanian and Rumanian, "shows in Rumanian and Albanian similarities in details which prove a connection between these two systems" (ILR 1969, p. 324).

The neuter gender: "The many correspondences in details with Albanian (among others, the appearance of some neuters as masculines in the singular and feminines in the plural) shows that the influence of the substratum is possible also here, but neither the linguistic material nor the structural oppositions lead to a definitive conclusion in favor of the substratum."[1]

The numerals between eleven and nineteen are in Rumanian formed according to the system *'unus supra decem'*: N. Rum. *unsprezece (un-spre-zece)* 'eleven', *doisprezece* 'twelve', etc. This is different from the Latin sytem: *undecim (un-decim), duodecim (duo-decim)* etc. The system used by Rumanian is also found in Albanian and in Slavic: Alb. *njëmbëdhjetë* and Old Slavic *jedinu na desete* 'eleven'. Most of the authors consider that the Rumanian system derives from Old Slavic. On the basis of its existence also in Albanian, the Baltic languages and partially in Armenian, Poghirc contends that it may as well originate from the substratum.

The personal pronoun: in Rumanian, the particle *-ne* in *cine, mine, tine, sine* is considered to derive from the substratum, cf. Alb. *-në,* Old Greek –νη and New Greek –να. "The perfect parallelism between the Rumanian, Albanian, and New Greek forms points to an autochthonous origin of *-ne* in Rumanian":

	absolut	*conjunct*
Rumanian :	mine	mă
Albanian:	mua (< mene)	më
New Greek:	(ε)μενα	με

"The Albanian pronoun presents also other interesting parallelisms with the Rumanian pronoun (the confusion between dative and accusative of certrain atonic forms, etc.) which would be worth to study" (ILR 1969, p. 326).

Suffixes

13 Rumanian suffixes are considered by Poghirc to originate from the

---

[1]ILR 1969 vol. II, p. 325; Miron, P., (edit) *Dacoromania*, vol. I, 1973, pp. 207– 208.

substratum. Six of these also exist in Albanian.

The confusion between the dative in both Rumanian and Albanian (also present in Greek, Armenian, and Iranian) is not considered to originate from the substratum because a similiar tendency appeared also in Vulgar Latin.

Vocabulary

There are several thousands of Rumanian words of unknown etymology, 10 - 15% of the Rumanian word stock.[1]A number of these originate from the pre-Roman substratum of the language. The criteria to decide which words belong to this category have been and still are discussed. Since the publication of the first edition of the present monograph, I.I. Russu published the results of his study of the pre-Latin elements of Rumanian (*Etnogeneza românilor*, 1981) with an extensive review of what is known about the subject. Russu uses the method of reconstruction of Indo-European roots and words: "Ancient Indo-European archetypes: roots and intermediary forms, primary formations, ′reconstructed′ and hypothetical, corresponding to forms unquestionably related in Sanscrit, Old Persian, Balto-Slavic, Germanic, Celtic, Latin, Greek, etc." [2] Poghirc (in ILR 1969, p. 319) used essentially the same principles (to look after etymologies among the rests of "Daco-Moesian", the Baltic languages, Armenian, as well as other Indoeuropean languages from which Rumanian could not borrow). He adds that only words may be taken into consideration, I.E. roots are not sufficient. Poghirc divided the "probable or possible" Rumanian substratum-words into 3 groups:

(1) "Words for which an etymology has been sought among words known from Daco-Moesian or other ancient Balkan languages." Thirty five words are placed in this group. The etymologies proposed are from Armenian, Balto-Slavic, Celtic, Dacian (threee words), Greek, Macedonian, Thracian, Thraco-Dacian (one word), etc. Most of them are very uncertain. Half (17) of these 35 words also exist in Albanian.

(2) "Rumanian words also existing in Albanian." This group is the largest, with 101 words.

(3) "Words of the substratum deduced from a comparison with other Indo-European languages." Five words with obscure etymologies are given here. They may originate from a variety of languages, including Germanic, Greek, Hungarian, Lithuanian, and Sanskrit. Two of them (*brînză* and *burtă*) may be connected with Albanian.

Poghirc created a separate group for geographical names north of the lower Danube assumed to originate from the substratum.

The result of this broad approach to the problem of the substratum of Rumanian is far from convincing. The origin from the substratum of the geographical names cannot be accepted (cf. below, pp. 245–246). But also group

---

[1]ILR 1969, vol. II, p. 327.

[2]I.I. Russu, *Etnogeneza românilor*, 1981, p. 111.

1 of words, with a proposed etymology from Daco–Moesian or other ancient Balkan languages, and group 3, with proposed Indo-European connections, contain very many dubious and even certainly false etymologies (cf. Russu, *Etnogeneza*, pp. 59–66). Also in the list of Russu, in which about 180 Rumanian words are given as probably deriving from the substratum, the etymologies are not more reliable. Illyés[1] analysed this word stock from the semantic viewpoint. He found that those Rumanian words which have an Albanian counterpart belong mainly to specific semantic categories: parts of the human body, shepherd terms and names of animals and plants encountered by a shepherd population in a mountainous region.On the other hand, words not found in Albanian are predominantly verbs and substantives of more general semantic content. This circumstance is, besides the uncertainty of etymologies, another reason for scepticism regarding the substratum origin of words not found in Albanian.

One difficulty is to decide whether a given Rumanian word may be a loan from Albanian or *vice versa* (cf., however, below, pp. 71–72). There are no unequivocal criteria; it is not entirely clear how to interpret the sound pattern of these words. Many of them have exactly the same form in both languages: Rum. *buză*, Alb. *buzë*, Rum. *călbează*, *gălbează*, Alb. *këlbazë*, *gëlbazë*; others show sound changes: Rum. *abur*, Alb. *avull*, Rum. *mînz*, Alb. *mës*. Albanian has sounds which do not exist in Rumanian, where they correspond to one or several Rumanian sounds: Alb. *th* – Rum. *ş*, *ţ*, or *c(i)*, Alb. *dh* – Rum. *z*, or *d*, etc. Rosetti assumes that the Rumanian sounds represent different sounds in Indo-Euroepan, which in Albanian evolved to a single sound, according to the sound laws of this language.[2] It is today generally accepted that most of the lexical elements existing in both Rumanian and Albanian are not loans but derive from a common language.

For all elements of language (phonetics, morphology, and vocabulary) which probably originate from the substratum of Rumanian, it is true that a large number of them also exist in Albanian: of seven phonetic features discussed above, at least three: the phonemes /*ă*/ and /*h*/, and the *kt* > *pt* (Alb. *ft*) change. Out of five morphologic elements discussed by Poghirc, the definite article and the particle *-ne* of the accusative of the personal pronoun are explained by the substratum, and also the neuter gender is in some way connected with it. In all these three cases, equivalents to the Rumanian forms are found in Albanian, reaching often into the smallest details. Out of 13 suffixes considered to originate from the substratum, six also exist in Albanian. Regarding vocabulary, the existence in both languages may be considered the most certain criterion for the inclusion of a certain word into the group of those coming from the substratum. There are about one hundred such words.

Thus, the method of broadening the field of investigation and taking a large number of (extinct and living) languages into consideration, gives many more or

---

[1] Illyés Ethnic Cont 1992, pp. 240 and 242.

[2] Rosetti ILR 1986, p. 242.

less possible etymologies. They are, however, very uncertain and are distributed over many different languages. On the other hand, there is one single language in which a large part of the elements considered to originate from the substratum of Rumanian are found – and that is modern Albanian.

F. The relationship between Rumanian and Albanian

Phonetics

Unstressed *a* > *ă, ë*.

Modern Northern Rumanian *ă* and Albanian *ë* are very similar, although not perfectly identical. This is verified also by X-ray studies.[1]

The tendency towards the reduction of the distinction of the degree of opening in an unstressed syllable is found in all Romance languages, strongest in Spanish, Portuguese, and southern Italian dialects. Moreover, there are differences between Albanian and Rumanian in the use of this sound. Referring to these circumstances, the theory of an independent development of *ă* in both languages was put forward.[2] There is, however, extensive evidence of close connections between Rumanian and Albanian also in this respect.

In both languages, *ă* developed from (1) unstressed *a* : Latin *familia* > N. Rumanian *fămeie, femeie,* Alb. *fëmijë;* Lat. *camisia* > N. Rum. *cămașă*, Arum. *cămeașă*, Alb. *këmishë;* Lat. *parens, parente(m)* > N. Rum. and Arum. *părinte;* Alb. *përint;* etc.; (2) from an *a* in front of a nasal: Lat. *canis* > N. Rum. *cîne, cîine*, Arum. *cîne*, Alb. *qën, qen;* Lat. *sanctus* > N. Rum. *sînt. sîn*, Alb. *shënt, shën,* etc. (From the phonologic viewpoint, *î* was in Common Rumanian a variant of *ă*.) (3) In both Albanian and Rumanian, *ă* developed not only from *a* but also, in certain circumstances, from any other vowel (*i, e, o* and *u*).

With certain exceptions, this sound does not appear in an initial position.

In a period corresponding to Common Rumanian, *a* appeared exclusively in a stressed syllable and *ă* only in an unstressed in both Rumanian and Albanian. In both languages, later development created several exceptions to this rule. Thus, in Northern Rumanian, stressed *ă* appears in the first person plural of the verbs in the first conjugation: *lucrăm* 'we are working'. The plural form of feminine nouns such as *cetate,* plur. *cetăți*, with stressed *ă*, developed after the period of Common Rumanian.

It is interesting that the Gheg dialect of Albanian created a series of nasal vowels while Tosc, the southern dialect, "followed the same way as Rumanian,

[1]For Albanian, by Anastas Dodi and for Rumanian, by A. Rosetti; cf. Brâncuş, G., "Albano-romanica, III. Vocala ă în română şi albaneză," *Studii şi cercetări lingvistice,* XXIV, 3, Bucureşti, 1973, pp. 291–292.

[2]Sandfeld LB1930; Petrovici, E., *Cercetări de lingvistică*, Cluj, 1965; Sala, M., ILR 1969 vol. II, p. 197.

creating a stressed vowel *ë*, similar to Rumanian *ă*." [1]

"The phonemization of *ă* occurred in relatievly identical circumstances in Rumanian and Albanian." [2] Thus, the opposition *a : ă* is found in the category of determination: N. Rum. *fată* 'girl', *fata* 'the girl'; Alb. *vajzë* 'girl', *vajza* 'the girl'. It also appears in gender: Common Rumanian *cumnatu* 'brother-in-law', *cumnată* 'sister-in-law'; and in certain grammatical cases: N. Rum. nominative-accusative *fată*, genitive-dative *(unei) fete*, Alb. *(një) vajzë* and *(e, i, një) vajze*, respectively.

In Albanian, however, *ë* has some functions which have no counterpart in Rumanian: the *ë : a* opposition is used to express number, e.g., sing. *vajzë*, plur. *vajza*. This is most probably a later development because otherwise final unstressed *a* changed to *ë*. Further, *ë* is used in Albanian also in forming of nouns (abstract nouns derived from the participle): *vdekë* 'dying', *pritë* 'waiting.'

Later development changed the Albanian *ë* in many cases, while the number of such cases in Rumanian is much less. Thus, regarding this sound, Rumanian is more conservative than Albanian.[3] This is in accord with the idea that Albanian is a continuation of an ancient Balkan language and as such, continues the phonologic system of that language (of which *ë* was a part). The ancestors of the Rumanians, on the other hand, abandoned this language (adopting Latin), preserving only some elements, among which is the vowel *ă*. In these circumstances, since most of the phonologic elements of Rumanian are of Latin origin, *ă* may be regarded a "borrowed" sound in this language.[4]

The preservation of Latin *ŭ*

Latin	**Albanian**	**Rumanian**	**Italian**	meaning:
furca	furkë	furcă	forca	fork
cruce(m)	kryk	cruce	croce	cross
bucca 'cheek'		bucă 'cheek'	bocca	mouth

The evolution of the Latin consonant groups ct and cs

In spite of much research concerning this phonetic evolution, many problems,

[1] Rosetti ILR 1986, p. 228.

[2] Brâncuş, G., "Albano-romanica III. Vocala ă în română şi albaneză," *Studii şi cercetări lingvistice*, XXIV, 3, 1973 p. 294.

[3] Ibid., p. 295.

[4] Brâncuş Albano-romanica 1973, p. 295: ... "regarding *ă*, Rumanian is beyond comparison more conservative than Albanian. This observation lends support to the idea that in Rumanian, *ă* is a borrowed sound (borrowed by Danubian Latin from the language of the autochthonous population), while in Albanian, *ë* is transmitted directly, together with an inherited phonologic system."

including such basic questions as the origin of the change (Greek? substratum? internal evolution? [1]) and its development (direct or through intermediary stages?) are still not sufficiently understood.

Similarities between Rumanian and Albanian in the treatment of these consonant groups suggest an effect of the substratum:

Latin *ct* > Rumanian *pt*, Latin *cs* > Rum. *ps* (when *k* was in a stressed syllable) and *s* in an unstressed syllable:

Latin:	**N. Rumanian:**	**Arumanian**	meaning:
pectus	piept	k′eptu	breast
directus	drept	d(i)reptu	right, direct
nocte(m)	noapte	noapte	night
luctare	lupta	alumtu	to fight
coxa	coapsă	—	thigh
maxilla	măsea	măseauă	molar (tooth)

In Albanian, the situation is partly similar but more complicated:
Latin *ct* > Albanian *it* (after *a* and after pre-palatal vowels):
Lat. *directus* Albanian *dreite, tractare* > *traitoj.*
Lat. *ct* > Alb. *ft* (in other cases):
lucta > *luftë, cotoneum* > *ftua.*
Lat. *cs* > Alb. *fs* (when *k* was in a stressed syllable):
coxa > *kofshë, koshë, laxa* > *lafshë, lash.*
Lat. *cs* > Alb. *s* (when *k* was in an unstressed syllable):
axungia > *ashung*, *fraxinus* > *frashër, laxare* > *lëshonj.*[2]
It appears that Albanian treated Latin *ct* as this group was treated in the western Romance languages when *kt* was preceded by *a* and *e*, and according to the way it was treated in Rumanian in other cases: *directa* > *drejtë*, but *lupta* > *luftë*. The following evolution may be assumed: *ct* > *Xt* > *ft* > *pt.*

M. Sala[3] tried to explain the developments of Latin *ct* and *cs* in Rumanian by internal evolution, without the influence of the substratum. This theory is

---

[1]Greek: A. Rosetti, H. Lausberg; substratum: O. Densusianu, I.A. Candrea, S. Puşcariu, O. Nandriş, C. Poghirc, M. Bartoli, W. Meyer-Lübke, H. Barić, Vl. Georgiev, P. Naert; internal evolution: Sala, M., "Evoluţia grupurilor latineşti *ct* şi *cs* în română," *Studii şi cercetări lingvistice*, XXIV, 4, pp. 343–354; and I. Iordan.

[2]Sala, M., "Evoluţia grupurilor latineşti ct şi cs în română," *Studii şi cercetări lingvistice*, XXIV, 4, p. 344.

[3]Ibid., pp. 343–354.

based on general considerations. According to B.Malmberg, the changes of Latin *pt, ct,* and *cs* in the Romance languages are the result of a tendency towards an open syllable. Sala considers that Rumanian may present the first stage of this evolution, the second stage would be found in Italian and the third, in the languages which have *i* . E.g.: Latin *lactem,* Rum. *lapte*, Ital. *latte*, French *lait.*

Poghirc (ILR 1969, p. 323) explains the *ct* > *pt* change by the substratum: the groups *pt, ps* were, in the Romance languages in general, as weak as was the group *ct*: in Late Latin, there are *ipse* > *isse, optimo, scriptum, septembre* > *otimo, scritum, setembre,*[1] while in Rumanian, this group is resistent: Lat. *septem* > Rum. *şeapte.* It appears that the consonant group *kt* was eliminated from the speech of the ancestors of the Albanians and Rumanians: in the Rumanian words from the substratum, it does never appear, nor is it found among Daco–Moesian words,[2] and Albanian has *natë*, in contrast to Latin *noctem*, Lithuanian *naktìs*. There are also examples of *ks* > *ps* among ancient Balkan placenames: Axyrtos – Apsyrtos, Crexi – Krepsa, Kokkyx – Kokkyps.

Latin -lv-, -rv-, > Rum., Alb. -lb-, -rb-

Latin	**N. Rum.**	**Albanian**	**Italian**	meaning
salvare		shelbuem	salvare	to save
silvaticus	sălbatec	—	selvatico	wild
pulvis	pulbere	pluhur	polvere	powder
servire	şerb	shërbenj	servire	to serve

There is a CORRESPONDENCE BETWEEN THE PHONETIC STRUCTURE OF ALBANIAN AND RUMANIAN, especially regarding end-vowels:[3] -e was preserved; a > ă, ë; and -u, -o, -i disappeared.

Rhotacism (the change of intervocalic n to r)

In Latin, *n* had a strong and a weak form. During the early development of the Romance languages, in several areas, this consonant became de-nasalized, as a consequence of the decrease of pressure of the tongue during its pronunciation. Weak *-n-* disappeared often, e.g., in Portuguese and in Rumanian dialects. In the southern (Tosc) dialect of Albanian and in Northern

[1]Rosetti ILR 1986, p. 123.

[2]Poghirc in ILR 1969, p. 323.

[3]Meyer-Lübke, "Rumänisch, Romanisch, Albanesisch", *Mitteilungen des rum. Instituts an der Univ. Wien,* 1914, pp. 1–42; quoted by Sandfeld LB 1930, p. 127.

Rumanian it changed to *-r-*. In N. Rum., this can be shown in words as *cărunt* ′grey(ish)′, *mărunt* ′small′, etc. In contrast to this, Arumanian has *minut* and *cănut*.[1] Earlier, much more words in N. Rum. were affected by rhotacism. Thus, at least until the 16th century, Rumanian spoken in Moldavia as well as by the Rumanian inhabitants of adjacent Máramaros (Rum. Maramureş), and those of the region of the Munţii Apuseni, was rhotacized. In other areas, the weak *-n-* disappeared. Today rhotacism is only found among speakers of N. Rum. living in the region of the Munţii Apuseni.[2]

Also Northern Rumanian spoken in the Balkan peninsula has varied and is still varying in this respect. Rhotacism is found in the Rudnik–Drinjaca area while it is absent in the valleys of the Timok and the Morava.[3] Also Istro-Rumanian is rhotacized. (Today, the situation once existing can in many cases only be reconstructed on the basis of placenames.) It is interesting that in Albanian, this phenomenon is only found in the southern (Tosc) dialect: *zëri, gjuri, Shqiperi*, as opposed to Gheg *zâni, gjuni,* and *Shqypni* (′the voice′, ′the knee′, and ′Albania′, respectively).

Rhotacism appeared after the *an, am* > *în, îm* change, and does not affect the words of Slavic origin in Rumanian.[4] The question whether its development in Albanian and Rumanian is connected is not yet settled. Rosetti does not believe in a connection and denies also the role of the substratum in this case.[5]

Morphology
The postposition of the definite article

In classic Latin, the demonstrative pronoun is mostly put before the noun which it determines. In the Late Latin text "*Peregrinatio Aethereae*", *ille* is proclitic in 194 cases and enclitic in 80. In Rumanian and in Albanian, as also in Bulgarian, the definite article is enclitic; e.g., N. Rum. *cal* ′horse′, *calul* ′the horse′, *fată* ′girl′, *fata* ′the girl′.

Sandfeld[6] presented a survey of the possible explanations of this phenomenon which may be summarized as follows: The suffixed article is found also in the Scandinavian languages and in Armenian. Starting from the idea that it must be very unusual, one has assumed connections between all languages in which this phenomenon appears. Thus, a connection between the Scandinavian and the Balkan languages was assumed by B.P. Hasdeu; others evoked Thracian or Armenian influence to explain the definite article in Rumanian. However, this phenomenon is not extremely rare and one has also started from the idea that the

---

[1]ILR 1969, p. 207.

[2]Ibid., p. 208.

[3]Dragomir Vlahii 1959, p. 172.

[4]Rosetti ILR 1986, p. 229.

[5]Ibid., p. 230.

[6]Sandfeld LB 1930, pp. 165–173.

Balkan languages may have developed it independently from each other. On the basis of certain peculiarities in Russian dialects, it was assumed that the definite article of Bulgarian developed independently from Rumanian.

None of these theories can with certainty be disproved, because the feature developed entirely in an age from which no written records are known. It existed certainly in Common Rumanian. In Bulgarian, it developed later, after the 10th century. However, as pointed out by Sandfeld, Albanian, Rumanian, and Bulgarian have so many elements in common that it is scarcely possible that they would have developed just this feature independently from each other. Moreover, as stated by Çabej:

> It is known that in Albanian and in Rumanian, as also in Bulgarian, the definite article is enclitic and that only these languages have also a proclitic article. It is worth noticing that these two languages coincide in the use of this element of speech in the smallest details of its syntactic position, which contradicts the assumption of a spontaneous (separate from each other) evolution in these languages.[1]

It is of interest to review this problem in some detail:

(a) The article is not used when the noun is reigned by a preposition: N. Rum. *au mers la pădure* ′they have gone to the forest′, Alb. *vate në pallát* ′he has gone to the palace′.

(b) the use of a double article: Rum. *omul cel bun,* Alb. *njeriu i mire* ′the good man′.

(c) the use of a possessive article with the possessive determiners when these are used without a noun: Rum. *un frate al meu* ′a brother of mine′

(d) The correspondence of the possessive article in gender and number with the preceding noun (denoting the person or thing possessed): Rum. *o fată a vecinului* ′a girl of the neighbour′, Alb. *kopshti i luleve* ′the flower-garden′.

(e) The article used with the possessive determiners also appears as the determinative before a genitive: Rum. *ai palatului,* Alb. *të pallatit* ′those of the palace, the people from the palace′; Rum. *a cui e această casă?* Alb. *e kujt është ajó shtëpi?* ′whose is this house?′

The differencies are the result of later development. For instance, in Albanian, the determinative is also used before a genitive or a possessive pronoun which follows the suffixed article: Alb. *shtëpia e plakut* ′the house of the old man′, *shtëpia e mia* ′my house, the house of mine′. In modern Northern Rumanian, this is not the case: *casa bătrînului* ′the house of the old man′, *pământul grîului* ′the earth of wheat′, *popa său* ′his priest′, etc. In Arumanian, as well as at an earlier stage of Northern Rumanian, however, as shown by old texts, the construction still present in Albanian is the rule: N. Rum. *pămîntul al grîului, popa al său,* etc.

---

[1] Çabej, E., "Unele probleme ale istoriei limbii albaneze", *Studii și cercetări lingvistice* X, p. 531.

Similarly, while modern N. Rum. has *al, a,* and *lui* (with the function of the genitive) and *cel, cea* (with adjectival function), Albanian has only *i, e,* but in the earliest N. Rumanian texts, *al, a,* often appear before adjectives instead of modern *cel, cea.*

Adjectives

In Rumanian as well as in Albanian, the feminine plural of the adjectives is used in a neutre sense: Rum. *toate*, Alb. *te gjitha* 'all'. N. Rum. *e cinstit în toate* 'he is honest in everything'.

The indefinite pronouns

Rumanian and Albanian have similar systems of creating indefinite pronouns: Rumanian forms pronouns by adding *-va* (from Latin *volet*), Alb. by adding *duaj, dua* ('will; love'): N. Rum. *careva* 'someone', *cineva* 'somebody', *undeva* 'somewhere', *cumva* 'somehow', etc. Alb. *kude* 'wherever', *kurdo* 'whenever', *kushdò* 'whoever, everybody', *sado* 'any amount', etc.

Also *adverbs* may be formed in the same way in the two languages: Rum. *niciodată* 'never', *tot aşa* 'in the same way'; Alb. *asnjëherë* 'never', *gjithashtu* 'in the same way', etc.[1]

The personal pronoun

The personal pronoun (*eu, tu, el, ea,* 'I, you, he, she') in the accusative (*mine, tine, sine* 'me, you, him, her') contains the particle *-ne*. This has a counterpart in Albanian (*-ne*) and in Greek (ε)μενα. There is a perfect parallelism among these three languages as regards the absolute and the conjunct forms.[2]

The feminine forms of the pronoun may be used in a neutre sense in Rumanian: *o cunosc* means both 'I know her' and 'I know that, I know it'; *una* means 'one (feminine)' and 'one thing', for instance: *una e s-o vrei şi alta s-o faci* 'it is one thing to want (will) it and another to do it'. Also *asta* means both 'this (feminine)' and 'this one, this thing'. Albanian *ajo* 'she' and *ketó, kejó* 'this one (feminine)' are used in the same way, e.g., *tsh do nga ketó* 'what do you want for this'.

The ordinal numbers

are in Rumanian formed in a way which is different from that used in the other Romance languages. Arumanian *ntînŭ,*, Northern Rumanian dialectally and in

---

[1] Rosetti ILR 1986, p. 233.

[2] ILR 1969, p. 326; cf. above, p. 57.

old texts *întânu;* modern literary language *întâi* 'first', from Vulgar Latin **antaneus* (cf. *ante* 'in front of, before').[1] This is similar to Albanian: *parë* 'first', from *para* 'in front of, before'.

Word formation

Several ways of forming of words are common to Rumanian, Albanian and Bulgarian, for instance:

Rumanian	**Albanian**	**Bulgarian**	meaning
nici un	asnjë	nieden	'no one', lit. 'neither one'
nicicând	askurrë	nikoga	'never', lit. 'neither when'

Suffixes

The following suffixes may originate from the substratum of Rumanian:
-a, -ac, -andru, -esc, -eşte, -eş, (-aş, oş), -ăni, -îrlă, -man, -oane, -(o)ma, -unţ(ă), -(u)ş(ă), -z(ă). [2]
Six of these 14 suffixes are also found in Albanian:

(1) *-a*, an enclitic, deictic and emphatic particle used in demonstrative pronouns and adverbs, may be of Latin origin. It is interesting that in Albanian, it only exists in the southern (Tosc) dialect, which also in several other aspects is more closely related to Northern Rumanian than the northern Albanian (Gheg) dialect.

(2) *-esc* is a very important suffix, which forms adjectives: *firesc* 'natural', from *fire* 'nature'; *bărbătesc* 'masculine', from *bărbat* 'man'; *românesc* 'Rumanian', etc. The variant of this suffix, *-eşte,* forms adverbs: *fireşte* 'naturally' *româneşte* 'like a Rumanian, after the manner of Rumanians', etc. In Albanian, the corresponding suffixes are *-ish* and *-isht,* e.g., *çobanisht* 'like a shepherd'.

(3) *-eş (-aş, oş)* may originate from the substratum but other etymologies have been proposed, among others, from Hungarian. However, a Hungarian borrowing is not possible in Albanian.

(4) *-oane*: N. Rum. *lupoa(n)e*, (from *lup* 'wolf') and Albanian *ujkonje* (from *ujk* 'wolf) 'she-wolf'.

(5) *-(u)ş(ă)*: in Albanian, *-sh* forms diminutives. This may have been the case once also in Rumanian.[3]

(6) *-ză, -ţă,* Alb. *-zë, -cë,* form diminutives and collective nouns: Rum.

---

[1]Rosetti ILR 1986, p. 337.

[2]ILR 1969, pp. 362–364.

[3]Ibid., p. 363.

coacăză ′black currant; gooseberry′; Alb. *kokazë* ′sweetmeat, from *kokë* ′berry, fruit′.

The verb

In certain constructions, the infinitive is replaced by a verbal noun derived from the perfect participle:[1]

Northern Rumanian	*Albanian:*	meaning:
trebuie făcut	duhet bërë	′it must be done′
e de mirat	është për t′u çuditur	′it is to be surprized at′
am de legat	kam për të lidhur	′I have to bind′

This construction is always used in the Tosc dialect; in Gheg, the verbal noun, preceded by *me*, developed into a regular infinitive: *me fjet* ′to sleep′, *me hangr* ′to eat′, etc. In Northern Rumanian, the counterpart of this form is *a dormi, a mînca,* etc., i.e., the Rumanian infinitive, which is different from the infinitive in all other Romance languages.[2] In Arumanian, the infinitive is always long, it is in most cases used as a substantive: *cîntári, beári, acupiríri,* etc. There are similiarities between Rumanian and Albanian also in the use of the infinitive.

Phraseology

Rumanian has a series of expressions in common with Albanian:

Rumanian	**Albanian**	meaning:
n-am când lit.: ′I have not when′	nuk kam kur lit.: ′I have not when′	′I have no time′
e cu cale lit.: ′it is with way′	ishtë me udhë lit.: ′it is with way′	′it is proper, it is convenient′
îmi vine rău lit.: ′it comes me bad′	i erdhi keq lit.: ′it comes me bad′	′that hurts me′

To strengthen the sense of a noun, ′great thing′ may be added: Rum. *mare lucru*, Alb. *pun′e madhe*: Rum. *am o poftă de ţigări mare lucru* ′I have a great

[1]Rosetti ILR 1986, p. 238.

[2]Sandfeld LB 1930, p. 131 The tendency to replace the infinitive i discussed below, in the section on the Greek influence on Rumanian, p. 89.

desire for cigarettes´, Alb. *i bënet një kal pun´e madhe* ´a huge horse appeared before him´. Also in Macedonian, ´great thing´ may be added with the same effect.

Latin *uvula,* the diminutive of *uva* ´grape´, is in both Rumanian and Albanian called ´little man´: Rum. *omuşor,* ´little man, dwarf; uvula´, a diminutive of *om* ´man´. Alb. *njerith* ´uvula´, from *njeri* ´man´. This is found also in Bulgarian: *mǎžec* ´little man; uvula´, from *mǎž* ´man´.

Several Latin words are in Rumanian used with a changed meaning, according to the meaning of their Albanian counterpart:

Latin **albina* ´bee hive, bee swarm´, > N. Rum. and Meglenorum. *albină,* Arum. *algină* ´bee´. The shift of sense in Rumanian to ´bee´ seems to have been induced by Alb. *bletë*, which has both the sense of ´bee´ and of ´beehive´.

Latin *dolor* ´pain´, N. Rum. *dor* ´pain; sorrow, grief; love, torment of love; longing, yearning; striving´. The extension of sense in Rumanian is also found in the Albanian word for pain: Alb. *dhëmp* ´pain´, *dhëmbem* ´I am regretted´, *dhëmshurë* ´loved´.

Latin *habere*, Rum. *a avea* ´to have´. The participle of this verb is used in Rumanian to express the notion of ´rich, wealthy´: *avut.* In Albanian, *i pásurë* ´rich´ is the past participle of the verb ´to have´. In early N. Rum. texts, the past participle of *a şti* ´to know´ was used in the sense of expert, learned, erudit.´[1] In Arumanian, this is still in use. The same is the case in Albanian: *dij* ´to know´, *i diturë* ´learned, erudite´.

Latin *talis* ´such´. It is possible that Rumanian *tare* ´strong´ is the continuation of this Latin word, with a different sense. Albanian *atillë* (from *talis*) means ´such´, but in the dialect of Borgo Erizzo, it also has the sense of ´strong´. [2]

Vocabulary
Changes of meaning of Latin words shared by Rumanian and Albanian:

Latin	meaning	**Albanian**	**N. Rum.**	meaning in Albanian & Rumanian:
conventus	district court, session, agreement	kuvëndoj ´I discuss´	cuvânt	word
cuneus	wedge	kuj	cui	nail
draco	dragon	dreq	drac	devil

[1] In modern N. Rumanian, *ştiut* means ´well-known´.

[2] Sandfeld LB 1930, p. 72.

falx	sickle, scythe	felqinë	falcă	jaw, cheek
horreo	I fear, I am shocked	urrèj	urăsc	I hate
mergo	I submerge	mërgonj	merg	I go
palus, padule	marsh	pyll	pădure	forest
sessum (sedeo, sedere, sessum est)	sit	shesh	şes	low-land
sella	chair	shalet ´saddle´	şale	loins, small of the back

Remarks: *conventus:* Latin *uerbum* became in the Christian terminology the correspondent of Greek λογος and was replaced by other terms, such as *conuentum, fabula, parabola* (ILR I, 1965, p. 62).

Latin *mergo*: the change of meaning is old, as shown by the Latin text: "*imargebam ... in quartum decimum annum*" ´I was in the 14s´; cf. Daicoviciu, C., *Dacoromania* V., Cluj, 1927/28, pp. 477–478; quoted by ILR II 1969, p.158.

These are examples of parallel changes of sense of Latin words, not found in the other Romance languages but shared by Rumanian and Albanian. They must be considered in the following contexts: (a) changes of meaning in Vulgar Latin (for example, *mergo* and *veteranus* have been also used in the senses which now are the rule in Rumanian and Albanian); (b) of the geographic situation of Balkan Latin, which made a considerable Greek influence possible (e.g., ομιλεω has also in Greek the two senses ´meeting´ and ´conversation´). (c) In the background of these changes of meaning are also universal, generally human ways of thought and association, the socio-cultural and historical characteristics of the speakers, as well as general psychological aspects. These factors made the changes possible. Such factors are at work in all human societies and several single examples of similar development of sense may be found in other languages.

In Rumanian and Albanian, however, there are not only single examples but a high number of parallel changes of sense, most of which are not known in Greek, Vulgar Latin or in the modern Romance languages and are not simple, readily explicable "common sense" changes. Therefore, they cannot be explained by chance or by general socio-cultural or psychological factors only. As also stated by Sandfeld, they were created in a period of common and simultaneous development of the two languages. This must have been the period (or part of that period) of the Latin influence on Albanian and the Romanization of the ancestors of the Rumanians.

The question of Albanian loanwords in Rumanian

Before discussing this question, it must be emphasized again that the large majority of common elements in Albanian and Rumanian derive from an ancient language, spoken once by the ancestors of both populations. However, the extensive similarity between the two languages regarding the Latin influence (see above) can only be explained by contact during several centuries of Roman domination. A symbiosis between Vlachs and Albanians in the region of Ulcinj – Ragusa – Prizren in the 13th, 14th, and 15th centuries is documented in Serbian deeds of gift (cf. above, p. 38). (From earlier periods, no deeds of gift are known.) There are also Rumanian loanwords in Albanian (cf. above, p. 39). Consequently, it would not be surprizing to find Albanian loanwords in Rumanian. This possibility is also admitted by Rosetti.[1] One would not expect a large number of such words, because these peoples′ way of life and their level of civilization were similar.

The important Northern Rumanian word *sat* ′village′ shows a phonetic peculiarity of Albanian, namely the loss of its first vowel : Latin *fossatum* ′ditch, entrenchment′ > Alb. *fshat* ′village′ > (modern) N. Rum. *sat* ′village′. In N. Rum. texts from the 16th century, there is *fsat*, with the sense in *Codicele Voronețean* of ′*lăcaş în câmp*′ ′dwelling, house in the field′.[2] In contrast to the northern dialect, in the corresponding Arumanian word the vowel in the first syllable is preserved, because this dialect borrowed the Greek form: Latin *fossatum* > Greek (we give here the New Greek form) φουσατο ′army′ > Arum. *fusáti, fusăți* ′trenchwork′.[3]

In the case of *sat,* the sound pattern proves its borrowing from Albanian. Otherwise, there are no certain criteria, and about a number of Rumanian lexical elements one may only assume with more or less probability a borrowing from Albanian: *droaie* ′great number, multitude; crowd, heap′ (Poghirc: "probably a recent loan from Albanian", not accepted by Russu); *ghimpe* ′thorn′ (Poghirc); *grapă* ′harrow′ (Puşcariu; not accepted by Poghirc); *moş* ′old man, ancestor′ (G. Meyer and E. Çabej; not accepted by Poghirc). Rosetti mentions *gresie, hameş, moş,* and *pîrîu,* but adds: "We have no criteria to prove this; the possibility should not, of course, be excluded." [4]

Weigand[5] considered that the following Northen Rumanian dialectal words

[1]Rosetti ILR 1986, p. 240.

[2]Ibid., p. 182.

[3]Caragiu Marioțeanu Dialectologie 1975, p. 259.

[4]Rosetti ILR 1986, p. 240.

[5] Weigand, G., *Balkan-Archiv*, III, 215-218; quoted by Rosetti ILR 1986, p. 254.

used in certain areas in Transylvania may have been borrowed from Albanian:

Albanian	meaning	**N. Rum. dial.**	meaning
ëma	mother	îmă	mother (16th century)
dhëndër, dhândër	son-in-law	dandăr	foreign man
farë*	family	fară (in Haţeg)	family
gjymture	band; link	ghiutură	band; link
shtezë	the lowest place in a ship	ştează	trough

* This word, also existing in Greek and in Bulgarian, is of Old Germanic origin (*fara*); cf. Sandfeld LB 1930, p. 97.

Rumanian words inherited from the substratum

The numerous correspondences between Rumanian and Albanian derive mainly from the same ancient language, once spoken by the ancestors of the Albanians and the Rumanians. The Albanians have largely preserved their original language, although they borrowed very many elements from Latin during six centuries of Roman domination in the Balkan peninsula. The ancestors of the Rumanians, on the other hand, changed their language to Latin, preserving only some elements from the ancient idiom. The correspondences regarding Latin elements, however – numerous expressions in common, changes of meaning of Latin words, etc. – must have been created during a period of close contact between the two populations, during the age of Latin influence.

Regarding vocabulary, these same possibilities exist, but it is difficult to decide for each word whether it was present in the ancestral language (i.e., in the substratum of Rumanian) or borrowed at a later period. There are no reliable criteria in this respect.[1] However, it is most probable that THE OVERWHELMING MAJORITY OF THE LEXICAL ELEMENTS SHARED BY RUMANIAN AND ALBANIAN DERIVE FROM THE SUBSTRATUM, and are not loans. As stated by Treimer:

> die alban. Wörter zeigen erbwörtliche Behandlung im Rumänischen, sind also so alt wie seine romanischen Elemente, ein anderer Standpunkt kann sagen

[1]Rosetti ILR 1986, p. 240.

als bodenständig, noch älter.[1]

Poghirc (in ILR vol. II, 1969, pp. 327–356) discussed the lexical elements of Rumanian which may derive from the substratum, a total of 142. Russu gave an extensive presentation of such elements (*Etnogeneza românilor*, 1981), listing 198 words. Not a single of the etymologies from other idioms than the ancient Balkan language whose continuation is Albanian is certain, however. The only reliable criterion remains the presence of the word in question in Albanian. Rosetti (ILR 1986, pp. 240–255) presents "the common elements of the Rumanian and the Albanian vocabulary", without referring to the substratum. (In the index, p. 794, as "substratum languages", Dacian, Illyrian, and Thracian are given.)

In the following list, we use a similar approach. It must be stated that with our present knowledge, it is not possible to create a complete list of Rumanian words which unquestionably originate from the substratum. It is, however, probable that most of the words in the list belong to this group of words, but with the following reservations: (1) It cannot be excluded that a few of them may be borrowings from Albanian. (Those which have been considered probable or possible loanwords, above, pp. 71–72, are not taken up in this list.) (2) It is scarcely probable that all lexical elements inherited from the substratum of Rumanian still exist in Albanian. In the course of time, words disappear and may be replaced by synonyms or by loanwords. Therefore, a number of words which no longer are found in Albanian may derive from the substratum. The chance that this is so is greatest for lexical elements pertaining to the same semantic categories to which most of the words shared with Albanian belong: shepherd terms, animals and plants with which a shepherd population may be familiar. Future research will probably add a number of such lexical elements to this list. (3) A few etymologies are not quite certain: thus, Alb. *baltë* and *mágulë* and corresponding Rumanian *baltă, măgură,* may be early Slavic loanwords, *bollë* may have been borrowed from Serbo-Croatian. The connection of Rum. *noian* and Alb. *ujanë* may also be questioned.

Although only about half of these lexical elements are found in the southern dialects of Rumanian, they must have existed in Common Rumanian. Of all dialects, Northern Rumanian is best known and the southern dialects may have lost a number of ancient words and replaced them with loanwords.[2]

A list of words which have been assumed to originate from the substratum of Rumanian (Poghirc in ILR vol. II 1969, and Russu, *Etnogeneza* 1981) is presented in Illyés *Ethnic Continuity* 1992, pp. 231–239.

In order to facilitate the comparison of the Rumanian words with their Albanian counterparts (which in many cases are identical or very similar), we

---

[1]Treimer, C., in *Zeitschrift für romanische Philologie,* XXXVIII, p. 40; quoted by Rosetti ILR 1986, p. 241.

[2]Rosetti ILR 1986, p. 240.

give here a list of those sounds which, although existing in both languages, are written differently:

Albanian	**Rumanian**	the corresponding English pronunciation
c	ţ	as ts in ´curtsy´
ç	c(i), c(e)	as ch in ´church´
ë	ă	as e in ´term´ (approximately)
sh	ş	as sh in ´she´

Albanian *dh* is pronounced as *th* in English ´they´; Alb. *th* as *th* in ´three´; Alb. *j* as ´year´ (or *i* in Rum. *iad*); Alb. *xh* as *j* in ´jester´, Alb. *y* as *u* in French *mur* (cf. Nelo Drizari, *Albanian–English and English–Albanian Dictionary,* New York, 1957, p. IV.)

WORDS SHARED BY ALBANIAN AND RUMANIAN PRESENTED BY SEMANTIC CATEGORIES

1. Man: parts of the human body

Rumanian	meaning	**Albanian**	meaning
buză	lip; rim, edge	buzë	id.
ceafă	nape (of the neck), backhead	qafë	neck, throat, windpipe, gullet
ciuf, ciof	tuft (of hair), shock; crest (of birds), hair	çufkë, xhufkë çupë	tuft, fringe long hair
grumaz	neck; nape; back, throat	gurmas (grumas), -zi	id.

2. Man: sex, age, family relations

Rumanian	meaning	**Albanian**	meaning
copil	child, infant	kopil	knight; bastard

ghiuj	(peior.) gaffer, old fogey	gjysh	old; grandfather
moş	old man	mishë, motshë	age
spîrc, spîrci	(1) beardless (2) boy, kid	spërk	beardless; raw, callow youth

3. Clothes

Rumanian	meaning	**Albanian**	meaning
brâu	girdle, belt	brez (< bren-zë)	band, bundle, connection
căciulă	(high) fur cap (fig.) head	kësuljë	id.

4. Words pertaining to animal husbandry (sheep stock)

Rumanian	meaning	**Albanian**	meaning
baci	shepherd in charge of a sheepfold	baç	id.
balegă	dung, manure	baigë, bagjë, bagëljë (<baljëgë)	id.
bască	sheep´s wool	bashkë, baskë (Gheg): mashkë	id.
bâr	interjection with which the shepherd urges on the sheep	berr	sheep, small cattle
cursă	trap, snare, pitfall	kurthë	trap, ´Fang-eisen´
căpuşă	sheep louse/tick (Me-lanophagus ovinus)	këpushë	louse
ciut, şut	hornless, poll; single-horned	shut	hornless

ciută	(zool.:) hind, female hart	shutë	id.
fluier, fluieră	little whistle pipe, shepherd´s flute	flojere	flute
daş	lamb of the house	dash	ram
gălbează, călbează	sheep pox; liverworts (Hepaticae)	gëlbazë, këlbazë	id.
mânz	foal, colt	(Tosc:)mës, mëzi (Gheg:) mâz, maz	id.
muşcoi, mâşcoi	mule	mushk	id.
rânză	stomach (of ruminants)	rrënd, rrâ, rrëndës	id.
sarbăd	sour (about milk)	tharbët, tharptë, thartë	sour
spânz, spânt, spâns	(1) horses´ disease with enlargement of the spleen (2) Hellebore	shpendër	hellebore
strepede	cheese maggot	shtrep	worm
strungă	sheepfold	shtrungë	id.
ştiră	sterile	shtjerrë	lamb, young cow
ţap	he-goat, billy-goat	cap, cjap, sqap, cqap, etc.	id.
ţarc	fold, pen	cark, thark	id.
urdă	soft cow cheese	urdha	cheese
viezure, viezune, viezine	common badger (Meles taxus or vulg.)	vjedhullë, vjetullë, vjedull, vidhëzë	id.

zară	the whitish, sourish liquid which remains of milk after the forming of butter	dhallë	sour milk
zgardă	dog collar	shkardë	dog chain

Remark: *brânză,* without an Albanian counterpart, is, however, connected with *rânză* (Rosetti ILR 1986, p. 253, referring to Barić).

5. Human dwelling

Rumanian	meaning	**Albanian**	meaning
argea	room (made in the earth)	ragal	hut
cătun	hamlet, small village	(Tosc:) katund (Gheg:) katun, kotun	id.
gard	fence; enclosure, pilework	gardh, gard	hedge, fence
vatră	hearth, fireplace; house, dwelling	(Tosc:) vatër, vatra (Gheg:) votër	id.

6. Tools

Rumanian	meaning	**Albanian**	meaning
burduf (-h)	skin, a primitive leather bag made of the hide of oxen, sheep, etc., or a bladder	burdhë	bag, sack
gresie (dial.): gre(a)să	grit stone; whet-stone	gërresë	grater, shredder; drawing knife
ţeapă	stake; point of a pile	thep	peak

7. Animals

Rumanian	meaning	**Albanian**	meaning
barză	stork	bardhë i bardhë ´white´	the white one (feminine)
cioară	crow (Corvus) rook (C. Frug-ileus)	sorrë	id.
cioc	beak; rostrum	çok	beak
ghionoaie (ghion + oaie /motional suffix/)	woodpecker (Picus)	gjon	little owl (Athene noctua)
guşă	coop, maw, gizzard (of birds); med.: goitre, wen	gushë	neck, comb of the cock
măgar	ass, donkey (Equus asinus)	magar, margac magjar, gomar, gumar	id.
murg	dark-bay horse	murk, murgu	dark
năpârcă	(common) adder, viper (Pelias berus)	nepërkë, nepkërë, nepërtkë	adder (Viperina) snake, viper
pupăză (pupă + -ză /diminutive suffix/)	hoopoe, hoopoo (Upupaepops)	pupë, pupzë, pupcë, pupa	´Wiedehopf´ upupa
şopârlă	lizard (Lacerta)	shapi	id.

8. Plants

Rumanian	meaning	**Albanian**	meaning
brad	fir (tree) (Abies alba)	bredh (primary form: brad)	id.
brustur(e)	common bur(dock) (Arctium Lappa)	brushtull(ë)	Calluna vulgaris
coacăză	black currant	koqë koqëzë	berry, fruit, grain sweetmeat
copac	tree	kopac	knot (in wood) stump, stub
ciump, ciomp	knot in wood, stump	thump, thumbi	thorn
curpen, curpăn	tendril; stem; species of Clematis	kulpër(ë), kurpul, kurpën, kurpër	wild Clematis
ghimpe	thorn	gjëmp, gljimp, gljëmbë	id.
leurdă	garlic (of the forest)	hudh(ë)rë, hurdhë	id.
mărar	dill (seed) (Anetum graveolus)	maraj, mëraje	Foeniculum officinale
mazăre	pea (Pisum sativum)	modhullë	id.
mugur(e)	bud, burgeon; med: small excrescence, fig.: offspring	mugull	cutting graft, offshoot
sâmbure	(bot.:) kernel; stone; main substance, nucleus	sumbull, thumbull, thumbëz	button

9. Agriculture

Rumanian	meaning	**Albanian**	meaning:
buc (dialectal)	chaff, husk	byk	id.
grapă	harrow	grep	hook

10. Nature, geography

Rumanian	meaning	**Albanian**	meaning
baltă	marsh, moor, morass	baltë	mud, mire, bog swamp, marsh
bară	swampy ground	bërrak(ë)	id.
bâlc	swamp, bog, marsh; narrow and swampy valley in the mountains	pellk, pellgu	swamp, bog, marsh; puddle, plash, mud hole
groapă	hollow, cavity; grave	gropë	id.
ciucă	peak, summit	çukë	id.
mal	lakeside, border shore; coast, beach, bank	mal	mountain
măgură	hill, hillock	mágulë	hill, hillock; pile
noian	multitude, sea; immensity; abyss	ujanë ujë	ocean water
pârâu, pârău	brook, rivulet	p(ë)rrua	id.

11. Popular mythology

Rumanian	meaning	**Albanian**	meaning
bală, balaur	dragon, monster (bală also: beast)	bollë	large serpent (< Serbo-Croatian?
gogă (dialectal, in Oltenia)	ghost, hobgob-blin; old hag	gogë	phantom, ghost; spectre

12. Miscellaneous

Rumanian	meaning	**Albanian**	meaning
abur(e)	steam, vapour; breeze	avull	vapour
bumb bumbărează	button coccyx	bumbrëk	kidney
druete (dialectal /Oltenia/)	wood	dru, plur: drutë	id.
fărâmă	small piece; morsel, bit; jot	thërrimë (Gheg also: tërrimë)	id.
grunz	lump, clod	grundë, krundë	bran, pollard; sawdust
lete (pe) îndelete	free time, leisure leisurely	leh(ë)të	light weight
scrum	ash	shkrum	id
spuză	(1) burning ash (2) eczema	shpuzë	burning ash

13. Adjectives and adverbs

Rumanian	meaning	**Albanian**	meaning
băl, bălaş	fair, blonde	balash, balosh	white, with a white spot on the forehead

gata	ready, finished, completed	gat gatuaj	id. finish, prepare, cook

14. Verbs

bucura	to gladden, to please	bukuronj (Bukurisht: placename in Albania).	to make beautiful
ciupi	to pinch, nip	çupis	id.
scăpăra	to strike, throw; sparkle, lighten	shrep shkrepës	id. flint

Out of these 89 words, 24 are specifically related to shepherding. To the shepherd terminology in the strict sense of the word must be added the names of plants and animals encountered by a population living in high mountains, as well as adjectives of general significance but which also have a distinct sense pertaining to shepherding: Albanian *balash, balosh* means ′white′, but also ′with a white spot on the forehead′ obviously pertaining to animals. Also words such as *cătun* and *argea* denote basic conditions for a shepherd population. The total number of words of significance for the everyday life of shepherds among these 89 words common to Rumanian and Albanian is at least 60 = 66 % of all. Of the rest, most denote basic human notions and conditions, such as parts of the human body and family relations.

The number of these words is considerable. I.I. Russu[1], after rigorous control, estimated the number of inherited Latin words in Rumanian (excluding derivations) to be 1550; those 89 words from the substratum, shared with Albanian, make up about 6% of the inherited (pre-Slavic) word stock.

Many of these lexical elements are among the most important words of the Rumanian language. Estimations can only be approximative because of the uncertainty as regards the substratal origin of a number of words. The following studies may give some idea about the issue: studying the main word stock of Rumanian ("*fondul lexical principal*") A. Graur[2] considered that 22 of the words assumed to derive from the substratum belong to this set of words. (This may not apply exactly to the words presented here, where only those existing in Albanian are taken into consideration.) Another indicaton of the great significance of these words was given by Macrea[3], who stated that they were most productive,

[1] *Dacoromania* I, 1973, p. 196.

[2] "Încercare asupra fondului principal al limbii române", 1954, pp. 48–55; quoted by Poghirc, ILR 1969, p. 364.

[3] *Dacoromania* X, 2, (Cluj), p. 37; quoted by Poghirc in ILR 1969, p. 364.

giving each an average of 4 derivations (as compared to words of Latin origin, somewhat more than 3, and of Slavic origin, about 2 derivations).

Semantic groups:	*Number of words:*		
Popular mythology	2		
Adjectives	2		
Agriculture	2		
Clothes	2		
Unspecific verbs	3		
Tools	3		
Human dwelling	4		
Unspecific nouns	8	—	9%
Man	8	—	9%
Nature, geography	9	—	10%
Animals	10	—	11%
Plants	12	—	13.5%
Terms of shepherding	24	—	27%
Total:	*89*		

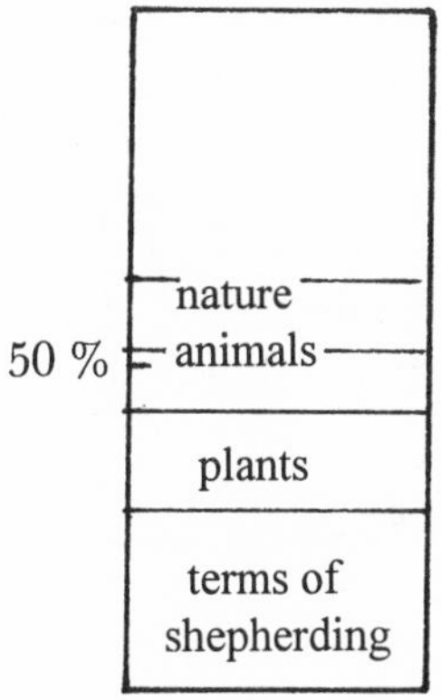

Fig. 1. The number and proportion of lexical elements shared by Rumanian and Albanian according to semantic groups.

G. The relationship between Rumanian and Dalmatian

Dalmatian, whose last speaker died on the island of Veglia in 1898, is partly known from records of the last remnants of the language made by Ive, Bartoli., and others; further, from archives found in Ragusa (Dubrovnik) written in Dalmatian. Studies of the placenames of Dalmatia, as well as Dalmatian elements transferred to Venetian and Croatian also contributed to this knowledge. There were two main dialects: a northern (also spoken on the island of Veglia), and a southern, which included the dialect of Ragusa. Dalmatian was spoken in the northwestern parts of the Balkan peninsula, especially along the coasts and on the islands. These areas were among the first to be colonized by the Romans, and were populated mostly by colonists from Italy.

The area of Dalmatian was adjacent to that of the Vlachs in the mountains east of the river Drina, and also to the territory inhabited by the Albanians. The river Drina in Serbia (after 395 AD the frontier between the western and eastern empires) became in the course of time the dividing line between the territories of the Rumanian and Dalmatian languages.[1] As a predominantly shepherd population, the Vlachs were from the social as well as from the ethnic viewpoint very different from the population of the Dalmatian coasts and islands.

Bartoli considered that Dalmatian belonged to the East Latin group of the Romance languages. However, this is not entirely true.[2] The vowel system of Dalmatian was, at the beginning of the 7th century, probably the same as that of the Western Romance languages. Thus, for example, the development of Latin /*ŭ*/ was different from that in Rumanian. The consonant system was different from that of the Western Romance languages and showed similarities to that of Rumanian (cf., for instance, the preservation of *p, t, k*, and of *pt*). Latin *ct, cs* changed to *pt, ps* only in Lat. *octo* > Dalmatian *guapto,* respectively Lat. *coxa* > Dalmatian *kopsa.* (In most other words, it was later simplified to *t* , under the influence of Venetian.)[3]
Also the *gn* > *mn* change, usual in Rumanian, appears only in single Dalmatian words: Lat. *cognatus* > Dalmtian *komnut*, Rum. *cumnat*; there are also examples of the *mn* > *au* change: Lat. *columna* > Dalmatian *kelauna*; Lat. *damnum* > Rum. *daună.*

The conservativism of Dalmatian regarding the Latin consonant system is explained by the fact that this system changed in the West in a period when Dalmatia was separated from the rest of the Romance languages by the Slavic occupation of the Balkan peninsula.

The great difference between the socio-cultural circumstances of the Dalmatians and those of the mainly shepherd Albanians and Vlachs explains that

---

[1] Mihăescu, H, *Limba latină în provinciile dunărene ale imperiului roman,* 1960, p. 32.

[2] Cf., for example, Hadlich, R.L., *The Phonological History of Vegliote,* 1963, p. 86.

[3] Ibid., p. 85.

the Dalmatian language does not belong to the idioms which constitute the Balkan Linguistic Union (cf. below).

However, Dalmatian, spoken in an area of the Balkan peninsula adjacent to Italy, shows features characteristic of both Italian dialects and Balkan Latin. It was considered a link between Italian and Rumanian:

> A notre avis le vegliote doit être consideré comme un parler intermediaire entre le roman d'Italie et celui de la péninsule balkanique. Par sa phonétique et son lexique il se rapproche tantôt de l'un, tantôt de l'autre. Sa position géographique nous autorise aussi à voir en lui la transition de l'italien au roumain.[1]

Significant are the lexical similarities, words and fine variations of meaning, SHARED BY ITALIAN DIALECTS, DALMATIAN, ALBANIAN, AND RUMANIAN. As shown above (p. 48), these are relics of the age when there was a continuum of Latin-speaking populations from Italy through Veglia and the other Dalmatian isles, and the Istrian peninsula, to the Balkans. To the examples given above, the following may be added here (Densusianu, HLR 1975 p. 227):

Latin **excotere*, Dalmatian *skutro*, Rumanian *scoate* 'to take/draw/pull out, to produce': Dalmatian *blaj me skutro joint daint*, N. Rum. *vreau să-mi scot un dinte* 'I want a tooth to be pulled'.

Dalmatian (the Ragusa dialect) *lundro*, Alb. *l'undrë*, Rum. *luntre* 'boat' and *luntre, luntri,* etc. in (mosty southern) Italian dialects.

Lat. *singulus*, Dalmatian *sanglo*, Rum. *singur* 'alone; only': Dalmatian *sanglo signaur nuestro,* Rum. *singurul stăpân al nostru* 'our only Lord'. *Singulus* was in most other Romance languages replaced by *solus*, although it appears in a number of dialects.

It should be remembered that the Dalmatian language is not known in detail and it is therefore impossible to decide more exactly its relation to Rumanian.[2]

H. The Balkan Linguistic Union

The populations of the Balkan peninsula have had intensive, mutual contacts with each other for many centuries. With the exception of the Croatians and the Turks, they have adhered to the same Church (after 1050 AD theGreek Orthodox) and have continued the traditions of Byzantium. They were exposed to Greek and Byzantine civilization, and absorbed a large amount of Greek material and spiritual culture. Some of these peoples were predominantly shepherds and their wanderings may have contributed to the spread of elements of civilization and popular culture. As a result, these populations have very many features in

---

[1]Densusianu HLR (1975), p. 226.

[2]Ibid., p. 227.

common in all fields of human activity: architecture, costumes, foods, popular art and literature, popular beliefs and, last but not least, language.

The most ancient populations of the Balkans are the Greeks and the Albanians. The ancestors of the Rumanians (of the Northern Rumanians, Istrorumanians, the Arumanians and the Meglenites) also belonged to the ancient populations of the Balkan peninsula. At present, however, the great majority of them are living north of the lower Danube and have no direct contacts with the Greeks and the Albanians. Slavs (ancestors of the Bulgarians, the Serbians, the Croatians, and the Slovenes) have been living in the Balkan peninsula since the 6th century AD. The Turks, coming from Asia Minor, dominated large parts of the peninsula from the 14th century on but occupy at present the southeastern corner only. The Balkan languages belong to different Indo-European groups: Greek, Romanized Illyrian, Thracian or other ancient Balkan populations, Slavic; as well as Turkish (Osmanli), the only non-Indo-European group.

The similiarities in phraseology and syntax are most numerous between ALBANIAN, RUMANIAN, AND BULGARIAN, these are by certain authors called Balkan languages OF THE FIRST GRADE, THEY ARE IN THE CORE AREA OF THE BALKAN LANGUAGES[1]. (Serbo-Croatian belongs to those of the second grade, in the peripheral zone *[Randzone]*). "Quite often, only vocabulary and morphology change and the manner of expression remains essentially the same throughout all the territory occupied by these languages."[2] Balkanisms appear equally in the speech of Northern Rumanians living in the Timok valley, south of the Danube, in Transylvania, Muntenia or Moldavia.[3] Rosetti[4] presents the correspondences between Rumanian and Albanian under the heading "Balkanisms". He states that it is not always possible to know the origin of a certain feature: they may be the effect of the substratum, or of the prolonged and close symbiosis between the different populations, influencing each other, of which most influence emanated from Greek, which is explained by the superior Greek civilization.

Out of those nine Balkan features discussed by Rosetti, five were presented above, under the heading "The relationship between Rumanian and Albanian," p. 60, because they are characteristic of these two languages and are most probably explained by the effect of the substratum of Rumanian, i.e., by Proto-Albanian. The definite article appeared in Latin in the 7th century AD; its postposition, also present in Albanian, is probably explained by Greek influence. The change in the use of the infinitive has the same explanation; these changes will be therefore presented under the influence of Greek, in the following section.

The first author who called attention to the peculiar relationships existing

---

[1]Cf. Solta, *Einführung in die Balkanlinguistik...*, 1980, p. 7.

[2]Sandfeld LB 1930, p. 6.

[3]Obviously, Common Rumanian contained all these elements; later, Arumanian was exposed to a strong Greek influence; the speakers of this dialect are surrounded by a Greek population to which many of them are being assimilated.

[4]Rosetti ILR 1986, p. 259.

among the Balkan languages was Kopitar, in *Wiener Jahrbücher der Litteratur*, XLVI, 1829. Later, F. Miklosich, H. Schuchardt, G. Meyer, and G. Weigand have assembled much material in this field. A detailed, systematic presentation of the intimate relationships between Greek, Albanian, Rumanian, Bulgarian, Serbo-Croatian, and, to a much lesser extent, Turkish, was published in 1930 by K. Sandfeld (*Linguistique Balkanique – Problèmes et résultats*, Paris). A shorter survey was more recently written by Solta (*Einführung in die Balkanlinguistik mit besonderer Berücksichtigung des Substrats und des Balkanlateinischen*, 1980).

The idea of a "Balkan Linguistics" has been criticized by A. Graur, who argued that this cannot exist in the same sense as, for example, "Indo-European linguistics" or "Romance linguistics":

> Remplacer dans la linguistique la notion de parenté par celle d′ ′affinité′, comme on veut le faire maintenant, c′est accorder a la phonétique et même au vocabulaire et à la syntax le pas sur la morphologie; c′est, par conséquent, remplacer l′essentiel par le superficiel.[1]

Graur considered that one only can talk about "relstionshipes of borrowings, of influences, but not about Balkan linguistics".

However, in the last decades, scientific journals of Balkanology have been published and congresses are oganized (since the first Congress of Balkanology in Sofia, 1966), particularly in the Balkan countries.[2] The investigation of the features shared by the Balkan languages seems quite justified. The results are valuable information about problems of interaction between languages, as well as language change, and may also contribute to the elucidation of historical problems. Rosetti presents these relationships in detail (Rosetti ILR 1986, pp. 225–60) under the heading "The Balkan Linguistic Union" (*Uniunea lingvistică balcanică*). His articles pertaining to this problem were published in one volume in 1985: *La linguistique balkanique suivie par le nouveau en linguistique dans l′oevre de A. Rosetti,* Bucharest.

I. The Greek influence upon Rumanian

Morphology and syntax

The verb: (a) The construction of the future tense

The future tense is in Greek, in the southern (Tosc) dialect of Albanian, in

[1] A. Graur, "Coupe d′oeil sur la linguistique balkanique", *Bulletin linguistique*, Bucureşti, IV,1936, pp. 31–45; quoted by Russu LTD 1967, p. 191.

[2] Cf. , for example, Solta, *Einführung in die Balkanlinguistik...*, 1980, p. VII. Solta gives also a theoretical discussion of the problem.

Bulgarian, in Serbo-Croatian, and in Rumanian constructed by the use of an auxiliary with the original sense 'will'. This is not unusual, being also found in English, in the Scandinavian languages, in French dialects, etc. The Balkan languages have, however, also many details in the construction of the future tense in common.

In Greek, Θέλω + infinitive in the construction of the future tense is found since the first centuries AD; in Bulgarian, the oldest texts have *hošta* 'I want' + infinitive, and Serbo-Croatian, *ću dati* or *da-ću* 'I want to give'. In Rumanian, *voi cînta*, in old texts often *cînta-voiu* 'I want to sing' is usual.

Because of the decrease in the use of the infinitive, Θέλω γράφειν became Θέλω νὰ γράφω (not being used as a future, the modern sense of this is 'I want to write'.) The counterparts of this construction are found in Bulgarian and in Rumanian. In N. Rumanian, *voiu să scriu* 'I shall write' is in old texts used parallel with *voiu* + infinitive: *vedea veți cum nu va să poată*, and, on the same page, *vedea veți cum nu va putea* 'you will see that he will not be able'.[1] In Serbo-Croatian, the construction of the type *'voi să scriu'* means in general 'I want to write', but in areas adjacent to Rumanian and Bulgarian, it has the sense of the future ('I shall write').[2]

In Middle Greek, the construction Θὲ νὰ γράφω appears, in which Θὲ is an abbreviated form of the third person of the verb Θέλει. This has a perfect counterpart in Albanian: *do të shkruaj* 'I shall write', where *do* is the third person singular of *dua* 'I will' (*dua të shkruaj* means 'I want to write'). The construction is similar in Northern Rumanian: *'o să scriu'*, where *o* is an abbreviated form of *va*, the third person singular of *voiu*. Arumanian preserved this form: *va si scriu*. This verb is a synonym of *vrea* 'want' but its origin is non-Latin: it derives from the noun *voie* 'will, volition', a Slavic loanword.[3]

Later, the conjunction να disappeared in Middle Greek: Θὲ νὰ γράφω became Θὲ γράφω. The same development is seen in Albanian,where *do shkruaj* often appears parallel with *do të shkruaj*; as well as in the southern subdialect of Arumanian, where *va scriu* is found together with *va si scriu*. In Bulgarian, this is the most usual construction, especially in Macedonia (*k'e, k'a, če piša*). In N. Rum., however, this development is not found.

The future tense may also be formed with the auxiliary of the counterparts of 'have' (Latin *habeo*): Alb. (Tosc) *kam me shkruem*, N. Rum. *am să scriu*, Bulg. *imam da piša* 'I shall write'. Also this is found in Byzantine Greek.[4] In old N. Rum. texts, there is also *am* + *a* + infinitive: *n'am a te lăsa* 'I shall not let you', which is the perfect counterpart of Alb. *kam* + *me* + infinitive. In Albanian, the admirative, constructed by the Gheg infinitive without *me* and with *kam* put after, was originally future tense and existed all over the territory of Albanian. The

---

[1]Sandfeld LB 1930, p. 182.

[2]Meyer-Lübke, *Toblerabhandlungen*, p. 112, quoted by andfeld LB 1930, p. 182.

[3]Lombard, A., *La langue Roumaine. Une présentation,* 1974, p. 275.

[4]Dietrich, Untersuchungen, 246; quoted by Sandfeld LB 1930, p. 184.

construction of the future by the auxiliary corresponding to ′have′+ infinitive is ancient in this language and the type ′will′ + infinitive is an innovation, probably coming from Greek.[1]

(b) The tendency to replace the infinitive

In Greek, the infinitive is used only in the unusual construction of the future tense Θέλω γράφει and is otherwise not used as a verbal form, being preserved only as a substantive. This is present already in the translations of the Bible from the first centuries AD.

In the other Balkan languages, the situation of the infinitive is as follows: Albanian: In the Tosc (southern) dialect, the infinitive is only used in some isolated cases, as *do me thënë* ′that is to say′. In the Gheg dialect, on the other hand, the infinitive, preceded by *me*, is used as in other languages.

Rumanian: (a) Northern Rumanian has two forms of infinitive: the longer form has become a substantive (*lucrare* ′work′), while the shorter one, often preceded by *a* for example *a lucra* ′ to work′, may, in many instances, be used as the infinitive in the other Romance languages. It is, however, in the majority of cases replaced by a subordinated clause with the verb in the subjunctive, and introduced by the conjunction corresponding to English ′that′. "Plus le style est aisé, populaire, moins on trouve d′infinitifs."[2] Also Arumanian preserved the infinitive, as N. Rum., with the ending *-re*, as a verbal substantive and in a petrified state in *va h′i* ′may be′, lit. ′it will be′, but replaced it in all other cases by subordinated clauses. In Meglenitic, the constructions with subordinated clauses prevail, although the infinitive may be used in those cases it also is used in Bulgarian. In Istro-Rumanian, whose speakers are living in close contact with Croats and Italians, the infinitive is used as in other languages and the substitution by subordinated clauses is unusual.

In Bulgarian, the infinitive is used in isolated cases only.

In Serbo-Croatian, the use of the infinitive is the rule, although it may be substituted by subordinated clauses.

This situation suggests that the tendency to evade the infinitive started in Greek and spread northward.[3] What is of most significance is not the partial disappearanec of the infinitive but the fact that ALL BALKAN LANGUAGES REPLACE IT EXACTLY IN THE SAME WAY, i.e., THAT A HOMOGENOUS SYSTEM OF SUBORDINATED CLAUSES TO REPLACE IT DEVELOPED IN THESE LANGUAGES.[4] "The conjunctive is in these languages introduced by the conjunctions *të, da*, and *să* (the use of *să [< si]* with the conjunctive is also characteristic, instead of *că*

---

[1]Sandfeld LB 1930, p. 185.

[2]Lombard Langue Roum 1974, p. 285.

[3]Sandfeld LB 1930, p. 175; Rosetti ILR 1986, p. 238.

[4]Ibid.

[< quod], which would be expected)..."[5]

The word sequence in these clauses follows also the same system in the above mentioned languages: "it is a rule without an exception that the verb follows immediately the conjunction and may only be separated from it by a negative, an adjunctive pronoun or a particle." [2]

In Greek, Albanian, and Rumanian, clauses with a final sense are constructed with the above mentioned conjunctions and the subjunctive. The Slavic languages have no subjunctive, but Bulgarian formed one by *da* + verb. For example: Greek δός μου νὰ πιῶ 'give me (something) to drink', Alb. *a-me të pi*, N. Rum. *dă-mi să beau*, Bulgarian *daj mi da pija* 'id.'.

> Characteristic is the procedure of replacing the infinitive forms with those of the conjunctive and the fact that the phenomenon appears in a handful of languages which may be grouped in a "linguistic union". The concordance between the languages of the "linguistic union" must be explained by the influence of one language on the other, and not only by the fact that the phenomenon appears among languages spoken in the same region (Meillet, *Revue internationale des études balkaniques*, I, p. 29 ff.). The facts from southern Italy make it possible to prove this assertion. In the Italian dialects spoken today in the south of Calabria and in Terra d'Otranto, where Greeks have been living since the antique era, the infinitive, without having disappeared, is not popular; the tendency is to replace it with personal formations introduced by the conjunctions *mu, mi, ma*, and *pemmu* (*<per modo* = New Greek διά ἵνα): *vulia mu sácciu 'volevo sapere'*"[...] etc.[3]

The phenomenon does not appear in the other Italian dialects. Not even in the northern dialect of Albanian did this usage become as common as in the southern, Tosc dialect; and it does not exist in Serbo-Croatian. In Rumanian, it exists in practically its entire area, from the Arumanians in the south through the Timok valley and in entire Rumania; thus also in Transylvania and in Moldavia. (In small areras of Maramureş and Crişana, the infinitive is preferred.[4] This cannot, however, be explained by the distance of these areas from the Greek territory, but it may be conditioned by a Hungarian influence – the Istro-Rumanians, living together with Croatians and Italians, also use the infinitive.)

In Greek, Albanian, Rumanian, and Bulgarian, να, *të, să*, and *da*, respectively, + subjunctive are used to express a wish or an order: e.g., N. Rum.: *nevasta să-şi cinstească bărbatul* '(that) the wife should respect her husband'.

---

[1]Rosetti ILR 1986, p. 238.

[2]Sandfeld LB 1930, p. 177.

[3]Rosetti ILR 1986, p. 237.

[4]Ibid., p. 238.

Vocabulary

Greek words were transferred to Balkan Latin at least beginning with the first century AD, and this continued through the Middle Ages. Especially many words were transferred to Rumanian during the Byzantine era. The rendition of the Greek sound υ in Rumanian indicates the age of borrowing: in borrowings before the 10th century, it corresponds to *u* (Greek στῦλος > Arumanian *stur*, Greek τρυφή > N. Rum. *trufă, trufie*); after that century, to *yu* or *i*: Greek μυστρίον > N.Rum. *mistrie.*[1] For words not containing this sound, there are no certain chronologic criteria.

Old loanwords from Greek are, in Rumanian and Bulgarian (and those underlined also in Albanian): *broatec, bunceag, ciul, ciumă, ciutură, busuioc, colibă, corabie, farmec, frică, jur, martur, papură, proaspăt, putină, sterp, stup, stur, trufă.* [2] "The similar treatment of some sounds in Greek words in southern Italy and of the corresponding sounds in words of Greek origin in Rumanian is explained by the contacts between the Greek language spoken in southern Italy and in the Danubian region."[3]

Some examples of Greek lexical elements in Rumanian will be mentioned here, out of those 18 given by Rosetti (ILR 1986 pp. 214–215). Most of these are also found in Albanian, many also in southern Italian dialects as well as in Bulgarian.

Northern Rumanian *amăgi*, Arumanian *amayiă, amaiă* 'to deceive; to seduce' < Ancient Greek μαγεύω 'to enchant, to charm', found also in several Italian dialects, and in Sardinian.

N. Rum. *cuteza*, Arum. *cutidzari* 'to dare' < Greek κοτταβίζο 'jouer au cottabe', Albanian *kuxoj, guxoj*.

N. Rum. *mîngîia* 'to caress, to console; séduire', Albanian *méngji* 'medicine, Zauberei', *mëngjim* 'healing' < Greek μαγγανεύω 'user de philtres'.

N. Rum. *sterp*, Arum. *sterpu*, Meglenitic *sterp* 'sterile', Albanian *shterpë* 'sterile, which does not give birth this year' < Greek στέριφος 'unfruchtbar'.

N. Rum. *urmă*, Arum. *ulmă, urmă*, Meglenitic *urmă*, 'trace', Italian *ormare* nach-'spüren', *orma* 'trace', Alb. *gjurmë* 'footprint' < Greek ὀρμός 'Geruch'.

N. Rum. *zeamă*, Arum. *dzamă*, 'juice; sauce, sap', Albanian *dhjamë* 'fat, grease; juice' < Greek ζέμα 'decoct, juice'.

A list of Greek lexical elements which exist in all Balkan languages is given by Sandfeld (LB 1930):

---

[1] Ibid., p. 213.

[2] Ibid., p. 212.

[3] Rosetti ILR 1986, p. 213, referring to I. Fischer, "Observations sur la forme et la chronologie de quelques emprunts grecs en latin vulgaire", *Revue roumaine de lingustique,* XIX, 1974, fasc. 6, p, 509–517.

Greek	Albanian	Bulgarian	Serb-Cr	Rumanian	meaning
ἀργάτης worker	argát	argát(in)	argatin	argat	farm hand, servant
δάσχαλος	dhaskál	daskal	daskal	dascăl	teacher
δάφνη	dháfen (dafíne)	dafin	dafina	dafin	laurel tree
δρόμος	dhrom	drum	drum	drum	way, road
χαλύβα	kalive	koliba	koliba	colibă	hut
κάματος work, labor,	kamate gamate	kamato	kamata	camătă	usury
καράβι	karáf	kórab (Old B: korabli, korabi)	korablja	corabie	ship
κεραμίδα	qeramidhe	keramida, garamida	ćeramida	cărămidă	brick
κρεββάτι	krevat	kervát	krevet	crevat (Mold.)	bed
ποτήρι	potír	potír	putir	potir	cup, bowl
τριαντά–φυλλον	trëndafil, trandafil	trandafil	trando-vilje	trandafir	rose
ζογράφος	zográf	zográf ´painter of churches´	—	zugrav	(house) painter
μωρέ, μορή (μωρός simpleton)	(masc) moré (fem) mori, mojë	moré, mori, mari	móre	măre, mări, măi, mă	hey you!

Also many verbs were borrowed, often derived from the aorist.[1] The subjunctive of the aorist has an important role in Greek as present perfect and is

[1]Tense denoting simple occurence, without limitations as to continuance, etc.

used also in cases in which other languages use the infinitive:[2]

Greek	**Alban.**	**Bulgarian**	**Serbo-Croat.**	**Rumanian**	meaning:
κυβερνω εκυβερ–νησα to govern	qivërris	—	—	chivernisi	manage, save, provide for
λείπω, ἔλειψα	lipsem	lipsam	lipsati	lipsi	to be missing
παδεύω, επαιδευσα	pedheps(Calabria) to correct	pedépsvam	pedepsati	pedepsi	to punish
σώνω, εσωσα	sos ′to be enough′	sósvam to be enough	—	sosi	to arrive

In Rumanian, these verbs have taken the accent of such verbs as *vorbí*; thus: *pedepsí, sosí,* etc. Albanian and Bulgarian preserved the accent on the syllable where it is in the subjunctive of the aorist in Greek: Alb.: *qivërrís*, Bulg.: *pedépsvam,* corresponding to Greek να χυβερνησω and να παιδεψω, respectively.

A large number of Greek verbs were borrowed by N. Rumanian in the 18th and early 19th century, when Ţara Românească and Moldavia were vassal states of Turkey and were governed by Greek lords originating from a district of Constantinople called Fanar (the Fanariot-period). With these, the total number of verbs of Greek origin in N. Rum. is about 100.[2]

As shown by their sound pattern, many N. Rum. words of Greek origin were transferred to Rumanian via Bulgarian and in a smaller number also via Albanian and Turkish.

Thus, Greek καλίβα > Bulgarian *koliba* > N. Rumanian *colibă*, (but Albanian *kalive*); and Greek καράβι > Bulgarian *korab* > N. Rum. *corabie* (but Albanian *karaf*). If these words had been borrowed directly from Greek, the N. Rum. forms would be **călivă* and **cărave*, respectively. Also *călugăr* ′monk′, *horă* ′dance′, and *ieftin* ′cheap′, originally Greek words, were by Rumanian borrowed from Bulgarian.

[1]These examples are given on the basis of a list completed by Miklosich; quoted by Sandfeld LB 1930, p. 19. Cf. also Lombard, A., *Le verbe roumain.* Étude morphologique, II, Lund, 1955, pp. 802–803.

[2]Lombard Verbe 1955, p. 802.

An example of a Greek word transferred to N. Rum. via Albanian is *mătrăgună*: Greek μανδραγόρα Albanian *matërgonë* > N. Rum *mătrăgună* ′deadly nightshade (*Atropa Belladonna*)′.

In many cases, the same Greek word appears in the Balkan languages in different forms. This is explained by the fact that different variants of the corresponding Greek words were borrowed. Thus, Greek φαρμαχον gave N. Rum. *fármec* ′charm, spell; enchantment′ (with the accent on the first syllable), while Arumanian, Albanian, and Bulgarian borrowed the Greek form φαρμάκι, resulting in Arum. *fărmac*, and Albanian *farmák*.[1]

A *suffix of Greek origin* for forming of names is known in Rumanian: *-ache,* from Greek -άχης: Michalache, Vasilache, etc.

Loan translations

Besides the borrowing of lexical elements, the Greek influence resulted also in a large number of loan translations (calques) in the Balkan languages:

Latin *conventus* ′district court, session, agreement′, Albanian *kuvendój* ′I discuss, I hold conversation′, N. Rum. *cuvânt* ′word′. Old Bulgarian *suboru* ′meeting′ developed in modern Bulgarian to *sbor* ′meeting; word, conversation′, with the verb *sborúvam* ′to talk′. Also Serbo-Croatian has *zbor* ′conversation′ and *zboriri* ′to talk′. In Greek, there are ὁμιλία and ὁμιλεω modern μιλω and it is very probable that the change of sense: meeting > word originated from Greek.

N. Rum. *a cununa,* Albanian *kunurzój* or *vë kunorë*, Bulgarian *vencavam*, Serbo-Croatian *vjencati* ′to crown; to marry′ (N. Rum. *cununie* ′wedding, marriage, ceremony; bride′s or bridegroom′s wreath′). This expression originates from στεφανόνω, a Greek marriage ritual.

N. Rum. *binecuvânta* ′to bless, to cross; to praise′, Bulg. *blagoslavjam*, Serbo-Croatian *blagoslaviti*, Russian *blagoslavljati* were all constructed according to Greek ευλογϖ βλογω.

N. Rum. *săptămâna mare*, Alb. *java e madhe*, Serbo-Croatian *velika nedelja* ′Passion week′, lit. ′great week′, reflect Greek η μεγαλη ἐβδομασ. This expression is also found in Hungarian: *nagyhét* (cf. also *nagypéntek* ′Good-Friday, lit. ′Great Friday′). Rumanian and Serbo-Croatian have, parallel with this expression, also ′Passion Week′: *săptămâna patimilor* and *strasna nedelja*, respectively.

N. Rum *săptămâna brânzei*, Bulgarian and Serbo-Croatian *sirna nedelja*, Russian *syrnaja (nedelja)* ′Shrovetide′, lit. ′the week of cheese′, on the pattern of Greek ἡ τυρινή (ἑβδομας) the week of cheese′.

N. Rum. *buric* ′navel, umbilical cord; the centre of something′, for example *buricul satului* ′the centre of the village′, Arum. *buriclu a păduril′ei* ′the interior

---

[1]Sandfeld LB 1930, p. 23.

of the forest', Albanian *kërthíjëza e Afrikëzë* 'the interior of Africa'. Greek ὀμφαλός has the sense of both 'navel, umbilical cord' and 'centre'.

N. Rum. *buză* 'lip; rim, edge, border; mouth, opening'- Arum. *budza* and Albanian *buzë,* as well as Greek χειλος have since ancient times the sense of both 'lip' and 'rim, edge'.

"He quarrels with his wife" is expressed by saying "he eats himself with his wife" in Greek: τρωγετα με την γυναικα, in Albanian: *hahetë me shoqenë*, in N.Rumanian: *se mănâncă cu nevasta*, and in Bulgarian: *jade se sŭ ženata.*

Greek στρώνω 'to lay out, to strech out' is also used in the following senses: στρώνω τό τραπέζι 'to lay the table' and στρώνω το χρεββάτι 'to make the bed'. N. Rum. *a aşterne patul,* or only *a aşterne*, Bulg. *postilam postelja*, Alb. shtrój 'to make the bed'; Rum. *aşternut,* Bulg. *postelja, postelka,* Alb. *shtrúarate* and Rum. *strat,* Alb. *shtrat* (< Latin *stratum*) 'bed'. There are also N.Rum. *a aşterne masa*, Bulg. *postiljam masata*, and Alb. *shtroj* 'to lay the table'. Rum. *a aşterne* and Alb. *shtroj* 'to spread (out), to lay' derive from Lat. *sterno, -ere, stravi, stratum* 'to lay out, to strech out; to level, to calm; to cover', *sternere lectum* 'to lay pillows in a resting place', *sternere torum* 'the make the bed'. Thus, Lat. *sternere* had at least one of the above mentined senses ('to make the bed'). This sense is, however, not found in the other Romance languages, only in Rumanian. It seems obvious that the the situation in Rumanian, Albanian, and Bulgarian developed under the influence of Greek στρωνω with its two senses.

Here are some other examples of calques from Greek to Rumanian, Albanian, and Bulgarian:

Greek	**Rumanian**	**Albanian**	**Bulgarian**
ψήνω to bake ψημένος ripe	coace bake; ripen copt baked; ripe	pjek to bake pjekur baked; ripe	—
ὅλο κλαίει he weeps all the time	totdeauna – always tot plânge – he weeps all the time	gjithënjë always gjith qan – he weeps all the time	vse-edno – always; all the same vse place – he weeps all the time
'ςπολλά ἔτη (να ζήσης) to many years σπολλάτι thank you	la mulţi ani to many years* mulţumi to thank, to have enough	për shumë mot to many years*	za mnogo godini – to many years*

* A toast: "to live a long time!"

In Rumanian, *astfel* ′so, thus, in this way′ may be used instead of a demonstrative pronoun with the verb ′listen′. This usage is frequent in Greek: το βασιλόπουλο ακούντας έτσι ′when the prince heard this′; in the New Testament, St. Mark, 2. 12: ούτως ουδέποτε είδαμεν ′we never saw it on this fashion′(in the Vulgate: *nunquam sic vidimus*). The same is the case in Albanian and Rumanian: *si pa djali ashtú* ′when the boy has seen this′, and *auzind astfel împeratul* ′when the emperor heard this′.

The Greek influence exerted through translations of the Bible

In Rumanian, Albanian, and Bulgarian one says ′I ask a word of you′, I say a word to you′ with the sense of ′I ask something of you′ and ′I say something to you′, respectively: Alb.: *do të të pjes dembëdhjetë llafë* ′I will as you twelve questions′, Rumanian *am să-ţi spun o vorbă* ′I have something to say to you′, *te-aş întreba de o vorbă* ′I would like to ask you a question′, lit. ′... to say a word, to ask you a word′, respectively.

It is very usual in all Rumanian dialects to add *de zile* ′of days′ to the words *săptămână, lună,* and *an* (′week′, ′month′, and ′year′, respectively): *un an de zile* ′a whole year′, etc. This is the case also in Serbo-Croatian: *mesac dana* ′a month (of days)′, in the south-western dialects of Bulgarian: *cela edna nedela dni* ′a whole week′, and in the northern dialects of Albanian: *një javë dit* ′a week (of days)′. It is very probable that these usages (the addition of "of days′" to year etc., and "a word" instead of "something") originate from Hebrew and were conveyd to the Balkan languages by the Greek translations of the Bible.

Rosetti (ILR 1986, pp. 256–258) mentions 26 such cases, including expressions such as "don′t intermingle", "unsteady whether", "to have the right to something", "to frighten" (′to put somebody into the earth′), "to annoy somebody", etc. These are only a very small part of the Greek influence on Rumanian and the other Balkan languages; Papahagi collected not less than 451 (fourhundred and fiftyone) such common features. Sandfeld stated (LB 1930, p. 205): "one would not exaggerate saying that it is an exception when these languages differ completely as regards phraseology." [1]

---

[1] Some more important monographs dealing with the relationships between the Balkan anguages (the "Balkan Lingustic Union") are the following:

Puşcariu, S., "Studii şi notiţe filologice", *Convorbiri literare*, 38, 1904, p. 461 ff., and 39, p. 50.

Papahagi, P., "Parallele Ausdrücke und Redensarten im Rumänischen, Albanischen, Neugriechischen und Bulgarischen", *Jahresbericht des Institutes für rumänische Sprache,* Leipzig, 14, p. 113 ff.

Philippide, A., *Originea românilor* II, 1927, Iaşi, p. 691 ff.

Çabej, E., "Parallele Ausdrücke und Redensarten in den Balkan-sprachen", *Revue internationale des études balkaniques,* Beograd, 2, 226 ff.

Solta, G.R., *Einführung in die Balkanlinguistik mit besonderer Berücksichtigung des Substrats und des Balkanlateinischen*, Darmstadt, 1980.

Jokl, *Litteris*, 4, 195 ff.

Sandfeld, K., *Linguistique Balkanique,* Copenhagen, 1930.

Summary and concluding remarks

The age in which the Balkan languages borrowed this large amount of Greek elements and elements of speech from one another, cannot be determined in all cases. The ancestors of the Rumanians and the Albanians received the first Greek influence on their language during the age of Balkan Latin. These words are to be considered Latin, although of Greek origin: for example, *angelus, baptizare, blasphemare, pascha,* etc. Summarizing the results of a study by H. Mihăescu, Coteanu and Dănăilă conclude that "almost all words of Ancient Greek origin found in the Rumanian language were, in fact, borrowed by the Latin language and, with rare exceptions, their evolution in Rumanian was identical with that of the inherited Latin terms."[1] After the age of Balkan Latin, the Byzantine period followed. Beginning with the 6th–7th centuries, a large number of Greek words were transferred to Rumanian, e.g., *ieftin, folos, a lipsi, a mirosi, a părăsi, proaspăt, prisos,* etc. Words transferred latest in the 10th century are found in all Rumanian dialects. That this era, beginning with the 6th century, was significant and must have been of considerable duration is shown by the fact that the Bulgarian language contains most of the typical Balkan elements shared by Albanian and Rumanian. The speech of the Bulgarians cannot have significantly been influenced by Greek (or Albanian and Rumanian) before the 6th century, when the Slavs migrated in large groups to the Balkan peninsula. In the first South Slavic texts, written in the 10th and 11th centuries, a considerable number of Greek words appear, many of which belong to religious terminology.

It is obvious that the parallelisms between the Balkan languages can only be explained by the influence of one language on the other; it is not sufficient to state that several peoples were living in the same territory (e.g., in the "Carpatho-Danubian area"). A situation of virtually general bilingualism must be assumed; many people knew Greek and many of them also one or more other neighbouring languages. The local character of these parallelisms is indicated by the fact that for instance, Serbo-Croatian is a much less of a typical Balkan language than Albanian, the northern dialect of Albanian is less affected than the southern, and also Bulgarian shows some dialectal differences in this respect, Balkanisms being more numerous in Macedonia.

In the centuries in question, the ancestors of the Rumanians cannot have been living north of the Danube or even along both shores of it, not even in northern Serbia, where placenames and geographgical names of Rumanian origin still are extant. The fact that Rumanian belongs to the Balkan languages of the first grade can only been explained if one considers that they lived in (parts of) Macedonia and adjacent areas.

Rosetti, A., *Istoria limbii române,* 1986 ("definitive edition"), pp. 256–258.

Rosetti, A., *Linguistique balkanique*, (a collection of the author's articles about the subject), Bucureşti, 1985.

[1]Mihăescu, H., *Influenţă grecească asupra limbii române până în secolul al XV-lea,* 1966; quoted by Coteanu & Dănăilă Introd Lingv 1970, p. 221.

J. The contact of Rumanian with South Slavic

The Bulgars, a Turk people from the steppes north of the Black Sea, subjugated during the 7th century the Slavs living in the northeastern parts of the Balkan peninsula and founded, in 679, the Bulgarian Empire. During the 8th and 9th centuries, Bulgaria expanded in a western and southwestern direction, occupying Serdica (Sofia), part of the Timok valley and Macedonia. The Bulgarians were Christianized in 865 AD. (A short summary of the early history of Bulgaria was given above, pp. 21–26).

The Serbs occupied the region of the rivers Lim, Ibar, the Western Morava and the lake Scutari in the course of the 7th and 8th centuries. At the end of the 11th century, they expanded eastward and their new centre became Ras, in the region where Novipazar is today. There was the seat of the Nemanja-family whose documents, from the beginning of the 13th century, contain much information about the Vlachs living in their territory (cf. above, pp. 26–29). The Serbs also expanded in a southern direction and occupied the region of Peć, Prizren, Kosovopolje, and finally, in the middle of the 14th century, parts of Epirus and Thessaly.

Between the Bulgarians in the east and the Serbs in the west, in the centre of the Balkan peninsula, an intensively Romanized region was preserved for a long time after the migration of the Slavs to the Balkans. This circumstance is considered to have been of decisive importance, leading to the differentiation of the initially uniform South Slavic language.[1]

1. A CHRONOLOGICAL SURVEY OF THE SOUTH SLAVIC INFLUENCE

The question of the oldest Slavic loanwords

East Latin borrowed the name of the Slavic tribe *Slovene* in the form *Sclavus* or *Sclavinus*; plur. *Sclavi* or *Sclavini* at the time of the first contacts with the Slavs. The word is attested to in Latin texts from the 6th century onwards. The Northern Rumanian form is *şchiau,* plur. *şchei*, Arumanian *şcl'eau.* From East Latin, it was transferred to Albanian: *shqa*, plur. *shqe* (which in that language means 'Bulgarian') and to Byzantine Greek: Σκλαβοι.

Five words are with considerable certainty accepted as being of Slavic origin and borrowed during the East Latin period:[2]
*altiţ*ă 'string of ornaments on a peasant shirt; shirt'
daltă 'chisel' (shows Slavic consonant group without metathesis).

---

[1] van Wijk, Weigand, cf. Sandfeld LB 1930, p. 144.
[2] Mihăilă Studii 1973, p. 22.

mocirlă 'marsh, morass'
scovardă 'pancake'
smântână '(sour) cream' (shows the *an* > *ân* change).

There are a few words from this early period which may be of Slavic origin or transferred to Rumanian via Slavic. They also may have been borrowed simultaneously by South Slavic and Rumanian from a third language and four of them (*baltă, gard, măgură,* and *mătură*) may derive from the substratum:

baltă	marsh, moor, morass	*mătură*	broom
gard	fence	*stăpân*	master, sovereign
jupân	boyard, master, mister	*stâncă*	rock
măgură	hill, hillock	*sută*	hundred

The oldest Slavic loanwords in Rumanian show the sound patterns of South Slavic before the end of the 8th century:

(1) Slavic **ū*, **ŭ*, correspond to Rum. *u*: Old Slavic **magula* > Latin **magula*, Rum. *măgură;* sŭta (Old Slavic *cъto* > *sŭto*) > Latin **suta* > Rumanian *sută*, **metŭla* > Latin **metula* > Rumanian *mătură.*[1]

(2) Slavic *a* (later changed to *o*) corresponds to Rum. *a* : Old Slavic **slavěne* > Latin *sclavus*, Rum. *şchiau.*

(3) The Slavic consonant groups *talt, tart*, are preserved: Rum. *daltă.*

A number of early Slavic loanwords, existing in Common Rumanian, are listed by Matilda Caragiu-Marioţeanu (p. 261):

Slavic	**Arumanian**	**N. Rumanian**	meaning
rana	aránî	rană	wound
nevěsta	niveástî (mveástî)	nevastă	woman, wife,
lěnĭ	leáni	lene	idleness, laziness
skapu	scúmpu	scump	expensive

[1]Pătruţ, I., *Studii de limba română şi slavistică,* 1974, p. 106. Rosetti ILR 1986, p. 251 does not accept the Slavic etymology of *măgură* (Albanian *magulë* 'hill'): there is Sardinian *moγoro* 'small hill'.

trupŭ	trupu	trup	body
lopata	lupátî	lopată	shovel; spade
pola	poálî	poală	hem; coat tail; foot (of a hill)
pragŭ	pragu	prag	threshold

This oldest stratum of South Slavic loanwords, common to all Rumanian dialects, contains about 70 words.[1] These existed in Common Rumanian, before the separation of the dialects around 1000 AD. Some of these words underwent formal or semantic changes during the process of borrowing. Common Rumanian constructed new words by adding Latin prefixes to Slavic lexical elements: South Slavic *vrteti* 'to turn, to twist, to wind etc.' was borrowed and prefixed with Latin '*in*': N. Rum. *învârtesc*, Arum. *anvîrtescu*, Meglenitic *anvărtes*, 'I whirl, spin: dance, etc. Slavic *plesti* 'to plait, to braid', became by the same procedure N. Rum. *împletesc*, Arum. *mpletescu*, Meglenite *amplites* 'I knit, weave'. An example of a Slavic word borrowed by Rumanian with a changed sense is *loviti* 'to hunt; to seize' > N. Rum. *a lovi* 'to strike, to hit, to attack'. Slavic *koža* 'skin' > Common Rumanian **cojă* (Arum.and N. Rum. *coajă*) 'shell, crust, rind'.[2]

The chronology of the Slavic loans in Rumanian

(1) Most Rumanian words of Slavic origin show metathesis of the groups *talt, tart:* N. Rum. *brazdă, grădină, grajd*, etc. This change occurred in Old Slavic in the 9th century.

(2) In most of these words which contain the wowel in question, Old Slavic *a* is rendered by *o* : *clopot, coș, gol.* This Slavic *a* changed to *o*, probably in the 8th - 9th centuries.

(3) The vocatives in *-o* appeared in Slavic in the 9th century, from which Rum. *fato, Silvio, badeo.*

(4) Slavic *in* corresponds to Rumanian *ę* into the 12th century.

(5) Slavic *y* corresponds to Rumanian *i* from the end of the 11th century.

(6) Bulgarian *ǫ* (nasal o) corresponds, until the 11th century, to Rumanian *un, um.* In words borrowed from the 12th century on, the corresponding groups are *în, îm.* In all Rumanian dialects, there are words of Slavic origin containing *un, um (scump, muncă,* etc.) sa well as *în, îm*. However, in the placenames of South Slavic origin of Rumania, only *în, îm* are found: e.g., Dâmbova, from Old Slavic *dǫbova* 'with oaks', Glâmbo(a)ca, from Old Slavic *glǫboka* 'deep'. This shows that the Slavic placenames were transferred to N. Rum. earliest during the 12th

[1] Popović, I., *Geschichte der serbokroatischen Sprache,* 1960, p. 200.

[2] Popović GSKS 1960, p. 200.

century. (Placenames with *un, um* exist, of course, but these were given by a Rumanian population using a Rumanian word, e.g. Dumbrava.)

(7) The Slavic consonant groups *tj, kt′, dj* appear in Rumanian as *št, žd* (written *şt, jd*), a specific Bulgarian feature.

(8) Bulgarian *ě* resulted in Rumanian *′a (ea).*

(9) Slavic *r, l* > Rumanian *îr, îl.*

There are LATIN WORDS WHICH WERE TRANSFERRED TO RUMANIAN VIA SLAVIC: Latin *matūrus* > Bulg. *mátor*, Serbo-Croatian *mátor* (with the accent on the first syllable) > Rum. *mátur* ′adult; mature′ (in case of inheritance from Latin, it would be **matúr*). Similarly, Latin *secūrus* was not inherited by Rumanian but borrowed via Serbo-Croatian: *sígūran,* as shown by the place of the accent in N. Rum. *sígur*. N. Rum. *oţet* < Latin *acetum* ′vinegar′ contains a Slavic *o* instead of Latin *a*, and *ţ* (ts) instead of *c(e).*[1]

The age of the most intense Slavic influence on Northern Rumanian

After the separation of the Common Rumanian population into a northern and a southern group around the year 1000, the northern group was exposed to a powerful South Slavic (predominantly Bulgarian) influence. To those 70 lexical elements borrowed during the Common Rumanian period, were, in the following centuries, added thousands of Slavic words. These show the sound pattern of Middle Bulgarian (12th century – early 13th century). They are found all over the territory where Northern Rumanian is spoken.

The Slavic influence after the 13th century

The more recent Slavic elements of Northern Rumanian are characterized by features of the respective Slavic language and by the fact that most of them only exist in certain areas, namely in the vicinity of the Slavic language in question. The Serbo-Croatian influence is found in the region adjacent to the territory of the Serbs, mostly in the Banat. Most of them are dated to the 15th century or later periods. (Ancient Serbian elements in Rumanian are few.) Ukrainian elements appear in the northeastern parts of the Northern Rumanian territory. They date earliest from the 12th–14th centuries, as indicated by the fact that they show the *h* > *g* change which took place in Ukrainian in that period.[2]

---

[1] Ibid.

[2] Mihăilă Studii 1973, p. 46.

2. THE SOUTH SLAVIC INFLUENCE

Phonetics

The palatalization of the labials in spoken Rumanian, as well as the palatalization of the dental occlusives (*d, t, n*) in certain N. Rum. dialects were, indirectly, caused by Slavic influence.

The *e* > *ie* change at the begining of a syllable: *el* 'he', pronounced *iel*, is explained by the fact that in Slavic, the palatal vowels (*ě, e, ı, i*) are iodized.

The surd laryngeal spirant *h* disappeared early in Vulgar Latin; it probably never existed in East Latin.[1] In contrast, it is found in all Rumanian dialects. It may originate (a) from the substratum and/or (b) from the large Slavic word stock borrowed by Rumanian containing *h* (e.g., Old Slavic *xari* > Rum. *har*).[2]

The change of Latin *sce, sci* into rum. *şte, şti* (Latin *piscem* > Rum. *peşte,* Lat. *scio* > Rum. *ştiu*, etc.) may be caused by Slavic influence.[3]

Rosetti explains the iodization of *e* , the appearance of *h* , as well as the loan translations (see below) by Rumanization of a large number of Slavs who, learning Rumanian, preserved certain traits of their original language.[4]

Morphology
Declension

The feminine form of the vocative: *soro, Anico*, reproduces the vocative of the Slavic feminine nouns ending in *-a* : nominative, *glava*, vocative, *glavo*. In Slavic, the masculine nouns ending in *o* have, in the vocative, *-e*. The Rumanian vocative in *e* probably comes from Latin (*lupe*, in Vulgar Latin: Alexandre) but its use was reinforced by the Slavic vocative.[5]

The numerals

The formation of the cardinal numbers from 11 to 19 is similar in the Slavic languages, Albanian, and Rumanian: Old Slavic *jedinu na desete*, Alb. *njëm-bëdhjetë,* Rum. *unsprezece* 'eleven'; lit. 'one over ten' or 'one on ten'. Slavic *na* corresponds to Rum. *spre*. The numbers 20, 30, 40 etc. are also formed similarly in these languages: Old Slavic *duva deseti*, Alb. *njëzet* 'twenty, a score', but *tridhjetë* 'thirty', N. Rum. *douăzeci* 'twenty', *treizeci* 'thirty', etc. For the numerals in between (21 to 29, 31 to 39, etc.), Arumanian preserved the Latin system: *triginta quinque*: Arum. *treidăţiţinţi* 'thirty five', while Northern Rumanian borrowed the Slavic system with 'and' (Slavic *i*, N. Rum. *şi*): *treizeci*

[1]ILR 1969, p. 38.
[2]Rosetti ILR 1986, p. 277; ILR 1969, p. 321.
[3]Popović GSKS 1960, p. 23 (referring to E.Petrovici).
[4]Rosetti ILR 1986, p. 269.
[5]Ibid., p. 278.

şi cinci 'thirtyfive'. Common Rumanian had most probably the system corresponding to that of Arumanian. Arumanian preserved also Latin *viginti* 'twenty', and it is assumed that Common Rumanian formed the numerals between 21 and 29 according to the Latin system: **vigenţiunu*, **vigenţidoi*, etc.[1]

The word for 'hundred' was transferred to Rumanian from Old Slavic: *sŭto* > N. Rum, and Arum. *sută*, after the 9th century. The Rumanian system is, in its details, closer to Slavic than to Albanian and it is generally considered that it is a loan translation from Slavic.[2]

The verb

The shortening of the infinitive (*cântare* > *cânta*) occurred most probably under the influence of the short forms of the Slavic infinitive (without *-ti*).[3]

The reflexive, a simple future, and the tense of a reported utterance

Although the reflexive form was used in Vulgar Latin, the Rumanian system of reflexives cannot be explained from Latin. It must have reached its high development through Slavic influence. In Rumanian, the passive is often replaced by a reflexive construction: *cerul este acoperit de nori* 'the sky is covered by clouds', but also *cerul se acopere de nori* 'the sky covers itself by clouds'. The reflexive is also used in expressions as 'they say', 'one never knows'. In many cases, Rumanian developed reflexive constructions where the other Romance languages use non-reflexive: *m-am născut* 'I was born', lit. 'I bore myself', according to Bulgarian *rodil săm se* (in contrast to Italian *sono nato*, French *je suis né*); Rum. *a se ruga* 'to pray', after Slavic *moliti se* (in contrast to Latin *rogare*); Rum. *a se jura* 'to swear', after Slavic *kleti se* 'to swear' (but Latin *jurare*, French *jurer*, Ital. *giurare*); Rum. *a se teme* 'to be afraid', after Slavic *bojati se* 'to be afraid', (but Latin *timere*), etc.The classification of the reflexive in the Slavic languages can also be used in Rumanian.[4]

Through Slavic influence, A SIMPLE FUTURE of the verb developed dialectally in Rumanian: *viu la tine mâine* 'I shall come to you tomorrow', lit. 'I come to you tomorrow'.[5]

In the western Romance languages, the verb of the subordinated clause must be put in the same tense as the verb of the principal phrase which reproduces the saying of the other person, e.g., *il m'a dit qu'il était malade'* he told me that he

---

[1]Coteanu Morfologia numelui 1969, p. 156–157.

[2]"This is the type of loan-translation that one might expect from people who had learned another language tolerably well, but had carried over into it some previous habits of word formation and syntax" (R.A. Hall, Jr., *External History of the Romance Languages*, 1974, p. 92.) Cf. also Rosetti ILR 1986, pp. 279–280, and Sandfeld LB 1930, p. 148.

[3]Křepinský, M., and Beneş, P., in *Studii şi cercetări lingvistice,* VI, 1955, p.255; quoted by Rosetti ILR 1986, p. 280.

[4]Rosetti ILR 1986, p. 282; Popović GSKS 1960, p. 207. The reflexive has six forms: objective, eventive, dynamic, reciprocal, passive, and impersonal.

[5]Popović GSKS 1960, p. 207.

was sick'. Rumanian has a different rule, borrowed from Slavic: the tense of an utterance is generally retained when the utterance is reported: *mi-a spus că e bolnav* 'he told me that he was sick', lit. 'he told me that he is sick'.[1]

The aspect of the verb

In Slavic, the aspect of the verb is of great significance. It is expressed by particles in front of the verb. The imperfective aspect expresses action not completed (either continuous, or repeated) while the perfective aspect expresses completion of action. In Rumanian, as in the other Romance languages, the verb expresses time, without indicating the duration of the action. The imperfective or perfective character of an action is expressed in different ways, of which one (expression by prefixes) developed under the influence of Slavic: *pre-*, in *preface, prelucra* 'to remake, to change, to process', *răs-*, in *răscumpăra* 'to redeem, to expiate; to buy back'.

Vocabulary: Qualitative aspects

The lexical elements of Slavic origin in Rumanian concern all fields of human activity and material culture, including also abstract notions. Particularly significant are the semantic groups of words which denote things of basic importance for all human beings: *gât* 'neck; throat', *obraz* 'face, cheek', *stomac* 'stomach' and family relations: *maică* 'moder; nun', *maşteră* 'stepmother', *nevastă* 'wife, young woman',[2] *rudă* 'relative'. Even *baştină* 'motherland, native land; origin, descent' is of Slavic origin, as well as such an important part of speech as the affirmative *da* 'yes'. Historically important semantic groups are the religious terminology of Slavic origin (presented below, pp. 113–114) and that of words pertaining to social life and state organization. Of the last mentioned category, the following may be mentioned as examples:

pravilă	law	zaveră	revolt, rebellion
poruncă	order	răscoală	" "
silă	compulsion, force, violence	război	war

[1]Lombard Langue Roum 1974, p. 280.

[2]Popović (GSKS 1960, p. 197) quotes S. Puşcariu: "Wenn *nevastă* 'junge Frau, Ehefrau' slavischen Ursprungs ist, so stammt dieses Wort aller Wahrscheinlichkeit nach aus der Zeit, in der die Rumänen anfingen, sich mit Slavinnen zu verheiraten. *Mi-am luat o nevastă* bedeutete also anfänglich nicht 'ich habe mir eine Frau genommen', sondern 'ich habe mir ... eine slavische Frau genommen'."

zapis	deed	năvăli	to rush (at), to attack, to invade
sfat	piece of advice; council	sabie	sword
obşte	community, people; council, assembly	steag	flag
gloabă	fine (sum of money fixed as penalty for offence)	strajă	sentry, guard

Bourciez described the intimate relationships between Slavs and Rumanians as reflected by the Slavic loanwords:

[many important words pertaining to material civilization, such as *zid* ´wall, barrier´, *sticlă* ´glass, bottle´, *coasă* ´scythe´ etc. were borrowed from Slavic] D´autre part, l´adoption des termes slaves relatifs à la vie intellectuelle et morale montre combien intime a été le mélange des populations. A coté du lat. *tempus* (roum. *timp*), on s´est servi de préférence de l´a. sla. *vremę* (roum. *vreme*), et voici quelques autres emprunts: roum. *slovă* ´a.sl. *slovo* ´écriture´, *războiu* = *razboj* ´guerre´, *rană* = *rana* ´blessure´, *ciudă* = *čudo* ´miracle´, *groază* = *groza* ´épouvante´, *nădejde* = *nadežda* ´espoir´, *noroc* = *naroku* ´bonheur´, etc. Il en été de même pour les termes se rapportant aux cadres de la vie sociale (roum. *jupîn* = *a.sl. županŭ* ´maitre´, *slugă* = *sluga* ´serviteur), et pour un grand nombre d´adjectifs usuels: roum. *drag* = *a. sl. dragŭ* = ´chéri´, *bogat* = *bogatŭ* ´riche´, *mîndru* = *madrŭ* ´orgueilleux´, *gol* = *golŭ* ´nu´. Enfin beaucoup de verbes furent empruntés, comme a.sl. *saditi* ´planter, *izbaviti* ´sauver´, (roum. *sădi, izbăvi*), *darovati* (roum. *dărui*) à coté du lat. dare, et il est caractéristique de voir un terme tel que *amare* disparaitre devant a.sl. *ljubiti* (roum. *iubi*). L´impersonnel qui marque la nécessité, roum. *trebuie* ´il faut´, vient aussi de la a.sl. *trěbovati*.[1]

Quantitative aspects

Before discussing the magnitude of the South Slavic impact upon Northern Rumanian vocabulary up to the 13th centrury, it should be pointed out that a considerable part of the words of Slavic origin was replaced during the last two centuries by other, predominantly Romance words. This was the result of a conscious attempt to "re-Romanize" the language. U. Weinreich, who does not believe that purism and standardizing tendencies are a major factor in the history of languages, cites Rumanian as one example (the other being Czech) where such

[1]Bourciez, E., *Éléments de linguistique romane,* 1967, pp. 194–195.

tendencies "did attain signal successes".[1] Nevertheless, in spite of the elimination of a large number of Slavic words in modern times, statistics made from different viewpoints show the tremendous impact of South Slavic on the vocabulary of Northern Rumanian.

(1) Macrea studied the vocabulary of Eminescu. Out of 3607 different words used by the great poet (1850–1889), he found that 48.68% of the words were of Latin origin and 16.81% were from Slavic. Regarding frequency, out of a total of 33.846 words, 83% were of Latin and only 6.93% of Slavic origin.Of course, as Mihăilă remarks, this method disregards the practical importance of the words. Thus, Eminescu used the international word of Latin origin *amor* very frequently, while *plug* 'plough', used daily by millions of peasants, occurs in his poems only twice.[2]

(2) Popović quotes Puşcariu: "... in einem Verzeichnis von 5765Wörtern, auf nur 1165 lateinischen Ursprungs die imposante Anzahl von 2361 slavischen Wörtern kommt (die übrigen sind türk., ngr., magy. und thrak. Herkunft), also 2/5 des Wortschatzes slavisch sind..." (Popović goes as far as to affirm: "In bezug auf den Wortschatz ist das Rumänische keine romanische, sondern eine slavische Sprache...")[3]

(3) A large sample of lexical elements (a total of 24.311, excluding derivations) were studied, on the basis of the dictionary of Candrea, by Macrea. Out of these, 20.68% were found to be of Latin and 16.45% of Slavic origin, a ratio of approximately 10 Latin to 8 Slavic.[4]

(4) The main word stock ("*fondul lexical principal*") of N. Rumanian was studied by Graur. Out of 1419 words considered to belong to this group, 58.21% were of Latin and 21.49% of Slavic origin.[5]

(5) I.I. Russu gives the following figures about the basic elements ("Grundelemente", "wenn man nur die Grundwörter zählt, aus denen die Familien der Ableitungen gebildet werden") of the Rumanian word stock: 160 (170) "autochthonous", 1550 Latin, "more than 2000 Slavic."[6] According to this, about 42% of the basic lexical elements of Northern Rumanian are of Latin origin and at least 54%, more than half, derive from Slavic.

---

[1]Weinreich Lang Cont 1964, p. 103.

[2]Quoted by Mihăilă, G., *Împrumuturi vechi sud-slave în limba română,* 1960, p. 250.

[3]Popović GSKS 1960, p. 199.

[4]Macrea, D., "Circulaţia cuvintelor în limba română", *Transylvania*, 73, 1942, Sibiu, pp. 11–14, 22; Macre, D., "Contribuţie la studiul fondului principal de cuvinte al limbii romîne", *Studii şi cercetări lingvistice*, V, 1954, 1–2, pp. 12–13; quoted by Mihăilă Împrumuturi 1960, p. 252.

[5]Graur, A., *Încercare asupra fondului principal lexical al limbii romîne*, 1954; quoted by Mihăilă Împrumuturi 1960, p. 253.

[6]*Dacoromania* I, 1973, p. 196.

The semantic influence of South Slavic

There are cases in which the meaning of a Slavic word was borrowed by Rumanian: Rum. *lume* 'light; world', from Latin *lumen* 'light'. The second sense developed in Rumanian on the analogy of Old Slavic *světŭ* 'light; world, universe'. The existence of this sense in all Rumanian dialects indicates its presence in Common Rumanian.[1] The origin of the double sense of this word is Oriental; Russian *svět* still preserves both senses, as well as Hungarian *világ*, while in modern Bulgarian, the sense 'world' is found only.

There are also many loan translations (calques), i.e., Rumanian adopted South Slavic expressions in more or less literally translated forms:

N Rum. *untdelemn* 'oil, olive oil', lit. 'wood butter', cf. Old Slavic *drěvěno maslo* 'vegetable oil', lit. wood butter'.

N. Rum. *destul* 'sufficient, enough', < *de sătul*; cf. Bulgarian *dosta* 'sufficient, enough', < *do* + *sit* (Old Slavic *sytŭ*).

N. Rum. *fruntaş* 'chief' < *frunte* 'forehead'; cf. Bulg. *cělnik* 'leader' < *celo* 'forehead'.

N. Rum. *a înlemni* 'to be dumbfounded', lit. 'to become of wood' (*lemn* `wood'); cf. Bulg. *sdărvjavam se* 'to become numb, as of wood' (*dărvo* 'wood').[2]

Among loan translations, there are also some verbs:

N. Rum. *binevesti* was formed according to Slavic *blagovestiti*, N. Rum. *preacurvi* corresponds to Slavic *preljubodeiti*, N. Rum. *încurţi* to Slavic *vodvoriti (se)*.[3]

South Slavic prefixes and suffixes

There are very many prefixes and suffixes of South Slavic origin in Rumanian, and they are often very productive. They are found in all dialects, which indicates their presence in Common Rumanian. Rosetti enumerates six prefixes:

(1) *ne-* (from South Slavic *ne-*) has the function of Latin *in-*, which was replaced in Rumanian by this Slavic prefix: *nemulţumit* 'not content, unsatisfied'.

(2) *po-* (from South Slavic *po-*) has the function of increasing an action or a trait, in verbs borrowed from Slavic; together with adjectives, *po-* appears in old texts as well as in popular speech today: *poneagră* 'even more black'.

(3) *pre-* (from South Slavic *pre-*) has the function of changing position or to repeat, change or strengthen an action. With adjectives, it forms superlatives; from this comes the adverb *prea* 'too', e.g., *prea mult* 'too much'.

(4) *pro-* indicates an anticipation of the action expressed by the verb. This prefix is productive in Meglenitic, but much less so in N. Rum.

(5) *răs-* (from South Slavic *raz-*) has the function of Latin *re-* (indicating

---

[1] *Grai şi suflet*, 2, 234; quoted by Sandfeld LB 1930, p. 85.

[2] Rosetti ILR 1986, pp. 292–293; Rosetti mentions 25 loan translations.

[3] Lombard *Verbe* 1955, p. 798.

repetition) and Latin *dis-* (indicating detachment, taking apart); it is also used to indicate an action of great intensity.

(6) *ză-* (from South Slavic *za-*) shows that the action has been finished.

Some examples out of 28 suffixes mentioned by Rosetti are:

-alnic (< South Slavic *anĭnikŭ*) forms adjectives: *strădalnic*, from N.Rum. *strădui* ′to strive′.

-an (< South Slavic *-anu*) forms mostly nouns denoting a quality: *codană* ′flapper, bobby-soxer′.

-ar (< South Slavic *-arĭ*) forms names of agent: *fugar* ′refugee′.

-ean (< South Slavic *-jan-ino, ěn-ino*), a very productive suffix, forms ethnic adjectives and nouns: *sătean* ′villager′, *apusean* ′westerner′, as well as family names: Bolintineanu, Sadoveanu, etc.

-enie (< South Slavic *-ene*) is also a very important suffix in Rumanian; it forms nouns denoting an action: *afuresenie* ′ban; curse of the Church; excommunication; curse′, or a state (of mind): *şiretenie* ′slyness; cunning; craftiness′.

-ic, -ice, -ici, -uş (< South Slavic *-iko, iče, and -uše*, respectively) form diminutives.

-nic (South Slavic *-nikŭ /ĭnŭ + -iko-/*) forms adjectives: *trainic* ′durable′.

"The fact that a very large number of words are formed by Slavic prefixes or suffixes shows how intense the Slavo-Rumanian symbiosis has been."[1]

3. THE RUMANIAN INFLUENCE ON BULGARIAN

Changes in usage may be caused by structural, as well as by socio-cultural factors. It is difficult to determine with certainty how many of those constructions which show similarities between Bulgarian and Rumanian were actually transferred from Rumanian. This occurred, without doubt, in many cases; in other intances, the Rumanian influence may only have contributed to the change.

Capidan considered that Rumanian was the most important single factor in the development of those peculiarities in Bulgarian which are not found in the other Slavic languages.[2] He assumed the following Rumanian influence on the *phonetics* of eastern Bulgarian:[3]

(1) The change of *a* to unstressed *ă*.

(2) The change of unstressed *e* to *i*.

(3) Stressed *e* is in eastern Bulgaria pronounced *ea* when followed by *a*,

---

[1]Rosetti ILR 1968, p. 319. In the definitive edition of Rosetti′s monograph (1986), this statement is omitted .

[2]Capidan, T., *Limbă şi cultură*, 1943, p. 229; quoted by Macrea Studii 1970, p. 12.

[3]Capidan, T., "Raporturile lingvistice slavo-române. I: Influenţă română asupra limbei bulgare", *Dacoromania*, 1922–1923, III, pp. 129–238.

o, or *u*; followed by *e* or *i*, it is pronounced *e*. Cf. N. Rum. *seară* 'night', and *seri* 'nights'.

Morphology and syntax

A characteristic feature of Bulgarian is the loss of a number of cases in the declension: while the Slavic languages preserved six or seven cases, Bulgarian has only a few (one, two, or three, depending on the gender of the noun). It is probable that this occurred through the influence of Rumanian.[1]

The construction of the dative in Bulgarian: *na* + accusative (*šče go koža na sini* 'you will tell my son') is also, most probably, the result of Rumanian influence:

> Since Bulgarian deviates structurally from all other Slavic languages in using the preposition *na* to express the genitive–dative, while Rumanian, especially Arumanian, reflects the situation in Latin and is very similar to the other Romance languages, the only conclusion which may be drawn is that Bulgarian borrowed the Proto-Rumanian system of genitive–dative.[2]

The Rumanian vocative with the definite article, *-le,* was transferred to Bulgarian and Macedonian: *božele* 'God!', *sestrole* 'syster!'.[3]

The postposition of the definite article in the Balkan languages was discussed above (pp. 64–66). In Bulgarian, it developed quite late: it is not yet found in the texts from the 11th century, and became general in the texts written in the 17th century. Most probably, it is the result of Rumanian influence. This is, among other circumstances, shown by the fact that Bulgarian borrowed Rumanian forms with the article: *drakulu* > *drakula,* etc.[4]

Also the general use of subordinated clauses instead of the infinitive (cf. above, pp. 89–91) is considered to have developed in Bulgarian under the influence of Rumanian.[5]

Vocabulary

The oldest Rumanian loanwords in Bulgarian belong to Ancient Bulgarian. The second influx of lexical elements occurred in the 12th–13th centuries, the era also of the most intense Bulgarian influence on Northern Rumanian. More recent loanwords were borrowed from the sub-dialect of Muntenia, from the 18th century on.

---

[1]Rosetti ILR 1986, pp. 279 and 394; *"influenţă romanică"*.

[2]Coteanu, I., *Morfologia numelui în protoromână (româna comună),* 1969, p. 54.

[3]Popovič GSKS 1960, p. 208.

[4]Skok, P., "O bulgarskom jezika u svjetlosti balkanistike", *Jugoslovenski Filolog*, kn. XII, 1933, pp. 73–146; quoted by Rosetti ILR 1986, p. 233. Cf. also Sandfeld LB 1930, pp. 170–171.

[5]Cf., for example, Macrea Studii 1970, p. 12.

The total number of words of Rumanian origin in Bulgarian is almost 200. The largest semantic group is that of the shepherd terminology; [1] there are also groups of names of animals, plants, objects of everyday use, parts of the human body, food, abstract words, etc. The placenames of N. Rum. origin in Bulgaria are discussed above, p. 31; cf. also map No. 3.

There are also similar expressions and calques from Rumanian: "great thing" (Rum. *mare lucru*) may be added to strengthen the sense of a noun im Macedonian; Bulg. *măžec* 'uvula' is the diminutive of *măž* 'man', as is Rum. *omuşor* 'uvula' the diminutive of *om* 'man' (cf. above, p. 69). Bulg. *počinal* 'deceased', from *počivam,* may be a loan translation of N. Rum. *răposat* 'dead, deceased', from 'to rest, to repose, to pass away'.[2]

The significance of the South Slavic influence

H.Schuchardt wrote in a letter in 1893: "der Beweis, dass das Rumänische eine romanische Sprache ist, ist noch nicht erbracht".[3] At present, after the "diligent work of two generations of scholars" (Rosetti ILR 1968, p. 281, omitted in the 1986 edition), Rumanian is generally considered a Romance language, although one with exceptionally large amounts of non-Roman, in the first place, South Slavic, elements. It contains thousands of South Slavic loanwords, many of which are of primary importance; calques, prefixes and suffixes, Slavic features are found in phonetics, syntax; and even in morphology.

It is evident that Rumanian could not have been affected to such a high degree by Slavic but in close and durable symbiosis with Slavs.[4] It does not seem too venturesome to assume that if this had continued some – not very long – period of time, the Rumanian language would have disappeared in South Slavic.[5]

The large number of words pertaining to social and church organization among the Bulgarian loanwords indicates that it was not only a question of two ethnic groups living in close contact (similar to the Vlacho-Albanian symbiosis), but LIVING IN A WELL-ORGANIZED STATE. This state cannot have been other than Bulgaria, founded in 679 AD, Christianized in 865 AD (cf. above, p. 20). This

---

[1]Rosetti ILR 1986, pp. 395–396; out of about 140 Bulgarian words of Rumanian origin enumerated, 33 belong to the shepherd terminology.

[2]Sandfeld LB 1930, p. 87, note 1.

[3]To G. Weigand; cf. *Balkan-Archiv*, I, V; quoted by Rosetti ILR 1968, p. 281. Rosetti stated in this connection: [the South Slavic languages will change the Rumanian language] "increasing its Balkan character *in such a way that the diligent work of two generations of scholars will be needed to bring to light the eminently Latin features of the Rumanian language"* (emphasize added). - In the definitive (1986) edition of this monograph, the passage emphasized here was changed to the following: ..."*but will not obscure the eminently Latin features of the Rumanian language.*"

[4]Popović GSKS 1960, p. 199 (referring to the South Slavic impact on Rumanian vocabulary): "Es ist klar, dass ein solches für das Romanentum der Rumänen fatales Ergebnis nur in einer festen slavisch-romanischen Symbiose entstehen konnte."

[5]Popović GSKS 1960, p. 208.

influence began therefore earliest in the 8th century (words pertaining to state organization) and towards the end of the 9th (pertaining to church organization). It is of course impossible to delineate a period of time which is sufficient for the development of the South Slavic impact on Rumanian (and especially Northern Rumanian). It was exerted already during the Common Rumanian period, which ended around 1000 AD. It not only continued, but was intensified after the separation of Arumanian from Northern Rumanian: the strongest Bulgarian influence on the northern dialect was exerted in the 11th and 12th centuries (cf. above, p. 101).

During this period, approximately from the end of the 7th century to the end of the 12th, the two populations lived in close symbiosis in the Bulgarian state. The geographical extension of this state has been described above (p. 22); it was south of the lower Danube, extending towards the southwest to Macedonia etc. (see also maps 4 and 5). During the 9th century, Bulgaria also occupied what is today Muntenia and southern Transylvania. This period lasted less than a century, which is a totally insufficient time to explain the South Slavic impact on Northern Rumanian.

K. The Rumanian religious terminology

During the last centuries of the Roman Empire, the most important socio-cultural influence on the Romanized populations was without doubt exerted by the Christian religion. This could not, of course, happen without a lasting effect upon the language. In the 3rd century, most of the fundamental terms of Christianity began to be created, mainly on a Greek and Latin basis. In many cases, the new faith required new expressions: "The new system of thought called for and created not quite a new language, but certainly new forms of expression."[1]

Repeated many times on different occasions during the religious services, the new terms were adopted by the language of the people. In the Romance languages about 30 religious terms were borrowed directly from Greek.[2] From the viewopoint of Rumanian, the Greek terms which were transferred to Balkan Latin are to be considered Latin words. Some examples of Rumanian religious terms directly inherited from Latin are:

Latin	**Arumanian**	**North. Rum.**	meaning
altarium	—	altare	altar, sanctuary
angelus	—	înger	angel

[1]Löfstedt, E., *Late Latin*, 1959, p. 68.
[2]ILR vol. I, 1965, p. 61.

baptizare	păteḑu	boteza	baptize, to name
basilica	băsearecă	biserică	church
*blastemare	blastimu	blestema	to curse, to excommunicate
carnem legare	cârleagă	cârneleagă	last but one week of Advent fast
caseum legare	căşleadze, căşleagă	câşlegi	carnival
commendo	—	comânda	to make a sacrifice (relig. sense only in Rumanian)
comunicare	—	a cumenica	to give (or receive) the Eucharist
crux	cruţe	cruce	cross, Crucifix
deus	—	zeu	god
draco		drac	devil
paganus	pîngînu	păgân	heathen
Paschae	paşte	paşte	Easter
peccatum	—	păcat	sin; guilt; misfortune
quadragesima	—	păresimi	Lent
sanctus	—	sânt	saint

The religious terms show the changes of Late Latin in all Romance languages, including Rumanian. In Rumanian, they also show some Balkan Latin features, such as the *d* > *dz* (*z*) change (Latin *deus* > Arumanian *dzeu*, N. Rum. *zeu*) and the word *basilica* > *biserică.* This word "is preserved in the Rumanian, Dalmatian, and Albanian languages, which proves that it was a popular and widely spread word".[1] Although the word itself is not entirely unknown in the western Romance languages, its use in the sense of ′church′is a peculiarity of Balkan Latin.

[1]Mihăescu Limba lat. 1960, p.277.

A number of Christian terms of Greek origin are found equally in Albanian, Bulgarian, and Rumanian; some were also borrowed by Serbo-Croatian:

Greek	meaning	***Albanian***	***Rumanian***	***Bulgarian***
ἀγίασμα	holy water	ajazmë	agheasmă	agiazma, ajazma
ἀχάθιστος	prayer for the dead	—	acatist	akatist
ἀναφορά	wafer, Eucharist bread	naforë	anafură	nafora
ἀφοριζω	to excommuni cate, to curse	—	afurisi	aforesvam
εἰκόνα	icon; image, picture	ikonë	icoană	ikona
λειτουργία	lithurgy, mass	(Tosc) liturgji	liturghie	liturgija
καλόγερος	monk	kallojér, kallogjër	călugăr	kaluger
ἡγούμενος	prior	igumén, gumén	igumen	igumen

Remark: *akatist, napora, kaluger*, and *igumen* are found also in Serbo-Croatian.

It is obvious that the religious terms of Latin (and Greek) origin concern many BASIC NOTIONS of the Christian faith. Another, larger, group of religious terms in Rumanian, those of SOUTH SLAVIC ORIGIN, pertain mainly to the ORGANIZATION of the Church. The exact age of these loanwords cannot always be determined, but they are earliest from the end of the 9th century, when the Bulgarians adopted the Christian faith (cf. above, p. 22). Most of these terms were, of course, borrowed later, during the 11th and the following centuries.[1] Many of the corresponding Old Slavic words are found in texts. The direct continuation of Old Slavic (Old Bulgarian) is Middle Bulgarian, the most important variant of

[1]Mihăilă Studii 1973, p. 126.

Slavonic (in French, *slavon*, in German, *Kirchenslavisch*), which dominated in Muntenia and Moldavia during the 14th–16th centuries. The Slavonic texts perserve in general the Old Bulgarian forms.

Mihăilă[1] presented 79 examples of Rumanian religious terms originating from this source. They are divided into the following groups: (1) fundamental notions of Christianity, (2) evil spirits and heathen gods, (3) designations of the saints, (4) Church hierarchy, (5) monastic life, (6) church, monastery, and (7) divine service. Thirtythree of these examples are of Greek origin, 2 are loan translations from Greek, and one derives from Latin.

Some examples: *duh* 'soul; spirit; ghost', *rai* 'paradise', *idol* 'idol, image', *iad* 'hell', *sobor* 'synod, group of priests; prayer, service', *episcop* 'bishop', *vladică* 'bishop', *popă* 'priest', *mănăstire* 'monastery, cloister', *jertfă* 'offering, sacrifice', *prohod* 'funeral service, requiem, burial'.

It must be added that, besides the rich Christian terminology, several words concerning popular heathen beliefs of the South Slavic populations were also borrowed by Rumanian: N. Rum. *vrajă* 'charm, spell: magic, witchcraft', *basm* 'fairy-tale' (cf. Slavic *bajati* 'to conjure'), *moroi* 'ghost, phantom', *vârcolac* 'werwolf; vampire; ghost', *zmeu* 'dragon'.[2]

The Christian terms of Northern Rumanian are divided into two distinct groups: (1) those adopted by the ancestors of the Rumanians during the period of the Roman Empire, latest in the 5th or 6th century, and (2) a larger group, borrowed from Bulgarian much later. This must have a counterpart in the socio-political conditions of the speakers of Rumanian. The existence of the Latin Christian terms indicates that they were Christianized already during the Roman age, before the 6th century; (a rich religious life, with several dioceses, bishops, churches, etc. is attested from those centuries in the Roman provinces of the Balkan peninsula). The enormous impact of Bulgarian terms pertaining predominantly to church organization indicates that the Vlachs were organized into the Greek Orthodox Church by the Bulgarians.[3] This cannot have occurred but after the end of the 9th century, since the Bulgarians were Christianized in 865 AD.

This is a very significant socio-cultural fact and completes the picture of an intensive symbiosis with the Bulgarians, which is shown by the Rumanian language in general. The connections between the Church and the state were intimate in those days. The strong Bulgarian influence on the Vlachs' religious terminology would therefore be very difficult to explain if one assumed that the Vlachs, in a period starting with the 10th century, lived outside the Bulgarian state.

Northern. Rumanian *cârneleagă*, Arum. *cârleagă* 'last but one week of

[1]Ibid., pp. 127–132.

[2]Popović GSKS 1960, p. 204.

[3]Rosetti ILR 1986, p. 286. ("the Slavic terms show that the organization of the religion occurred in the period after the 9th century.")

Advent fast' and *câşlegi* 'carnival' testify to connections also with the Albanians as regards religious terms. *Cârneleagă* (< Latin *carnem-ligat*) means literally 'the binding of meat'; these words must be connected with Albanian *e lidhura* (Gheg *e lithmeje)* 'carnival', from *lidh* 'to bind'.[1]

L. Common Rumanian (*româna comună*)

This ancient period of the Rumanian language has been referred to in the preceding presentation, among other things, in the context of Arumanian and the other dialects.

The Northern Rumanian, Istro-Rumanian, Arumanian, and Megleno-Rumanian dialects once formed a single language without any significant dialectal divergences. This language, which is not documented in written texts, was reconstructed on the basis of the present day dialects; it is called Ancient Rumanian *(străromână)*, Primitive Rumanian *(română primitivă)* or Common Rumanian *(română comună)*. The latter term is used here, since it conveys the most important information about this stage of the language.[2]

The starting point of the common period is the age when the Balkan Latin dialect from which Rumanian developed, started to show its own, specific features, distinct from the rest of the Balkan Latin idioms. The common period ended when the originally homogenous population, living in a relatively small area in close contact with each other started to separate. It is generally considered that this was caused by the Arumanians migrating towards the south. There is some disagreement among different authors over this question: the beginning is assumed by Coteanu (ILR 1969, p. 15) to be the 5th century, by Weigand the 7th century, by Stati (in *Dacoromania* 1973, p. 213) the 8th century. Weigand puts the end of Common Rumanian in the 9th century, Stati, in the 11th century.

There are some data which help to define the end of the common period: one is the report by the Byzantine chronicler Cedren about some Vlach wayfarers, who in 976 AD killed David, the brother of Samuil, the Bulgarian co-regent, between Kastoria and the lake Prispa. These Vlachs were southern Rumanians.[3] The other circumstance is the presence of Hungarian words in Northern Rumanian, which do not exist in Arumanian. Assuming that a Hungarian influence was not possible before the 12th century, Coteanu[4] considered that "the separation of Arumanian from Dacorumanian could not have occurred before the 12th century".

---

[1]Sandfeld LB 1930, p. 73, referring to Puşcariu in *Dacoromania* I, pp. 437–438. Cf. also Rosetti ILR 1986, pp. 155 and 257.

[2]Rosetti ILR 1986, p. 321; ILR 1969, p. 17.

[3]Rosetti ILR 1986, p. 322; Coteanu Morfologia 1969, p. 20.

[4]Coteanu Morfologia 1969, p. 20.

According to Rosetti,[1] the common Rumanian period started in the 7th and 8th centuries, when it is generally agreed that Latin gave way to the Romance languages, and it ended in the 10th century. This seems to be the most plausible thesis.

Common Rumanian was reconstructed on the basis of the present day Rumanian dialects – primarily Northern Rumanian and Arumanian. Every old element found in at least one of the dialects is considered to have been part of the common idiom. Some characteristic features of it will be summarized here, mainly on the basis of descriptions given by Rosetti ILR 1986, pp. 321–159, ILR 1969, pp. 189–212, Tagliavini Lingu Neolat 1969, pp. 365–374, and Caragiu-Marioţeanu Dialectologie 1975, pp. 86–124.

Phonetics
The vowel system

Unstressed Latin *a* > Rumanian *ă*: Lat. *camisia* > Arum. *câmeaşă*, N. Rum. *cămaşă* 'shirt'. Also unstressed Latin *o* changed to *ă* in monosyllabic Latin grammatical words, such as Lat. *quod* > N. Rum, Arum. *că*, Latin *contra* > Arum. *cîtrî*, N. Rum. *cătră*. In words borrowed from Slavic, *-o* also changed to *ă* : Old Slavic *sito* > Arum., N. Rum. *sită*, *sŭto* > *sută*. As "a characteristic feature of the Balkan languages",[2] *ă* appears also in Albanian, Bulgarian and Serbo-Croatian dialects.
Stressed *e* (Latin *ĕ*) was diphthongized: *ye*:

Latin	**Arumanian**	**N. Rumanian**	meaning
heri	a(i)eri	ieri	yesterday
ferrum	h'er	fier	iron

This change is spontaneous (i.e., it is not caused by the influence of another sound on *e*). It seems to appear in grammar books in the 5th century AD.[3]

In contrast to Arumanian, Northern Rumanian diphthongized also *e* in the position as the first sound in a syllable: *ieftin* 'cheap'. This occurred later than the above-mentioned change and under the influence of South Slavic.

Stressed *o* followed in the following syllable by *e* or *a* was diphthongized: *oa* . Latin *coda* > Arum., N. Rum. *coadă*; also in early Slavic loanwords: Old Slavic *kosa* > Arum., N. Rum. *coasă*. Stressed *e* followed in the next syllable by *a (ă)* or *e* was diphthongized after the 6th century: Latin *herba* > Arum., N.

---

[1]Rosetti ILR 1986, p. 322.

[2]Ibid., p. 591.

[3]Rosetti ILR 1986, p. 328, referring to Elise Richter, *Beiträge zur Geschichte der Romanismen*, Halle, I, 1934, p.138.

Rum. *iarbă*, Latin *petra* > Arum. *k'atră*, N. Rum. *piatră*. These diphthongs "constitute the originality of Rumanian, in which *e* and *o* have the role of semivowels, as *i* for example in *ia'*".[1]

Later, diphthongs with *i* as the second element appeared: *ai, îi, ei, oi, ui*. The vowel system of Common Rumanian was as follows:

i ă u
e o
a

The *an* > *ăn*, *am* > *ăm* change precedes rhotacism and with some exceptions of very early borrowings from Slavic, does not affect the Slavic loanwords. Later, this *ă* developed into *î* : Latin *manus* > Arum., N. Rum. *mână*, (but Istrorum. *mără*), Latin *angelus* > N. Rum. *înger*, etc.

Unstressed Latin *o* showed a tendency to change to *u* already inVulgar Latin (*o* and *u* are confounded in many texts). This continued in Rumanian: Vulgar Latin *oricla* > Arum. *ureacl'a* , N. Rum. *ureche* 'ear', Latin *romanus* > N. Rum., Arum. *rumân*, Arum. also *rămân, arrămănu, armân*.

Of consonants, the following may be mentioned:

Latin *d* followed by *i* in a hiatus[2] changed in the Latin period; in Latin grammar books from the 5th century AD it is written *dz, z*, or *i*[3] . In Arum., *d* > *dz* if followed by *ia*, or by unstressed *io, iu*. In N. Rum. (except a few sub-dialects) *dz* later changed to *z*: Latin *medius* > Arum. *'nedz*, N. Rum. *miez*, Latin *hordeum* > Arum. *ordzu*, N. Rum. *orz*. If followed by stressed *io, iu d* changed to *ǵ*, later *j*: Latin *deorsum* > Arum. *(n)ǵos*, N. Rum. *jos*. Latin *d* + *e, i* changed similarly, after the 6th century: Latin *decem* > Arum. *dzaţe*, N. Rum. *zece*, Latin *deus* > Arum. *dzău*, N. Rum. *zeu*.[4]

The change of Latin *t* + *i* in a hiatus was recorded from the 5th century on.[5] Later development went in two ways: (1) If followed by *ia*, or by unstressd *iu*, *t* changed to *ts*: Latin *matia* > Arum. *maţă*, N. Rum. *maţe*. (2) If followed by stressed *io, iu*, Latin *t* changed to *č*: Latin *fetiolus* > Arum. *fičor*, N. Rum. *fecior*, Latin *titionem* > Arum. *tičuni*, N. Rum. *tăciune*. - The assibilation of Latin *t* + *e, i* occurred after the 6th century: Latin *terra* > Arum., N. Rum. *ţară*, Latin *teneo* > Arum. *ţin*, N. Rum. *ţin*.[6]

Latin *i* (*j*) followed by stressed *o, u* > Rumanian *ǵ* : Latin *jocus* Arum. *ǵoc*, N Rum. *joc*, Latin *adjungere* > Arum. *aǵundziri* N. Rum. *ajunge*. In

[1]Rosetti ILR 1986, p. 565.

[2]Break between two vowels coming together not in the same syllable.

[3]Ibid., pp. 335 and 113.

[4]Ibid., p. 335.

[5]Ibid., pp. 335 and 113.

[6]Rosetti ILR 1986, pp. 335, referring to A. Rosetti, *Recherches sur la phonétique du roumain au XVIe siècle*, Paris, 1926.

parts of the N. Rum. territory, *ǵ* changed to *j*.[1]

Latin *k* + *i* in a hiatus was palatalized in the 2nd century AD. Later, it developed as follows: followed by unstressed *io, iu*, it changed to *ts*: Latin *socius* > Arum., N. Rum. *soţ*. Followed by stressed *io, iu*, it changed to *č*: Latin *petiolus* > Arum. and N. Rum. *picior*.

The palatalization of *k* ′ (+ *e, i*) is attested in Latin in the 5th century.[2] In Northern Rumanian, it changed to *č*: Latin *cera* > N. Rum. *ceară*. In Arumanian, the general rule today is *ts* in this position: *ţeară*, *ţer*. There are, however, in certain parts of the Arumanian area, reports of the use of *č* instead of *ts*, and Rosetti considers that the pronunciation *ts* is recent.[3]

Latin *s* followed by *i* and *e* in a hiatus, changed to *š* : Latin *camisia* > Arum. *cîmeaşă*, N. Rum. *cămaşă*, Latin *caseus* > Arum., N. Rum. *caş*.

In the Latin group of consonants: *br* , *b* changed to *u* or disappeared: Latin *cibrum* > Arum. *ţir*, Meglenitic *čur*, N. Rum. *ciur*. (This is why *Abrud* [placename in Transylvania, cf. below, chapter III, p. 181] cannot be inherited from Latin *Abruttus* but must have been handed down to Rumanian by an other language.)

Latin *cl, gl* : The *l* in these groups disappeared in most of the N. Rum. territory, but not in Arumanian and Istrorumanian: Latin *clavis* > Arum. *cl′ae*, N. Rum. *cheie*, Latin *glacies* > Arum. *gl′eţ*, *gl′aţă*, N. Rum. *ghiaţă*.

The Latin group *st* followed by *e* or *i* changed to *št*: Latin *castigare* > Arum. *cîştigari*, N. Rum. *câştiga*. Followed by *i (e)* in a hiatus, *st* changed to *š*: Latin *pastionem* > Arum. *pîşuni*, N. Rum. *păşune*. The word *christianus* is an exception: Arum. *crişţin*, N. Rum. *creştin*, "because the word penetrated late into the language and was not adapted to the words from the old stock."[4]

Intervocalic *l* > *r*: Latin *mola* > Arum., N. Rum., Istrorum. *moară*, Latin *fil(um)* > N. Rum. *fir*. This change did not affect the Slavic loanwords.

As a result of the action of a iot on the preceding consonant, the following new phonemes appeared: */č/ /ǵ/ /ţ/, /ḑ/ /ş/, /ń/ /l′/.*

The phoneme */h/* probably existed in this period in words from the substratum but had a subordinate role until strengthened by */h/* in several Slavic loanwords.

The consonant system or Common Rumanian had 22 phonemes:

/p/ /b/ /t/ /d/ /c/ /g/ /ţ/ /ḑ/ /č/ /ǵ/ /f/
/v/ /s/ /ş/ /n/ /n̄/ /ń/ /l/ /l̄/ /l′/ /r/ /r̄/[5]

---

[1] Rosetti ILR 1986, pp. 337, 340.

[2] Rosetti ILR 1986, p. 340. When the first Latin words were transferred into German, *k* was not yet assibilated, as shown by: Latin *cellarium* > Old German *kelari*, Lat. *cista* > Old German *kista*, Lat. *vicia* > Old German *wicka*. (The senses of these words are cellar, coffin, and vetch, respectively.)

[3] Rosetti ILR 1986, pp. 340, 343.

[4] Ibid., p. 346.

[5] ILR 1969, p. 201.

Morphology

The neutre disappeared in Latin and reappeared probably in the period of Common Rumanian. It is expressed with the endings of the masculine nouns in the singular and that of the feminines in the plural, as well as by Latin *-ora*: N. Rum. *scaun* 'stool', *scaune* 'stools'; *ochi – ochiuri.*[1]

For an exhaustive presentation of Common Rumanian, cf. Rosetti ILR 1986, pp. 321–359.

The conclusion is formulated in the following quotations:

> The comparison of the Daco-Rumanian dialect with Arumanian (because Istro-Rumanian is only a branch of the Daco-Rumanian dialect and Meglenitic is a branch of the Arumanian dialect...) reveals the former unity of the primitive language from which the two dialects developed.[2]

> The innovations (more than conservation of features) shared by the four large Rumanian dialects are so many and of such importance that it is impossible to attribute them to mere chance, which would have been the case if the four dialects would have developed in the areas they occupy at present, without any contact with one another. Thus, one must admit that the territory of formation of Proto-Rumanian was more or less extensive but uniform.[3]

M. The dialects of the Rumanian language

1. THE FOUR DIALECTS: NORTHERN RUMANIAN, ISTRO-RUMANIAN; ARUMANIAN, AND MEGLENITIC

Northern Rumanian

Although this term is not unknown (cf., for example, Bourciez, *Éléments de lingustique romane*, 1967, p. 548: "*roumain du Nord*"), the designation "Daco-Roman" has been used generally when speaking about the Rumanian dialect found north of the Arumanians and the Meglenites. However, this term may cause misunderstanding. It is based on the circumstance that the northern dialect of

[1]Rosetti ILR 1986 p. 351.

[2]Ibid., p. 321.

[3]Tagliavini, C., *Le origini delle lingue neolatine. Introduzione alla filologia romanza* (5th edition), Bologna, 1969, p. 373.

Rumanian is at present, among other areas, also spoken in the territory which between 106 and 275 AD was Roman Dacia. It is, however, also spoken south of the Danube and during the Middle Ages, its Balkan territory was much more extensive. It included large parts of Serbia and Bulgaria; cf. above, p. 22. The most important reason not to use the designation "Daco-Roman" is that it can be used (and has been used) with the implication that the northern dialect of Rumanian is based on the Dacian language. Thus, for example, C. Daicoviciu (1969) stated categorically that he regarded the term "Daco-Roman" not only in its geographical sense and continued: "For us, the term implies, in the first place, the genetic character of the Daco-Romans, i.e., A ROMANCE POPULATION ON A DACIAN ETHNIC BASIS" (*romanitate pe temelia etnică dacică*).[1] This cannot be regarded adequate, in the first place because our knowledge of possible Dacian elements in the Rumanian language is very scanty. It is uncertain whether such elements exist at all.

An exhaustive presentation of Northern Rumanian was written by Alf Lombard: *La langue Roumaine. Une présentation*, 1974. In the following survey this, as well as Matilda Caragiu-Marioţeanu's *Compendiu de dialectologie română (nord- şi sud-dunăreană)*, 1975, were used in the first place.

Northern Rumanian is the mother-tongue of more than 20 million people in Rumania, to whom must be added smaller or larger groups living in adjacent countries. It is the most highly developed dialect of the Rumanian language. It is characterized by a tremendous impact of Slavic (cf. above, pp. 98–108). From the 18th and especially the 19th century on, it has absorbed many French, Italian and Classic Latin words.[2] Northern Rumanian also contains, in contrast to Arumanian, a considerable amount of Hungarian and a smaller number of German elements, the result of Rumanian contacts with these peoples in Transylvania. Its Balkan characteristics are the same as those found in the other (southern) Rumanian dialects (cf. above, p. 86). As a result of the various foreign influences, many synonyms are organized to a principle involving a double scale, Latin versus Slavic: *timp–vreme* 'time', but there are many words included in the synonymic pattern based on a triple scale, for example *repede–iute–rapid,* three words derived from Latin (inherited), Slavic, and French (which borrowed it from Classic Latin), respectively, to express the notion of 'fast'.[3]

The speakers of *Istro-Rumanian* are the remnants of the Vlachs whose northwestern migration during the Middle Ages ended in Istria. Their dialect is closely related to Northern Rumanian. Their numbers were very low already in the 19th century. P. Kandler gave the figure of 6.000 in 1846, while in 1862,

---

[1]Daicoviciu, C., *Dacica* 1969, p. 434 (emphasis in the original).

[2]"In the case of Roumanian, the prestige of French was so great as to introduce thousands of French words – a process still going on – and to make much of the Roumanian vocabulary simply of French lexicon with Roumanian endings" (R.A. Hall, Jr., *External History of the Romance Languages,* 1974, pp. 198–199).

[3]Cf., for example, Lombard, A., *Latinets öden i Öster* (The Destinies of Latin in the East), Lund, 1967.

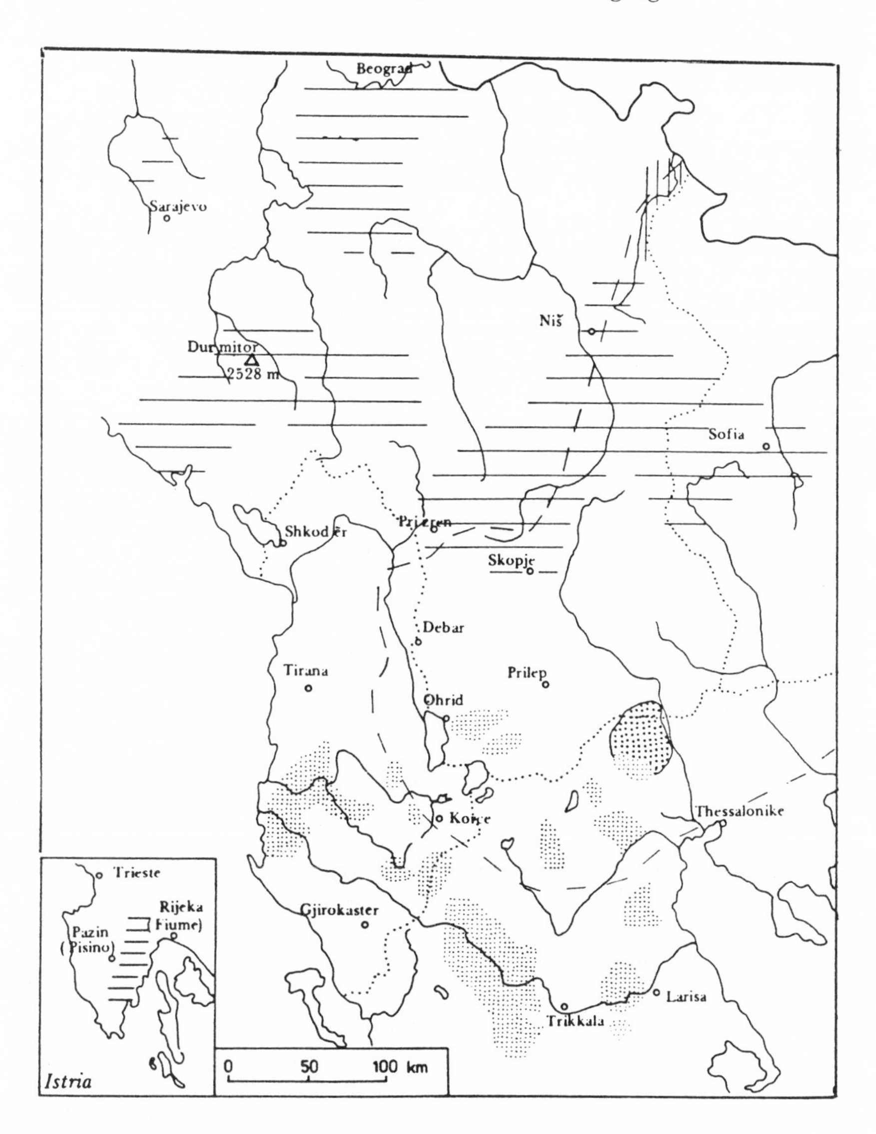

Map 7. The Rumanian dialects in the Balkan peninsula

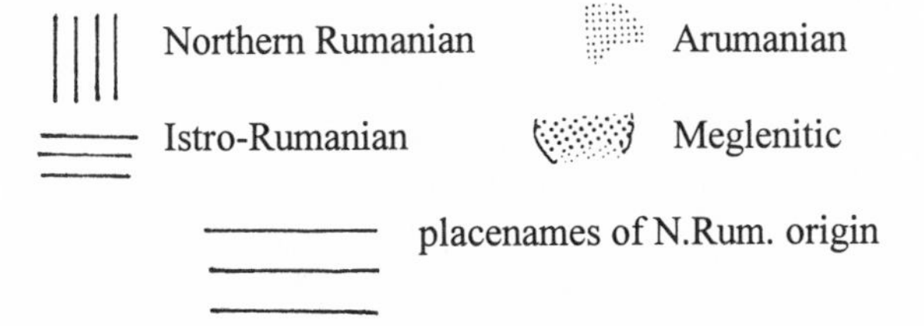

years 1959 to 1961 (A. Kovačec) is 1.250 to 1.500. The Istro-Rumanians are all bilingual and are being increasingly assimilated into the surrounding Croatian and Italian populations. Once, they were shepherds, and vestiges of this fact are left in the language of Croatian shepherds in the region of Zadar, who use Rumanian numerals when counting their sheep: *dô, pâto, šasto, šopće, zéci.*[1] The Istro-Rumanians used to call themselves *vlåş, vlås*; and their language, *vlåski*. The surrounding populations call them *ciribiri*.

Arumanian or *Macedo-Rumanian,* the main southern dialect of Rumanian, is spoken by the Arumanians, who are living on both sides of the Pindus mountains in Greece, in Albania and in Bulgaria. According to the Brockhaus Encyclopedy (1966), their total number in the entire Balkan peninsula is 400.000.[2] Also the number of this population is decreasing, as that of the speakers of the other Rumanian dialects in the Balkan peninsula.

This group of Vlachs call themselves *ar(u)mânu, rumănu, rămănu* (< Latin *romanus)*. Their neighbours call them Vlachs; the Greeks use the designation Κουτσοβλαχοι, which means 'limping Vlachs'; the Bulgarians say *belivlasi* 'white Vlachs'. The Albanian name of the Arumanians is *rëmër* (from Latin *romanus*) or *çoban*. The Serbians call them *ţinţars*, probably because of the high frequency of *ţ* (ts) in the Arumanian dialect.

The Arumanians have always been predominantly shepherds. In ancient times, they were moving flocks to an Alpine pasture in the spring and then to nearby lowlands in the autumn, but they were also seminomadic or nomadic (wandering) shepherds. There was still between the two World Wars a group of Arumanians who were nomads.[3]

Arumanian is the only Rumanian dialect south of the Danube with a literature of its own; the first text whose age is known dates from 1731.

The *Megleno-Rumanians* or *Meglenites* are living in the plain of Meglen north of Thessaloniki, mostly in Greece, partly in Macedonia. This dialect is closely related to Arumanian. The number of the Meglenites was, at the beginning of the 20th century, estimated around 20.000, but emigration, especially to Turkey after the first World War (they are Mohammedans) has reduced their number. Assimilation to the surrounding Greek and Slavic population thereafter has resulted in the practical extinction of this group.

The Meglenites are a group of speakers of Rumanian who lost their name derived from Latin *romanus*; they call themselves Vlaşi; their neighbours call them Vlaşi or Meglenites.

The importance of the southern dialects in the study of the history of the

---

[1]Puşcariu, S., *Studii istroromâne*, II, 1926, p. 6; quoted by Caragiu Marioţeanu Compendiu dial 1975, p. 191; which also is the source of the data about the number of the Istro-Rumanians (p. 190).

[2]Caragiu-Marioţeanu Compendiu dial 1975, p. 216.

[3]Capidan, T., *Românii nomazi*, 1926, quoted by Caragiu-Marioţeanu Compendiu dial 1975, p. 219.

Rumanian language was summarized by Macrea as follows:

> Being very close to primitive Common Rumanian (*româna primitivă comună*) in several respects, Arumanian, Megleno-Rumanian, and Istro-Rumanian must be regarded living historical documents of our language from the period before our first written documents.[1]

Although the theory that the speakers of these dialects originate from the areas north of the lower Danube has been presented (cf., for example, the discussion by Macrea: "Despre dialectele limbii române", *Limba romînă*, V, 1, 1956, pp. 14–15), there is no evidence for this. It is now generally recognized that they always lived south of the Danube. A survey of the discussion of the question whether Arumanian, Meglenitic, and Istro-Rumanian should be regarded as dialects or separate languages is given by Cazacu (*Studii de dialectologie română*, 1966, pp. 9–32). Cazacu´s conclusion is that they must on the basis of genealogic and structural criteria be considered dialects of the same language (Rumanian). Matilda Caragiu-Marioţeanu (*Compendiu dial* 1975) also presents them as dialects.

Area	**Hungarian**	**Saxon**	**Rumanian**	**other**	total c:a
Szekler	150.000 93.7%	?	?	–	160.000
Saxon	?	65.000 76.5%	15.000 17.6%	–	85.000
Counties	210.000 52.5%	20.000 5%	170.000 42.5%	?	400.000
Partium	140.000 46%	–	90.000 30%	80.000 26%	300.000
total c:a	500.000 52.3%	90.000 9.4%	280.000 29.3%	85.000 8.9%	955.000

Table 3. The ethnic situation of the Transylvanian Principality at the end of the 16th century. Because of the scarcity of data, only approximate figures can be given. (After *Erdély rövid története*, red. B. Köpeczi, in an article by G. Barta, p. 238.)

[1] Macrea, D., *Limba romînă*, V., 1956, p.73.

Nationality	Counties & Fogaras	Szekler	Saxon	Transylvania total
Rumanian	781.791 74.5%	54.246 14.5%	207.810 51.8%	1,043.650 57.2%
Hungarian	159.396 15.2%	303.975 81.5%	25.063 6.2%	488.434 26.8%
German	49.166 4.7%	1.163 0.3%	141.425 35.2%	191.754 10.5%
other	58.696 5.6%	13.528 3.7%	26.953 6.8%	99.187 5.5%
total	1,049.049	372.912	401.251	1,823.025

Table 4. The ethnic situation of Transylvania (without the Partium) according to the census made in 1850–1851 (shortly after the Freedom Fight against the Habsburgs, in which very many Hungarians were killed or expelled from the country. (After *Erdély rövid története*, red. B. Köpeczi, in an article by Zs. Trócsányi & A. Miskolczy, p. 371.) Absolute numbers and proportions are given.

2. THE SUB-DIALECTS OF NORTHERN RUMANIAN

When discussing the Rumanian dialects in Transylvania, it must be remembered that in this province, the proportion of the Rumanians was earlier much lower (for example, in the 16th century, only around 30%, see Table 3) and they lived mainly in the mountainous areas of the southern Carpathians, the Transylvanian Alps, and Máramaros (Maramureş).

The first systematic studies of the sub-dialects of Northern Rumanian spoken north of the lower Danube and in Dobrogea were carried out by Gustav Weigand (1860–1930), whose *Linguistischer Atlas des dacorumänischen Sprachgebietes* appeared in 1909 in Leipzig. In general, Weigand's conclusions have been confirmed by more recent research, although the *Rumanian Linguistic Atlas*, published in the 1930's, added much new material.

The literary language in Rumania is based on the sub-dialect spoken in Muntenia. On the basis of the *Rumanian Linguistic Atlas*, Emil Petrovici summarized the phonetic differences of the other sub-dialects as follows:[1]

The different pronunciation of *ge (gi)* and *ci*; the preservation of *dz* (which in Muntenia changed to *z*), and of *-n-* in certain words: *a încuna* instead of a

[1] Petrovici, E., "Repartizarea graiurilor dacoromîne pe baza Atlasului Lingvistic Romîn", *Limba romînă*, III, 5, 1954, pp. 5–17.

încuia: the change of *ia* to *ie*, of *-e* to *-i*, and of *o* to *uă;* the palatalization of *d, t, n* in front of *e* and *i*. To this, the following may be added: *mîine* instead of *mîini;* the velar *g* in *sugit* and the velar *k* in *înkid*; the palatalization of the velar *c* in *călk'îi*, etc., the palatalization of *f, v (> s, z)*; the change of *-ea* to *e;* the palatalization of the labials; the different treatment of Latin *a + n:* in Muntenia, *îi (cîine),* in Moldavia and other areas, *î (cîne).*[1]

Some commentaries to these differences between the sub-dialects:

(1) *a încuna, călcâne,* etc., are old forms which existed in Common Rumanian and are still found in the dialects south of the Danube. Northern Rumanian, with the exception of the Banat, has innovated (*încuia, călcâi*). This innovation is quite recent: in placenames and personal names found in Latin and Slavic documents written in the 15th century, forms in *-n-* are the rule.[2]

(2) The palatalization of the dentals had occurred in several areas already in the 15th century. This is shown in Hungarian documents from Transylvania, where some Rumanian placenames are recorded: the Rumanian name of a village in Hunyad county (Rum. Hunedoara), Cârneşti, was written *Kernyest* (1447 AD); Bădeşti, a former village near Temesvár (Rum. Timişoara) > *Begyest*, etc.[3]

(3) The only phoneme written differently in different areas in the 15th century was, as far as it is known today, *z* – *dz*. Documents from Moldavia, the Banat and Transylvania show *z*, while those from Muntenia have *dz.*

Vocabulary

There are many lexical elements which in the southern sub-dialect, corresponding mainly to Muntenia, are different from those used for the same notion in other (nothern) areas, for example:

Muntenia	**Northern areas**	meaning
ficat	mai	liver
varză	curechi	cabbage
gresie	cute	whetstone
năduşeală	sudoare	sweat
zăpadă	nea, omăt	snow

---

[1]Todoran, R., "Cu privire la repartiţia graiurilor dacoromîne", *Limba romînă,* V. 2, 1956, pp. 38–50. Todoran also presents some variations in morphology of minor importance and restricted to three areas.

[2]Petrovici Repartizarea graiurilor 1954, p. 16.

[3]Ibid.

burtă	foale, pântece	belly
rinichi	rărunchi	kidney
porumb	cucuruz	maize

The following words are considered roughly to delineate the eastern (Moldavian) sub-dialect; [1] although their isoglosses do not coincide:

Moldavia	**Muntenia**	meaning
ciolan	os	bone
mancă, mamcă	doică	(wet) nurse
omăt	zăpadă	snow
cori	pojar	measles
hulub	porumbel	pigeon
pântece	burtă	belly
moş with the sense of ′uncle′	moş	gray-headed man; forefather, ancestor
a pisca	a ciupi	to pinch
păpuşoi	porumb	maize
chelbos	chel	bald(-headed)

The following words are characteristic of a northwestern sub-dialect but, as shown on map No. 3 by Petrovici,[2] here too, the isoglosses show wide divergence:

Northwest	**Muntenia**	meaning
piţig	pisc	peak, summit
goz	gunoiul din ochi	rheumy
chefe	perie	brush

[1] Petrovici Repartizarea graiurilor 1954, p. 9.

[2] Ibid.

prunc	băiat	boy
sclab	slab	weak
pântece	burtă	belly
şi	să	(sign of the conjunctive)

In this area (part of Transylvania) appear a series of lexical elements of Hungarian origin, such as for example:

Northwest	**from Hungarian**	meaning
ciont	csont	bone
mai	máj	liver
cuştălesc	kóstolok	I taste
feşteală	festék	colour, paint
sabău	szabó	tailor

The following words appear characteristic of the Banat, although many of them are used also in other areas:[1]

Banat	**Muntenia**	meaning
nea(ua)	zăpadă	snow
uică	unchiu	uncle
lopăţiţă	spată	weaver's reed
golumb	porumbel	dove
cozeci	pojar	measles
arghelă	herghelie	stud (farm)
foale	burtă	belly

Of German origin: *farbă* (< Farbe) 'colour,' *şnaidăr* (< Schneider) 'tailor,' etc.

[1]Petrovici Repartizarea graiurilor 1954, map No. 4.

Petrovici concludes that Northern Rumanian may be divided into five subdialects: that of Muntenia, Moldavia, the Banat, Crişana, and Maramureş. This division is chiefly based on differences in the vocabulary and phonetics; of the last-mentioned differences, the pronunciation of *ge (gi)* is considered the most important.

> THUS, TRANSYLVANIA HAS NO DIALECTAL AREA OF ITS OWN, NOT EVEN ON THE BASIS OF PHONETICS.[1]

About the vocabulary, Petrovici stated the following:

> Regarding Transylvania without the Banat, Crişana, and Maramureş, it is very difficult to find words which would exist in the territory of this province only. Only if we consider Transylvania together with the Banat, Crişana, and Maramureş as a unit, opposing Muntenia and Moldavia taken together, is it possible to find maps on which the former frontier between Transylvania and the Banat on the one hand, and Muntenia and Moldavia on the other, represent a dialectal frontier. The isoglosses, however, do not coincide exactly with the former frontier. Thus, regarding the words *cireadă, bolnav, herghelie*, the corresponding words beyond the mountains[2] are *ciordă, beteag, stavă* (in the Banat, *arghelă*). In such cases, there usually appear new words, of Hungarian origin in Transylvania (for example, *ciurdă*), and of Turkish origin in Muntenia and Moldavia (*herghelie*). It should be mentioned that the form *arghelă*, found in the Banat, passed (from Turkish) into the Banat subdialect through Serbian.
> Transylvania forms, in most cases, a single lexical area together with one or two of those four adjacent provinces: once with Moldavia, once with Muntenia, but more often with the Banat, Crişana, and Maramureş. Most often, however, Transylvania is divided into several (three or four) lexical areas, as was also the case on the maps presented here. We all know the dialectal distribution of those three terms *zăpadă, omăt*, and *nea* (see maps No. 1, 2, 3, and 4) which divides Transylvania into three areas: one southern in which *zăpadă* is said, as in Muntenia; one northeastern, where *omăt* is said, as in Moldavia, and one western, where *nea* or *neaua* is said, as also in the Banat and in Crişana.[3]

---

[1] Petrovici Repartizarea graiurilor 1954, p. 15 (emphasis added).

[2] I.e., in the intra-Carpathian territory.

[3] Petrovici Repartizarea graiurilor 1954, pp. 9–11.

Oltenia, Muntenia	**southern Transylv.**	**Moldavia**	**east Tr**	**s.-w. Tr**	**Banat**	**Crişana**	**n-.west Transylv.**	**Maramureş**
ge (gi)	ge (gi)	z	z	z	z	j	j	approx. ge (gi)
încuia					încuna			
		-e > i stressed ia>ie					stressed ia > ie	
					palatalization of d, t, n before e, i		palatailization of d, t, n before e, i	
z	z	dz	z	dz	dz	z	z	z
ci	ci	s	ci	ci	s	ci	ci	c
						o- > uă		
palatalization of labials: Oltenia: - Muntenia: (+)	+ (south-east)	+	+	—	—	north: + south: –	+	palatalization of f, v (> s, z)
epenthesis of i in the plural					velar g in *sugit,* velar k in *înkid*	palatalization of c in călc'îi -ea > ę		

Table 5. Phonetic peculiarities of the Northern Rumanian sub-dialects.
(On the basis of E.Petrovici, "Repartizarea graiurilor dacoromâne pe baza Atlasului Lingvistic Romîn", *Limba Romînă*, III, 5, pp. 5–17 (1954), and R. Todoran, "Cu privire la repartiţia graiurilor dacoromîne", *Limba romînă*, V, 2, pp. 38–50 (1956).

Oltenia, Muntenia	Banat	Crişana
Possessive article: *al, a; ai, ale*	—	—
—	1sr person sing., 1st and 2nd person plural of *'a fi'*: *(eu) mi-s* *(noi) ni-s* *(voi) vi-s*	
—	Formation of conditional in *ręş* (obsolete)	—
—	—	Formation of the past tense of the condiitonal mood with *'a vrea'*
—	—	Form. of the conjunctive with *şi* (not *să*)

Table 6. Morphological peculiarities of the Northern Rumanian sub-dialects. (Transylvania, including Maramureş, and Moldavia have no distinctive morphological features.)
(On the basis of Todoran, R., "Cu privire la repartiţia graiurilor dacoromîne," *Limba română*, V, 2, pp. 38–50.)

Petrovici concludes as follows:

> Transylvania has no sub-dialect of its own, but those four (or five) sub-dialects extend from the south, the east, the southwest and the northwest (the sub-dialect of Maramureş from the north) towards the centre of Transylvania.[1]

On the basis of phonetic peculiarities in texts from the 16th century, two sub-dialects may be distinguished within Northern Rumanian: a northern area with northern Transylvania, Maramureş, and Moldavia, and a southern area, comprising southern Transylvania and Muntenia.[2] Texts written in the Banat

[1]Ibid., p. 17.

[2]Rosetti ILR 1986, p. 539. – It should be stated that in the 16th century, Rumanian was spoken in a much smaller part of Transylvania as compared to the situation today. The population living in the central parts of the province was predominantly non-Rumanian.

coincide partly with the northern and partly with the southern sub-dialect. The differences in phonetics were in that period probably somewhat more pronounced than today.[1] An investigation of the vocabulary used in the 16th century texts resulted in the delineation of essentially the same areas as those established by phonetic criteria.[2]

The absence of dialects in Northern Rumanian is remarkable and unique among the Romance languages:

> The Rumanian language, in contrast to other Romance languages, has a much more unitary character, a fact which has been emphasized repeatedly.[3]

In a note, Cazacu quotes the observation of J. Boutière:

> Ce qui frappe dès l'abord, lorsqu'on examine ces cartes (de l'ALR) ... c'est leur unité, au moins relative, qui confine parfois à la pauvreté; nous sommes, la plupart du temps bien loin de l'exubérante richesse que présentent d'autres atlas linguistiques, et notamment celui de Gilliéron.[4]

N. The way of life of the early Rumanians as reflected by their language

Among lexical elements originating from the substratum of Rumanian, shepherd terms predominate; in the Latin word stock, terms pertaining to urban life are practically non-existent and several Latin words changed their meaning in a direction explicable only in the setting of a shepherd community. This has been shown above, but there are other circumstances also indicating that the Vlachs were mainly shepherds, even after the separation of the dialects.

These circumstances are:
(1) The use of shepherd terms to express general human conditions.
(2) Ancient Vlach placenames and names of mountains in the Balkan peninsula.
(3) Documents on the shepherd Vlach population in Serbia (12th–15th centuries).
(4) Considerable numbers of shepherd terms of Rumanian origin in at leat 12 European languages. (This will be discussed below, see "The wanderings of the Vlachs outside the Balkan peninsula.")

(1) In the Rumanian language, several expressions connected with general human conditions and activities derive from the shepherd terminology:

---

[1]Rosetti ILR 1986, p. 540.

[2]Florica Dumitrescu, *Contribuţii la istoria limbii române vechi*, 1973, pp. 48–69.

[3]Cazacu, B., *Studii de dialectologie română*, 1966, p. 148.

[4]Boutière, J., "Quelques observations sur les cartes lexicologiques de l'Atlas linguistique de la Roumanie", *Études romanes dédiées à Mario Roques...*, Paris, 1946, p. 194.

(a) ′To wean′ is expressed by a term taken from the realities of shepherd life: *a înţerca* lit. ′to put in a fold;′ ′to wean′. This word contains Latin *in-* and a word from the substratum: *ţarc* ′fold, pen′ (cf. above, p. 76). In contrast, in French, for example, ′to wean′ is expressed by a word the sense of which in Latin is ′to separate′: French *sevrer* ′to wean′ (< Latin *se-parare* ′to separate′).

(b) *arete*, from Latin *aries* ′ram′, may in N. Rumanian signify ′male destined for reproductive function′, for example: *cocoşul acesta l-am lăsat de arete* ′we have preserved this cock for reproduction′.[1]

(c) The word *strungă* ′sheepfold′, from the shepherd terminology, may also be used in the sense of ′gap between two teeth′; (*strungăreaţă* has only this sense).

(d) *chiag* ′rennet′, from Latin *coagulum*, is used in such expressions as *se închiagă un gând* ′a thought is being formed′, lit. ′a thought is being coagulated, clotted′; *chiagul unei societăţi* ′the cement of a society′; *a prins chiag* may be said of somebody who has consolidated his or her economic situation, etc.[2]

(e) To say that two persons are of the same age, one may say *suntem de aceeaşi iarbă*, lit. ′we are of the same grass′ – as two lambs which started grazing at the same time. ′Don′t occupy yourself with things you don′t understand′ may be expressed by *paşte iarba pe care o cunoşti*, lit. ′feed upon the grass you know′.

(f) The word for ′to graze, to feed′ – *paşte* – is used in several everyday expressions: *ce paşti aici*? ′what do you seek here?, *mă paşte moartea* ′there is death ahead for me′, *mă paşte norocul* ′luck is close at hand′, *mă paşte gândul* ′the thought worries me′, etc.

> Seul un peuple où la vie pastorale a joué un rôle capital peut dire: *mă paşte un gînd* litter. ′une pensée me paît′; il y a à la base de cette expression l′image d′un troupeau de brebis qui broute jusqu′au dernier brin d′herbe, jusqu′à ce qu′il ne reste plus rien.[3]

(g) Also *oaie* ′sheep′is used in everyday expressions: *o face de oaie* ′he makes something foolish′, *prea e de oaie* ′it is a very stupid thing′, *suge la două oi* is said of somebody who makes a profit out of two sources, etc.

(2) The names of Northern Rumanian origin in the Balkan peninsula of small villages (*cătun*-s), as well as the names of mountains of the same origin, must have been left by a population living in the high mountains. These names were found by the Slavs when they populated the area, before the 8th century (cf. above, pp. 29–32).

(3) Although from a later period (the 12th to the 15th centuries), there also are documentary descriptions of this population: they are mentioned in the earliest

---

[1] Puşcariu, S., "Le rôle de la Transylvanie dans la formation et l′évolution de la langue roumaine", *La Transylvanie*, 1938, p. 53.

[2] Ibid., p. 52.

[3] Ibid. p. 53.

deeds of gift from Serbian monasteries known today, and are consistently described as shepherds or carters, often living in symbiosis with Serbians or Albanians (cf. above, pp. 26–29, 38).

O. The wanderings of the Vlachs outside the Balkan peninsula

Above, pp. 36–37, the protracted wanderings of the Vlachs in almost the entire Balkan peninsula were described. Here I will present their northward migrations to rather distant territories.

In the course of time, part of the Vlach population settled down as peasants. However, large numbers of them continued to be shepherds throughout the Middle Ages and even later, while migrating to new territories. This is, besides historical records, shown by the Rumanian lexical influence on a series of Europen languages: Slovakian, Czech, Polish, Ukrainian, Russian, Hungarian, and Transylvanian Saxon. This is the result of the migrations of the Vlachs to territories north of the lower Danube; the Carpathian mountains, the Munţii Apuseni in Transylvania, the sub-Carpathian Ruthenian area, Slovakia, Moravia, southern Poland, the Ukraine, and southern Russia. It must be pointed out that the Vlachs did not borrow shepherd terms from the Slavs[1] or from any other population with the exception of the other *par excellence* shepherd population of the Balkan peninsula, the Albanians.

The largest semantic category of Rumanian lexical material borrowed by languages of southeastern Europe is that of the shepherd terms. Other groups are: plants, animals, parts of the body, family relations, human qualities and defects, clothes, food and drink, occupations, tools, habits, administrative and military terms, and even abstract notions.

In Hungarian, the oldest Northern Rumanian influence consists mainly of shepherd terms: *berbécs* 'ram', *brindza* 'cheese', *cáp* 'he-goat', *cigája* 'breed of sheep with prime wool', *esztrenga* 'fold, pen', *esztena* 'shepherd cottage', *furulya* 'flute', *csobán* 'shepherd in charge of a sheepfold', *mióra* 'sheep', *mokány* 'spunky, plucky', *pakulár* 'shepherd', *orda* 'soft cheese', etc.

The same is the case with the German language of the Transylvanian Saxons: *batsch* 'shepherd in charge of a sheepfold', *berbetsch* 'ram', *tschurde* 'flock', *stine* 'shepherd cottage', *strunge* 'fold, pen', *prents* 'cheese', *zare* 'butter milk', *zer* 'whey', *flur* 'flute', etc.

---

[1]Mihăilă Studii 1973, p. 19. Popović GSKS 1960, p. 201, mentions *dobitoc* 'animal, beast' (cf. Macedonian *dobitok* 'cattle'), *bivol* 'buffalo, Bos bubalus', *jivină* 'animal; wild beast', and *cocoş* 'cock' – all Slavic words borrowed by N. Rum. These could be regarded as exceptions; however, they also belong to the rich *agricultural* terminology of Slavic origin in Rumanian.

In Ukrainian, there are: *afyra* and *afina* 'blueberry', *armaš* 'provost marshal', *harmasar* 'stallion', *arsyca* 'intense heat', *bracar* 'bracelet', *bryndza* 'cheese', *bukata* 'piece, bit', *kam* (adverb) 'about, around, nearly', *kamašy* 'shirt', *kapestra* 'halter, bridle', *karuš* 'carter', *karuca* 'cart, waggon', *kl'ag* 'rennet', *kip* 'image', *frika* 'fear', *kodaš* 'last, lagginbg behind', *fruntaš* 'leader', *mai* (adverb) 'more', *makriš* '(cock) sorrel, sharp dock', *malaj* 'maize flour', *mamaliga* 'maize porridge', *merend'a* 'victuals, food', *popušoja* 'maize', *sapa* 'ho', *sapaty* 'to hoe, to dig', *tryfoi* 'clover, trefoil', *turma* 'flock', *cariyna* 'tilled land', *vatra* 'hearth', *dzama* 'juice', *dzer* 'whey', etc.

In Russian: *barbos* 'bearded', *bryndza* and *brynza* 'cheese', *malaj* 'maize flour', *mamaliga* 'maize porridge', *placynda* 'pancake', *urda* 'soft cheese', *cygeika* 'sheep', *kalauz* 'guide', *papuša* 'doll puppet', *carina* 'tilled land', *caranin* 'peasant', *mors* (from Rumanian *mursă* 'beauty-spot; Schönheitspflästerchen; Honigwasser'), *džok* 'play', etc.

In Polish: *afyra* 'blueberry', *jefer* 'blueberry', *bacza* 'shepherd in charge of a sheepfold', *barda* 'hatchet', *berbeč* 'sheep', *bryndza* 'cheese', *bukat* 'piece, bit', *kalarasz* 'horseman', *kalcun* 'bennet', *koliba* 'hut', *kornuta* '(long)horned', *koszar* 'barn, stall', *fujara* 'flute', *kokonica* 'young woman', *domna* 'lady', *domnica* 'princess; sweetheart', *linta* and *lenta* 'lentil', *maczuga* 'club, bludgeon', *malaj* 'maize flour', *mamalyga* 'maize porridge', *mierynda* 'victuals, food', *strygoń* 'ghost, phantom', *traista* 'bag', *urda* 'soft cheese', *dziama* 'juice', *dzer* 'whey'.

A systematic study showed 30 terms of Northern Rumanian origin used by the Slovakian shepherds in the north and the northeast of Slovakia and Orova. Macrea[1] mentions the following of these: *ghaleta* and *geleta* 'bucket', *kl'ag* 'rennet', *putyra* and *putina* 'vat', *merinda* 'victuals, food', *demikat* 'soup with crumbed bread', *kornuta* '(long)horned', *kulastra* and *kuljastra* 'beest(ings)', *carek* and *carok* 'fold, pen', *rumegat'i* 'to chew, to rumigate', *meridzat'i* '(from Rumanian *a meriza* 'to let the cattle rest at noon'), *murgana* ' (from Rumanian *murgană* 'sheep with black streaks'), *cigaja* 'sheep with fine, soft wool', *laja* (from Rumanian *laie)* 'black sheep', *strunga* 'sheepfold, pen', *bryndza* 'cheese', *urda* 'soft cheese', *bača* 'shepherd in charge of a sheepfold'.

Almost all these terms are also found in the Czech language.

In Moravia and in Galicia, personal names of Rumanian origin were found by Drăganu: Puyne, Bacs, Cerbul, Gropa; in Galicia: Plina, Runkur, Stremtura, Florea, Pascu, Botez, etc.

[1]Macrea Studii 1970, pp. 11–18.

Rumanian	meaning	**Rumanian**	meaning
afină	bilberry	joc	play; pastime; dance
armăsar	stallion	linte	lentil (Lens esculenta)
arşiţă	intense heat	mai (adverb)	more
baci	shepherd in charge of a sheepfold	malai	maize flour
barbă	beard	măciucă	club, bludgeon
bardă	hatchet, block bill	mămăligă	maize porridge
berbece	ram	merinde	victuals; food
brăţară	bracelet	mioară	ewe lamb
brânză	cheese	mocan	shepherd; boor, cad
botez	baptism, Christening	mursă	mouche, beauty spot
bucată	piece, bit	păcurar	shepherd
cam (adverb)	about; almost	păpuşoi	maize
călăraş	cavalry man, horseman	pâine	bread
călţun	(herb)bennet (Geum)	plin	full; compact; fat
cămaşă	shirt	putină	vat
căpăstru	halter, bridle	runc	forest pasture
cărăuş	carter, waggoner	sapă	hoe
căruţă	cart, waggon	stână	sheepfold, pen

cerb	stag	strigoi	ghost, phantom; wizard
chiag	rennet	strâmtură	narrow passage, gorge
chip (< Hung. kép)	image, face, shape	strungă	sheepfold
cioban	shepherd	traistă	bag
ciurdă	herd, flock	trifoi	clover (Trifolium)
coconiţă	lady	turmă	flock
codaş	last; lagging behind	ţap	he-goat
colibă	cabin, hut, hovel	ţarină	field under cultivation
cornută	mouse ear (Cerastium arvense)	ţigaie	breed of sheep with prime wool
coşar	barn; stall; hovel; hut	urdă	soft cow cheese
floare	flower	vatră	heart; house; home
fluier	whistle, pipe	zară	butter milk
frică	fear, anxiety	zeamă	juice; souce; soup
groapă	pit, cavity	zer	whey

Table 7. List of Rumanian lexical elements transferred to Hungarian, Transylvanian Saxon, Ukrainian, Slovakian, Czech, Polish, and Russian.

The total number of Rumanian words in the Slavic languages is about 400. The highest number is found in Bulgarian (almost 200); this language also shows phonetic and structural changes of Rumanian origin (cf. above, pp. 108–110). The Slavic languages north of the Danube show lexical influence only.

Some suggestions regarding the age of these words are given[1] (a) by the rhotacized forms *putyra (< putină), afyra (< afină)* in Ukrainian, Polish, Slovakian, and Czech. Rhotacism was probably widespread in the 10th to the 13th centuries; later, it was restricted to certain smaller areas; (b) by the forms *kl′ag* in Ukrainean, Polish, and Slovakian, *gl′ag* in Czech: *cl* in Latin words changed in N. Rum. to *k′* before the 16th century; (c) *dz* in *dzeama*, *dzer*, in Ukrainian and Polish, *bryndza* in all northern and eastern Slavic languages. In Northern Rumanian, the *dz > z* change was, as shown by the first written texts, almost complete in the 16th century. It should be pointed out that these criteria are not unequivocal, both rhotacism and *dz* existed also after the 16th century in certain areas of Northern Rumanian. Historical records may give some help: Vlachs are first described in the Balkan peninsula at the end of the 10th century, in Moldavia, at the end of the 11th century, and in Muntenia, somewhat later; in Transylvania, beginning with the 13th century. In Slovakia, Vlach shepherds appeared, according to Drăganu, already during the 10th to the 11th centuries (via Pannonia), but their presence there (and in Moravia) is attested by Czech and Slovakian historians only from the 16th century on.

According to Macrea, these Rumanian terms were borrowed "in the period of great dispersion" of the Vlachs, "between the 10th and the 13th centuries."[2]

That the Vlachs came to the above mentioned areas as wandering shepherds is obvious; no peasant population could have made such extensive migrations. This appears also from the analysis of the Rumanian loanwords from the semantic viewpoint: the largest single group of these words belongs to shepherd terminology and of the rest, a large part, names of plants, animals, tools, etc., are connected with shepherd′s way of life.

The Vlach population had its own organization, led by its own leaders (*cnezi, cătunari, celnici*), and had with them everywhere the *jus valachicum,* developed in Serbia. In the Balkans, many of their leaders attained high ranks in society as administrators, clerks, church leaders, and also as chiefs of their own local state organizations : cf. the "Valachies" described in Byzantine sources, as well as the Asăneşti-family, the founders of the second Bulgarian empire. The rank and file were, however, mainly shepherds. In the course of time, more and more of them settled down as peasants. In Slovakia, Bohemia, Poland, the Ukraine, and Russia, they were eventually assimilated into the surrounding Slavic populations. The above mentioned Rumanian impact upon the language of these populations is the only memento of them today.

---

[1]Macrea Studii 1970, p. 17.

[2]Macrea, Studii 1970, p. 17, referring to works of Drăganu and to D. Macrea, *Probleme de lingvistică română,* 1961, pp. 50–53: "The loan of shepherd terms occurred certainly in the period of great dispersion of the Rumanians, of whom a number have reached, in the west, Istria, where they still exist today: the Istrorumanians, others in the south of the Balkan peninsula: present day Arumanians and Meglenites, others to the east of the Dniester and others northward as far as to Moravia and Silezia, all of which happened betweeen the 10th and the 13th centuries."

Chapter III

THE THEORY OF THE DEVELOPMENT OF RUMANIAN NORTH OF THE DANUBE

A. Introduction

The definition of the theory of Daco-Roman continuity

This theory assumes that present day Rumanian is the direct descendant of Latin spoken at one time, i.e., in AD 106–275, in the territory of the Roman province of Dacia Traiana, present day Oltenia and most of Transylvania.

Within this framework opinions vary between archaeologists, historians, and linguists; and also in time. Until the early 1970s, only the former province of *Dacia Traiana* was considered in this context (C. Daicoviciu). Thereafter, however, certain archaeologists and historians started to declare that areas *extra provinciam*, such as Muntenia and Moldavia, also belonged to the ancient Daco-Roman areas. On the other hand, the evidence of early Vlachs (Rumanians) in several parts of the Balkan peninsula is too strong to be neglected; particularly linguists have assumed a very large area of formation for the Rumanian language and people, both north and south of the lower Danube, from the central areas of the Balkans to northern Transylvania.

About the history of the theory

Poggio Bracciolini, Italian humanist, travelled in Eastern Europe and discovered with surprise the Vlachs, a population whose language resembled very much his own, Italian. His writing from 1451 was, as far as this is known today, the first thesis about the origins of the Rumanians. Bracciolini knew of the Roman province of Dacia Traiana and believed that the presence in the same territory of a population speaking a Romance language can only be explained by assuming a direct continuity between Trajan's Romans and this population. This has been called "historical logic" and is by many people still considered plausible. During the centuries following Bracciolini, many similar records appeared about the Vlachs and their language.

These ideas were taken up and developed during the 17th and 18th centuries by the first Rumanian chroniclers of importance: Miron Costin, Dimitrie Cantemir, and others. Cantemir (1673–1723) affirmed that Emperor Trajan annihilated or ousted all Dacians from the conquered territories north of the lower Danube and that the Rumanian people was the descendant of the Romans –

mostly of noble families transferred from Rome to Dacia Traiana; not of a mixed, Roman and Dacian, population. He assumed, nevertheless, the existence of some Dacian words in the Rumanian language.[1]

As pointed out by Armbruster:

> Der Sinn und Wert dieser Anschauung liegt in ihrer politischen Absicht, als theoretische Begründung praktischer Unternehmen zur Wiederzusammenführung der 'Romano-Moldo-Wlachen' aus der Moldau, der Walachei und aus Siebenbürgen in einen einzigen einheitlichen rumänischen Staat.[2]

During the second half of the 18th century, these views were further developed and propagated by the "Transylvanian School" (*Şcoala ardeleană)*, whose main protagonists were P. Maior, Gh. Şincai, and S. Micu-Klein. Emphasizing the Latin origin of Rumanian, these writers considered the Slavic elements of language alien. They wrote Rumanian grammars and histories, occupied themselves with education, literature, etc. and launched the development of national consciousness among the Rumanians. The political importance of this activity was also very great:

> History and language were the most important arms with which Micu, as also Şincai and Maior, has sought to argue for the right of the Rumanian people to a life in freedom and equality with the other nationalities of Transylvania.[3]

The ideas of the Transylvanian School have had, and still have, an enormous influence on Rumanian historical thinking.

B. The theory of continuity in modern times

In *Istoria Romîniei,* C. Daicoviciu (editor), Edit. Acad. RPR, Bucharest, 1960, the theory of the "formation of the Rumanian language and the Rumanian people" is summarized as follows:

> The Rumanian people was formed in a prolonged process which was made possible by the colonization and Romanization of Moesia and Dacia. Two elements are found on the basis of this ethnogenesis: the autochthonous

---

[1]Cf., for example, Dacoromania II, 1974, p. 263. These words are: *stejar, grăesc, privesc, nemeresc, pădure, cărare,* and *heleşteu.* None of them is, however, Dacian: four are of Slavic origin, two derive from Latin and one from Hungarian.

[2]Dacoromania II, 1974, p. 75.

[3]Macrea, D., "Samul Micu", *Limba romînă,* III, 1956, p. 9. Cf. also Dami, A., "La controverse de la continuité daco-roumaine", *Humanitas Ethnica, Ethnos,* 5, 1967, p. 268; and Grecu, V., *Şcoala ardeleană şi unitatea limbii române literare,* Timişoara, 1973.

population with a Thraco–Daco–Moesic language and the Roman element, represented by the colonists of Rome, who settled in this Daco–Moesic territory during the centuries of Roman domination, and by the Romanizing influence of this domination.
The birth of the Rumanian people in the territory of its fatherland (*naşterea poporului romîn pe teritoriul patriei sale*) was in the first place made possible by the continued existence of a Latin-speaking population in the entire territory between the Haemus mountains and the Northern Dacian Carpathians ALSO AFTER THE OFFICIAL ABANDONMENT OF DACIA. In fact, this continuity was ascertained, its main foci being the Romanized centres of the former province of Dacia and the valley of the lower Danube, including Dobrogea. It continued without interruption, in time and space, not only until the massive settlement of the Slavs in Dacia and in the Balkan peninsula, but also after.
During this period, the Moeso–Danubian Roman population (*romanitatea moeso-danubiană*) of urban, rural, and pastoral character contributed effectively to the completion of the Romanization of the territories north of the river, by unceasing intermigrations of the population from one shore to the other as well as by contacts of political character (temporary domination of the Romano–Byzantine Empire north of the Danube), of economic and cultural character (the propagation of Christianity in the Latin language) which the Empire maintained with the territories beyond the Danube.
After the end of the Romano–Byzantine domination on the southern side of the Danube (about the year 600), and as a consequence of the symbiosis of the autochthonous Romance population with the Slavs who settled in Dacia and in Moesia, the process of Rumanian ethnogenesis in a more restricted sense of the word started in the entire Daco–Moesian territory, lasting about two or three centuries (from the 7th to the 9th century). The contacts between the Romance population of Moesia and Dacia were not interrupted in these centuries either, but were preserved, though from now on the common Latin language spoken by this population started to sever itself from popular Latin when going through the first stage of the common Rumanian language (the so-called Ancient Rumanian (*străromâna*).[1]

Considering the fact that the Slavic elements in the Rumanian language show predominantly Bulgarian traits, and the frontier of Bulgarian was approximately the same as today, the early Rumanians are said to have been living in the Balkans only in the small area between the Haemus mountains (the Jireček-line), the lower Danube, and the Bulgarian–Serbian frontier.

From this small area of the Balkan peninsula – it is true that it was strongly Romanized – those waves of Romance population are alleged to have started which, according to another theory, that of the linguist A. Philippide, led to the

[1]Daicoviciu, C., (red.) *Istoria Romîniei*, 1960, pp. 806–807.

re-Romanization, from the 7th century on, of the territories north of the Danube, where at present 17 million people speak Rumanian. The probability of such a massive migration, starting from a limited area is, however, very small.

Therefore, the area on both sides of the Danube (the "Daco–Moesian territory," *spaţiu daco-moesic*) is said to have been the region in which the ancestors of the Rumanians lived and where the Slavo–Rumanian symbiosis took place:

> The phonetic, lexical, and grammatical changes in the Daco–Moesian Rumanian language (*romanica daco-moesică*) took place in the long interval between the 7th and 9th centuries. This language was carried towards the south by the Vlachs, the ancestors of the Arumanians mentioned by Byzantine historians of the 10th century as having arrived from the Danubian regions, from the vicinity of Dacia. Thus, at this period, the formation of the Rumanian language was completed.[1]

Another summary of the theory of continuity is given in an article by C. Daicoviciu (1967):

> Die slawische Toponymie Rumäniens, besonders die im Banat, in Siebenbürgen, in Oltenien und Muntenien zeigt dieselbe südslawischen phonetischen Kennzeichen, wie auch im Wortschatz der rumänischen Sprache vorkommenden slawischen Elemente. Folglich muss die Urheimat der rumänischen Sprache nördlich des Kammes des Haemus-Gebirges und zwar bis in Gebiete, zu denen die Romanisierung vordrang, also BIS NACH DACIEN HINEIN, und bis östlich der heutigen Grenze zwischen Jugoslavien und Bulgarien gesucht werden.
> Von diesen donau-moesischen Gebieten her sind im Laufe des frühen Mittelalters (etwa im 7.–9. Jahrhundert, also nach dem Eindringen der Bulgaren) romanische Schafhirten nicht nur nach Süden, Südwesten und Westen, in die Balkanhalbinsel (die Vorfahren der heutigen Arumänen, Megleno-Rumänen und, auf der Istrien-Halbinsel, der Istro-Rumänen), sondern auch nach Norden, in das gebirgige Dazien gezogen.[2]

It appears that the above authorities do not believe in the theory that the Rumanian language originated exclusively from Latin spoken in Dacia Traiana but assume a larger or smaller area also south of the lower Danube as its area of formation. The question is then, which was this area?

---

[1]IR 1960, p. 797.

[2]Daicoviciu, C., "Der Ursprung des rumänischen Volkes im Lichte neuesten Forschungen und Ausgrabungen", published originally in *Forschungen zur Volk- und Landeskunde,* Sibiu (Hermannstadt), 1967; in *Dacica* 1969, pp. 544–558 (the passage quoted here is found on pp. 553–554).

> The territory of formation of Common Rumanian was defined above (p. 321).[1] According to Densusianu, (H.d.l.r., I, 289), this territory would have comprised Moesia, Illyria,and Dacia; Puşcariu (Ét. de ling. roum., 112) puts the territory of formation of the Rumanian language on both shores of the Danube ("a large territory, south and north of the Danube", LR I, 255, Treimer (*Literaturbl. f. germ. u. rom. Phil.*, LXII, col. 64–65) in Illyria, Dardania, and Paeonia, and Philippide (*Orig. Rom.*, II, 385), in the Balkan peninsula.
> The areas of the Timok and Morava remained Romanized until the 13th and 14th centuries. In these regions, although to a lesser extent as compared to Dalmatia, a large number of Roman placenames were preserved (see the enumeration in *Orig. Rom.*, I, 453, by Philippide); the Romanized population was preserved during the period of the Byzantine domination along the road of great penetration in the Balkan peninsula, Via Egnatia (Margulies, A. Slavic. Ph., XL, 197 ff.) [2]

It is interesting to follow Rosetti's argument about the territories north of the Danube as a part of the Rumanian ancient homeland. The arguments are taken from archaeological finds and a reference to the assumption that not all citizens of Dacia Traiana have left the province in 275 AD. There is also a difference between the 1968 edition and the definitive (1986) edition regarding the territories north of the Danube:

> The presence of a Romanized population (Vlachs...) in the western parts of the Balkan peninsula is normal. It does not exclude the persistence of a Romanized element north of the Danube in those regions which once were under Roman rule. The existence of a Rumanian population north of the Danube (at Dridu, Urziceni, and Bucov, Ploieşti) in the 9th and 10th centuries is, as a matter of fact, proved by archaeological excavations (Nestor, Don. archéol. 407–410).
> M. Besnier, L'Empire romain, de l'avenement des Sèveres au concile de Nicée, Paris, p. 243 (Histoire romaine. IV, 1): the evacuation of Dacia "ne fut pas complète ... La masse des paysans ne bougea pas ... Ainsi s'explique la persistence si tenace de la race et de la langue latines dans la contrée que Trajan avait conquise". After the official abandonment of Dacia by Aurelian, a part of the Romanized population – with the exception of the soldiers, functionaries and a considerable part of the town-dwellers and of those who were living in the countryside – remained in their places, in the Banat (C. Patsch, Banater Sarmaten, Akad. d. Wissenschaft. in Wien, Anzeiger 1925, nr. XXVII, p. 215.) For the conditions in which this Romanized population

---

[1]On this page, this territory is defined a follows: [the Rumanian dialects: Arumanian, Meglenitic, Northern Rumanian, and Istro-Rumanian] "were originally a single language, descendant of Oriental Latin, which was once spoken in the Romanized Danubian provinces, Moesia Superior and Inferior, Dacia, and Pannonia Inferior."

[2]Rosetti ILR 1986, p. 323.

survived in Dacia under the domination of the barbarians, until the arrival of the Slavs, cf. Daicoviciu, Transylv., p. 79 ff.[1]

In the year 535, the diocese of the bishop of Skopje comprised the provinces Dacia Ripensis, Dacia Mediterranea, Moesia Superior, Praevalis, Macedonia Secunda and the eastern part of southern Pannonia, thus, also the provinces enumerated above (M. Friedwagner, ZRPh., LIV, 663). "We are forced to admit that at least part of the ancient Rumanians lived south of the Danube" (Puşcariu, LR, I, 270).
This territory, restricted and enlarged in the course of time (in 235–238, Moesia Inferior was abandoned because of the incursions of the migrating peoples, and in 268 were Dacia and Moesia Superior abandoned; in 377, the Huns occupied Pannonia: Philippide, Orig. rom., I, 854), does not comprise the regions in which the Rumanian language was to be extended later (*unde limba română era să se întindă mai tîrziu*): eastern Transylvania, Bucovina, Moldova, Basarabia, Ţara Românească and Dobrogea. [2]

The argument of Puşcariu against the theory of a Balkan origin of the Rumanians is quoted:
If the Rumanians of modern Rumania were the descendants of some migrating shepherds who, as some people pretend, came form the Balkan peninsula during the Middle Ages into regions inhabited by other populations, their fate would have been, beyond doubt, the same as that of those Vlach groups who disappeared in the masses of Hungarians and Slavs in Ancient Pannonia and in the northern Carpathians.[3]

As was mentioned above, before the 1970s, historians as well as linguists considered that the Rumanian language developed (also) in the territory of the former province of Dacia Traiana. (C. Daicoviciu explicitly stated this, criticizing the attempts at extending the theory of continuity to areas beyond the frontiers of this province.) Also Rosetti stated, in the earlier editions of his *Istoria limbii române,* that Muntenia, Moldavia, and other areas once *extra provinciam* did not belong to the territory of the Daco-Romans (see above). However, in the definitive edition (1986), this statement was omitted. This is the expression of a change in policy during the first years of the 1970s, as shown by a similar inconsistency in a textbook of history:
Istoria României. Compendiu, 1969, stressed the importance of the distinction between those areas which once belonged to the Roman Empire and those which remained *extra provinciam.*

---

[1] Ibid., p. 199.

[2] Rosetti ILR 1968, pp. 215–216. (In the 1986 edition, the last sentence was omitted.)

[3] Puşcariu, S., *Limba română,* vol. I, 1940, p. 361; quoted by Rosetti ILR 1986, p. 200.

> We must not forget that the problem of continuity appeared for a very long time ago in the science of history and that it has a well-defined content, which we are not allowed to change according to our own wishes. This problem pertains exclusively to Roman Dacia: it was for THIS territory that the followers of Roesler denied the preservation under Roman rule of the Dacian population, for THIS territory was Daco-Roman continuity denied after 271 AD, in THIS territory were "brought", also by Roesler's partisans, from the territory south of the Danube, the Rumanians in the 9th–13th centuries. The problem of continuity is thus a problem regarding Roman Dacia.
> Does this mean that in Muntenia and in Moldavia no continuity of human life existed? Not at all! Muntenia and Moldavia were never left deserted, but there one cannot talk of Dacian continuity under Roman rule, only of continuity of the free Dacians. There is not and cannot be a Daco-Roman continuity after the abandonment by Aurelian because of the simple reason that between 106–271, Muntenia and Moldavia not having been occupied by the Romans, little more than a bare beginning of Romanization can have occurred there, and the abandonment by Aurelian changed almost nothing of the situation in these territories. The Dacian population of Muntenia and Moldavia was Romanized much later.
> This is the reason why the issue of continuity must be restricted exclusively to the territories which belonged to Roman Dacia and particularly to the intra-Carpathian areas.[1]

In the third (1974) edition of the same textbook a very different view is found:

> Does this mean that in Muntenia and in Moldavia no continuity of human life existed? Not at all! Muntenia and Moldavia never remained desert; also there, there was a Dacian continuity under Roman rule, continuity of DacoRoman life, because southern Moldavia and Muntenia belonged to the Roman province of Moesia Inferior.[2]

History

1. THE ARGUMENTS IN FAVOUR OF ROMANIZATION NORTH OF THE DANUBE

C. Daicoviciu[3] assembled the following arguments in favour of "the possibility of a real Romanization" of Dacia Traiana:

---

[1] *Istoria României. Compendiu.* M. Constantinescu et al. (red.), 1969, p. 105.

[2] *Istoria României. Compendiu,* Ş. Pascu (red.), 3rd edition, 1974, p. 87.

[3] Daicoviciu, C., "Romanizarea Daciei", *Apulum,* VII, 1, 1968, pp. 261–271; in *Dacica*, 1969, pp. 427–437. The following survey (1–13) is based on this article.

(1) The Dacians were exposed to Roman civilization at least a century before their subjugation by the Romans, and Romanization continued also after the abandonment of the province by Rome.

(2) The colonization there – as shown by the facts that very strong army units were used and that the process was highly organized, – was a deliberate effort made by the Roman state to build a bastion in the midth of *barbaricum.*

(3) The spread of Christianity during the 4th century among the population left by the Romans in the province. "That this propagation of the new religion occurred in the Latin language is shown by the basic terms of Latin origin in the Christian terminology of Rumanian."

(4) Those of the foreign colonists who did not speak Latin, were compelled to learn it in order to be able to communicate with the other inhabitants.

(5) There are two historical records about "the Roman character of the province": (a) Eutropius (VIII, 6, 2) tells us that when Emperor Hadrian (117–138) planned to leave Dacia, he was told not to do so, "to evade handing over many Roman citizens to the barbarians". (b) Zonaras (Annal., XI, 21, II, p. 510, ed. Bonn): "And from that time on, from the conquest of Dacia, the Dacian people and their province became Roman."

(6) The absence of any racial sentiment and any opposition based on a uniform language. The Dacian language, with its many dialects was no obstacle to Romanization, on the contrary, affirms Daicoviciu, it was advantageous to change to a language known by the entire population.

(7) A large number of inscriptions (almost 3000), of which most are Latin, attest to the presence of the Latin language in the province. Daicoviciu asserts that the frequent appearance of non-Latin names in the inscriptions is no indication against Romanization because this has, in the 2nd and 3rd centuries, counterparts in other Roman provinces. The statistics made by A. Kerényi (*Die Personnamen von Dazien,* Budapest, 1941) show that the great majority of the names were of Roman origin.

(8) Among colonists coming from 20 provinces, some were from Italy, as shown by the situation in the capital, Ulpia Traiana, where this was studied:

> An investigation of the personal names in Ulpia Traiana revealed some whose territory of origin is certain, among which was Italy (families such as Varenii, Cominii, Domitii, Servii, etc.). An investigation which will be necessary to make also about the rest of the communities of Dacia will result in the same statement: the number of people from Italy, settled in Dacia either as veterans, as handicraftsmen or as businessmen (among whom there were certainly also farmers) is much higher than is generally believed (p. 432).

(9) A large number of Dalmatian miners contributed to Romanization.

(10) The high number of military units: at the beginning, three, then one, and later, two legions, and a "considerable number of auxiliary units". The majority of these came from the western provinces, in a period when the auxiliary units

were increasingly Romanizaed. Through the *canabae,* these units were starting points of Romanization.

(11) The increase in the standard of living, from which also the indigenous population benefited, may have brought them close to the Romans.

(12) The archaeological finds show that the Roman buildings in Dacia were of the same style as those in the western parts of the empire.

(13) The progressive Romanization of the province is reflected in the successive organization of municipia and of colonies.

(14) "In the most suitable moment of the maturation of this process of Romanization, the institution of the Concilium III Daciarum by Severus Alexander crowns this transformation of 'barbarian' Dacia into Dacia Romana" (p. 436).[1]

2. THE ABANDONMENT OF DACIA BY THE ROMANS

The record about the Roman retreat from Dacia Traiana was written about 100 years after the event, by Eutropius. This writer was the *magister memoriae* of Emperor Valens (364–369). Eutropius wrote in 369 a history of Rome: *Breviarium ab urbe condita.* The most important sources of this work were Suetonius, Livius, and a history of the Empire also known by other authors. Writing about Emperor Aurelian, Eutropius tells us the following:

> IX, 13, 1. After him, Aurelian, who originated from Dacia Ripensis, took the power in the Empire: [...] he defeated very bravely the Goths, thanks to several lucky wars, he restored the Roman power to the former frontiers.
> IX, 15, 1. [...] He abandoned the province of Dacia, created by Trajan beyond the Danube, since the whole of Illyricum and all of Moesia were devastated, and he had no hope of keeping it. He took the Romans from the towns and

[1]Historical and archaeological treatises published during the last decades in Rumania defend the theory of continuity. Out of the large number of books on this theme, the following, more important volumes may be mentioned:

Condurachi, E., Daicoviciu, C., *The Ancient Civilization of Romania,* 1971.

Constantinescu, M., Daicoviciu, C., and Pascu, Ş., *Istoria României, Compendiu,* 1969; 3rd edition: 1974.

Daicoviciu, C., *Dacica,* Cluj, 1969 (a collection of the author's articles). Daicoviciu, C. (red.), *Istoria Romîniei,* vol. I, 1960.

Giurescu, C.C. (red.), *Istoria României în date,* 1971.

Giurescu, C.C., and Giurescu, D.C., *Istoria românilor din cele mai vechi timpuri pînă astăzi,* 2nd edition, 1975.

Miron, P. (red.), *Dacoromania. Jahrbuch für östliche Latinität,* vol. I, 1973.

Pippidi, D.M. (red.), *Dicţionar de istorie veche a României (paleolitic - sec. X),* 1976.Giurescu, C.C., (ed.) *Istoria României în date,* 1971.

Protase, D., *Problema continuităţii în Dacia în lumina arheologiei şi numismaticii,* 1966.

Protase, D., *Autohtonii în Dacia,* 1980.

from the fields of Dacia and placed them in the middle of Moesia; and, what before was to the left, is now to the right of the Danube, as it flows into the sea.[1]

Historians who believe in Daco-Roman continuity cannot, of course, accept the idea that all Latin-speaking inhabitants have left Dacia Traiana. Thus, for example, V. Iliescu, one of the editors of *Fontes Historiae Daco-Romanae*, comments in a footnote the above text as follows:

Since he wanted to save the prestige of the Romans and at the same time not to diminish the figure of Aurelian, who is praised by the author to have restored the empire, Eutropius "augments" (*lărgeşte*) the operation of evacuation of Dacia and creates in this way the illusion of a total evacuation, in the same way as he, in connection with Trajan, talked about a total colonization of Dacia. And in this way, a false tradition was created, taken up by Festus and then put into circulation.[2]

3. THE "SILENCE OF HISTORIANS"

After the record by Eutropius, no Roman population north of the lower Danube is mentioned for 800 years, until the second half of the 11th century, when Vlach soldiers were first recorded in Moldavia. This silence has been used as an argument against the theory of continuity. It is, however, only an argument *ex silentio*; it has been pointed out repeatedly[3] that the absence of records about a Roman population cannot in itself be regarded as proof of the absence of such a population. The following explanations have been offered:

When discussing these regions in their works, the Byzantine and the western chroniclers occupied themselves only with the events of war or with dominating ethnic elements, and only if these were interesting for their friendly or inimical attitude towards Byzantium or the Western world. [...] Of course, the possibility cannot be excluded that the Byzantine authors had the autochthonous population in mind when using archaic expressions or the name of some dominating peoples, since it might be possible that the

[1]Eutropius, Breviarium ab urbe condita; - Fontes Historiae Daco-Romanae, vol. II, Bucureşti, 1970, p. 38: IX, 13, 1. *"Post eum, Aurelianus suscepit imperium, Dacia Ripensis oriundus: ... quoque Gothos strenuisse vicit, Romanam ditionem ad fines pristinos varia bellorum felicitate revocavit."* IX, 15, 1: ... *"Provinciam Daciam, quam Traianus ultra Danubiam fecerat, intermisit, vastato omni Illyrico et Moesia, desperans eam posse retineri; abductosque Romanos ex urbibus et agris Daciae, in media Moesia collocavit; et est in dextra Danubio in mare fluenti, cum ante fuerit in laeva."*

[2]Fontes II, p. 39, note 11.

[3]Cf., for example, Daicoviciu Dacica 1969, pp. 552 - 553; IR 1960, p. 780.

chroniclers meant, without saying it explicitly, the masses of local peoples when they wrote about those numerous *"nationes"* and *"gentes"* over which (also according to the chroniclers of the age) Huns and Avars reigned.[1]

G. Ştefan[2] affirmed that even in the light of the historical records, "the theory of a total evacuation of the north-Danubian province proves false". His and other authors´ arguments in favour of this may be summarized as follows:

(1)The fact that the Huns dominated over several populations, among which there might have been also Romans. Travelling north of the lower Danube, the Byzantine envoy Priscus found villages (κῶμαι) comprised of huts (καλύβαι):

> Thus, this was a sedentary population of peasant farmers, not of Hunnish origin, without any political significance but only with an economic one, because politics and war belonged to the affairs of the Huns.
> We may talk about a kind of symbiosis between the dominating Huns and their subjects (Sarmatians, Goths, Gepidae, beyond doubt, also Romance groups). [...]
> One may also observe the progress attained by the Hunnish society thanks to the contact with the Roman civilization. The court of Attila, the dwelling place of Onegesios, the bath constructed by a prisoner from Sirmium are only some examples. We also may add the fact that there was an organized office, that several languages were spoken at the court of Attila. About this, Priscus writes: "because the Scythians are mixed and besides their own language, they try to speak the language of the Huns, or that of the Goths or that of the Ausoni, when some of them have to do with the Romans." This is not the place to once again discuss the question of the Ausoni and their language. For us, the statement by Priscus that this language was used for the understading with the Romans (όσοις αὐτῶν πρός Ρωμαίους ἐπιμιζία καί οὐ ῥαδίως τις ἑλλενίζει τῆ φωνῆ), and not with the Byzantine Greeks, is sufficient. It was thus a Romance language (*o limbă romanică*), probably Latin spoken in the Romanized region of the Danube valley (the two Moesiae and Daciae, Pannonia, which together with north-Danubian Dacia and Scythia Minor, constitute the territory of the Danubian Roman population).

(2) The persecution of king Hellenos (?) would have been "caused by the hatred against the Romans", but it did not succeed in suppressing the Christians. In fact, Epiphanios writes (70, 15, 4): "and even though it would appear as if all Christians had been expelled, SOME BELIEVERS REMAINED THERE." Such affirmations give us the right to ask whether the hatred against the Romans was directed against the Roman state or only against the Roman subjects of the Goths.

---

[1]IR 1960, p. 780.

[2]In Fontes II, pp. VI–X.

(3) Talking about the propagation of Christianity among the Goths, [Sozomenos, an historian living in the 5th century] says that it was spread among the Goths as well as among "those who earlier were their neighbours along the shores of the Ister", an information which deserves to be remembered. Who were earlier the neighbours of the Goths the author refers to? Sarmatians, Carps, Daco-Romans? An opportunity to meditate and an incentive to go into the problem more deeply is offered us also by the affirmation that under the influence of Christianity, "they (the Goths) adapted themselves to a more civilized and better life".[1]

(4) Zosimos, IV, 34, wrote that Theodosius defeated the Carpo–Dacians and forced them to return to their places. Gh. Ştefan considers this to be of great significance: ..."being repelled, they returned to their places, an incontestable proof of continuity."

(5) The story of Chilbudios is told by IR 1960 pp. 738–739 as follows:

During their incursions into the Empire, the different Slavic tribes often brought with them as prisoners, groups of Thraco-Romanized population (*populaţie traco-romanizată*) from the territory south of the Danube. The Latin language was used north of the Danube, and in this context an important record was left by Procopios. Narrating the attempt made by the Ant [a Slavic tribe] Chilbudios to appear as if he were the general with the same name who died, Procopios shows how he was exposed by general Narses, "IN SPITE OF THE FACT THAT HE SPOKE LATIN and that he learned to imitate many of the habits of the Roman general Chilbudios ..." The fact that the false Chilbudios learned the Latin language north of the Danube can only be explained by the presence there of a Romance population and by the use of the Latin language among the different groups [emphasis in the original].

(6) The episode recorded by Theophylaktos Simokattes and Theophanes Confessor about the shouting of the words "*torna, torna, frater!*", during a march of a Byzantine army unit in the region of the Haemus mountains refers to a Romanized population:

...all repeated in the language of the local peoples (*în limba băştinaşilor*): "*torna, torna*", i.e., return, as if it had been the sign of peril. The words are evidently Romance. Since the author shows that they were uttered in the language of the local population of the Balkans, it is obvious that these people were Romance (*este evident că aceştia erau romanici*). [2]

(7) In a work written at the beginning of the 7th century, the author, Mauricius,

---

[1] Fontes II, p. XI.

[2] Fontes II, p. XIV. The description of the episode itself is found on pp. 538 and 604.

gives advice regarding the tactics to be followed by the Byzantine army in the battles with the Sclavini and the Antes north of the Danube. In chapter XI, 31, Mauricius writes:

> We must beware of those so-called refugees, sent to us to show the ways and to find somebody; although they are Romans, with time, their mode of life changed, they forgot their own people and show more affection for the enemy. The difficulty is to understand the exact significance of the word refugees. Are they some inhabitants of the Empire who fled to the Slavs and were used by these to deceive the Byzantine army? Or are they somehow Romans originating from the north of the Danube, because, "in the course of time, their mode of life changed", in the course of the symbiosis with the Slavs? [...] The problem remains open.

In a note to this text, however, V. Iliescu gives the following commentary to the word *refugees* (ῥεφούγους):

> The Latin technical term used shows a juridic notion. The author talks about Romance elements north of the Danube, who fled across the Danube, home, to the Empire but served as guides for the Byzantine troops north of the Danube, these places being known for them, because their flight occurred a not very long time before.[1]

(8) Also the record written by Auxentius Durostorensis, who stated that the Gothic bishop Ulfila preached in Greek, Latin, and Gothic, has been assumed to prove the presence of a Latin-speaking population north of the lower Danube:

> Having done these and similar things, and shining with glory for forty years in the episcopate, he preached, by apostolic grace, without interruption, in the Greek, Latin, and Gothic languages in the one and only Church of Christ.[2]

C. Daicoviciu wrote about this in 1941 the following:

> Even the Christianity of the Goths propagated by Ulfila and other missionaries is, with good reason, connected with the Daco-Roman, Christian population north of the lower Danube, for to whom would Ulfila have preached in Latin if not to these people?[3]

In a note to the above-mentioned text, in *Fontes Historiae Daco-Romanae*, II, (p. III, note 1) the same opinion is found:

---

[1]Fontes II, p. 561, note 5.

[2]Ibid., p. 110.

[3]Daicoviciu Dacica 1969, p. 525.

The preaching in three languages, and especially in Latin, attests to the continued presence of a Latin-speaking population north of the Danube.

4. THE NATURE OF CONTACTS ACROSS THE LOWER DANUBE DURING THE 4th–6th CENTURIES

After the abandonment of Dacia Traiana in 275 AD, the lower Danube became again the frontier of the Roman Empire. What was the relation between the Empire and the territories north of the lower Danube after the end of the 3rd century? According to *Istoria Romîniei,* 1960 (p. 647):

> The lively connections between the populations of the Dacian territory and the Roman provinces situated between the Danube and the Balkan mountains were an important factor in the preservation of the north-Danubian Roman population (*în menţinerea romanităţii nord-dunărene*).

The maintenance of contacts across the Danube was, according to IR, made easier by the following circumstances:

> It was possible to evacuate Dacia without a hurry, the evacuation was organized and certain terms could be imposed upon the new rulers.[1]

It is also assumed that because the territories south of the Danube were poorer than those north of the river, the Romans needed the products of the north, which must have led to exchange between themselves and the population living in the north.

What are then the material proofs of these assumptions? On the basis of what is found in *Istoria Romîniei*, 1960, and an article by D. Tudor,[2] the arguments may be summarized as follows:

Commercial contacts

Themistios (317–388 AD) mentions the existence of commercial contacts between the Romans and the Goths:[3]

> ...The exchange is shown to have been very active as proved by the continued circulation of Roman coins and the presence of some Romano–Byzantine

[1] IR 1960, p. 647.

[2] Tudor, D., "Preuves archéologiques attestant la continuité de la domination romaine au nord du Danube après l'abandon de la Dacie sous Aurelien (IIIe–Ve siècles)", *Dacoromania* I, 1973, pp. 149–161.

[3] Oration No. X; in Fontes II, p. 60; cf. IR 1960, p. 650.

products far in the territory of Dacia.

As shown by archaelogical finds, Sucidava, on the northern shore of the Danube, has had economic contacts with Dobrogea, the Balkan peninsula, the Near East, and also with Dacia

> ...by some periodical markets organized in the same way as in other periods, on the shore of the Danube, supervised by the garrison. Many weights were found here, one of which was used for the checking of coins of precious metal from the barbarian world. In Sucidava, imitations of Romano–Byzantine bronze coins circulated, made by the populations of Dacia.[1]

Military operations

Procopios[2] recorded that during the 3rd, 4th, and 5th centuries, the Roman emperors raised forts (mostly single towers, *monopyrgia)* not only along the southern shore of the lower Danube, but "here and there, also on the other shore".

Emperor Diocletian (284–305) conducted a series of military actions, reaching from the Danube far into the Valachian plain, which led to an increase of the Roman influence north of the lower Danube.

Constantine the Great (306–337) occupied the southern parts of present-day Oltenia and Muntenia, probably up to the Furrow of Novac (*brazda lui Novac*, see map No. 8). This was the greatest expansion of the Empire north of the lower Danube after the abandonment of Dacia Traiana; it lasted for about 40 years. Constantine also built a 2400 m long bridge across the Danube, between Oescus and Sucidava.

> It must be emphasized that a bridge of such dimensions could not have been constructed only to serve the needs of a modest fortress such as Sucidava, but rather with the aim of serving a domination which must have been exercised in the large territory reconquered in the south of the ancient province of Dacia.[3]

Remnants from this bridge, and a *miliarium*, 1479 m from Celei at the Danube were discovered by archaeologists. The road from Sucidava to the Furrow of Novac was repaired, as well as that between Oescus and Serdica. The tower of Sucidava (on the place of present-day Celei–Corabia) was repaired. Excavations made there showed jewels,weapons, and many other objects which belonged to the soldiers stationed there. In the town, objects of metal, mirrors, amphorae for wine and many other articles were found; several imported from the region of the Aegean Sea. These finds testify to civil urban life in Sucidava. Sucidava, with a

---

[1] IR 1960, p. 664.

[2] Procopius: *De aedificiis*, Fontes II, pp. 458–474; quoted by IR, p. 650.

[3] Tudor, D., Dacoromania I, 1973, p. 156.

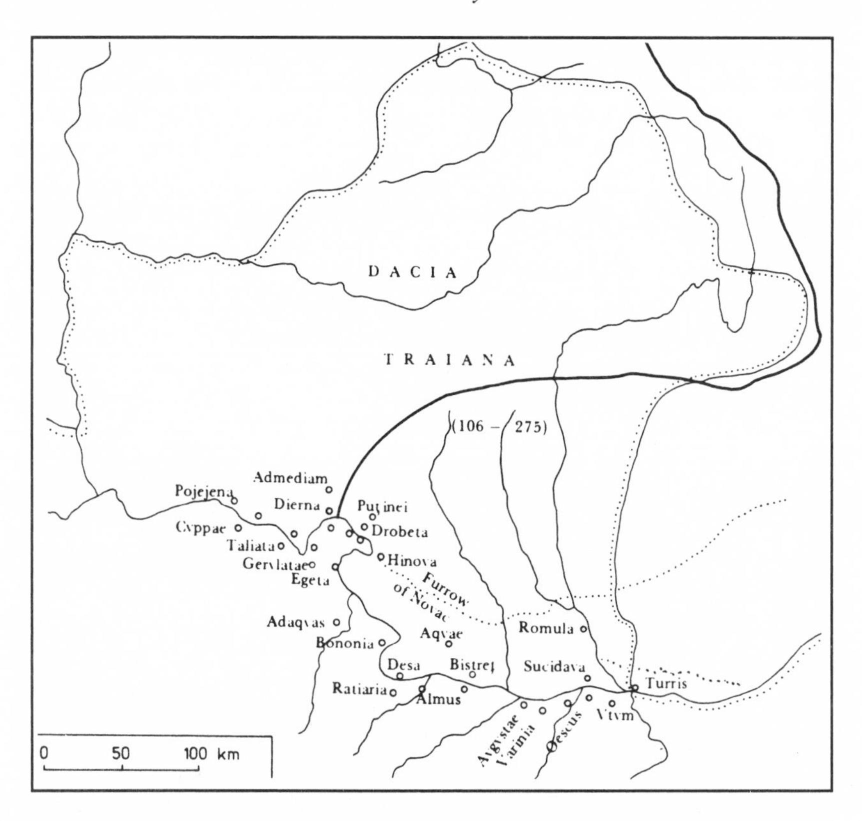

Map 8. The Roman fortresses along the lower Danube in the 3rd to the 6th centuries AD and the area occupied by the Empire for about four decades in the 4th century (between the Danube and the Furrow of Novac).
(On the basis of the map [fig. 2] in Tudor, D., "Preuves archéologiques attestant la continuité de la domination romaine au nord de Danube après l´abandon de la Dacie sous Aurélien [IIIe–Ve siècles]," *Dacoromania* I, 1973, pp. 149–161.)

Roman garrison between 275 - 450 AD,[1] was probably the centre of defense along the lower Danube. In the 5th century, it was burnt down twice by the Huns and then left by Byzantium, until Emperor Justinian (527–565 AD) restored it, "in order to cut the road of the barbarians towards the territory south of the Danube, as affirmed by Procopios (de Aedif. IV, 6)."[2] Another large military station, mentioned in written documents as well as shown by archaeological finds, was Drobeta (Turnu Severin). At the beginning of the 5th century, the military units stationed there were called *cuneus equitum Dalmatarum et auxilium*

[1] Ibid., p. 156.

[2] Tudor, D., Dacoromania I, 1973, p. 156.

primorum Daciscorum. Material finds show modifications of the camp, the construction of new buildings in the 3rd and 4th centuries. About four miles north of Drobeta, at Puţinei, a *castellum* was built. In Dierna, a prefecture of the *Legio XIII Gemina* was installed. The camp, 35 by 35 metres, was excavated before the town Orşova, later built on this place, was inundated by the artificial lake serving the new hydroelectric power station of the Iron Gate. A large number of coins from the epoch of Diocletian (284–305) and from that of Constantine the Great (306–337) were found within the camp. Dierna had to defend the valley of the Danube against attacks coming from the valley of the Cerna. At Turnu Măgurele, remains of a fortress, fragments of earthenware, and a number of coins were found. At Pojejena de Sus, on the northern shore of the Danube, bricks from the 4th century with the inscription *leg(io) VII Cl(audia) C(uppis)*, were excavated.

During the period between the abandonment of Dacia Traiana and the Hunnish invasion, at least 14 Roman fortresses existed along the northern shore of the lower Danube (see Map No 8).

> Thus, for about 170 years, the Romans dominated, by these fortified centres distributed from Baziaş to Galaţi, over an important part of the territory along the Danube.[1]

In the early 6th century, the Byzantine state expanded, reaching again the lower Danube. Many towers and towns in the Balkan peninsula were re-built. Procopios mentions the names of more than 600 such places and states that some of the towers were built on the northern shore of the lower Danube. These were: Litterata or Lederata, a powerful fortress in the Banat, the ruins of which still are visible; the castle of Zernes (former Dierna); Daphne; as well as a tower at Turnu Măgurele, whose ruins still exist. In the *Novella of Justinian*, Recidiva is mentioned as an important political and religious centre. It is not known which place was meant by this, but it may be Sycibida-Sucidava. In Sucidava, some objects of the Byzantine style were found, which date, according to coins, from the 6th century. There is also a stratum of ash, 20–40 cm thick, from the end of the 6th century, in which Avar iron shafts were found. The Avar devastations mark the end of the Byzantine power in the region of the lower Danube.

The *Novella* of Emperor Justinian is considered an important document on the policy of Byzantium regarding south-eastern Europe in the 6th century, showing that the Byzantine state had plans referring to territories north of the lower Danube:

> (XI) Thus, since in our time, with God's help, our state became greater, and our fortresses exist on both shores of the Danube, and Viminacium as well as Recidiva and Litterata, which are beyond the Danube, were again put under our power, we have considered it necessary to place beside Pannonia, in our

[1] Ibid., p. 160.

most lucky fatherland, the glorious prefecture, which was organized in Pannonia, because Pannonia Secunda is not far away from Dacia Mediterranea but large territories separate Macedonia Prima from Pannonia Secunda.

(XLI) The disposition to Bonus, the questor of the army, states who has to investigate the appeals from those 5 dioceses: Caria, Cyprus, the Cicladian isles, Moesia, and Scythia. [...] "We know that we took recently a sacred decision by which we have put under the rule of your highness these five dioceses, Caria, Cyprus, the Cicladian isles, Moesia and Scythia..."

(CXX) "We advise the holy Churches in the towns Odessos and Tomis to sell buildings in order to ransom the war prizoners..."

Edict XIII, chapter XI. About taxes to be collected and punishments in case of disobedience in this respect. It is also possible that "the entire military unit will be sent away from the country and placed into the areas beyond the river Istros or Danube, in order to guard the frontiers there..."[1]

It is asserted that Emperor Justinian's (527–565) policy led to a strengthening of Romanity (an assumed Roman population) north of the lower Danube:

> ...the document of foundation of the archiepiscopate Justiniana Prima, contained in the *11th Novella* of Emperor Justinian and dated 535 AD, disposes that some localities on the other [northern] side of the Danube be put under the authority of the archiepiscopate Justiniana Prima and under the administration of the Illyrian prefect's office. Two *civitates* are mentioned by their older name. *Recidiva* and *Litterata* (probably former *Arcidava* and *Lederata),* about which it is explicitly stated that they are on the farther side of the Danube (*quae trans Danubium sunt*) and that they were again in the possession of the empire (*nostrae iterum dicioni subactae*).[2]

The conclusion drawn from all this is that the Roman bridge-heads and fortresses on the northern shore of the Danube, as well as the annexation of certain territories of the Valachian plain, contributed to the preservation of the connections and to the strengthening of the Roman population in the north by lively contacts mediated by "emigrants, merchants, prisoners of war, mercenaries, marriages, etc."[3]

> La présence continuelle et de longue durée de la domination romaine dans une grande partie de la Dacie méridionale même après l' abandon officiel de la province sous Aurélien offre un matériel documentaire de toute première importance pour la discussion des problèmes historiques si disputés comme la continuité de la romanité au nord du Danube, la formation de la langue et du peuple roumain, la diffusion du christianisme dans l'ancienne Dacie

---

[1]Fontes II, p. 386.

[2]IR Compendiu 1974, p. 78.

[3]IR 1960, p. 649.

> trajane, etc. Si l'on veut aboutir à une solution définitive en ce qui les concerne, historiens, archéologues et philologues doivent nécessairement partir de cette réalité archéologique.[1]

* * *

5. THE *GESTA HUNGARORUM*

The question of the ethnic situation in Transylvania in the 10th century is not connected with the problem of Daco-Roman continuity. In that period, Vlachs were living in many areas of the Balkan peninsula, also south of the Jireček-line, where they must obviously have migrated. The time span of eight centuries without records about a Romance population north of the Danube would decrease to about seven centuries, if Vlachs would have been living in Transylvania in the 10th century. It is only because the problem concerns the early history of the Vlachs, and refers to the last century of Common Rumanian, that a brief survey may be warranted.

In several works on Rumanian history, the ethnic situation in Transylvania in the above mentioned period is presented mainly on the basis of the *Gesta Hungarorum.* IR, vol. II, writes, under the heading "The first political formations of a feudal character in the territory of our country" (pp. 42–44):

> Anonymus, the notary of King Bela III, gives us interesting information concerning the political situation of Transylvania in the first half of the 10th century. It is true that Anonymus wrote his work, "The feats of the Hungarians" (*Gesta Hungarorum*) towards the end of the 12th century, but he used other historical records from the end of the 11th century, as well as the sources he had access to as a person of high rank in the Royal Court, while the oral tradition was still alive in his period. Moreover, it should not be forgotten that Anonymus included records concerning later periods when referring to the first half of the 10th century; a custom practised by many other medieval historians. But what is in the first place to be retained from the record of Anonymus is the basis of the narrative, the essential instead of the details. In this respect, historical criticism arrived at the conclusion that the things Anonymus described deserve to be trusted, that they reflect the reality of the period to which they refer.
>
> As also mentioned in volume I (p. 804), Anonymus described three political formations, three principalities (voivodates): one in Crişana, led by "prince" *(voivod)* Menomorut, which comprised the territory between the rivers Mureş and Someş, with its centre in the forests of Biharea; the second in the Banat, between the Mureş and the Danube, the leader of which was "prince" Glad, who probably had his seat in the fortress of Cuvin (Keve), between the Timiş and the Danube, and the third in Transylvania proper extending from the gate

[1] Tudor, Dacoromania I, 1973, p. 160.

of the Meseş mountains to the springs of the rivers Someş, led by "prince" Gelu, who had his centre near Cluj.

Fighting is said to have been especially fierce around the fortress of Satu Mare (Hung. Szatmár), which was subdued after a siege of three days, and Biharea (Hung. Bihar), occupied on the thirteenth day of siege.

In the Banat was the principality (voivodate) of Glad, who also tried to defend his possession, concentrating his large army of equestrians and pedestrians formed by Cumans, Bulgarians, and Rumanians (*Cumani*[1] *et Bulgari atque Blachi*). Since he was subdued, Glad fled to the fortress (*castrum*) of Cuvin (Keve) followed by the invaders who at first conquered this fortress and later that of Orşova.

The attacks of the Hungarians were thereafter directed towards Transylvania proper where the principality inhabited by Rumanians and Slavs (*Blasii et Sclavi*) was situated, led by the Rumanian prince (*quidam Blachus*) Gelu. Since the Hungarian tribes were not arrested at the gate of the Meseş mountains, they penetrated into the pincipality of Gelu, pursuing the army of the prince until the river Almaş, where a battle took place; being defeated, Gelu tried to flee to his fortress (*ad castrum suum*) near the Someş but was killed not far from the river Căpuş, and the Hungarians and the autochthonous population, "shaking hands", came to an agreement, electing Tuhutum as their leader, the leader of the Hungarian tribe.

In his story, Anonymus presents the events in such a way that the merits of the main hero of his work, prince Árpád, comes to light as much as possible. The similarity of the events which have led to the defeat of the above-mentined princes – in the way they are described by Anonymus – raises some suspicion regarding the veracity of the narrative. Even if the details of the described events were not true – these must be regarded with some reservation (for example the names of the princes, derived very probably by the historian from the existing placenames in the principalities in question), the core of the story deserves to be taken into consideration, the more so because certain descriptions have been verified by records from other sources: the existence of the successor of Glad, prince Ahtum, by the Legend of Saint Gerard, the events in Transylvania in the first years of the 10th century, by chroniclers from the 13th and 14th centuries, the occupation of the fortress of Biharea, the events concerning Gelu etc., by the latest archaeological excavations.

Thus, we may consider that the existence of some political formations, some voivodates, led by "princes", i.e., voivodes, in the territory of Transylvania at the beginning of the 10th century was a reality.[2]

[1]Footnote in IR: "Anonymus confounds the Cumans with the Petchenegs, the latter were present at the frontiers of the Hungarian kingdom in the period his chronicle refers to."

[2]IR vol. II, pp. 43–44.

D. The archaeological finds in post-Roman Dacia Traiana

The theory of Daco-Roman continuity is mainly based on archeological finds excavated in present day Rumania

> As a matter of fact, earlier and more recent investigations have disclosed numerous direct proofs of the existence of the Daco-Roman population in Dacia in the centuries following the retreat by Aurelian from Dacia. They belong to archaeology and their number is increasing in direct proportion to the intensification of the investigations. [...]
> As is natural, continuity was probably more intense and is easier to detect in the areas near the Danube, considering the presence of the Roman Empire along the northern shore of the river beginning with Constantine the Great. Thus, it has been fully proved in the Banat, on the basis of written records as well as by archaeological discoveries. Here, the products of late Roman origin and imperial coins from the period after Aurelian until the 6th century are present in almost all localities known from the Roman period, sometimes even in the ruins of the old buildings. [...]
> In the rural areas, particularly in the eastern regions of Dacia, [...] a popular culture was formed already in the Roman period, in which the traditions of the autochthonous Dacian culture combined with Roman cultural forms. With this popular culture the Daco-Romans embarked upon the new historic evolution opened up by the liberation of Dacia from the domination of the Roman state.[1]

A comprehensive survey of the archaeological finds considered to indicate the persistence of a Romanized population in the territory of former Dacia Traiana is *Problema continuităţii în Dacia în lumina arheologiei şi numismaticii* (The Problem of Continuity in Dacia in the Light of Archaeology and Numismatics) by D. Protase, Bucharest, 1966. In the Foreword to this monograph, the author states that "we have collected and selected here all the archaeological and numismatic material published or yet unpublished which was known to us up to 1964–1965." According to the Preface written by C. Daicoviciu, Protase's monograph is

> ... a systematic and critical presentation of the concrete proofs of the persistence of the Dacian and the Daco-Roman populations in the territory of our present socialist country, which is the fundamental premise of the autochthoneity of the Rumanians in their several thousand year old fatherland.[2]

---

[1]These quotations are from IR 1960, pp. 616, and 628–629.

Protase gives a detailed presentation of what he calls "the vestiges of the Daco-Romans in Dacia between 271 and 450 AD" (pp. 103–198). In the introduction to this chapter, the following statement is made:

> Emphasizing that the problem of continuity is not resolved by admitting only fragmentary remains of the Romanized population in Dacia, C. Daicoviciu showed convincingly that the Rumanian people could have been formed only by the survival en masse of the north-Danubian Roman population and by its development in uninterrupted contact with the Roman element south of the Danube, and supported (*alimentată*) continually by them.

Protase's monogaph is of great value, because it gives a systematic and exhaustive presentation of the archaeological finds existing up to the mid 1960s considered to prove Daco-Roman continuity. In the decades after the publication of this monograph, very much new material was excavated in Rumania. It would take too much space to discuss these; only some of these more recent finds will be used here. The nature of all the discoveries is essentially the same, in the sense that the material shows traits characteristic of Roman products, Roman provincial traditions, Roman style, etc.

The ethnic attribution of the different sites is mainly based on the style of the objects, often earthenware, and, in the case of the cemeteries, also on funeral rites and rituals. For each site, the relevant text will be quoted or summarized below. In the Foreword to his monograph (p. 10), Protase mentions that he in general adopted the opinions of the authors who described the material in question.

The possibilities of establishing the period in which the different settlements and cemeteries were in use are in many cases fairly good, since the style of the material contents often shows elements characteristic of a certain period. The maximum time span during which the different settlements and burial sites might have been in use is shown in *Figures 2* and *3* (p.232) according to data compiled from the above-mentioned monograph by Protase.

1. SETTLEMENTS

Archiud (Erked):

> The Roman earthenware and the late changes easily observed in their forms and style, the supply caves similar to those found in the Daco-Roman settlement at Obreja, as well as the absence of Gothic or Sarmatian cultural

[2]Protase PCD 1966, p. 7 (written by C. Daicoviciu in July, 1965). In the original: ..."*prezentarea sistematică şi critică a dovezilor concrete asupra stăruirii populaţiei dacice şi daco-romane pe meleagurile ţării noastre socialiste de astăzi, premisă fundamentală a autohtoniei românilor în patria lor multimilenară.*"

Settlements		Cemeteries	
Archiud	(Erked)	Alba Iulia	(Gyulafehérvár)
Bezid	(Bözöd)	Chilia	—
Bratei	(Baráthely)	Bratei	(Baráthely)
Cioroiul Nou	—	Cipău	(Csapó)
Cipău	(Csapó)	Iernut	(Radnót)
Cluj-Mănăştur	(Kolozsmonostor)	Lechinţa de Mureş	(Maroslekence)
Comolău	(Komolló)	Mediaş	(Medgyes)
Iernut	(Radnót)	Moigrad	(Mojgrád)
Mugeni	(Bögöz)	Proştea Mică	(Kisekemező)
Noşlac	(Nagylak)	Sărăţeni	(Sóvárad)
Obreja	(Obrázsa)	Sf. Gheorghe	(Sepsiszentgyörgy)
Porumbenii Mici	(Kisgalambfalva)	Stăneşti	—
Răcari	—	Soporul de Câmpie	(Mezőszopor)
Reci	(Réty)		
Sarmizegetusa	(Várhely)		
Sebeş	(Szászsebes)		
Sic	(Szék)		
Soporul de Câmpie	(Mezőszopor)		
Verbiţa	—		
Veţel	(Veczel)		

Table 8. Settlements and cemeteries where archeological remains attributed to "Daco-Romans" were described. (On the basis of D. Protase, *Problema continuităţii în Dacia în lumina arheologiei şi numismaticii,* 1966, pp. 104–132. The Hungarian names of the places in Transylvania are given in brackets.

elements justify the attribution of this settlement from the 3rd to the 4th centuries at Archiud to the provincial population to which probably groups of free Dacians were added, in the second half of the 3rd century.

Bratei (Baráthely): see below, p. 166.

Cioroiul Nou:

> ...fragments of bottles and of black earthenware of Roman style, similar to those discovered at Sucidava, in the cultural stratum of the 4th and the 5th centuries AD. The coins of silver and bronze form a continuous series from Nerva until the period of Constantine, and thus confirm the life of the Romam population in this settlement also after Aurelian.

Cluj-Mănăştur (Kolozs-Monostor):

> The earthenware, mostly made by hand, rarely on the wheel, is of grey colour, porous or fine, fragments of red vases are rare. Regarding the forms, grey jars (*dolia*) of the Roman provincial tradition predominate, as well as different kinds of grey-blackish pots without a handle and usually without ornaments. Among the few pieces of earthenware, there is none of the Sântana de Mureş-Cerneahov type, while the forms and the techniques show the powerful tradition of provincial Roman pottery (*puternice tradiţii ale olăriei romane provinciale*).

Iernut (Radnót):

> The pottery preserves to a large extent the style of the provincial Roman pottery, but shows at the same time non-Roman technical and ornamental elements, specific to the period immediately after the abandonment of Dacia by the Romans.

Mugeni (Bögöz):

> Most numerous are the vases of Roman provincial tradition, grey and red, but fragments of vases showing the style of the Sântana de Mureş–Cerneahov culture, as well as Dacian vases are also found. As shown by the material contents, elements from the Sântana de Mureş culture penetrated to this settlement during the second phase of its existence.

Noşlac (Nagylak):

> In one of the cavities, a comb made of bone with a curved back was found, with characteristic rivets, and decorated on both sides with the usual

concentric circles.
The earthenware from this settlement includes some red-yellow fragments of the Roman style, numerous fragments of grey, fine vases with a metallic shine and sometimes with shiny, geometric patterns, pieces of large, grey jars *(dolia),* decorated by strips of curly lines; and there is an appreciable quantity also of grey-blackish pieces, made by hand or on the wheel.
On the basis of the earthenware and the comb mentioned above, the settlement is dated to the 4th–5th centuries and is considered to have belonged to the Daco-Roman population.

Obreja (Obrázsa):

This settlement was inhabited during the Roman domination and also after, in the 4th century,
...which is proved by a fibula of the type "with onion heads", found among the pottery of the best Roman provincial style. The continuation of the settlement in the 4th century is also indicated by some grey, fine fragments, with patterns achieved by polishing, and also by the information that after the first World War, some coins (now lost) were found which, according to the description given by the villagers who discovered them, seem to be from the period of Constantine.

Porumbenii Mici (Kisgalambfalva):

...red and grey provincial Roman pottery and a large bronze coin of Commodus. Other objects discovered in this settlement are: a Denar of Vespasian, a funeral lion, and two rings of Roman type, one of silver with an inlaid stone and another of gold, decorated by two granulated triangles (the stone is not preserved), and also grey and red earthenware of strikingly Roman style. There is no grey earthenware of metalllic shine in this settlement.
In some sections, only GREY earthenware of Roman style is found, no red. This would be the only indication of the continuation of the settlement after the Roman retreat from these areas, until the end of the 3rd century.

Răcari:
During the Roman period, Răcari was a *vicus* on the way to become a town.
A roman camp built of stone was found there.

...in the period after Aurelian, but probably not before Constantine the Great, the doors of the camp were blocked by "barbarian" walls and over the wall of enclosure, which has fallen into ruins, a wall of earth mixed with old debris was erected, at some places 2.5 metres high. Within the old military camp cabins were dug and huts of wood were constructed from which

Tocilescu collected a rich archaeological material which dates from the 4th–6th centuries (fibulae, objects of bronze, and pottery) specific to this late period, which is deposited, still not published, in the National Museum of Antiquities. Regarding the period of Roman domination in Dacia, the coins found in the camp start with Vespasian and end with Decius, and then, after a pause of some decades, the bronze coins of Diocletian, Constantine I and his son, Valens, Theodosius II and Justinian I appear.

Sarmizegetusa (Grădiştea) (Várhely):

The archaeological excavations made in the former capital of Roman Dacia revealed modest but incontestable vestiges of the poor, local population who, after the retreat of the Roman authorities, sought shelter among the ruins of the old town. In Sarmizegetusa, finds suggest that the forum and some buildings were used, for the needs of a shabby life, also AFTER Aurelian.

Sebeş (Szászsebes):

During the excavation made in 1960, at the "bridge of Pipoc", a cavity was emptied which contained pieces of Roman bricks, a bronze fibula with the legs inverted below, as well as fragments of grey vases, intensively burned, with a surface of metallic shine. On the basis of the pottery and the fibula, the cavity dates from the 4th century AD. To the same period belongs a hut, on the side of a kiln with a cover of burned clay, fastened on the bank of the Secaş.
From the limited number of excavations made so far, one may conclude on the basis of the uninterrupted succesion of the remains of material culture, that the autochthonous element continued to exist here during the Roman occupation and that a Daco-Roman population was present here also after the retreat by Aurelian.

Sic (Szék):

A settlement inhabited during the Roman domination in Dacia and attributed to the Dacians was found on the territory of this village in 1963.

...Roman provincial pottery was discovered, associated by fragments of vases made by hand of rough paste of dark grey colour, some of them showing ornaments specific to the late Dacian *La Tène*.
In our opinion, the settlement in Sic continued to exist also after the abandonment of Dacia by the Romans, until the beginning of the 4th century. This is definitely indicated by the numerous fragments of vases made by hand of a rough paste characterized by the cut off (right) or arched form of the base, and the absence of ornamentation.

Soporul de Câmpie (Mezőszopor):

A small settlement used during a short period, probably in the second half of the 5th century. Fragments of vases of a greyish black colour, mostly without ornamentations, were found there.

> The presence of the huts from the 5th century in the territory of the old, abandoned, Daco-Roman cemetery proves that its inhabitants did not know that the place was once used as a cemetery, and that they came from an other place, possibly from an adjacent area. Without having at present more exact material proof, the facts that these huts form a small group, are situated in a remote region and lack material characteristic of the migratory peoples, are valid indications that they belonged to some elements of the indigenous [*băştinaşă*] population.

Verbiţa:

A settlement from the period of Roman domination "and, possibly, also from the times following the official abandonment of the province."

Veţel (Veczel):

A fragment of a silver fibula, dated to the 4th century, with the inscription "*Quartine vivas!*" was found there (cf. below, p. 180).

A general characterization of these settlements is given by Protase as follows:

> It is interesting to note that this type of settlement ceased to exist after the end of the 4th century; there is no continuation into the following century. The disappearance of these settlements may have been caused, if not by economic circumstances, by the same disturbances which led to the termination of life in the towns. No doubt, the preservation of the Daco-Roman population in the old settlements after the evacuation of the Roman state apparatus from Dacia is a phenomenon of much larger proportions, something which will be brought to light by future archaeological excavations and investigations (*care va fi pus în lumină de viitoare săpături şi cercetări arheologice*).[1]

2. CEMETERIES.

Alba Iulia (Gyulafehérvár):

[1]Protase PCD 1966, p. 134.

> In the years from 1898 to 1915, five tombs of inhumation were discovered [...] among many other tombs with inventaries from the 11th to the 13th centuries, equipped with sarcophagi made of RE-USED Roman bricks. In the tombs, bracelets of the Roman style, bronze fibulae of the type "with onion-heads", necklaces of characteristic forms and two bronze-coins of Constantine I (306–337) were found.
> The tombs, partly deranged by the burials in the 11th to the 13th centuries, are found in the territory of the former Roman town Apulum, in its very centre, and obviously date from the times following the retreat of the Romans from Dacia. The funerary inventary and particularly those two coins of Constantine I found IN THE TOMBS indicate that these are from the 4th century AD. The uniformly Roman style of the tombs and the total absence of any foreign element exclude their attribution to a migratory population.

Thus, as pointed out also by Kurt Horedt, the public buildings in the centre of the Roman town had lost their original function and were now used as cemeteries.[1] Horedt summarized in 1982 the signs of life in the former Roman towns in Transylvania, stating that one finds a uniform, although fragmentary picture, determined by the same kinds of finds.

> Siedlungsreste sind sehr spärlich und könnten nur in sicher datierten Schichten abgegrenzt werden. Sie müssten bei Stadtkerngrabungen festgestellt werden, die aber nur unter bestimmten Voraussetzungen bei gelegentlichen Bauarbeiten durchgeführt wurden und bisher keine Ergebnisse in dieser Hinsicht erbrachten.[2]

Bratei (Baráthely):

A cemetery of cremation, which dates from the second half of the 4th century (and possibly to the beginning of the 5th). This is the largest cemetery from the period following the abandonment of Dacia Traiana by the Romans. It was found in Bratei, 7 kilometers east of Mediaş (Hung. Medgyes), on the bank of the river Târnava Mare (Hung. Nagyküküllő). This cemetery is considered particularly significant:

> Of particular significance in proving the continuation of the Daco-Roman population is the cemetery at Brăteiu, along the Tîrnava Mare, a cemetery of cremation dated to the time span between 380 and 454...[3]

Therefore, it will be described in some detail. But first, a survey over the material

---

[1]Horedt, K., *Siebenbürgen in Spätrömischer* Zeit, 1982, p. 62.

[2]Ibid., pp. 69–70.

[3]Giurescu & Giurescu Istoria rom 1975, p. 147.

remains found at Bratei:

As on several sites in Transylvania, remains from many different periods and populations, from the neolitic to the 13th century inclusive, were excavated at Bratei. The following survey is based on the article by R. Harhoiu, in *Dicţionar de istrorie veche a României*, edited by D.M. Pippidi, 1976, pp. 99–102.

SETTLEMENTS

Settlement No. 1 (4th–6th centuries AD). Pottery made on a wheel ("a development of Roman pottery") and by hand ("of Dacian origin"), and a small quantity of fine, grey earthenware, "indicating the presence of a Germanic element". Settlement No 2, in four levels:

(a) 4th–6th centuries, of the same character as settlement No 1.
(b) 6th–7th centuries, showing traits of the Ipoteşti–Ciurel–Cândeşti culture.
(c) 7th–8th centuries, showing traits of the first phase of the Dridu culture.
(d) 12th–13th centuries; pottery made on a wheel; agricultural and other kinds of tools; vases and cooking vessels of the Petchenegs.

CEMETERIES

Celtic tombs from the 3rd and 2nd centuries BC.
Cemetery No 1, 4th–5th centuries (see below).
Cemetery No 4, similar to the preceding .
Cemetery No 3, 6th–7th centuries, with 300 tombs of inhumation; Gepidic.
Cemetery No 2, 8th century, showing the rite of cremation (85% of the tombs) as well as that of inhumation (15%). Considered to have belonged to the first phase of the Dridu culture.

Cemetery No 1 was described by Ligia Bârzu in a monograph published in 1973.[1] The following survey is mainly based on this monograph.

Between the years 1959 and 1969, 353 tombs were excavated in this cemetery; another 100 were destroyed in 1970, in the course of work on this site, which now is a sandpit.

The cemetery is 72 meters long and 55 meters wide. At the beginning, the tombs formed regular rows, but this order was not always kept. Tombs placed one upon the other are especially frequent in the middle of the cemetery. This may be explained by the custom according to which members of one family were buried near to one other; after some time, space was no longer sufficient for this practice.

The funeral rite was cremation. The cavities in which the remains were laid down are of different types:

Ritually burned cavities are found in 270 cases (77.5%). Most of these tombs are rectangular or oval, but two are almost entirely round and one is cross-shaped.

Not burned are the cavities of 78 tombs (22.5%). Sixtyone of these are oval or rectangular, 9 are round, 6 are bottle-shaped and one is conical.

---

[1] Bârzu, Ligia, *Continuitatea populaţiei autohtone în Transilvania în secolele IV – V (cimitirul 1 de la Bratei)*, 1973.

The size of the cavities is the following: length, 120 – 150 (180) cm, bredth, 40 – 60 cm, depth (measured from the original surface), 20 – 50 cm.

Orientation in space: in a north to south direction are placed 78% of the burned cavities of rectangular or of oval shape, and somewhat more than half of the cavities which are not burned. Twenty-two percent of the burned cavities and less than half of those not burned are placed in an east to west direction.

Contents of the tombs

A large amount of animal bones were found in these tombs. The figures given by Ligia Bârzu are based on the analysis of 220 tombs (about 63% of all) made in 1966 and 1969. Most of the bones belong to big, domesticated animals, the number of which is estimated by L. Bârzu as follows: 349 oxen (*Bos taurus*), 120 porcs, 77 animals like sheep and goats and 27 horses. Other animals are rare: there were 3 dogs, 4 deers, and one wild bore (*Sus scrofa ferus*).

1. Earthenware

I. Made on a wheel.

a. Of rough paste.

1. Pots, of Roman origin, also found in the Sântana de Mureş culture.
2. Large storing vessels are found in almost all tombs. They are known from the Roman period and also from the Sântana de Mureş culture.
3. Bowls, very frequently found also in sites of the Sântana de Mureş culture.
4. Amphorae are more numerous than the bowls. In the Sântana de Mureş culture, amphorae are rare. According to L. Bârzu (p. 39), "This form is provincial Roman and represents the realization of the red Roman amphorae in a grey paste, of a late period." They indicate, according to the same author, that workrooms which preserved the techniques of the Roman provincial pottery existed in Transylvania in the 4th century.
5. Jugs – a small number of fragments were found.

b. Of fine paste.

This type is represented less (about 15%) than the pottery made of a rough paste. The Bratei cemetery reveals in this respect a different situation as compared to the sites of the Sântana de Mureş culture. The forms are largely the same as those in the group made of a rough paste. They must be products of local workshops, which thus produced pottery "of purely Roman tradition" in the 4th century and in the first 2 or 3 decades of the 5th. The pots and the bowls, as well as the jugs are similar to those found in the Sântana de Mureş culture, but the jugs are also found in Roman cemeteries.

c. Imported earthenware.

About 5% of the pottery found at Bratei were imported. These vessels were made of a fine paste, burned red; there also are enamelled vessels, mostly amphorae and jugs. These were probably made in Pannonia, a province well-known of the production of enamelled vessels in the 4th century. At Bratei, there is a large variety of forms, while in the Sântana de Mureş culture, the amphorae prevail. This is considered another indication suggesting that the population at

Bratei was different from that of the Sântana de Mureş people.
II. Earthenware made by hand.

Although present in almost all tombs, this type is not found in very large amounts. According to differences in the paste and the burning, 3 types may be distinguished. Regarding forms, the pot without handles is most frequent; there is also the censer (*căţuia*) and the lid. The censer is of typical Dacian tradition:

> These forms are of the most authentic Dacian tradition and confirm, in the possibly most certain way, the Daco-Roman character of the cemetery at Bratei.[1]

One form of these vessels, of Roman origin, shows an ornamentation usual in the pottery of the free Dacians who migrated to Transylvania from the west. The significanec of this kind of pottery at Bratei is that it shows a clear influence from the free Dacians:

> Regarding the similarities between this type of earthenware and that made by hand in the culture of the western Dacians, we believe that it is not wrong to affirm that one may regard in it a substantial contribution from the group Cipău "Gîrle".[2]

2. Pieces of metal

These are few in the cemetery No 1 at Bratei. There are pieces made of iron, silver, and bronze. Objects of iron include farming implements, handicraft utensils and other tools, one weapon, "*fusaiol*"-s,[3] fibulae, clasps, etc. One entire plough-share and a fragment was also found; they are of the type of the provincial Roman style of Pannonia. Sickles are of the type found among the free Dacians as well as in the Roman world. Of some joiners tools, one is known from the material remains of the free Dacians, the rest from the Roman Empire. Of the awls, one variant, of Roman origin, as well as most of the *fusaiol*-s are also found in the Sântana de Mureş culture. Only 19 fibulae were found at Bratei. All are of the type "with the leg inverted below"; most of them have counterparts in the Sântana de Mureş culture or in the territory of present day Hungary. The same is true about 8 clasps of iron.

3. Objects of glass

All objects of glass were imported; they are quite numerous. There are vases,

---

[1]Bârzu Cemet 1973, p. 51.

[2]Ibid., p. 52.

[3]A *fusaiol* is a round object, mostly made of clay, with a small opening in its middle part; it served as a weight for the spindle. Its shape and the material it was made of changed in the course of time.

bracelets and pearls. The vases are of several types, most of which have counterparts in Western Europe, in the Sântana de Mureş culture and/or in the territory of present day Hungary. One of the centres of production of these vases was Cologne, but they were also made in Pannonia; those found at Bratei were most probably imported from that province.[1] Pearls are also of several types, and almost all have counterparts in the Sântana de Mureş culture and/or in Hungary (from the Hunnish period). Certain types were widespread in Europe, and are characteristic of the "barbarian" world of the 4th century (Bârzu Cemet p. 72).

4. Objects made of bones; tiles and bricks

These are mostly combs varying in size from 5.2 x 5.2 cm to about 10 x 8 cm. "Combs of this kind are characteristic of some late Roman settlements and cemeteries and particularly of the area of the Sântana de Mureş-Cerneahov culture" (p. 74). The number of tiles and of bricks is quite high. They are made of a very rough paste and are bulky. "These tiles are different from the classical Roman tiles by the quality of the paste, the burning as well as by the bulkiness" (p. 75). Ligia Bârzu assumes that their presence in this cemetery indicates the existence of an older settlement in the vicinity, from which those who used the cemetery took the tiles.

(End of the detailed report on the Bratei cemetery; the description of the other cemeteries continues.)

Cluj (Hung. Kolozsvár, German Klausenburg)

Roman sarcophags were re-used; material remains are scarce, but a Christian symbol (a plain cross), nails, and a pair of ear-rings indicate that these tombs date from the period after the Roman era.[2]

In the territory of former Napoca and in present day Mănăştur, 3 km from the centre of the town, a total of 26 Roman coins from the period after the Roman domination in Dacia (up to the end of the 4th century) were found.[3]

Iernut (Hung. Radnót):

Not far from the place of a *villa rustica*, about 12 urns of cremation were found in 1961 during work on a thermo-electric power station. Only one tomb could be saved, the others were destroyed during the work. The urn preserved from this tomb, now in the Museum of Archaeology in Cluj, is described as follows:

Made on a wheel, of red-yellowish paste, with a rounded rim and a supporting

---

[1] Bârzu Cemet 1973 p. 69.

[2] Horedt, K., *Siebenbürgen in spätrömischer Zeit,* 1982, p. 66.

[3] Horedt Spätrömische Zeit 1982, pp. 67–68.

Village	Period (centuryAD)	Settle-ment	Cemetery	Population
Bezid	2nd ½ of 3rd, and 4th	+	(none)	Sântana de Mureş; free Dacians "Roman provincial cultural influences"
Chilia	2nd ½ of 3rd	+	95 tombs	free Dacians, "powerful Roman influence"
Cipău	4th	+	5 tombs of inhumation	Dacians and "Daco-Iazyges"
Cipău	5th–6th	+	(none)	"of other ethnic character"
Comolău	end of 3rd - 4th century	+	(none)	free Dacians
Mediaş	end of 3rd	+	1 urn of cremation	Carps
Reci	4th century	+	1 tomb of inhumation	Sântana de Mureş or Daco-Carps
Stăneşti	2nd ½ of 3rd	(none)	1 urn of cremation	free Dacians

Table 9. Settlements and cemeteries where archaeological remains of free Dacians and other non-Roman populations, who migrated to the territory of former Dacia Traiana after 250–275 AD, were found. (On the basis of D. Protase, *Problema continuităţii în Dacia în lumina arheologiei şi numismaticii,* 1966, pp. 104–132.)

ring on its base, the urn preserved is a pot without handles, which in shape, colour, and paste technique, continues the series of the red Roman pots from the time of the province, and has close analogies in the cemetery at Soporul de Cîmpie. [...] A certain degeneration in the making of the paste, as compared to the red Roman provincial pottery, may be observed in the case of the urn from Iernut.[1]

Lechinţa de Mureş (Maroslekence):

A tomb from around 300 AD:

The urn, made beyond doubt in the Roman pottery-workshops at Cristeşti, contained cremated human bones and a silver fibula with the head made of a semicircular plate, and the leg inverted below. Analogous to some samples from the Gothic inhumation cemetery at Sântana de Mureş, it represents one of the earliest of this type of fibulae. [...] The funeral rite and the style of the urn are clearly Roman provincial, which shows that the deceased belonged to a community of Daco-Roman population, in spite of the Gothic fibula, which came from the east.[2]

Moigrad (Mojgrád):

Before the First World War, in the territory of the Roman municipium [...] among the ruins of a Roman building equipped with a hypocaust, A. Buday discovered 17 tombs of inhumation, of which 6 were boxes of bricks connected by mortar and 11 without a sarcophag, the deceased having been laid down directly in the cavity. The tombs, most of which were plundered and scattered, did not contain any objects. [...] The assumption that they date from the period after the retreat by Aurelian which is supported only by the fact they were found among the ruins of a building from the 2nd or the 3rd century, encounters real and multiple difficulties.[3]

Proştea Mică (Kisekemező)

A tomb with the skeleton of a man was discovered there in 1958. The pottery found in this tomb is described as follows:

...fragments of vases made by wheel, of fine or porous paste and well-burned; of red-yellowish or dark-grey colour. Among the fragments of vases there is also a rim which, as suggested by its form, seems to originate from a grey fruit-dish, of the kind known from the settlements of Roman Dacia.
According to the coin of Philip the Arab, the tomb is from the second half of the 3rd century AD, but according to the fibula, it must date from around 300. The contention that the deceased belonged to a community of Daco-

[1]Protase PCD 1966, p. 116.

[2]Protase PCD 1966, p. 117. In a note (No 272), Protase mentions that C. Daicoviciu agreed with this interpretation, while K. Horedt, in *Untersuchungen zur Frühgeschichte Siebenbürgens,* Bucharest, 1958, p. 20, as well as I. Nestor, in *Istoria Romîniei*, 1960, p. 688, do not believe that this tomb belonged to a Daco-Roman.

[3]Protase PCD 1966, p. 119 ("*întîmpină reale şi multiple dificultăţi*").

> Romans, as indicated by the pottery, whose forms and techniques strongly resembled the Roman forms and techniques, appears entirely justified.[1]

Sărăţeni (Sóvárad):

Two tombs of cremation, which date beyond doubt from a period when the Roman camp was abandoned, possibly the second half of the 3rd century or more probably the first half of the 4th. These tombs, as suggested

> by the funeral rites and the vase made by hand, may belong to some elements of the Romanized provincial population, who stayed on in the eastern part of Dacia, abandoned by the Romans.

Sfântu Gheorghe (Sepsiszentgyörgy):

On a hill called "Eprestető", on the eastern shore of the Olt, two tombs, one of cremation and the other of inhumation, were discovered in 1959. This type of tomb of cremation was usual in Dacia Romana, being found also at Apulum, Porolissum, Moreşti, Sebeş, and Cinciş. The cemetery at Bratei, from the 4th century (see above), is of the same type. It is not found in areas which remained *extra provinciam.*

> Because of this, we consider the tomb at "Eprestető" to have belonged to a Daco-Roman, a supposition supported also by the style of the earthenware.[2]

It is uncertain whether this tomb is really from the period after the abandonment of the province by the Romans:

> If the fragment of the grey, polished vase, with a net-pattern, really belonged to the inventary of the tomb, then this must be dated to the end of the 3rd century or, more probably, to the first half of the following century, in any case, after the retreat of the Romans from this region.

Soporul de Câmpie (Mezőszopor):

Three urns of cremation were discovered in the territory of this village in 1960, but only one of them was preserved (without its contents), the others were destroyed and lost.

> The urn which was recovered, 0.34 m high, without handles, was made on a wheel, of fine, hard and resistent paste, *without a metallic polishing.* In the

[1]Protase PCD 1966, pp. 124–125.

[2]Protase PCD 1966, p. 128 (the following quotation is from the same page).

Daco-Roman cemetery (2nd to 3rd centuries) discovered at "Cuntenit", this kind of pot is not found. According to its form and style, which shows strong reminiscenses of the Roman provincial pottery, the urn may date from the end of the 3rd century AD, after the official abandonment of the province. [...] The funeral rite of cremation and the style of the urn suggest that those buried here were Daco-Romans.[1]

3. OBJECTS OF CHRISTIAN CHARACTER IN POST-ROMAN DACIA

It seems that Dacia Traiana did not take part in the large-scale spread of Christianity during the 3rd century, which characterized the Balkan provinces and also Gallia, Britannia, and the Iberian peninsula. (In the western Asian and northern African territories of the Roman Empire, the new religion had been propagated effectively already before 200 AD.) Discussing the causes of this, Protase stresses the importance of the fact that the socio-economic structure of Dacia Traiana was different from that of other Roman provinces; it was closer to the "barbarian" form of life in free Dacia than to a system of a Roman community.[2] Other factors, according to Protase, may have been the stronger supervision exercised by the authorities in this remote province as compared to other regions, and also the interruption of contacts with Asia Minor in the mid-second century.

Protase considers that the significance of the objects of Christian character from the 4th century is that they can be used as a "testimony of the theory that a numerous Roman population existed in Dacia after Aurelian."[3] In IR 1960, the fact is pointed out that, in the 4th century, Christian communities appeared along the Danube and that dioceses were founded in the Danubian provinces: in Marcianopolis, Naissus, Sirmium, Siscia, Durostorum, Tomis, etc. The gains of territory north of the lower Danube in the 4th century, during the reign of Constantine the Great are said to have made the propagation of Christianity in the regions north of the lower Danube possible.[4]

Protase described ten objects of Christian use. Some more important data about these are given in table 10. (Protase omits objects found along the Danube, which may have been imported there during the years of domination by the Empire and are therefore not relevant in this context.)

The style of these objects is similar to those made in the period in question in Italy, northern Africa, the Balkan provinces and Pannonia; they were, "far from

---

[1]Ibid., p. 129.

[2]Protase PCD 1966, pp. 142–143.

[3]Ibid., p. 141, "*mărturie în sprijinul tezei dăinuirii în masă a populației romanice de după Aurelian*".

[4]IR 1960, pp. 629–630.

No. Description of object	found in (place)	(year)	dated	Christian trait	similar objects found in
1. Clay lamp	Alba Iulia?	about 1837	4th century	Latin cross	
2. Donarium (“*Ego Zenovius votum posui*”)	Biertan	1773	”	“Chrismon”, style of text	Pannonia, Italia
3. Funeral altar (re-used)	Cluj	1927	”	plain cross	
4. Bronze lamp	“near Dej”	about 1914	5th - 6th cent	Christian crucifix	Oriental provinces
5. Precious stone: “The good shepherd”	“Transylvania”	about 1886	?	contents of picture	
6. Clay lamp	“Transylvania? Banat? South of Danube?”	about 1952	4th - 5th cent	Chrismon	Balkan peninsula, Italy
7. Clay lamp	“Transylvania?”	?	”	Latin cross	Northern Africa
8. Precious stone: “The good shepherd”	Turda	1830 - 1840	4th century	contents of picture	
9. Clay lamp	Turda?	about 1925	4th - 5th century	Late Roman style	Sucidava, Dobrogea, Asia Minor, Egypt, etc.
10. Funeral monument (re-used)	Zlatna?	?	4th cent. ?	“a sign in the form of a cross”	

Table 10. Objects of Christian character from the 4th to 6th centuries found in the territory of former Dacia Traiana, according to D. Protase, *Problema continuităţii în Dacia în lumina arheologiei şi numismaticii,* 1966. pp. 144–151.

being local products", imported from some of these provinces.[1]

Protase assumed, as other Rumanian archaeologists, that the owners of these objects were "Daco-Romans". Other authors, e.g., A. Alföldi, considered that they belonged to the Goths or, as F. Lot, did not attribute any importance to them.[2]

Protase gives the following arguments in favour of his opinion:

(1) All objects of Christian use f rom the 4th century were found in the territory of the former province of Dacia Traiana. It is true that two inscriptions were found also in Slovakia, but only one of these can be accepted as having been Christian, and they "belong to *Pannonia Romana*, from where they may have been imported to Slovakia in a late period."[3] Three objects of Christian character were found on the Great Hungarian Plain, but

> ...they are objects of precious metal and may have reached the places in question from the region of the Danube in Pannonia either as a result of the offensive of Constantine the Great or in connection with a possible Roman occupation of some areas on the northern side of the river during the same period.
> (2) Without exceptions, the Christian relics from post-Roman Dacia were discovered in large urban centres (Apulum, Napoca, Potaissa, Ampelum) or rural settlements (Biertan) during the times of the Roman occupation in Dacia. On the other hand, they are (with the exception of the lamp from Dej) grouped in the central and in the southwestern parts of intra-Carpathic Dacia [...] where Roman life, in all its manifestations, reached the greatest development in the era of the province, and where no Gothic archaeological complexes from the period after the abandonment by Aurelian were found so far. On the other hand, unequivocally Christian objects are totally absent from the eastern parts of Transylvania, north of the Tîrnava Mare and in the upper valleys of the Olt and the Mureş, where archaeological remains of the Goths are more frequent.[4]
> The vestiges of Christianity from the territories of the old province can in no case belong to the newly arrived Goths, and the assumption that they were left by some elements who came later from the Empire is plainly contradicted by the fact that they were discovered in former Roman towns and rural settlements. The only reasonable conclusion is that they belonged to some communities of Daco-Roman population which remained in their territories atfer 271 and which, by their Roman provincial life style constituted a

---

[1]Protase PCD 1966, p. 154.

[2]Ibid., p. 155.

[3]Ibid., p. 155, note 382.

[4]Ibid., pp. 157–158.

favourable medium for the propagation of the new religion in Latin shape in a simple, popular form, without any higher ecclesiastic organization.[1]

4. ROMAN COINS FOUND IN POST-ROMAN DACIA TRAIANA.

As in the case of the objects of Christian use, Protase excludes from the discussion coins found along the Danube (in the Banat and in Oltenia) since these territories were for some periods also after 271 AD occupied by the Empire.

The circulation of coins between 271 and 450 AD was subject to considerable fluctuation, by which three periods may be distinguished:
(1) *271-305 AD.* The number of coins is very low, in absolute numbers as well as compared to the period of Roman domination. According to Preda,[2] 60 finds were made in entire Rumania, i.e., about 17 finds for each decade of the period. The total number of coins from this period is somewhat more than 100. Two thirds of the finds were made in the area of the former Roman province and one third in areas which remained *extra provinciam.*
(2) *306-392 AD.* The circulation of Roman coins increases sharply. Most finds are from the period of Constantine the Great, who occupied an area north of the lower Danube (cf. above, p. 155). Most of the coins were made in Siscia and in Sirmium. From this period, which ends with the Hunnish invasion, almost 300 isolated bronze coins were found in Transylvania. Ten hoards of coins, which were either entirely accumulated during this period or whose accumulation ends in this period were found in Transylvania, 19 in the Banat, and 2 in Oltenia. The total number of discoveries from this period is, according to Preda, "about 200" approximately 26 for each decade.[3]
(3) *393-450 AD.* The number of coins is much lower than it was during most of the 4th century. The proportion of gold coins increased. Thus, in Transylvania, at least 11 isolated gold coins, 11 isolated bronze coins, and about 30 gold coins in hoards were found. In the Banat, the number of gold coins is about 5, that of bronze only small and there are an unspecified, low number of gold coins in hoards. In Oltenia, about 40 isolated bronze coins, no gold, and about 480 bronze coins in hoards were discovered. However, the finds from Oltenia are almost exclusively from the surroundings of Sucidava and belonged to the soldiers of the Roman garrison stationed there.

The gold coins are considered to have been owned by the peoples who dominated the country – the Goths, the Gepidae, the Huns – representing tribute

[1]Ibid.

[2]Preda, C., "Circulaţia monedelor romane postaureliene în Dacia", *Studii şi cercetări de istorie veche şi de arheologie*, 26, 4, 1975, p. 445.

[3]Ibid., p. 447.

paid to them by the Roman or the Byzantine Empire.[4] In the following, the circumstances will be summarized which, according to Protase,

> ...may be used as valid arguments in favour of the continued existence, in the territories north of the Danube and in the interior of the arch of the Carpathian mountains, of the Daco-Roman peoples, who always maintained monetary commercial contacts with the Romano-Byzantine world.[2]

(1) The coins were found throughout a large territory and not restricted to some areas with one particular population: "the attribution of the coins to a population which did not occupy the entire territory of the former province is *a priori* excluded."

(2) In general, the Goths did not put bronze coins in their tombs, although a few such cases are known, for example, at Cerneahov. Several hoards of gold and silver (but no bronze) coins were found among the material remains of the Goths.

> The bronze coins with a small, almost negligible intrinsic value, were used in the first place by the autochthonous population, accustomed from earlier times to the advantages of a commerce based on an exact monetary system, and to a lesser extent by the Goths, who appreciated not the coins as such but the precious metal it contained.

(3) The coins were mainly found in the vicinity of Roman camps, urban centres, rural settlements, or in places where vestiges from the Romans were found, or in settlements and cemeteries of the autochthonous population founded at the end of the 3rd century or in the 4th century.[3] However, on the same page, Protase states that "late Roman coins found in places where no kinds of remains from the 2nd and the 3rd centuries or from the following period are mentioned in the literature, are numerous." This may, according to Protase, in many cases be explained by our lack of knowledge of such remains because of lack of archaeological investigations in the places in question.

> (4) Regarding the hoards of coins hidden in the 4th century, it has been pointed out rightly that there are some among these which by their particular composition may contribute the the solution of the problem of Daco-Roman continuity in Dacia.These are the hoards which IN A CERTAIN PROPORTION comprise silver and bronze coins also from the times after Aurelian. In fact, IF we exclude the import of these hoards from the Empire to the Daco-Roman territories and IF we do not take some reservations regarding their INTEGRITY or the UNITY of some of them into account, we have a group of hoards with

[1]Protase PCD 1966, p. 192.

[2]Ibid., p. 198.

[3]Ibid., p. 195; *"aşezări şi cimitire autohtone"*.

a probatory value for Daco-Roman continuity. We talk about the generally known hoards of coins from Hunedoara, Pasul Vîlcan, Reghin (?), Nireş, Orşova, and Borlova.[1]

These hoards contain mostly *denarii* from the 1st to the 3rd centuries and, after a gap, a few coins of bronze from the first half of the 4th century.

The successive owners of such monetary estates, transmitted from generation to generation within the same family or population, could not have been others than the autochthonous elements, people who lived in Dacia Romana and remained in their settlements after the abandonment by Aurelian.

To another group of hoards belong those which were accumulated exclusively during the 4th century and contain mostly bronze (and a few silver) coins.

It must be admitted that these, either because they are small, (Bran-Zărneşti, Sarmizegetusa, Ungurei, etc.), or because they were buried in places where no traces of Goths, Iazyges, or of Romano-Byzantine domination were shown, also belonged to the autochthonous population. The hoard which contains 15 pieces of bronze found at Cipău in a hut which belonged to the settlement of the free Dacians who came from the west of the country confirms in general the view that the small hoards represent monetary collections of the autochthonous population.[2]

The total volume of the monetary circulation does not seem to have been sufficient to satisfy the needs of the economy and it must be assumed that exchange *in natura* was used extensively in the entire period between 271 and 450 AD. [3]

5. THE LATIN INSCRIPTIONS

Two objects from the the 4th century AD with Latin inscriptions were found in Transylvania:

(1) An *ex voto*, made of a *tabula ansata* of bronze, with the inscription in three lines:

EGO ZENO
VIVS VOT
VM POSVI

(*Ego, Zenovius, votum posui* 'I, Zenovius, have placed [this] present'), and a disc of bronze with the monogram of Jesus Christ (X + P). It was found in 1775 in

[1] Protase PCD 1966, p. 197.

[2] Ibid., p. 198.

[3] Ibid.

the woods and fields, about 3 miles from Biertan, nearMediaş (Hung. Medgyes), together with fragments of a jar and a tureen of bronze. Made in the Roman Empire, these objects probably belonged originally to a bronze chandelier from an altar.[1] The significance of this find is, according to C. Daicoviciu, as follows:

> This Donarium cannot have been placed in Biertan for any other reason than the existence there of a Christian community around the sanctuary of a Christian cult place. Who were these Christians, is a question which must be discussed in more detail. In the first place, the Latin language used in the votive inscription gives us an answer sufficient in itself: the believers spoke Latin, i.e., [they are] ROMANS or ROMANIZED people. But these could not, in the heart of Transylvania, have been other than the Daco-Roman population who stayed on in spite of the order of retreat given by Aurelian.
> Even if we would admit (in excessive prudence), that a Gothic Christian community existed at Biertan, we ask why Zenovius wrote the inscription in Latin and not in Greek, if he was a missionary from the Orient, or in the Gothic language, if he was a local Goth? The answer is easy to give: because he either was a Daco-Roman himself, or because he addressed himself to his believers in a language which they knew and spoke. These believers, even if they were Goths or only Goths *(chiar dacă erau goţi sau numai goţi)* could, however, know this language only from their subjects living in the region of Biertan.This also leads us to the only valid historical conclusion: the admission of the existence of a Daco-Roman population speaking Latin, which adhered to the Christian faith in Dacia Superior after Aurelian.[2]

In *Istoria României. Compendiu,* 1974, these ideas are presented again:

> ...settlements and cemeteries of the Daco-Roman tradition, from the 4th–6th centuries AD, for example Bratei, Biertan, etc. These are rural settlements of a population of farmers who used pottery of Roman provincial or Dacian tradition, bread ovens, Romano-Byzantine coins and the Latin language. In this context, the bronze inscription from Biertan is very important which, besides the monogram XP, shows the Latin text EGO ZENOVIVS VOTVM POSVI. We conclude from this that at Biertan, not far from Mediaş, a Christian community was constituted in the 4th century, using the Latin language, to which a person called Zenovius gave a chandelier with his name.[3]

In *Ancient Civilization of Romania*, by E. Condurachi & C. Daicoviciu, 1971, (p. 179), the following may be read about the Donarium:

---

[1] Protase PCD 1966, p. 144.

[2] Daicoviciu Dacica 1969, pp. 524–525.

[3] IR Compendiu 1974, pp. 76–77.

> We now have a whole series of remains bearing witness to the continued existence of a population of Daco-Roman stock throughout the whole of the former province of Dacia Traiana. [...] ...only a Daco-Roman population could have produced the various objects of Christian use which are dated to the same century – for example the *lucernae* or, even more strikingly, an *ex-voto* (*Plate 123*) bearing the monogram of Christ and the inscription *ego Zenovius votum posui.*

(2) The arch of a silver fibula, later changed to a ring, discovered in 1865 in the Mureş valley at Veţel, west of Alba Iulia (Hung. Gyulafehérvár). It shows the inscription: QUARTINE VIVAS; it does not contain Christian features.

E. The Rumanian language

1. THE THEORY OF CORE-AREAS

The appearance of the *Rumanian Linguistic Atlas* in the 1930s seemed to have provided linguistic evidence of the preservation of the Latin language in some regions north of the lower Danube. Puşcariu argued that the presence of Latin forms in the Transylvanian Alps imply the survival of a Latin-speaking population:

> ...si nous considérons la carte de l´ancienne Dacie trajane ... nous voyons que la région où les établissements romains étaient plus denses, et par conséquent la romanisation plus intense, coïncident avec la région où les mots d´origine latin se sont le mieux conservés.[1]

This theory has been accepted also by several other European scholars. E. Gamillscheg[2] believed that two areas in Rumania might be considered core areas, *"Kerngebiet"*-s of a Romance population: (a) a small strip of territory along the lower Danube, and (b) the region of the Munţii Apuseni in western Transylvania. The consideration which led to the hypothesis of the Munţii Apuseni as a *Kerngebiet* may be summarized as follows:

The Rumanian sub-dialect spoken there pronounces *sclab* instead of *slab, scloată, scloi, sclovă, sclugă*, etc. instead of *sloată, sloi, slovă, slugă*, etc. It is known that in certain areas of Vulgar Latin, *k* was put between *s* and *l*.

---

[1] Puşcariu, S., "Les enseignements de l´Atlas linguistique de Roumanie", Bucharest, 1936, extr. from *Rev. de Transylvanie*, III, 1936, p. 9; quoted by Rosetti ILR 1986, p. 199.

[2] Gamillscheg, E., "Über die Herkunft der Rumänen", *Preuss. Akademie der Wissenschaften, Sitzungsberichte*, Philos. -hist. Klasse, Berlin, 1940, pp. 118–134.

> Wenn nun heute für das allgemein rumänische *slab* hier *sklab(ŭ)* gesprochen wird, dann bricht in dieser Aussprache das altlateinische Lautsystem mit der gleichen Stärke durch wie im 5. Jahrhundert auf dem Boden Südfrankreichs oder Oberitaliens.

Moreover, *rinichiu* 'kidney' in Muntenia corresponds to the form *rărunchiu* in other parts of Rumania (also in the region of the Munţii Apuseni). The origin of these two forms goes back to the period of the Roman Empire: *reniculus* was said in Gascogne, in Sardinia, and in the south of the Roman Empire, while *renunculus* was preferred in northern France, in the provinces of Raetia, Noricum, and part of the Balkan peninsula. This suggests that the Rumanian population originated from at least two areas, one connected with the south and another situated within the area of *renunculus.*

According to Gamillscheg, the hypothesis of the Munţii Apuseni as an ancient dialectal area is strengthened by two names of rivers and two placenames of directly Roman origin in this region: Ampoi and Criş (rivers), and Abrud and Turda (placenames). The placenames in the valleys of the Arieş and the Ampoi indicate that 110 villages were founded by Hungarians, 87 by Rumanians, and 32 by Slavs. On the other hand, out of 17 names of mountains in the same region, only 4 are Hungarian, 13 are Rumanian, and none is Slavic. This would suggest that the mountains there were populated by Rumanians before the Slavs and the Hungarians settled in that region. To all this, Gamillscheg adds, with some reservation ("wenn auch seine Angaben durchaus nicht als einwandfreie historische Zeugnisse gelten können"), the text of Anonymus about a certain Gelu, a "Vlach", who is said to have been living in this region at the beginning of the 10th century. (The narrative of Anonymus is discussed above, p. 156, and below, p. 215–219).

The theory of an ancient Rumanian Core Area *(Kerngebiet)* in western Transylvania, put forward by Sextil Puşcariu in the 1930s, was referred to in 1975 by Giurescu & Giurescu:

> [the *Rumanian Linguistic Atlas* shows] ...the presence of some terms of Latin origin, such as for example *nea, pedestru,* and *june* only in the westen parts of Transylvania, from Maramureş and Crişana to the Banat, which do not appear in the rest of the Carpatho-Danubian region. This would not be possible if the Ancient Rumanians (*străromânii*) would have come from the Balkan peninsula. This was revealed and stressed by the Rumanian linguists Sextil Puşcariu and Emil Petrovici, as well as by foreign linguists. One of these, the Romanist K. Jaberg, showed that the map of the cited Atlas "speak a clear language: how could the Latin elements be preserved particularly well in the northwest of Rumania if the Rumanians would have come from Moesia?" And another leading Romanist, Ernst Gamillscheg, stated – also on the basis of the maps mentioned above – that one of the centres of formation of the Rumanian people was exactly the region of the Apuseni mountains,

from where the three rivers with such a characteristic Romance name as Criş, spring.[1]

2. OTHER LINGUISTIC ARGUMENTS IN FAVOUR THE THEORY OF CONTINUITY

The main linguistic argument for the theory of continuity is that based on data revealed by the *Rumanian Lingustic Atlas* in the 1930s. Other arguments based on language are as follows:

a) Rumanian religious terminology

Linguistics shows that in the territory of former Dacia Romana, the bearer of Christianity was the Latin language. In fact, in Rumanian, the basic terms of the Christian doctrine are clearly of Latin origin: *cruce, dumnezeu, creştin, înger,* etc. derive from Latin.
Of most significance in this respect is the term *biserică.* Only in the Rumanian language (and in Rhetoromance!) was this Latin word (from *basilica*) preserved, in the other Romance languages (French, Italian, etc.) the derivations of the Greek term *ecclesia* are used (in French, *église*, in Italian, *chiesa*). The explanation of this phenomenon is provided by the fact that in the 4th century, when the term *basilica* was replaced by *ecclesia,* the Daco-Romans no longer belonged to the Empire. If our Daco-Roman ancestors lived south of the Danube, in the Empire, that innovation would have penetrated also into the Rumanian language and the notion of 'church' would also here have been expressed by a word derived from Greek *ecclesia* (as happened, for example, in the case of the Albanians, in the Balkan peninsula, who have the term *'qeshë'*.[2]

In the third (1974) edition of IR Compendiu, the idea that early Christianity was spread in the former province of Dacia Traiana in the Latin language appears again (p. 77), but the passage about the word *biserică* is omitted.

b) A theory based on the Slavic influence

Emil Petrovici presented a theory summarized by IR 1960 as follows:
The treatment of *št, žd,* (Rumanian *şt, jd*) of the Common Slavic (*slava comună*) groups **tj, (*kt'), *dj,* the rendition of the Common Slavic vowels **ǫ, *ě, *ъ, *ь* by *în, ea, (a), o, e* is found also in the Slavic placenames of Dacia, while these reflexes are not present to the west of a line

[1] Giurescu & Giurescu Istoria Rom 1975, p. 151.
[2] IR Compendiu 1969, p. 92.

corresponding to the present day frontier between Bulgaria and Yougoslavia, where the corresponding reflexes are *č, k′, ć, dž, ǵ, d, u, (< *ǫ), e, (je, i) (< *ě), ă, (> a) (< *ъ, *ь)*. This fact is of decisive importance in establishing the territory in which the Rumanian language was formed.[1]

It is claimed that this proves that "the oldest and most numerous" (*cele mai vechi şi cele mai numeroase*) Slavic elements of Rumanian could only have been borrowed from the Slavs who lived east of the present day frontier between Bulgaria and Serbia, and north of the highest peaks of the Haemus mountains.

Petrovici remarks that this hypothesis is corroborated by the fact that the Greek language has a Slavic word (βλαχθι) to denote the Vlachs, which indicates that "in the early Middle Ages, South Slavs were living between the Greeks and the Rumanians."

c) The time span of the South Slavic influence

It is obvious that the South Slavic impact upon Rumanian must be the result of a close symbiosis lasting several centuries. Which centuries, and if there were periods of particularly strong influence, etc. are important issues in Rumanian history.

The sound patterns of loanwords and other circumstances indicate that already Balkan Latin was exposed to a certain Slavic influence, beginning with the 6th century. The number of words of South Slavic origin in Common Rumanian was relatively low (only about 70), and the South Slavic influence on Northern Rumanian became most intense AFTER the 10th century. All these facts are described by Rosetti.

In contrast to this, Rumanian historians and archaeologists affirm that the Slavic influence on Rumanian ended much earlier:

> With the retreat of the Bulgarian Empire to the south of the Danube, the Slavic element, which until then had been dominant, became secondary in the regions north of the Danube, and the Slavic population left in the territory of our country was, in a relatively short time, assimilated to the Proto-Rumanian (*străromânească*) population.[2]

Giurescu & Giurescu affirmed approximately the same: the Slavs were assimilated to the Rumanians between the 6th and the 10th centuries.[3] Eugenia

---

[1]IR 1960, pp. 792–793, referring to Petrovici, E., "Problema limitei sud-vestice a teritoriului de formare a limbii romîneşti", *Limba romînă*, IX, 1, 1960, pp. 79–83.

[2]IR 1960, p.747. — As shown above, the Bulgarian state dominated what today is Muntenia and southern Transylvania during most of the 9th century. The statement of IR implies therefore that the Slavs in these territories disappeared "in a relatively short time" after the 9th century, having been assimilated to a population which spoke Common Rumanian.

[3]Giurescu & Giurescu Ist Rom. 1975, p. 179.

Zaharia asserted that the archaeological finds indicate the complete assimilation of the Slavs to the Daco-Romans in the entire territory of present day Rumania already in the 8th century.[1]

d) The territory of the Slavo-Rumanian symbiosis

A crucial problem of the history of the Rumanian language is WHERE the tremendous South Slavic influence was exerted upon it. No serious linguist can deny that such influence was exerted south of the Danube, but if the theory of continuity is to be sustained, also north-Danubian areas must be assumed. Rosetti (ILR 1986, p. 265) formulated the following statement about this:

> The contact between the Slavs and the Romanized population of the Danubian provinces took place north of the Danube as well as south of it. Those who deny the possibility of the existence of these connections north of the Danube (Friedwagner, ZRPh., LIV, 659; Mustafčiev, Bulg. et Roum., 70 ff.; Skok, Sl., VIII, 624 ff.; [...], on the grounds that Dacia north of the Danube was a territory through which the migratory peoples passed and that the Romanized population could not remain in its old settlements, are making a mere assumption because, in fact, we have no direct information on the connections between the Romanized population and these peoples. For those who admit that the Rumanian language developed in a large territory of Roman colonization, the existence of contact between the Romanized population and the Slavs south of the Danube as well as north of it appears to be beyond doubt (cf. Popović, GSKS,[2] 118.)
> Drăganu, Rom. s. IX–XIV, 28 ff., as well as Jung, admit that the Romanized population was preserved in Dacia after Roman domination ceased. For the borrowings from Albanian, see Mladenov, Bălg.-alb. otnoš: Seliščev, Slav. nas. Vlach. Alb. and Jokl, Slavic., XIII, 281 and 609 [..].
> E. Petrovici considers that the territory "in which the victory of popular Latin over the Thracian language took place ... must be placed along the lower Danube, from the estuary of the Tisza to the sea. The Roman domination there lasted for at least 600 years." Şişmariov, Lb. mold., 26–28, states that the military units and the provincials crossed the Danube to the south but considers that the poor classes of the population could not have wanted to leave Dacia.

---

[1]Eugenia Zaharia, "Les sources archéologiques de la continuité daco-romaine", *Apulum*, XII, 1974, pp. 284, 287, and 293.

[2]GSKS = Geschichte der serbokroatischen Sprache. — Popović does not support this opinion. On p. 118, discussing the age of the placenames and the geographic names of Slavic origin in Rumania, he states: ..."die Lehnwörter sind jedoch im gegebenen Fall überhaupt zu unserem Zweck nicht nutzbar, weil *das Problem der sog. rumän. Urheimat /südl. oder nördl. der Donau/ noch offen bleibt* (s. Kap. II, § 22) und wir nicht wissen können, ob ein Lehnwort nördlich oder südlich der Donau aus dem Sl. ins Rum. eingedrungen ist..." (emphasis added).

3. OTHER ELEMENTS OF THE RUMANIAN LANGUAGE FROM THE VIEWPOINT OF THE THEORY OF CONTINUITY

Above, arguments based on the Rumanian language in favour of the theory of continuity were presented. In the following, the arguments put forward with the aim of defending this theory against objections based on the Rumanian language will be summarized.

a) The correspondences between Rumanian and Albanian

In IR 1960, this problem is summarized as follows:

> We have seen that the presence in the Rumanian language of some words which Rumanian shares with Albanian has been interpreted by some scholars who are against continuity as an indication that the fatherland of the Rumanian people was somewhere in the Balkan peninsula, in the vicinity of the Albanians. This argument is not valid. These words in common do not show the sound pattern and the sense they should as a result of living together (*convieţuire*). On the other hand, the Bulgarian linguist Dečev has rightly pointed out that in the case of a symbiosis between Rumanians and Albanians in the Balkan peninsula, the result ought to have been one common or [two] related languages (*o limbă comună sau înrudită*) and not two totally different ones. In reality, those few words which the Rumanian language shares with Albanian are not loanwords but were inherited by both languages from the ANCIENT INDO-EUROPEAN, CARPATHO-BALKANIC WORD STOCK.[1]

In the chapter on linguistic arguments for the theory of continuity, the following is added:

> Regarding the Albanian territory, Albanologists agree that it extended far towards the northeast. It must be noted that the ancient name of the most important town in the centre of the Balkan peninsula, Naissus, was mediated to the Slavs by an Albanian population, which changed it according to the sound laws of Albanian.[2]

Daicoviciu, Petrovici, and Ştefan (*La formation du peuple Roumain et de sa langue*, 1963) also restrict their discussion of this problem to the WORDS from the substratum, without mentioning the correspondences between Rumanian and

[1] IR 1960, p. 782. The first part of this in the original: "S-a văzut că existenţa în limba romînă a unor cuvinte comune cu limba albaneza a fost interpretată de unii cercetători adversari ai continuităţii ca o indicaţie că patria poporului romîn a fost undeva în Balcani, alături de poporul albanez. Argumentul este şubred."

[2] Ibid., p. 796.

Albanian in other respects. They conclude, referring to I.I. Russu, *Limba traco-dacilor,* 1967, p. 220, that these words

> ...constituent un bien commun que l'une et l'autre ont hérité de fond linguistique archaïque indoeuropéen (thrace, respectivement thraco-illyrien), propre à l'espace carpato-balkanique.

Rosetti, in *Istoria limbii române,* 1986, presents the Albano–Rumanian correspondences in great detail. His conclusion regarding the territory of contact between the two populations is cautious:

> It is not necessary to assume that the borrowing of the terms took place in the vicinity of Albanian. In spite of this, there are reasons to believe that the linguistic territory of the Albanians once extended beyond their present day territory towards the north (cf. above, p. 195 ff.) and that, consequently, the ancestors of the Albanians were neighbours of our ancestors.[1]

The very close correspondences between Rumanian and Albanian would not contradict the theory of formation of the Rumanian language north of the Danube if it could be shown that the same language was spoken in antiquity in Macedonia, in Serbia, western Bulgaria, Oltenia and Transylvania.In that case, the ancestors of the Rumanians could have inherited the ancient, pre-Roman elements from this language north of the lower Danube. (We disregard here the similarities also regarding the Latin elements.) This hypothesis is based on the ancient Greek and Roman terms "Thracian" and "Illyrian"; there is also the term "Daco-Moesian":

> Au fait, les éléments communs au romain et à l'albanaise s'expliquent parfaitment par parenté génétique, par le voisinage et la réciprocité d'influence possible dans l'antiquité entre l'illyrien ou thrace, comme ancêtre de l'albanaise, et le daco-moesien, substrat du roumain.[2]

This author (C. Poghirc) refers to the Balkan Linguistic Union and points out that the mutual influences among the Balkan languages must have been even greater during the first centuries AD than they are now. Finnish and Rumanian also have several words in common: Slavic words transferred to Finnish from Russian, and to Rumanian from Old Bulgarian. Poghirc argues that it would be unreasonable to conclude that Finns and Rumanians were neighbours as it is to assume that Albanians and Rumanians lived together.

---

[1]Rosetti ILR 1986, p. 259. — On p. 195 he refers to, Rosetti discusses the original homeland (i.e., the area inhabited before their partial Romanization) of the Albanians and concludes that this was in northern Albania and in adjacent areas towards the north-east, stretching approximately to the region of Niš.

[2]Poghirc, C., *Dacoromania* I, 1973, p. 202.

Is there any material evidence in favour of the assumption of the same language in a very large territory: Thracian, Thraco-Dacian, Illyrian, Daco-Moesian, or a "Carpatho-Balkanic word stock", as assumed by IR 1960? Unfortunately, very little is known about these ancient languages, which makes the answer to this question difficult. But Thracian and Dacian etymologies have been proposed for Rumanian words. Poghirc, in ILR 1969, pp. 329–335 and 355 considers that a Dacian etymology is possible in the following cases:

brusture ′common burdock′. Among other possibilities, the Dacian name of a plant *ribobasta, peripobasta, peripomasta,* (the name was preserved with an uncertain spelling), may come into question (cf. also Alb. *brushtull(ë),* above, p. 79).

mic ′small, little′ "seems to be attested in Thraco–Dacian"[1] in the placename Micia, in the name of a people Micenses, and in the personal names Miccos, Miccas, etc.

zîrnă ′black nightshade, *Solanum nigrum*′. The second half of the Dacian name προ–διαρνα may have had the meaning ′dark′. This word was connected with the Dacian placenames Dierna, Tierna, Zerna.

doină ′elegiac song; doina′. Many etymologies have been proposed. A connection between this Rumanian word and Lithuanian *daina*, Lettish *daina* ′popular song′ is generally accepted by investigators of the Baltic languages. E. Fraenkel believed that *doină* originated from Dacian.

This list of four words not only gives some examples of possible Dacian etymologies in Rumanian but contains ALL words for which such an etymology is discussed by Poghirc among words of unknown origin.

A Thracian etymology has been discussed, among other possibilities, in about twenty cases. Most of these are very uncertain, and there is no correspondence between the meanings of the proposed Rumanian words and that of the corresponding Thracian words. Many of these last mentioned words were preserved as placenames and their meaning is often unknown.

I.I. Russu[2] has tried to compose a Rumanian–Thraco-Dacian glossary. The Thracian lexical elements were compiled from Greek and Latin texts; their meanings are either known with some probability or are assumed. Among the Rumanian words in this list, 11 probably originate from the substratum of Rumanian: *baltă* ′marsh′, *brusture* ′common burdock′, *bucurie* ′joy′, *cătun* ′small village′, *colibă* ′hut′, *copil* ′child′, *curpen* ′tendril′, *gard* ′fence′, *groapă* ′cavity′, *spânz* ′hellebore′, *ţap* ′he-goat′.

In only one of these cases has the corresponding Thracian word a similar form: Rum. *gard,* Thracian *Gordion* (placename). The sense of this Thracian name is not known. Another Rumanian word of unknown etymology has been assumed to have a Thracian connection: Rum. *mare* ′great, large, big′, is similar

---

[1]ILR 1969, p. 332.

[2]Russu LTD 1967, pp. 137–143.

to - *maros, -merula* in Thracian personal names; however, the sense of these is also unknown.

b) The relationship between Rumanian and Dalmatian

The fact that the Dalmatian language does not belong to the Balkan Linguistic Union is said to show that "the Rumanian language was not formed near the Dalmatian".[1] Similarly, the differences between the two languages, for example those in the treatment of the Latin consonant groups *gn, ct,* and *cs*, are said to prove that the south-western part of Illyricum and Old Dalmatia had nothing to do with the formation of the Rumanian language.[2] It is emphasized that Rumanian and Dalmatian were always separated from each other:

> The Rumanian territory is isolated from the Dalmatian by an area occupied by the Slavic languages (Bulgarian, Serbo-Croatian, Macedonian, Slovenian) and Albanian. The isolation of the territories along the lower Danube does not, however, originate only from the period in which the Slavs migrated to the Balkan peninsula (the 7th century AD), but from the first years of Romanization of the regions along the lower Danube, starting during the reign of Augustus. [...]
> Towards the west, Romanization affected very slightly the mountain region in which relatively few Latin inscriptions were discovered and in which non-Romanized Thracians and Illyrians prevailed, ancestors of the Albanians and, by Slavification, of the Serbo-Croatians. This large, weakly Romanized mountain region separated the two strongly Romanized narrow areas of the Balkan peninsula: the Danubian and the Dalmatian regions, the latter region having been connected to Italy by very intense navigation on the Adriatic Sea which went on in antiquity and during the Middle Ages. The intense Romanization of these two regions is attested by thousands of Latin inscriptions that have been discovered in Dalmatia, Dacia, and Moesia.[3]

IR 1960 also contends that this intense Romanization along the lower Danube is indicated by the large number of Roman towns; about 40 are known to have existed between present day Belgrade and Tulcea on the shore of the Black Sea. In the 4th, 5th, and 6th centuries, eleven of these towns were residences of bishops: Singidunum, Margum, Viminacium, Aquae, Castra Martis, Ratiaria, Oescus, Novae, Abrittus, Appiaria, and Durostorum.

---

[1] IR 1960, p. 791: "*Limba română nu s-a format în apropierea dalmatei*".

[2] Russu LTD 1967, p. 218.

[3] IR 1960, pp. 794–795.

4. THE ABSENCE OF OLD GERMANIC ELEMENTS IN THE RUMANIAN LANGUAGE

Old Germanic populations – in the first place, Goths and Gepidae – were living in several areas of present day Rumania for many centuries after the Roman domination. This is known from written records and from rich archaeological material characteristic of these peoples. On the basis of the theory of Daco-Roman continuity, one would expect some Old Germanic influence upon Northern Rumanian. It is therefore understandable that several authors have assumed an Old Germanic origin of many Rumanian words. Thus, Diculescu assumed that 16 words, 15 personal names, and 5 placenames derived from Old Germanic. It has been shown, however, that these etymologies are based on mere phonetic similarity.[1]

According to M. Isbăşescu,[2] there are ten Rumanian lexical elements of which "a Germanic origin seems possible or at least more probable than the other etymologies which were proposed": *bâlcă* 'jug; pitcher', *bulz* 'chunk, lump; sawn log', *ciuf, ciof* 'tuft of hair, shock', *nasture* 'button', *rapăn* 'scurf, scab', *strănut* 'star', *strugure* 'grapes', *targă* 'barrow; litter', *tureci* 'trousers', and *zgudui* 'to shake'. None of these etymologies is generally accepted and almost all were rejected by scholars who have investigated the problem.

Gamillscheg assumed that *gard* 'fence, enclosure, pilework', was a loanword from Gepidic (*gards*; there is a similar word in Old Icelandic). This cannot be accepted, because the word also exists in Albanian *(gardh)* as well as in Old Slavic. The possibility that Rumanian *gard* is of Slavic origin cannot be excluded[3] but Albanian *gardh* is not likely to have derived from Slavic because Old Slavic *d* corresponds to Albanian *d*, not *dh*.[4] This word may derive from the substratum of Rumanian and may be related, on the Indo-European basis, with Lithuanian *gar̃das*, Gothic *garþs*, etc.[5]

The conclusion is given by Rosetti:

> One may say that none of the proposed etymological relationships is valid; most of them are contradicted by a clear explanation of the Rumanian word from other languages. Because of this, those few words for which no other etymology has yet been proposed besides the Germanic, have little chance of belonging to this group of words.[6]

---

[1] Rosetti ILR 1986, pp. 221–224.

[2] ILR 1969, p. 368.

[3] Mihăilă Studii 1973, p. 22.

[4] Ibid., p. 21; Rosetti ILR 1986, p. 249.

[5] Russu, Element autohtone 1970, Mihăilă Studii 1973, 21.

[6] Rosetti ILR 1986, p. 222. There are Old Germanic words in Rumanian which were borrowed by Vulgar Latin. Such words are found also in New Greek and in Albanian. One example is *tufă* 'bush, shrub; branch', attested to in Latin near Vegezio: *tufa*. It is also present

The absence of Old Germanic elements in the Rumanian language is thus generally recognized. According to Daicoviciu, Petrovici & Ştefan (*La formation du peuple Roumain et de sa langue*, 1963), this does not contradict the theory of continuity in Dacia, and the same opinion may be read in IR 1960.

> Le caractère de la domination des peuplades germaniques sur la Dacie, leur nombre restreint, l'absence de toute vie commune de longue durée avec les Daco-Romans...[1]

were not favourable for the penetration of Germanic elements into the Rumanian language. In IR 1960, it is also affirmed that "Germanic elements would have been transferred to Rumanian even in the case it had been formed in the Balkan peninsula."

On the other hand, a "Daco-Roman" element among the Gothic and Gepidic material remains in Transylvania is also asserted. Referring to IR 1960, p. 692, to investigations of Diculescu, Philippide, and Gamillscheg, Rosetti concludes:

> The permanent habitation of the populations of Germanic language north of the Danube and their symbiosis with the local Romanized populations are, thus, well-proved facts.[2]

5. ABOUT THE BALKAN LINGUISTIC UNION

Also the very close relationships between the Balkan languages (Greek, Albanian, Rumanian, Bulgarian, and Serbian) are in contradiction with the idea that the ancestors of the Rumanians lived as far away from the areas of these populations as present day Rumania. Explanations: a "Carpatho-Danubian language", lively contacts between the Empire and the territories north of the lower Danube etc., were discussed above, p. 186. But also the idea itself of a Balkan Linguistic Union has been questioned (cf. above, p. 87). However, Rumanian authors in general accept the idea of Balkan Linguistics (cf., for example A. Rosetti's volume entitled '*Balkan Linguistics*').

---

in Albanian: *tufë* 'bunch (of flowers)'. (Cf. Old Swedish *thuva,* modern Swedish *tuva* 'tussock, grassy hillock'; Norwegian *tuv* 'top, knot, tie'.

There are, of course, particularly in Transylvania and in the Banat, recent borrowings from the German (Transylvanian Saxon and Swabian) population of these regions.

[1]Translation of a passage in IR 1960, p. 782.

[2]Rosetti ILR 1986, p. 220.

6. EXPLANATIONS OF THE ABSENCE OF LATIN PLACENAMES AND GEOGRAPHICAL NAMES

a) Placenames

"Rumanian placenames which continue autochthonous antique names ... exist."[1] Eighteen such names were assumed by Poghirc to belong to this type of placenames; of these, a geographic correspondence (besides the phonetic similarity) may exist in the following cases: *Drencova, Hîrşova, Mehadia, Oltina,* and *Băroi.* Drencova, in the Banat, is believed to continue *Dric(c)a,* mentioned by Iordanes and possibly a tributary of the Danube. Another river, a tributary of the Tisza, is Δρέγκων or Δρήκων. Hîrşova is assumed to continue ancient Carsium in Dobrogea. Mehadia is assumed to originate from Latin Ad Mediam; although not from Latin *medius* but "probably from an autochthonous *Mehedia, Mehadia, with an intervocalic *h* not recorded by the Romans."[2] Oltina in Dobrogea continues ancient Altina, and Băroi, ancient Birea, Beroe. (This question is discussed in more detail below, p. 244.)

These hypotheses are not generally accepted, on the contrary, there is general consensus that no inherited Latin placenames exist in the toponymy of the territories north of the lower Danube. This is not, of course, favourable for the assumption of the persistence of a Roman population there until the arrival of the Slavs. However, several explanations have been offered:

> If examined critically, also toponymy gives the same answer in favour of continuity and an argument can by no means be constructed against this continuity from the absence of placenames directly inherited from the Geto-Dacian or the Latin language. This is because, in the first place, although its documentary value cannot be denied, the probatory value of toponymy (as also that of personal names) is not absolute. The giving of names in the Middle Ages to people as well as to places, was subject to many conditions and factors. Very often, personal names and placenames are translated from one language to the other, and the original name does not always remain in use. In the second place, the fact should be remembered that in the entire Balkan peninsula, all placenames and names of small and large rivers and streams are non-Rumanian, with the exception of some cases, such as Săruna (Salonic), Peşter(i), and Durmitor (mountains in Yougoslavia), etc. All these names, spread over a large territory and of relatively recent origin (with the exception of the important centre of Săruna) originate from the Vlach shepherds of the Peninsula and do not prove that the primitive fatherland of the Rumanian people was in the Balkan peninsula.[3]

---

[1]Poghirc in ILR 1969, p. 359.

[2]Ibid., p. 360.

[3]IR 1960, p. 786.

The fact that placenames of Slavic origin dominate in Rumania is explained as follows:

> A valid explanation of this phenomenon in our country may be found in the temporary political, military, and social domination of the Slavic conquerors over former Dacia, as well as in the result of the Slavo-Rumanian symbiosis and of the bilingualism which was created. Because of these circumstances, the Slavic placenames were able to supersede the Latin, the indigenous population *(băştinaşii)* adopted them, either by abandoning, in part, the old Daco-Roman names or adjusting part of these to the Slavic sound pattern. This may have been the case particularly in regions in which the indigenous people at a certain time were not in the majority among the sedentary farmers.[1]

Another possibility is mentioned by Rosetti:

> The fact that the majority of Rumanian placenames north of the Danube are Slavic is explained by the fact that the very numerous Slavic population translated older names of villages, as *Frumoasa* into *Dobra, Piatra* into *Kamenu, Repedea* into *Bistriţa, Cîmpulung* into *Dulgopol*, etc. [Rosetti refers here to Puşcariu, Capidan, and Iordan] and that the towns were founded BY FOREIGNERS, THUS, THE TOWNS ALONG THE NORTHERN FRONTIER OF ŢARA ROMÂNEASCĂ WERE FOUNDED BY TEUTONIC EQUESTRIANS AND THE MARKET-PLACES OF MOLDAVIA HAVE A MIXED POPULATION (FOR EXAMPLE BAIA).[2]

Also Puşcariu wrote about the translation of Rumanian placenames by the Slavs, and, in Transylvania, by the Hungarians:

> Le cas du fleuve Bistriţa est instructif. Son nom est d'origine slave, et il signifie 'rapide', en roumain 'repede'. Mais Repede est auhjourd'hui encore le nom d'un des affluents de ce fleuve, dans la région montagneuse de son cours, et que ce nom a été traduit par des Slaves établis plus tard sur ses rives par l'équivalent Bistryca. Il est arrivé ensuite ce qu'on peut observer bien souvent chez nous et dans d'autres pays: la population ancienne accepte la nouvelle dénomination officielle donnée par les conquérants.

And in a note:

> De même le nom du village de Dobroudja Camena n'est qu'une traduction slave, étendue aujourd'hui à la langue des Roumains, de l'ancien Petra , qui apparaît dans une inscription latine trouvée là-bas (C.T. Sauciuc: *O inscripţie*

---

[1]Ibid., p. 787.

[2]Rosetti ILR 1968, p. 215, emphasize added. — In the 1986 edition, the passage emphasized here was omitted and replaced by the word "later" (thus: "and the towns were founded later").

latină dans 'Analele Dobrogei', XV (1934), pp. 93–112)."[1]

Not all placenames based on Slavic lexical elements were given by Slavs. There are Rumanian derivatives of Slavic names: Cernăteşti (cf. Old Slavic *črŭnŭ)*, Pleşeni (cf. Old Slavic *plěšĭ)* "which may have been given by the respective Rumanian population."[2] Also placenames derived from personal names of Slavic origin may have been given by Rumanians: "If a name of river, such as Dîmboviţa originates from a population which spoke the Old Bulgarian language, the placename Crăeşti (Tecuci), for example, does not permit the same explanation because it derives from a personal name (Craiu), from the name of the owner of the estate (Iordan, Rum. Top., 53)."[3]

There are also placenames of Slavic origin given by Rumanians: for example Baia or Bivol, from words of Slavic origin borrowed by Rumanian. However, the number of placenames given by a Slavic population – such as for example Cobia (cf. Old Slavic *kobĭ*), Crasna (cf. Old Slavic *krasĭna*) Bălgrad, Bistriţa, Ialomiţa, Ilfov, Prahova, Predeal, Râmnic, Vlaşca, Zlatna, etc. is extremely high in entire Rumania.[4]

(b) River names

The following hypotheses have been presented concerning the names of the great rivers in Transylvania:

> Linguistic research has established that the names of the rivers Olt, Mureş, Someş, etc. derive from the names used during the Roman period: Alutus, Maris, Samus. These names preserve vestiges indicating that they were used by the Slavs who settled in our country during the 6th–7th centuries, but do not show any traces of having passed through a Germanic medium (*filieră germanică*). This fact shows that the Slavs did not learn these names from a Germanic population but from one which spoke Latin and which preserved the names of rivers used during the Roman domination.[5]

In this passage, it is accepted that the names of these rivers were borrowed by a Rumanian population from the Slavs. However, also attempts at explaining these names without borrowing from Slavic or Hungarian have been made. The argumentation is based on certain sound changes: *-si-* > *š* and *a* > *o* (or, sometimes, *u*). Thus, ancient Marisia and Timisia would have changed, in "late Daco-Moesian", to Mureš and to Timiš, respectively; ancient Samus to Someš

[1] Puşcariu, S., "Le rôle de la Transylvanie dans la formation et l'évolution de la langue roumaine", *La Transylvanie*, 1938, 41.

[2] Rosetti ILR 1968, p. 288.

[3] Ibid., p. 301.

[4] Ibid., pp. 301–302; Popović GSKS 1960, pp. 116–122.

[5] IR Compendiu 1969, p. 92.

and Alutus to Olt. A difficulty is *Tisia* which, according to this hypothesis, would have changed to something like **Tiš* (instead of *Tisa*). Poghirc, who put forward this theory, assumed that the *-si-* > *š* and the *a* > *o (u)* changes occurred in "late Daco-Moesian", between the 3rd and the 6th centuries. He explains the form of the *Tisa* by the possibility that the "autochthonous population" did not have the same sound on the place of *-si-* as in Marisia, Timisia, etc. The writing of this name (with *tz)* by Constantinus Porphyrogenitos in the 10th century is said to support this view.[1]

In the 1968 edition of ILR (p. 288), Rosetti mentioned the explanation given by E. Petrovici in 1951of the toponymy of Slavic origin in Rumania:

> The contradiction between the Romance character of the Rumanian language and the non-Romance – primarily Slavic, but also Hungarian, Cumanian and other – character of the old toponymy in the territory of the Rumanian language cannot be explained, I believe, other than by assuming the spread of the Romance (Rumanian) language in a territory where mainly Slavic was spoken (Petrovici, Lingv. R.P.R. [1951] 91.)

Rosetti commented upon this as follows: "which is not our opinion about the Slavo-Rumanian contacts and the explanation of the Slavic toponymy north of the Danube." He continues, however, with discussing certain regions, where, also according to Petrovici, "the population that spoke Rumanian settled among a relatively sparse Slavic-speaking people." Also the hypothesis that "the Rumanian element penetrated to southern Moldavia, coming from Transylvania, in the 11th and 12th centuries," is mentioned in this context. Regarding the toponyms of a Serbo-Croatian or Bulgarian sound pattern in Moldavia and Bucovina (e.g. Slănic), Rosetti considered that these "were introduced in this area by the Rumanian population in Moldavia in the 13th century." All these reasonings, beginning with the quotation of Petrovici (1951), are omitted from the definitive (1986) edition of Rosetti´s *Istoria limbii române.*

[1]C. Poghirc in ILR 1969, p. 359; and Dacoromania I, 1973, p. 198.

Chapter IV

A CRITICAL ANALYSIS OF THE THEORY OF CONTINUITY

A. A survey of opinions of Western scholars about the theory

1. Friedwagner, M., "Über die Sprache und Heimat der Rumänen in ihrer Frühzeit", in *Zeitschrift für romanische Philologie*, Halle, LIV, pp. 641–715:

Friedwagner stresses that the territory inhabited by the early Rumanians must have been unitary:

> Im ganzen aber wird an der Vorstellung eines *einheitlichen, zusammenhängenden Lebensraumes* bis zur Abwanderung des südlichen Zweiges schon aus zwingenden sprachlichen Gründen festgehalten werden müssen (pp. 713 – 714).

Regarding the main areas of early Rumanian:

> Dass der *Mittelpunkt* des urrumänischen Volkes (*centrul vieţii române*) einst im Donauraum und zwar südlich des Stromes lag, daran wird im allgemeinen von den Linguisten nicht mehr gezweifelt (p. 713).
> ...es ist illyrische Gegend, im Altertum Dardanien in sich begreifend, nach neuerer Bezeichnung das Land östlich von Montenegro: Alt- und Südserbien (in seinen früherer Grenzen) und Westbulgarien (p. 714).

About the possibility of development north of the lower Danube, Friedwagner writes:

> Nördlich der Donau glaubt man wohl mit Recht an römische Reste im südöstlichen Banat; möglich dass solche auch im südwestlichen Gebirge Transylvaniens und im nördlichen Oltenien (Kleine Walachei) sich halten konnten. Ob das in der dortigen Sprache sich noch nachweisen lässt, wird sich zeigen (p. 715).

Friedwagner concludes with the statement that if the Rumanians really were able to persist in those areas, this would be a lesser miracle than their ability to keep their language as unitary as it is today in spite of the large area which they inhabited in ancient times (if one assumes areas north of the Danube):

> ...dass bei so grosser Ausbreitung des Volkes in der Frühzeit die sprachliche

[...] Einheit möglich geworden ist (p. 715).

2. Popović, I., *Geschichte der serbokroatischen Sprache*, Wiesbaden, 1960: Dass die Rumänen südlich der Donau gesessen haben, lässt sich kaum bestreiten" (p. 62). "Die ersten sl. Elemente sind ins Rum. bereits in der ′urrumänischen′ Epoche eingedrungen, d.h. zur Zeit, als die rum. Sprache [...] noch eine geographisch-linguistische Einheit bildete (irgendwo auf dem Zentralbalkan) (p. 200).

However, Popović, after having stated that it is *a priori* not probable that all of the Latin-speaking inhabitants would have left Dacia Traiana in 271, concludes as follows:

> Wenn wir im Endresultat die heute herrschende Annahme einer rumän. Urheimat sowohl nördl. als auch südl. der Donau vetreten, so beruht das eher auf einer allgemeinen Überzeugung als auf sicheren sprachlichen Tatsachen. Feste Sprachargumente müssen erst von der künftigen Forschung erbracht werden, da uns die bisherigen nicht genügen können (p. 63).

3. Stadtmüller, G., *Grundfragen der europäischen Geschichte*, München – Wien, 1965:

Stadtmüller considered that the Rumanian language developed mainly south of the Danube and that the Rumanians (Vlachs) started to migrate to their present day territoriers in the 12th century. About Transylvania, Stadtmüller remarked:

> Für Siebenbürgen ist es wahrscheinlich, dass zuerst die Bulgaren dort sassen, danach kamen die Ungarn und später die Rumänen. Nach dem Sprachatlas von Puşcariu und nach Untersuchungen von Ernst Gamillscheg und Günter Reichenkron muss man jedoch mit der Möglichkeit rechnen, dass geringe Reste der Provinzialromanen auch nach der römischen Räumung der Provinz Dacia Trajana (271) in Siebenbürgen überdauert haben und dann seit dem 12. Jahrhundert durch einen gewaltigen Zuzug von Rumänen aus dem Inneren des Balkan verstärkt worden sind. An diesem Zuzug kann nämlich nicht gezweifelt werden. Er ist von nichtrumänischen und rumänischen Gelehrten überzeugend aus urkundlichen und literarischen Quellen nachgewiesen worden (p. 91).

4. Lombard, A., *Latinets öden i öster* (The destinies of Latin in the East), Lund, 1967:

Lombard considered the absence of Old Germanic elements the most important argument against the possibility of development north of the Danube. However, "the concordances between ancient times and the present are too striking and speak for a continuous existence of Latin north of the Danube, in ancient Dacia" (p. 7). Also dialectology – the theory of core regions – has, according to Lombard, "given some support" for the theory of continuity (p. 6). This author also stressed the significance of linguistics in solving historical and cultural problems. In the case of Rumanian, neither the chronicles, nor archaeology can give a reliable answer:

> The archaeological remains, such as the big *Tropeum Traiani* in Dobrogea and the rich finds in Transylvanian cemeteries say little more [than the chronicles and the Latin inscriptions] in spite of the efforts of Pârvan and Daicoviciu to get them speak (p.3).

Lombard was of the opinion that if it is true that the Latin language survived north of the lower Danube then "one must say that this is a unique case". The conclusion of this treatise is that the Rumanian language probably was formed south and north of the lower Danube.

5. Bourciez, É., *Éléments de linguistique romane,* Paris, 1967.

Bourciez considers that the entire population of Dacia Traiana does not seem to have left the province: until the period of Justinian, the mid-sixth century, there were contacts between Dacia and the Empire, since Byzantine authors from the 6th century recorded the building or restauration of bridge-heads on the northern shore of the lower Danube.

> Toutefois, c´est bien au sud de ce fleuve que doit avoir été, pendant quelques siècles, le siège principal des populations qui parlaient le latin d´Orient: elles étaient répendues en Moesie, en Dalmatie, et communiquaient largement avec l´Italie dont elles formaient le prolongement... (p. 135).

6. Tagliavini, C., *Le origini delle lingue neolatine. Introduzione alla filologia romanza,* Bologna, 1969.

Tagliavini emphasizes that the similiarities, especially the innovations shared by all four Rumanian dialects can only be explanied by a common, unitary area and that this must have been situated south of the Danube:

> Philological arguments indicate that Ancient Rumanian developed on the southern shore of the Danube. To this conclusion leads us the study of facts such as the concordances with Albanian which cannot exclusively be ascribed to a common substratum but must have developed during a period of symbiosis; the Bulgarian character (and only to a lesser degree, Serbian) of the old Slavic elements of Rumanian (all the northern Slavic elements, for instance, Ruthenian, are more recent), the absence of Old Germanic elements, etc. (p.373).
>
> Without denying the possibility of rests of Roman population north of the Danube, the majority of foreign linguists now consider that the territory of formation of the Rumanian language must have been approximately in

historical Serbia (p. 374).

7. Vidos, B.E., *Handbuch der romanischen Sprachwissenschaft*, 1975.
After the enumeration of facts of language (the concordances with Albanian, the Bulgarian influence, the lack of Old Germanic elements), Vidos continues:

> Auf Grund dieser sprachlichen und historischen Überlegungen nimmt man an, dass sich die romanische Bevölkerung nach der Räumung Daziens in das Gebiet südlich der Donau zurückgezogen hat, und dass das Rumänische hier auf dem Balkan entstanden ist. Da sich indes fast das ganze dakoromanische Sprachgebiet im Norden der Donau erstreckt, wird angenommen, dass die Rumänen im Lauf des Mittelalters von neuem aus der Balkanhalbinsel auf das linke Donauufer ausgewandert sind und das heutige Rumänien erneut kolonisiert haben.[1]

After these statements, however, Vidos refers to the data revealed by the *Rumanian Linguistic Atlas* (cf. above, pp. 180–181), and concludes that these prove that

> Die grosse Masse des Volkes, Bauern, Hirten, arme Leute, die noch heute den grössten Teil des rumänischen Volkes bilden, ist nicht auf das rechte Ufer der Donau ausgezogen.[2]

8. Pei, M., *The Story of Latin and the Romance Languages,* 1976.
Presenting the problem of the origin of Rumanian ("The Mystery of Rumanian"), pp. 137–143, Pei puts a number of questions and concludes that there is no sufficient evidence to give the answers. These questions "continue to plague Romance linguists and historians" (p. 137).

9. Izzo, H., "On the History of Romanian", *The Twelfth Lacus Forum 1985*, edited by Mary C, Marino and L. A. Pérez, Lake Bluff, 1986, pp. 139–147.
The most likely scenario is, according to Izzo,

> ... that Romanian is the language of what remained, after the South Slavic invasions of the 6th and 7th centuries, of the once thoroughly Latinized population of the Balkan peninsula between the Danube and Greece, somewhere in the area corresponding to modern Serbia, Macedonia or Bulgaria (not too far from where Macedo-Romanian is now spoken). After living among Slavs for several centuries they would have migrated across the

---

[1]Vidos Handbuch 1975, pp. 360– 361. In a note, the author refers to Friedwagner, Tamás, Gamillscheg, Puşcariu, Wartburg, Brătianu, Valkhoff, and Tagliavini.

[2]Vidos Handbuch 1975, p. 361. In the notes, Vidos refers to S. Pop, *La dialectologie. Aperçu historique et méthodes d'enquêtes linguistiques. I. Dialectologie romane*, p. 270 and S. Puşcariu, *Études de linguistique roumaine*. Klausenburg–Bukarest 1937.

> Danube into Romania after the nomads abandoned it, perhaps as late as the end of the 13th century. Although there is no proof that this last supposition is correct, it is at least plausible; and, unlike all the others, it accounts for precisely those facts which conflict with all the other hypotheses (pp. 144–145).

B. Inconsistencies

The essential features of the theory of Daco-Roman continuity were presented above in chapter III. Here, a number of contradictions and inconsequencies will have to be pointed out.

(a) The notion "Daco-Roman" is ambiguous

This is surprizing, because the term is the very base of the theory of continuity. The logical definition would be "Romanized (Latin-speaking) people, who, or whose ancestors, were once Dacians and lived north of the lower Danube"[1]. However, reading the literature, it may be observed that this is not as simple, as Protase also clearly explained the real situation:

> The notion of "Daco-Roman" may be understood in several different ways. It has an ethnic, and at the same time, a chronological sense. If we say 'Daco-Roman settlement' – in the case we do not know the ethnic composition of its inhabitants – we may think of four or even five possibilities: 1) settlement of local Dacians in the period and territory of Roman Dacia, 2) settlement of Roman colonists in Dacia, 3) settlement in which a mixed population lived, LOCAL DACIANS AND ROMAN COLONISTS, 4) settlement inhabited by Romanized Dacians, dated to the post-Aurelian period, 5) settlement of Romanized Dacians and Roman colonists from the same period.
> The term "Daco-Roman" is thus equivocal, if it is not qualified by some of the above specifications. We use it here because of its conciseness. Usually, by "Daco-Romans" one denotes the population of the Romanized Dacians, mixed with the Roman colonists.[2]

This ambiguity – because authors not always give the necessary specification– causes in many cases uncertainty about what is really meant. ALSO THE EXPRESSION "AUTOCHTHONOUS POPULATION" IS AMBIGUOUS: it is used to designate a Latin-speaking people, but also Dacians, free or living in Dacia Traiana. Vague and ambiguous terms are often used, such as "Carpatho-

---

[1]Using the term "Daco-Roman" in the present monograph, the author has always this sense in mind.

[2]Protase, D., *Autohtonii în Dacia*, vol. I. *Dacia romana*, 1980, p. 12.

Danubian" or "Carpatho-Balkanic" space, "Thraco-Illyrian", "Thraco-Dacian", or "Geto-Dacian", "Daco-Moesian" language. In the historical circumstances in question, it is very unlikely that a uniform language would have existed in the entire eastern half of the Balkan peninsula, thus, even "Thracian" (as a single language) is questionable.

(b) The change of opinion about the territory of the Daco-Romans

Until the early 1970-s, it was maintained that the Daco-Romans lived in the territory of former Roman Dacia – after these years, practically entire present day Rumania is claimed by historians as the ancient homeland of the Rumanian people (cf. above, pp. 143–144). The change is not explained, no new discoveries were made to warrant it. A comparison of the two texts in IR Compendiu shows that only a few words were deleted, *"dar acolo nu e vorba"* (but there is no question) is changed to its opposite *"şi acolo e vorba"* and in this way, the statement made in 1974 corresponds exactly to the opposite of what was said five years earlier. This refers to *Istoria României. Compendiu*, 1969 and 1974, but the change is seen also in other publications – also in the 1986 edition of Rosetti's ILR, passages which in 1968 clearly stated what areas were *not* considered as the ancient areas of the Daco-Romans are omitted (cf. above, p. 143). At the same time, a number of archaeological studies started to be published which asserted Daco-Roman continuity also in Muntenia and in Moldavia.

(c) Did the Daco-Romans flee to the mountains?

According to IR 1960, the Daco-Romans left their settlements during the 5th to the 6th centuries because of repeated harassments and it is therefore "easy to understand why all the ancient placenames, in contrast to the areas south of the Danube, disappeared in the territories of the former province of Dacia Traiana."[1] According to E. Condurachi & C. Daicoviciu *(Romania,* 1971, p. 182): "The steady disappearance of Daco-Roman farming settlements in the period up to 600 A.D. was a natural consequence of the repeated harassments of a population which had become accustomed to a settled and peaceable life." *IR Compendiu* 1969 (p. 100) writes that the Daco-Romans were, after the 6th century AD, forced to flee to remote valleys and mountains, and that "this is the only way to explain the oblivion of the old names of settlements and towns". In the third edition (1974, p. 83), the situation is described differently:

> After the emigration of the Slavs across the Danube, the relation of power north of the river changed in favour of the autochthonous Daco-Romans. These have left the mountainous and hilly regions, united themselves with the groups spread over the forest steppe and with a part of the Romance people

---

[1]IR 1960, p. 627.

> who came here (*cu o parte din romanicii veniți aici*) because of the attacks of the Slavs on the southern shores of the Danube. Because of their higher numbers, superior biological and economic capacities, a more united social organization, the Daco-Romans have assimilated the Slavs.

Thus, an admigration of Romance elements from the south is admitted here. The flight to the mountains is not denied, but at the same time, "groups spread over the forest steppe" are assumed. This is the start of a new concept, that of denying the idea of the flight to the mouintains explicitely. Several monographs dealing with archaeological materials claim now that the Daco-Romans never left their ancient dwelling places but lived together with the migratory peoples, for example with the Goths and with the Gepidae.

(d) Partiality

These changes of concept, without any material basis (for example, new discoveries) somehow reminds of the situation in earlier periods, when the study of the development of the Rumanian language and people was in the first place undertaken in order to prove the autochthoneity of the Rumanians in their present territories. I. Iordan wrote, for instance, (in connection with the study of the placenames), in 1952:

> In our country, the Daco-Roman placenames were, considered from a historical viewpoint studied for a long time almost exclusively with the purpose of proving the persistence of the Romance element in Dacia after this province was abandoned by Aurelian. Since the realization of such an aim presupposes the existence of a large number of Latin toponyms, possibly pre-Roman, i.e. indigenous but borrowed and preserved by Trajan's colonists and their descendants, the problem of continuity is complicated as regards toponyms by the Latin origin of a significant part of our geographic names. The difficulties are great – even for linguists and so much more for historians – particularly if these do not abandon the aim which is, because of circumstances, to a great extent purely political: if you consider the placenames as proof of national significance, you are inclined to find such evidence even where it does not exist. And I do not have in mind here only the peculiar or ludicrous etymologies of, for example, Slatina < *stella latina*, Târgovişte < *Târgul Vestei*, etc. from once upon a time.[1]

[1] Iordan, I., *Nume de locuri românești în RPR*, 1952, pp. VI–VII.

C. History

1. THE ROMAN COLONIZATION OF DACIA TRAIANA

The approximate frontiers of the Roman domination north of the lower Danube (the frontiers of Dacia Traiana) are shown on maps No. 1 and 9. These maps were drawn according to the description of the frontiers of Dacia Traiana in IR Compendiu 1974, p. 45, and the map given by Protase (PCD 1966, p. 156). The accuracy of these maps is not very high; they are based on the Roman *castra* built for the defence of the province.[1] It may be seen that not the entire territory of Dacia was occupied. The areas of what are present day Maramureş and Crişana were never under Roman rule, and the plains of the Banat were not colonized. The area of Dacia Traiana corresponds to less than 40% of the territory of what is today Rumania.

After the conquest in 106 AD, the new province was populated by people coming from the whole Roman world (*ex toto orbe Romano*), probably from 20 provinces. Some years later, Dacia was divided into two parts: *Dacia Superior* and *Dacia Inferior* (corresponding roughly to what is today Transylvania and Oltenia, respectively). The northern part was later divided into *Dacia Porolissensis* in the north and *Dacia Apulensis* in the south.

The new province was a Roman outpost in *barbaricum,* and as such, subject to many attacks. There are several records describing the wars with the free Dacians (in 144, 156–158 AD, etc.). During the Marcomann wars (166–180 AD), Dacia Traiana and Moesia Inferior were ravaged by Germanic peoples and the Iazyges. Records about wars give an idea about the great damage caused to the population of the Empire. Thus, Dio Cassius, LXXI, 16, 2 (in *Fontes* I, p. 703) stated about the Iazyges:

> The great power they still possessed, as well as the severe damages they have caused to the Romans were indicated by the fact that they returned one hundred thousand prisoners, after having sold many of them and many others died or suceeded to escape.

These peoples, as well as the free Dacians and the Carps, continued their attacks against the province during the 3rd century. Major incursions are recorded from the years 236, 245, and 254. However, new roads were still being built towards the mid-third century and in Sarmizegetusa, the bronze sculpture of Emperor Decius was erected. During the reign of Emperor Alexander Severus (222–235), Dacia received the "*Concilium Provinciarium Daciarum trium*" with its seat in Sarmizegetusa, which at the same time received the title of "*metropolis*". The chief of this Concilium was a chief priest, the "*sacerdos arae Augusti (nostri)*". Of those six priests who are named in the inscriptions, four are mentioned as

---

[1] IR Compendiu 1974, p. 45.

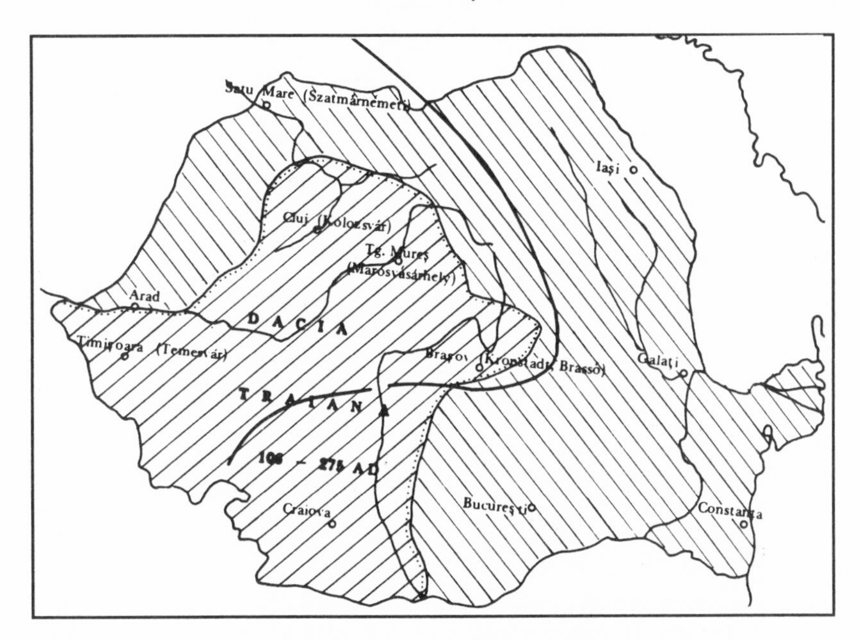

Map 9, showing the relation between the territory of Dacia Traiana and present day (1995) Rumania. The area occupied by the Roman Empire was less than 40% of the territory of Rumania. (See also the commentary to the question of the frontiers of Dacia Traiana, map No. 1, p. 14).

being Roman chevaliers. This is considered to indicate that, by that time, Dacia had the same status as the western provinces of the Empire.[1] During the 3rd century, the number of Oriental elements in the population increased. Many non-Latin people, mostly from the Near East, had their own organizations, according to their nationality or religion.

During the reign of Gallienus (253–268), eastern Transylvania was abandoned. Archaeological finds from this period, attributed to the free Dacians, were discovered in several places, indicating that these migrated to the areas left by the Romans.

The question of the number of Dacians living in Dacia Traiana

Remains of dwelling places and cemeteries of the Dacian type, with earthenware showing Dacian traits, and dated to the 2nd and 3rd centuries AD, were found in many places of the former province. But finds also show a serious discontinuity: for the two centuries preceding the Roman conquest, 235

[1] Daicoviciu Dacica 1969, p. 408.

settlements were verified. On the site of 87 of these, a settlement existed also during the Roman period, but only on one site (Slimnic, near Sibiu) has the direct continuation of the pre-Roman settlement been shown.[1] Such a serious discontinuity on the village level is difficult to reconcile with the thought of a flourishing population living in masses in the Roman province. It has been explained by the policy of the Roman state to concentrate the small indigenous settlements in larger and more stable communities, as well as the desire to move these into open places, where they were easier to supervise.[2]

There are no reliable methods to determine the approximative number of Dacians in the province. According to Strabo, the Dacians were in the period of Burebista able to raise 200.000 soldiers; later, about 40.000. IR Compendiu, 1974, (p. 59), asserts that in the time of Decebal, the Dacian population "must have numbered about half a million people". The number of prisoners taken by Trajan was estimated to 50.000 (Ioanes Lydus). But are these records reliable? If they are, did those 50.000 men represent the majority of the Dacian men, in other words, was Dacia really "deprived of men", as affirmed by Eutropius? There are no answers to questions like these.

In these circumstances, there is substantial room for speculation. Thus, the protagonists of the *Transylvanian School*, who were mainly interested in the Latin character of the Rumanian language, denied even the presence of Dacians in Roman Dacia. C. Daicoviciu believed in 1934 that there were not many Dacians left, but later he changed his mind: on the basis of settlements and cemeteries attributed to the Dacians that were discovered during the two decades after the war, he stated (in 1968): "we have the right to reckon with a numerous provincial Dacian population".[3] Giurescu assumed that 3/4 of the original population remained in the province after the Roman conquest:[4]

> Even if we admit, which is impossible, that all warriors perished, [...] their wives and children remained (we refer to the words *prunc, copil*, and *zestre*, which are Dacian), thus, roughly THREE FOURTH OF THE INITIAL TOTAL POPULATION REMAINED.

The argument based on "Dacian words" cannot be accepted – there are no certainly Dacian words in the Rumanian language (cf. above, p. 55).[5] The

[1] Iudita Winkler, "Procesul romanizării în lumină monumentelor epigrafice şi sculpturale din aşezările rurale ale provinciei Dacia", *Studii şi cercetări de istorie veche şi de arheologie*, 25, 4, 1974, pp. 497–515.

[2] Daicovicu Dacica 1969, p. 434.

[3] Ibid.

[4] Giurescu & Giurescu Istoria Rom 1975, p. 92.

[5] The etymology of *prunc* 'small child, infant', is not clear; explanations from Latin and Greek are not satisfctory (Rosetti ILR 1986, p. 175), *copil* belongs to the words from the substratum which Rumanian shares with Albanian *(kopil), zestre* is considered to derive from the substratum (Russu Etnogeneza 1981, p. 423).

preservation of ancient geographical names does not tell us anything about the number of the Dacians and even less is the significance of certain scenes on the column of Trajan showing Dacians returning to their homes. It is kown that many Dacians were taken to Rome and to other parts of the Empire as slaves and many others were dispersed throughout the Empire as soldiers.

Quantitative data are extant about a) Dacian personal names on the inscriptions and b) Roman army units in Dacia formed by Dacians.

a) Along with more than 2000 Latin names, about 60 Dacian ones are known from the province, and another 37 from other parts of the Empire. The Dacians may have had less opportunity to make inscriptions than the Romans had, but the figure is in any case extremely low.

b) The number of army units in Dacia, formed by Dacians, was very low:

> Regarding the Geto-Dacians, it is impossible not to take into account their quite small number in the Roman period (cf. the extremely small number of *alae* and *cohortes* formed by Dacians in the imperial Roman period, stated by Pârvan, Dacia, Cambridge, p. 190.)[1]

One may conclude that there are no hard facts on which to base any estimation of the number of Dacians in their old places or anywhere in the province of Dacia Traiana. There is nothing to indicate that they would have been living there in large numbers, the contrary seems more probable.

A comparison with the Balkan provinces, which were under Roman rule for a much longer time than Dacia Traiana, is of interest. Religious syncretism was widely practised there, but the indigenous beliefs prevailed stubbornly. Thus, in Bulgaria, about 2000 reliefs of the Thracian equestrian god were found, indicating a widespread worship of this god, while in Dacia Traiana, no traces of the indigenous Dacian religion exist:

> In many parts of the Empire, including Italia, Hispania,Gallia, Germania, Britannia, numerous indubitable proofs exist of the worship of indigenous gods having continued for a long time under varying forms and under their own original name, side by side of those from the Greco-Roman Pantheon, or even merging with these, while in Dacia Traiana not a single name of a Geto-Dacian god is known whose worship by the indigenous population continued. Here, everything is hidden under the forms of the Greco-Roman religious forms.[2]

The question of Romanization

There are very few facts regarding the degree in which the Latin language

---

[1]Daicoviciu Dacica 1969, p. 17

[2]Protase Autohtonii 1980, p. 252.

was spread in Dacia Traiana. It may be assumed that many of those people who have been brought to the new province knew Latin, but the mother tongue of a large number of them – coming from 20 provinces – must have been other than Latin. In an article published in *Apulum*, VII, 1, 1968 ("The Romanization of Dacia", pp. 427–437), C. Daicoviciu stated:

> The idea that the acceptance or the rejection of Romanization is, to a high degree, also a question of rather subjective judgment is not unfamiliar to us.

The short time span of the province (at most 169 years) has repeatedly been pointed out. According to I. Iordan, for example:

> Dacia was not completely Romanized and, in addition, was dominated by the Romans for only 165 years, in which time only part of the autochthonous population could have learned the Latin language, namely those who had economic, administrative and other kinds of contacts with the representatives of the new conditions.[1]

The arguments in favour of an intensive Romanization in Dacia put forward by C. Daicoviciu were presented above (chapter III, pp. 144–146). They are more or less valid, but they are only indications of the possibility of (a certain degree of) Romanization. There is nothing to prove that the majority of the population had Latin as their mother-tongue in the province; and this is the prerequisite of the creation of a Romance language. Moreover, when Hadrian was told not to leave the province, in the 120s, because there were "many Roman citizens" there, not even two decades had passed since the occupation of Dacia and under this short time there can be no question of any real Romanization. The Dalmatian miners lived in a limited area and also in a short time; after the Marcomann wars, in the 180s, these areas were largely abandoned. The record of Hadrian´s plans to give up the province witnesses against the belief that the Empire organized Dacia deliberately into a "safe bastion of Romanity", "planted in the midth of Barbaricum". The scope of Rome with the occupation of this territory was rather different: it was partly military and partly economic; above all, it aimed at the exploitation of gold and salt.

Life in this remote outpost of the Roman Empire was quite different from that in the other Roman provinces:

> In the inscriptions from Dacia, mostly acts of administrative and religious character are reflected, or the public and private manifesttions of the army. It is only on rare occasions that the sincerity and the kind of speech of the ordinary citizen or of the slave permeate through them.[2]

---

[1]Iordan, I., *Alexandru Philippide*, 1969, p. 104.

[2]Mihăescu Limba Lat 1960, p. 278.

A presentation of the many different peoples who assembled after 106 AD in Dacia Traiana is given by D. Tudor (*Orașe, tîrguri și sate în Dacia romană*, 1968). The inscriptions do not offer a reliable basis for the estimation of the Roman element, because inscriptions were in the Roman Empire predominatly made in the Latin language and non-Roman people often used Latin or Latinized names. Moreover, a large part of the inscriptions in Dacia were made by the army, and these do not indicate a sedentary, Latin-speaking population. There are indications that the number of non-Romans was high all over the province and that these were in the majority in extensive areas. In eastern Transylvania, the Dacians are considered to have been in the majority [1] and in the region of the gold-mines in the Munţii Apuseni, the population consisted mainly of Illyrians, Greeks, and Oriental peoples.[2]

On the basis of Latin inscriptions found IN THE RURAL AREAS, a numerous Latin-speaking population has been assumed there. Iudita Winkler[3] gives the following figures: the number of villages in the entire province is estimated to 500 and the population of a typical village is assumed to have been varying between 50 and 200 inhabitants. In only 160 (32%) of these villages were inscriptions found, in a total number of 230 (about 8% of all inscriptions found in Dacia Traiana). This is a small proportion, although similar figures were reported from other provinces, for example from Moesia Superior.[4] However, most of these inscriptions are of an official character, initiated obviously by the ruling Roman functionaries, priests and soldiers, who were not permanently living in the respective places but were strangers. Consequently, the inscriptions do not indicate a Latin-speaking population living in significant numbers in the rural areas of the province.

It is well-known that all over the Roman Empire, the centres of economic, political, and cultural life, AS WELL AS OF ROMANIZATION, were the towns. What was then the situation IN THE TOWNS OF DACIA? All towns had a mixed population, coming from many different areas of the Empire. Tudor stated about the capital, Sarmizegetusa: "The Roman element of Italian origin was not numerous and consisted mainly of the representatives of the floating group of functionaries."[5] Permanent inhabitants from Italy were very few in Dacia Traiana. The colonists from the Orient and from the other provinces were more or less Latinized or not Latinized at all. Thus, for example, at Sarmizegetusa, the inscriptions "testify to numerous *nationes* of civilians and soldiers".[6] At Apulum,

[1]Tudor, D., *Orașe și sate în Dacia Romană*, 1968, p. 283.

[2]Ibid., pp. 194, 197, and 203.

[3]Iudita Winkler, "Procesul romanizării în lumină monumentelor epigrafice și sculpturale din așezările rurale ale provinciei Dacia", *Studii și cercetări de istorie veche și de arheologie,* 25, 4, 1974, pp. 497–515.

[4]Mócsy, A., *Gesellschaft und Romanisation in der römischen Provinz Moesia Superior*, 1970, pp. 199–326.

[5]Tudor Orașe 1968, p. 101.

[6]Ibid., p. 76.

there were a large number of Augustales with non-Latin names, and all known names of the merchants there, in the largest town of the province, were of Oriental origin.[1] A great variety of gods were found there; especially those imported from the Orient were numerous and these gods "made a real assault with the aim of conquering the 'religious market' of the locality."[2] At Ampelum and at Alburnus Maior, the majority of the population were Illyrians, Greeks and Oriental peoples. Out of 68 free citizens living there, who are named in 25 documents published in CIL (*Corpus Inscriptionum Latinarum*), III, only 6 were with certainty and another 12 with some probability Roman citizens.[3] As shown by these texts, "their knowledge of Latin was not among the best".[4] In Potaissa, the majority of the gods in the Pantheon were Roman "which is natural in view of the presence of the 5th Macedonian *legio* in this place." But even here, a variety of different peoples were living, in the first place, of Oriental origin. Also in Napoca, colonists came mainly from Asia Minor and organized themselves in different associations (*Galatae consistentes municipio [Napoca], Collegium Asianorum,* etc.). These people preserved their ethnic and cultural identity throughout the period of the province: "Until the 3rd century inclusive, these [people] preserved the knowledge about their home country."

A general conclusion about the towns of Roman Dacia was given by Protase:

> In contrast to Italia and the western provinces, where some urban centres of the indigenous population continued to develop and became real Roman towns, in Dacia, the more important settlements, the town centres of the indigenous population ceased to exist with the Roman conquest. All the towns of Trajan's province were created from civil and military settlements as a consequence of Roman colonisation, and only borrowed the names of the old Dacian settlements: Sarmizegetusa, Apulum, Potaissa, Napoca, Porolissum, Drobeta, Dierna, etc. In Dacia, there was no Daco-Roman urban development. The towns (with the exception of the Greek towns along the black Sea) appeared in Dacia with the Roman domination and disappeared as such after its abolishment ...[5]

2. THE ABANDONMENT OF DACIA BY THE ROMANS

Eutropius recorded clearly that the Romans evacuated Dacia Traiana and

---

[1] Ibid., p. 159.

[2] Ibid., p. 165.

[3] Pólay, E., *A dáciai viaszostáblák szerződései,* 1972, pp. 71–72.

[4] Tudor Oraşe 1968, p. 198; the following data about Potaissa and Napoca are from the same monograph, pp. 215 and 229, respectively.

[5] Protase Autohtonii 1980, p. 252.

created at the same time two other provinces south of the Danube with the names Dacia Ripensis and Dacia Mediterranea. The scarcity of data does not permit to decide how much of the population may have been left north of the Danube. The validity of Eutropius´ record has been questioned (cf. above, chapter III, p. 147). It does not make sense to speculate about this problem. The scepticism of Rumanian authors may be appreciated, records of ancient chroniclers must be rigorously scrutinized; in too many cases, a critical analysis of the texts shows superficial descriptions, exaggerations, errors, etc.

The question of a total or only partial evacuation is not as important as it may appear to be. In many other provinces, Latin-speaking people were left behind after the retreat of the Roman army and administration. In Noricum, for example, there are lists of names of Roman peasants living in their old areas after the abandonment of that province by Rome. In the new surroundings, outside the Roman Empire, these groups of people were not strong enough to resist gradual assimilation to the surrounding, mainly Germanic population. Even more striking is the case of Britannia: England was under Roman rule from 43-45 AD to 410, i.e., under 365 years. Roman life there is attested by a number of material remains, such as about 100 towns, baths, a very rich system of roads, etc. Most significant is the fact that a large number of Roman placenames were preserved in England to our days: from Latin *castra*, there are today English place names ending in *–caster, –cester, –chester*, (Manchester, Lancaster, etc); Latin *vicus* > English *wick* (Warwick); Latin *colonia* > English *–coln* (Lincoln).[1] People who spoke Latin were most probably left in England in 410 AD, but, living outside the Empire, they eventually were assimilated to other populations; to the native people who continued to use their mother tongue during the Roman rule, and/or to the peoples which migrated there after the Roman retreat. The only thing we know certainly is that in spite of 365 years of Roman domination, abundant material remains of Roman style and customs, and even the preservation of dozens of Latin placenames, no Latin-speaking (Romance) population survived in England.

3. THE ´SILENCE OF HISTORIANS´

This is also one of the frequently mentioned arguments against the theory of continuity. However, the situation is in principle similar to the case of the records about the abandonment of Dacia Traiana by the Romans: the questionable reliability of ancient records and narratives. It is rightly pointed out (cf. above, p. 147–148) that the Byzantine and the western chroniclers did not give a systematic presentation of the circumstances in different territories and of

---

[1]Herbert Izzo ("On the history of Romanian", *The Twelfth Lacus Forum* 1985, pp. 139–147) has pointed out that it is appropriate to compare the situation of Dacia after the Roman retreat with that of post-Roman Britannia.

different times, but occupied themselves mainly with events and conditions that have had some relevance for their own country. In other words, the silence of historians is only an argument *ex silentio* and cannot be decisive. Again, the question is which populations lived north of the lower Danube in the centuries after the Roman retreat? Is there any evidence of "Daco-Romans"?

As shown above, pp. 147–151, a number of arguments were put forward in favour of a positive answer to this question. Unfortunately, none of these stands up to a critical examination. (1): The theory about the "Ausonian" language is only speculation without any material basis. (2) For the discussion of the record about bishop Ulfila, see below. (3) The reports of some Christians who remained in Dacia, and about the "earlier neighbours of the Goths" do not contain anything to warrant the conclusion that a Romance population is meant. (4) The Carpo-Dacians were forced to return to their places. This could suggest Roman continuity if it had been the question of a Romance population, but this people never lived in the Empire and did not speak Latin. (5) Chilboudios, if he was a prisoner taken by the Slavs in the territory of the Empire, had learned the Latin language there. (6) The words *"torna, torna, frater"* are Romance – but they were uttered in present day Bulgaria, south of the Danube, and the story has therefore no relevance for Roman continuity north of the river. (7) The theory about the refugees who "show more affection for the enemy" having been Romance elements, lacks any evidence. In this context it may be asked why the Byzantine author did not explicitly state that these refugees were Latin-speaking people living in *barbaricum,* if this had been the case?

Two of these arguments warrant a more extended discussion: the Latin language having been spoken in the Hunnish empire and the story of Ulfila, the Gothic bishop living in Muntenia in the 4th century.

(a) In the Hunnish Empire, several populations subdued by the Huns were living, of which the Sarmatians, the Goths and the Gepidae are well-documented. Ştefan adds that "beyond doubt, also Romance groups [lived there]", however, these were not living in former Dacia BUT IN PANNONIA. There, evidence of a Latin-speaking population exists from the time immediately before the invasion of the Huns: Latin inscriptions were made until the end of the 4th century. Pannonia, however, was of a considerable distance from Dacia and these two provinces were divided from one another other by the plains between the Danube and the Transylvanian Mountains (Munţii Apuseni). These plains were never under the rule of the Roman Empire. The presence of a Latin-speaking population in Pannonia has therefore nothing to do with the ethnic situation in Dacia.

(b) The record on Bishop Ulfila is quoted in a truncated way (above, p. 150–151). The entire relevant text leads to a totally different conclusion.

Auxentius Durostorensis tells us that Ulfila was 30 years old when he became bishop over the Goths (*in gente Gothorum de lectore triginta annorum episkopus est ordinatus*), "to lead and improve, to teach and to build in spirit the people of the Goths" (*ut regeret et corrigeret [et] docet et aedificaret gentem Gothorum*), "according to the Evangelical, apostolic, and prophetic directory, this saint, on the decision and order of Jesus Christ, led the people of the Goths" (*iste sanctus ipsius Cristi dispositione et ordinatione .. agentem ipsam gentem Gothorum secundum evangelicam et apostolicam et profeticam regulam emendavit...*).

Ulfila preached among the Goths for seven years; then a persecution of Christians started and Ulfila was forced to settle, together with a part of his congregation, south of the Danube, in the Roman Empire: "Living with his people in the territory of the Romans, he preached, besides those 7 years, another 33 years the truth..." (*Degens cum suo populo in solo Romaniae absque illis septem annis triginta et tribus annis veritatem predicavit...*).

To summarize: Ulfila preached for 7 years among the Goths (in a few sentences, Auxentius Durostorensis states three times: *"gentem Gothorum")*. Thereafter he was forced to settle in the Roman Empire where he preached for another 33 years of course, (also) in Latin. One may wonder why this Byzantine author did not mention a Latin-speaking population (if there had been such a population) among the believers of Ulfila, in view of the fact that he was so explicit regarding the Goths. Therefore, far from suggesting Romans living north of the lower Danube in the 4th century, the record of Auxentius Durostorensis rather makes this assumption more unlikely.

4. THE QUESTION OF CONTACTS ACROSS THE DANUBE

Commercial contacts and military operations in the 4th–6th centuries along the northern shores of the lower Danube and at some distance from the river towards the north are claimed to have strengthened the Roman population assumed to have been living in former Dacia Traiana (cf. above, pp. 151–153). An analysis of the situation shows, however, that no normal, everyday contacts could exist in that period between the populations south and north of the Danube. After 275 AD, the lower Danube became again the Roman *limes,* the frontier of the Empire against *barbaricum.* It was defended by a strong army and a fleet. The centuries to come were characterized by repeated incursions into the Empire of a number of barbarian peoples; Goths, Sarmatians, Huns, Avars, etc. The Roman Empire, and later, until about 600 AD, Byzantium, defended their own people and territories against them with varying success.

The communications across the Roman *limes* were described by Jireček as follows:

> An der Reichsgrenze war der Verkehr an der Donau, ebensogut wie an der persischen Grenze oder am Rande der Wüsten von Afrika strenge überwacht, nur an bestimmten Tagen und Orten unter militärischer Aufsicht gestattet. Die Ausfuhr von Waffen, Eisen, Gold, Getreide und Salz war überhaupt verboten.[1]

[1] Jireček GS 1911, p. 43.

Historical records, corroborated by archaeological finds, tell us about fortifying of the camps and the towns along the lower Danube, the establishing of bridge-heads and a number of *castra* on the northern shore of the river, military raids towards the north, as well as occupation of certain areas for periods of different lengths. The largest of these occupations was achieved by Constantine the Great: the territory probably up to the "Furrow of Novac" (*Brazda lui Novac*) was under Byzantine rule for about 40 years.

The fortresses on the northern shore of the Danube were the outposts of the Empire in *barbaricum* with the strict military purpose of DEFENSE. It appears clearly from the record of Procopios that during all this time, Byzantium made great efforts to defend its own territories against the invading barbarians and there was no question of an expansion northward.

Procopios from Caesarea was born around 500 AD. He described, partly as an eye-witness, the wars waged by the Romans against the Persians, the Vandals, the Goths, etc. His work *About constructions* (Περι κτισματων) was written in the years 553–555, from which we quote:

> IV, 3. Particularly in Europe [i.e., the Balkan peninsula], seeking to give help according to need, he [Emperor Justinian] realized works of which we have difficulties speaking and which also in writing can only be explained with difficulty. These [the works] were made taking into account the vicinity of the river Istros and the barbarians who threatened our country. 5. Hunnish and Gothic peoples have settled in its vicinity and the Tauric and Scythian peoples, as well as Slavs [...] and other kinds of wild men are roaming there with their herds or are living there. 6. Determined to resist those who incessantly sought reasons for war, and not doing anything half way, Emperor Justinian was forced to raise innumerable fortifications, to place very many sentries, and do everything which could set a barrier for cruel and wild enemies.
> IV, 14. Because he has fortified with walls the entire Europa [i.e., the Balkan peninsula] made it impossible for the barbarians who live beyond the river Istros to defy it.
> 33. Because the Emperor wanted to make of the Istros our most powerful defence of the entire Europe, he covered the shore of the river with dense fortifications, as we will show below, and has placed sentries all over the shores, with the aim powerfully to check the passing of the barbarians from those areas. 34. Not having relied on deceptive human hope, and considering that if the enemies succeed in trespassing the river in some way or other, they will invade the fields lacking defense, they will take as slaves all the young people and will destroy all the wealth, the Emperor was not satisfied with giving [his people] a collective security by the fortifications on the shores of the river but gave them also a special local one. 35. He made such dense fortifications in villages that every estate had its own fortification or was in the vicinity of a fortified place.

> IV, 5, 1. In this way, Emperor Justinian fortified all the territory in the interior of Illyria. Now, I shall show how he fortified the shore of the Istros, which is also called Danubios, with fortifications and garrisons of soldiers. 2. Aiming to check the trespassing of the Danube by the barbarians, previous Roman emperors covered the entire shore of this river with fortifications, not only on its right [southern] shore, but have built also on the opposite side small, fortified towns and towers. [. ..] 8. In this way, he entirely restituted to the Roman Empire the security which it had lost.
> IV, 6, 18. Emperor Justinian has re-built Pontes, which is situated on the right side of the river and impossible to conquer, and in this way he made the Illyrians secure. [Writing about two fortifications situated on the southern and the northern shore of the Danube]: 35. Emperor Justinian has restored these posts, which were demolished in the course of time, and in this way, he stopped the invasions of the barbarians there.
> IV, 11, 20. He [Emperor Justinian] has raised innumerable fortifications in Thracia, and thanks to these Thracia, earlier exposed to the invasions of the enemy, has now given protection.[1]

It appears clearly from the passages quoted above that between the end of the 3rd century and about the year 600, the Roman and the Byzantine empires had great difficulties in defending their own population from unceasing attacks from the north. Large parts of the Balkan peninsula were fortified; during certain periods, particularly under Constantine the Great in the early 4th, and Emperor Justinian in the 6th century, defense was more successful. In other times, many towns and smaller or larger areas in the Balkans were devastated. There cannot have been any attempts (and even less any possibility of success in case attempts had been made) to spread Roman or Byzantine culture or the Latin language in the territories inhabited by the barbarian peoples. The occupation of the southern part of Oltenia for 40 years was a short episode in the history of that province. The towns were not affected at all:

> The return of the Roman domination in the 4th century in the southern and southeastern parts of Dacia did not lead to a renewed urbanization of these territories.[2]

Commercial contacts existed between the Roman Empire and almost all of

[1]Procopios′ work *About constructions* is reproduced in *Fontes Historiae Dacoromanae,* II, 1970. The quotations given here are found on pp. 458–471 (in the Greek original and with a Rumanian translation).

[2]Tudor Oraşe 1968, p. 385. It goes without saying that Oltenia north of the Furrow of Novac, most of the Banat and entire Transylvania never were affected by these operations of the Roman army. As stated also by E. Popescu: "Im 4. und 6. Jahrhundert hat die römisch-byzantinische Herrschaft jenseits der Donau nur verhältnismässig kurz gedauert und dehnte sich lediglich über ein begrenztes Territorium des früheren Dakiens aus" (*Dacoromania* I, 1973, p. 70).

Europe north of it (cf. the survey of the impact of Roman culture and civilization on the peoples of Europe, below, pp. 220–223). Material remains of such contact were found also north of the Danube, not only in present day Rumania but also far away towards the north and the east. Commercial contacts often result in the transfer of lexical elements (cf. the many words of Latin origin in the Germanic languages) but rarely if ever have other effects upon language. Nothing has been discovered to indicate that the situation north of the lower Danube was different. Nothing has been reported to suggest that contacts through the temporary bridge-heads or through the annexed territories by "emigrants, merchants, prisoners of war, mercenaries, marriages, etc." (as assumed by IR 1960, p. 649; cf. also above, p.152) were different from those along the other frontiers of the Empire. Nowhere did such contacts contribute to or result in the preservation of the Latin language. Thus, one may conclude with Straka:[1]

> On ne trouve non plus aucune preuve tangible de la continuation des rapports lingustiques entre la Dacie et les régions romanisées au sud du Danube entre 271 et la fin du VIe siècle; la supposition de M.M. [H. Mihăescu] a ce sujet est donc une hypothèse qui n'est pas fondée sur faits objectifs. Enfin, en ce qui concerne les rapports entre les Balkans et la latinité occidentale par l'intermediaire de Byzance et du christianisme (rapports dont la Dacie semble d'ailleurs exclue), il ne pouvait s'agir que d'influences exercées par la langue officielle de l'État ou de l'Église, et c'est autre chose que les rapports directs avec le latin quotidien de l'ouest que les régions balkaniques avaient eus précédemment, avant leur detachement de l'Empire romain. Dans ces conditions, et contrairement à ce qu'en pense M. Rosetti (*Istoria limbii romîne*, vol. I, 3e ed., 1960, p. 49–50), il n'y a pas lieu de modifier en quoi que ce soit le point de vue de Bourciez *(Éléments,* § 50, 4) et le nôtre (RLR, 71, p. 276, et RLiR, 20, p. 253 et 258; v. aussi Väänenen, ouvr. c., p. 27) sur l'isolement linguistique des provinces de l'est à la suite de leur abandon par les Romains; rien ne semble infirmer, dans l'ouvrage de M.M., la théorie selon laquelle après 271, c'est-à-dire a partir du moment où de nouveaux colons ne venaient plus s'installer en Dacie, les changements linguistiques de l'ouest ne se propagaient plus dans le parler roman de cette ancienne province, qui de ce fait ne participait plus, depuis le dernier quart du IIIe siècle, à l'évolution linguistique des autre parties de la Romania et commencait à se constituer en une langue indépendante.

[1]Straka, G., in a critical review of H. Mihăescu, *Limba latină în provinciile dunărene ale imperiului roman,* in *Revue de linguistique romane*, Paris, XXIV, 1960, pp. 405–406.

5. THE *GESTA HUNGARORUM*

A considerable number of scholars, mostly Hungarian, have during the last two centuries occupied themselves with the problem of the *Gesta Hungarorum*. "It is not an exaggeration to talk about a special Anonymus-philology."[1] The author of this narrative was most probably the notary of the Hungarian King Béla III (1172–1196). This statement is based on the style of the text, the descriptions of the political situation in Hungary and the relations between Hungary and its neighbours, as well as on peculiarities in the general tendency of the work. All these suggest the situation at the end of the 12th century and the beginning of the 13th.[2]

The main written sources of this text were: *De excidio Troiae historia*, and *Gesta Alexandri Magni* by Dares Phrygius, the annals of abbot Regino, who died in 915 AD, the *Exordia Scythica*, which is an extract made in the 7th century from the work of Justinus, written in the 2nd century, the *Bible, Etymologiarum libri* by Isidorus Hispalensis, *Rationes dictanti prosaice* by Hugo Bononiensis. Similarities in style show that the author also knew the romantic gesta-literature which was in fashion in the 12th century in England, France, and Aragonia. Anonymus did not appreciate oral tradition, "the false tales of the peasants and the foolish songs of the minstrels."[3] He did not use the *Gesta Ungarorum* either.

The narrative is preserved in the Széchényi Library, Budapest, under the registration number *Cod. Lat. Medii Aevi 403*. It contains 57 chapters. The manuscript was first published by J.G. Schwandtner and M. Bél, in 1746. It was recently published again (*Anonymus Gesta Hungarorum,* Budapest, 1975). This edition includes a reproduction (photocopy) of the original manuscript, a Hungarian translation, and a study about the narrative by Gy. Győrffy, who summarized its contents as follows:

> In the first sentence of the prologue, the author refers to his own person: P. *dictus magister ac quondam bone memorie gloriosissimi Bele regis Hungariae notarius...*, then he writes about his studies, during which he became fond of the history of Troy and Greece as well as the work of Dares Phrygius. These works prompted him to write "the genealogy of the Hungarian kings and noblemen" and also record their wandering from Scythia to Hungary. The first chapter gives the description of Scythia, mostly word by word from *Exordia Scythica,* extracted from the work of Justinus. In the second chapter, the author explains the designation *Hungari* from the placename Hunguar (Ungvár). The 3rd to the 6th chapters narrate the election of chief Álmos in Scythia. The 7th to the 11th chapters contain the

---

[1]Karsai, G., *Középkori kútfőink kritikus kérdései* (Problems of our Medieval Sources), 1974, p. 45.

[2]Győrffy, Gy., "Anonymus Gesta Hungarorumának kora és hitelessége", *Irodalomtörténeti közlemények*, 1970, 7, pp. 1–2.

[3]Győrffy Anonymus 1970, p. 6.

description of the wandering of the Hungarians from Scythia to Pannonia. According to the author, the Hungarians crossed the river Volga (Ethyl) and the province of Suzdal (*in Rusciam, que Susudal dictur*) and arrived at the town Kiev (*ad civitatem Kyeu*) where seven Cuman leaders (*VII duces Cumanorum*) attached themselves with their peoples to the Hungarians, and the Russian leaders (*duces Ruthenorum*) offered to pay an annual tax (*tributum*) of 10.000 Marks. From there, they marched to the town Vlagyimir (*ad civitatem Lodomer*), then to Galicia (*in Galiciam*) where the leaders of Vlagyimir and Galicia opened the gates of their towns, honoured chief Álmos with a very precious gift and asked the Hungarians to move to Pannonia, describing the country and its inhabitants. The phases of the Hungarian *Landnahme* are narrated in 41 chapters. Of these, the 12th and the 13th discuss the crossing of the Carpathian mountains (*per silvam Houos*) and the occupation of Ungvár; the 14th to the 18th chapters describe the occupation of the region between the Tisza and the Tátra (*mons Turtur*). The 19th to the 23rd chapters depict the military operations against Menomorut, who reigned over the Kazars (*populus Cozar*) and whose country extended from the Tisza to the Maros. Interrupting this, chapters 24–27, inserted later, describe the occupation of Transylvania where the Vlach leader Gelou reigned (*dux Blacorum*). Chapters 28 and 29 again describe the military operations against Menomorut; chapters 30 to 37, the occupation of the area between the Tisza and the Nyitra; the largest part of which was ruled by the Czech chief Zubur, a smaller part by the Bulgarian chief Salan. Chapters 38 to 41 relate the occupation of the province between the Danube and the Tisza, dominated by the Bulgarian chief Salan, who was the vassal of the Greeks. Chapters 42 and 43 deal with the occupation of Dalmatia, Croatia, and the area of Zagreb. Chapters 44 and 45 deal with the conquering of the country of Glad between the Maros and the Danube and a military operation in the Balkan peninsula, which was dominated by the Romans, as well as with the completion of the military operation against Menomorut. Chapters 53 and 56 narrate the "wandering" military operations in the west during the period of prince Zulta, based partly on the annals of Regino. The last chapter, the 57th, describes how the frontiers of Hungary were drawn, and describes the settlement of alien peoples during the 10th century.[1]

The aim of Anonymus was not to give an objective account of the events but rather to emphasize the merits of his principal hero, Árpád, and his associates and by pointing out their deeds of prowess, to stengthen the legal right of the contemporary aristocracy – the descendants of Árpád and of his associates – to the land they owned.[2] Using the family tradition of noblemen and of high priests in the royal court, Anonymus also wanted to write the genealogy of the Hungarian

[1] GyőrffyAnonymus 1970, 7, pp. 1–2.

[2] Karsai Középkori kútfőink 1974, p. 44.

kings and noblemen.[1]

Since he wanted to prove the right to their land of as many contemporary families as possible, he described seven Hungarian and seven Cuman leaders, seven leaders of the army as well as five famous heroes. He asserts that the whole country and the territories which later became satellites or developed into a feudal relationship with Hungary were all conquered by Árpád and his associates, not taking the historical facts into consideration.[2]

How Anonymus invented names for his heroes

Anonymus had no sources for the fighting during the *Landnahme* 300 years earlier. Nevertheless, he wanted to show by descriptions of battles, made vivid by colourful details, how the ancestor of X or Y occupied the land which he owns.
Since the written sources only told him that Pannonia was once the country of the Romans, thereafter ruled by Attila, and the ancient *gesta* preserved only the name of prince Morot, personified from the name of the Moravian people, and he needed enemy leaders who were defeated by the Hungarians, he invented inimical leader images. On the basis of recurrent regularity, it may be concluded that Anonymus invented stories in order to explain several placenames known in his time. His method, related to a very widespread custom, is the following: the name of place X derives from the name of a famous person X, who was murdered in that place. [...]
Anonymus used this method to fabricate from the following geographical and placenames: the river Loborcy, the hills Turzol and Zubor, the tower of Gelou, and the village of Glad, names for the Bulgarian chief Loborcy, the Cuman Turzol, the Czech Zubur, the Vlach Gelou, and Glad, the leader of Vidin – each of whom, according to Anonymus, died in the respective place [named after him].
He also created new names from those found in his sources and split other names apart. He probably read in legends of the origin of the Hungarians in the ancient *Gesta* that the first mothers of the Hungarians (*a magyarok ősanyjai*) were the daughters of *Enech, Dula, and Belar,* and it seems that he fabricated, by putting together the first syllables *(ene-du-bel)* of these, the name of the maternal ancestor of Álmos: *Eunedubelianus.* In the ancient Gesta, *Menrot*, the first father (*ősapa*) is mentioned, who had several wives. Anonymus added to this the name of chief *Morout*, who reigned in Pannonia, thus creating *Menomorut,* the alleged leader of the Cazar people in Bihar, whom he later also attached to the family of Árpád.[3]

---

[1]Győrffy Anonymus 1970, p. 6.

[2]Karsai Középkori kútfőink 1974, p. 54.

[3]Győrffy Anonymus 1970, pp. 6–7.

What did Anonymus know about events 300 years earlier?

Comparing the story told by Anonymus with historical sources from the 9th century, Gy. Győrffy concluded that Anonymus knew very little about the real situation in the basin of the Carpathians in that century.[1] Thus, contemporary sources recorded two events in connection with the Hungarian *Landnahme.* In 896 AD, Emperor Arnulf appointed Braslav to the defence of Pannonia and of Paludarum urbs (Mosaburg, Blatinski grad, Zalavár); and in 907, the Hungarians defeated the Bavarian army at Bretslavspurc (German Pressburg, Slovakian Bratislava, Hung. Pozsony). Although a large part of the narrative describes battles in the period in question, it does not mention these events.

Győrffy lists the names of 21 historical persons (prince Svatopluk, bishops Wiching and Metod, Emperor Arnulf, etc.) who had important political functions in the second half of the 9th century in the basin of the Carpathian mountains. None of these is mentioned by Anonymus.

What did Anonymus know about the different populations living in the basin of the Carpathians in the 9th century?

Contemporary sources attest to the existence in the Carpathian basin in the 9th century of Avars, Danubian Slovenes, Bavarian-Franks, Moravians, Bulgarians, and Gepidae. Of these, Anonymus mentions only the Slavs and the Bulgarians. The name of the Moravian people appears in the Gesta only as that of prince Morout. On the other hand, Anonymus mentions a series of peoples who are not attested by other sources: Romans, Czechs, Greeks, Vlachs, Cozars, and Cumans. The anachronism in mentioning Cumans is also pointed out by IR (cf. above, p. 157, footnote 1). Anonymus writes about two different kinds of Cumans: (a) "Cumans" who associated themselves with the Hungarians before the end of the 9th century and were with them when they took possession of Hungary in 896 AD. These "Cumans" were probably the Kabars, a Turk people, who are known from other sources to have joined the Hungarians in that period. (b) According to Anonymus, Cumans helped the Slavic chief Glad in the Banat in his fight against the Hungarians:

> When they started to cross the river Temes, they were countered by Glad [...] the prince of the country, with a large army of pedestrians and equestrians helped by Cumans and Bulgarians and Vlachs.[2]

This is a projection of the situation at the end of the 12th century back to the 9th. In the time of Anonymus, Cumans were living on the plains south of the Carpathian mountains and made also incursions into Transylvania. They helped

---

[1] Ibid., p. 8.

[2] Cum vellent transire amnem Temes, venit obviam eis Glad ... dux illius patrie cum magno exercitu et peditum adiutorio Cumanorum et Bulgarorum et Blacorum.

the Bulgarians and the Vlachs in achieving independence from Byzantium and establishing the Vlacho-Bulgarian Empire in 1187 (cf. above, p. 25). An explanation of this erroneous record may have been the Slavic tradition which helds that the Hungarians ousted the Franks – the *Volochs* in the language of the Slavs – from the area of the Danube.

The Slavic ethnic name of the 10th century, Vlach, was, in its plural form: *vlasi*, borrowed by the Hungarian language with the sense 'Neo-latin, Italian, French', in the form *olasz(i)*; in the period of Árpád, this was the Hungarian name of the Neo-Latin peoples, thus also of the French, i.e., the Franks (cf. Latin Frankavilla > Hungarian Olaszi) and this is also at present the Hungarian name of the Italians.[1]

Conclusion

It has been argued that even if Anonymus made mistakes, he described the most significant circumstances in a trustworthy way (cf. above, p.157). Given the significant inconsistencies between reality as known from other sources and the *Gesta*, this conclusion is very questionable. The reasoning of IR may be analysed, however. The question is what is significant? For a present-day historian, records about the different peoples would be among the most important information. But for the author of this narrative, this seems to have been of minor significance: whether his Hungarian heroes defeated Slavs, Franks, Cumans, or Vlachs, cannot have been important to him. Also his knowledge of the peoples living in the territory is extremely scanty. Therefore, the mention by Anonymus of *quidam Blachus*, as well as his characterization of the alleged population in Transylvania (in chapter 25): "The inhabitants of that country are the most unworthy people of the whole world (*habitatores terre illi viliores homines esset toti mundi*) because they are Vlachs and Slavs"[2] cannot be accepted. The *Gesta* of Anonymus is not a reliable historical source but a narrative writtten according to the fashion of the age, a legend with very little contact with actual historical facts.

---

[1]Győrffy Anonymus 1970, p. 8.

[2]For an exhaustive discussion of Anonymus' *Gesta Hungarorum* see E. Illyés Ethnic Continuity 1988, 1992, pp. 11–32. Illyés analysed those ten placenames and names of rivers and streams in Transylvania mentioned by Anonymus. Out of these, four are based on Hungarian appellatives (Meszes, Almás, Kapus, Esküllő) and were borrowed by the Rumanians from Hungarian. Two are based on Hungarian personal names (one of which is probably of Slavic origin): Golou (today Gyalu), and Zyloc (today Zilah); both were borrowed by Rumanian. One ancient river name (Criş, Hung. Körös) was transmitted to Rumanian from Hungarian, and the other three (Timiş, Mureş and Someş) either from Slavic or from Hungarian. The river name Căpuş < Hungarian Kapus (cf. Hung. *kapu* 'door') cannot have been borrowed earlier than the 13th or 14th century, when the o > a change was accomplished in Hungarian (in case of an earlier borrowing, it should be *Copuş). Also Rumanian *Zalău* indicates that the borrowing of this Hungarian placename must have occurred after the time of Anonymus, since it reproduces a later form in Hungarian, without the end consonant: *Zilah,* pronounced *Zila'*. In the 13th century, it was *Zyloc*, this form appears also in the *Gesta Hungarorum*.

C. The Archaeological finds

1. THE INFLUENCE OF THE ROMAN MATERIAL CULTURE IN EUROPE

The enormous impact of Roman civilization on the populations of Europe is well-documented. Roman products were carried also to remote areas, such as Scandinavia and India. In most of Europe, the STYLE of manufactured products was powerfully influenced by the Roman patterns. The PROVINCIAL ROMAN STYLE, developed in the western provinces, spread soon over large areas *extra provinciam*, particularly among the Germanic peoples. In the Gothic style, which originated among the Goths north of the Black Sea and spread westwards, Germanic patterns were mixed with classical (particularly Hellenistic) and Oriental forms.

Influenced by the Roman Empire, many European peoples introduced the use of coins. After the period of Emperor Trajan (98–117 AD), silver coins were spread over the entire territory inhabited by Germanic peoples and towards the end of the 2nd century, such coins reached Denmark, Gotland, and the region of the lake Mälaren in Sweden. They were used in commerce (not only as jewels), and were found at thousands of places beyond the Empire. There are also finds showing that the Germanic peoples borrowed the Roman custom of putting gold coins in the mouth of the dead.

Elements of the highly developed Roman technique of building houses were also borrowed. When Julianus Apostata, in the second half of the 4th century, conducted a military expedition against the Alemannians, he found stone houses erected by this Old Germanic population according to Roman techniques.

The Goths living north of the Black Sea developed the Runic letters mainly on the basis of the Greek alphabet. The writing of these letters soon spread all over the territory inhabited by Germanic peoples, and they were used already in the 4th century in Scandinavia. The Old Germanic populations attributed also magic significance to them; the magic numbers coincide largely with those found in the eastern cult of Mithras.

In the 4th century, a Christian congregation existed among the Goths living in the territory of present day Muntenia. For 7 years, their bishop was Ulfila, who translated the Bible to the Gothic language (cf. the record of Auxentius Durostorensis, above, pp. 210–211).

The contacts of the Empire with the non-Roman world were many-sided. In the period of Trajan, for example, many Germanic tribes, such as the Frieses, the Bructeres, the Marcomanns, the Quades, were in a dependent position to Rome. In the course of time, friendly relations alternated with war.

Many men from the barbarian territories served as soldiers in the Roman army, a large part of whom certainly returned home after having been discharged. In the second half of the 4th century, half of the army officers in the Imperial army were of Gemanic origin. Men from the upper classes were often sent to Rome as envoys or as hostages. Especially the latter category had, during prolonged stays among the Romans, the opportunity of picking up Roman customs and absorbing Roman culture. The powerful influence of Roman culture and of the Roman state had far-reaching consequences for the policy of many Germanic tribes as regards their relations with the Empire. But also Romans, i.e., Roman slaves and prisoners of war were numerous in *barbaricum.* Prisoners of war taken by the Goths in Asia Minor propagated Christianity among the Gothic population.

All these reciprocal and prolonged contacts have had significant effects also on language, the vestiges of which are a number of lexical elements in the Germanic languages. Since wine was not produced in northern Europe but was imported from the Empire, the Germanic peoples borrowed Latin *vinum,* probably already during the 1st century AD, cf. English *wine,* German *Wein*, Swedish *vin*; Such words as English *pound*, German *Pfund*, English *mint*, Geman *Münze*, Swedish *mynt*, etc. were probably borrowed in the same period together with several Latin words designating weight and measure, obviously as a result of commerce with the Romans. German *kaufen*, Swedish *köpa* ′to buy′ originate from Latin *caupo* ′inn-keeper, tradesman′. In certain cases, even the names of Roman coins were preserved. Thus, the name of the Roman gold coin, *aureus,* is still in use in Scandinavia: Danish and Swedish *öre* (although it is now the name of a unity of lower value). Also the name of the *solidus*, the gold coin introduced by Emperor Constantine the Great is preserved in Europe: English *soldier*, German *Soldat* and *Sold*, etc.

The Roman cultural influence in Scandinavia

The material vestiges of the Roman influence on the peoples of Scandinavia will be summarized in the following, in order to give an idea about the extent of Roman cultural influence even in a far away territory in which any degree of Romanization is *a priori* excluded.

As early as during the first century BC, commercial contacts existed between the Empire and Scandinavia. These were particularly intense between the second half of the first century AD and about 400. At the beginning, imports to Scandinavia came mainly from Italy, e.g., bronze vessels from Capua, later also from other places, especially from Gallia. The great rivers were the most important roads of commerce: the Elbe, later the Odera, the Vistula, etc. Scandinavia also had commercial contacts with the regions along the northern shore of the Black Sea. Part of the imported Roman objects were transmitted to the population of the Scandinavian peninsula by the Germanic peoples living on the Continent, who were very responsive to Roman cultural influence.

Parallel with the beginning and the intensification of commerce, Roman influence on the material civilization of the people of Scandinavia appeared and increased rapidly. Thus, the short, double-edged sword, made after the model of the short Roman *gladius*, became the main weapon of men; the spear with flukes dated to the late Roman Iron Age, was introduced and the shield changed significantly. The style of the fibulae changed often, according to the Roman patterns. Clothes and ornaments were in a very high degree influenced by Roman style. The strap-clap was introduced from the Empire and soon replaced the belt-ring. An industry of pottery was built up in the Baltic Sea island of Gotland and produced for many centuries large amounts of beautiful pieces of earthenware. The style of these pieces shows influences from Roman bronze vessels.

Most of these objects were found in tombs which, accordingly, show a new style beginning with the end of the 1st century AD. (In the 1st century AD, inhumation was the main funeral rite, probably a Celtic influence.) Objects of different origin were laid down in the tombs. For example, on the Baltic Sea island of Öland, a sword, a pot of clay, two arrow-heads of bone and a glass cup of provincial Roman style were found in a tomb dated to the Roman Iron Age.[1] In a tomb probably from the 2nd century AD, excavated on Gotland, a vessel of clay of the typical Gotland style, two drinking horns with bronze mountings and a wine-scoop of provincial Roman style were found. Many Scandinavian tombs from this period contain imported Roman material: a total of about one hundred of the above-mentioned wine-scoops are known. The oldest are from the middle of the 1st century AD and were made in Italy, the newer ones, of which some are from the early 3rd century AD, were produced in the region of the Rhine.

Large numbers of silver *Dinarii* were found in Scandinavia; in Sweden almost 7000.

An interesting group of imported objects is that of small FIGURINES OF ROMAN GODS AND GODESSES, of which about 15 are known from Denmark and some also from Sweden. These were widespread in the Germanic world of those days. In Scandinavia, they were never found in tombs or in settlements but constituted single finds in the woods and fields. They were mass-produced in the Roman Empire, for the needs of the general populace. Their use may be compared to that of pictures of saints in the Catholic world today. These figurines were copied at least in one place (Öland), and it is not excluded that they were used also by the population of Scandinavia as cult objects.

Also LATIN INSCRIPTIONS were found in Scandinavia. Two swords with inscriptions are known, one from southeastern Sweden and one from Gotland, as well as two bronze vessels, all dated to the 2nd century AD. One is the so called Apollo Grannus vase, found north of the lake Mälaren in Sweden, with the inscription "APOLLONI GRANNO DONUM AMMILIVS CONSTANS PRAEF TEMPLI IPSIVS VSLLM". ('To Apollo Grannus was this gift given by his chief of temple Ammilius Constans.') Another bronze vessel with a similar inscription was found in Norway, east of Mjösen. These objects were most probably taken from temples in Gallia or Raetia by plundering soldiers.

---

[1] Stenberger, M., *Det forntida Sverige*, Stockholm, 1971, p. 371.

Conclusions

Objects of the kind discussed in this section may easily be transported to far away areas. They may give information regarding technology: the people of Öland were capable of producing figurines of Roman gods; economics – indicating commerce with the Empire, or suggesting that soldiers from the place in question may have served in the Empire. Regarding questions of the social circumstances in the area in question, not to mention the language or ethnicity of the people living there, they have no value.

2. THE MATERIAL REMAINS IN POST-ROMAN DACIA TRAIANA

There are two main problems: 1) Do the material remains found in the former province of Dacia Traiana warrant the conclusion that they were left by a Roman population, i.e., are they more specific than just showing a Roman influence also characteristic of archaeological finds from the period in other parts of Europe? 2) Regardless of the question of ethnicity, do the settlements and cemeteries show any continuity from the time of the Roman era to the following centuries?

I. THE QUESTION OF DACO-ROMANS

a) The settlements

Archaeological remains of an assumed "Daco-Roman" population were described from a number of sites in Oltenia and Transylvania. Protase presented more than thirty such sites (cf. above, pp. 159–173). The assumption of a Roman population is based on the Roman provincial style shown by the remains. However, at least at eight of these sites, (cf. table 9, p. 170), the existence of non-Roman peoples is shown. Among these are Chilia and Stăneşti in Oltenia, and Cipău, Comolău, Mediaş, Bezid, and Reci, in eastern Transylvania, which date from the middle or the 2nd half of the 3rd century, when the Romans left the *limes trans-Alutanus* and eastern Transylvania. To the abandoned areas, free Dacians, Carps, Iazyges, and Goths migrated. Instead of the continuation of the population from the Roman period, we see here the influx of non-Roman elements already in the mid-third century. The classification of these sites as "Daco-Roman" is simply wrong – en example of the ambiguity of this notion, cf. above, pp. 199–200.

Also at other sites, clearly non-Roman elements appear. At Archiud (Erked), in a settlement inhabited from the mid-third to the 4th century, the earthenware of Roman provincial tradition shows "increasing barbarization", and there are vestiges of the free Dacians. At Mugeni (Bögöz), elements of the Cerneachov culture appear towards the end of the 3rd century. In Sarmizegetusa, the once flourishing capital of Roman Dacia, changes made on the old Roman buildings, according to a "barbarized technique", may have been achieved by any population. Two of the sites (Cioroiul Nou and Verbiţa) are situated between the Danube and the Furrow of Novac in Oltenia. This area was in the 4th century re-conquered by the Empire (cf. above, p. 152 and map No 8), the existence there of Romans in that period would therefore not be impossible. Regarding the problem of the persistence of a Roman population in former Dacia Traiana, this is, however, of little relevance.

Horedt described 50 settlements in use in post-Roman Dacia Traiana. He distinguished two main groups: (a) a western group of settlements, in the valleys of the Mureş, the lower course of the Târnava, and the Someş, there are a kind of fibulae *(Zwiebelknopffibeln)* and combs with two rows, not found in the eastern group. The pottery is more like the Roman pottery. (b) The eastern group, found in the valleys of the middle course of the Mureş and the upper courses of the rivers Târnava, as well as in present day Covasna and Braşov counties, called the *Sfântu Gheorghe culture*, is clearly non-Roman, with influences from the Sântana de Mureş culture, and also from the east, the Carps.[1]

b) The cemeteries

The assumption of a Daco-Roman population in 13 cemeteries (cf. above, p. 164–173) is also based mainly on material of Roman style. In several sites, as also in the case of the settlements, clearly non-Roman material remains were found. Thus, at Sărăţeni (Sóvárad), vessels similar to Carpic vessels and the habit of putting several vessels in a tomb is characteristic of the Cerneachov culture. Cemetery No. 1 at Bratei contains material remains characteristic of the free Dacians, pieces of earthenware made by hand, e.g., the Dacian censer (*căţuia*), fragments of big vessels of supply decorated according to the classic period of the Dacian pottery. Also the large amounts of animal bones, not found in Roman and Illyrian cemeteries, is characteristic of the tombs of free Dacians (of the type Porolissum–Salca). Several details of the rituals, such as placing the inventary over the cavity, assembling of fragments of earthenware together with stones, animal bones, and other objects, are old Dacian customs. The ritual of burning of the cavities used at Bratei was also found in the cemetery excavated at Ocniţa, which dates from the period before the occupation of Dacia by the Romans. The funeral ritual of burned cavities is not Dacian and does not appear in significant numbers before the Roman conquest. It is found in Pannonia, Moesia, and Illyricum. Garasanin (quoted by Bârzu Cemet. 1973, p. 92), assumed that it is of Illyrian origin; it was, in any case, widedspread in Illyria. Big vessels of supply are abundant, and they are not of the Roman type. This cemetery does not continue one from the Roman period but was in use in the second half of the 4th

[1]Horedt, K., *Siebenbürgen in spätrömischer Zeit,* Kriterion, Bucharest, 1982, pp. 70– 82, with maps and figures.

(and, possibly, in the first quarter of the 5th) century. All these facts contradict the assumption of a Roman population having been buried here. Also the surroundings are other than Roman: only about 5 miles from Bratei, at Mediaş (Hung. Medgyes), a Carpic tomb of cremation which dates from the end of the 3rd century was discovered (cf. above, Table 9, p. 170). Products imported from the Empire suggest that the people who used the cemetery No. 1 at Bratei had commercial contacts with Pannonia. On the other hand, nothing among the finds suggests contact with the Roman towns along the lower Danube.[1]

About the two tombs discovered at Sărăţeni, Protase wrote in 1966 that they may have belonged to Daco-Romans (cf. above, p. 172). In a more detailed analysis, however, he stated that "if the observations at Sărăţeni are correct", the cremation was made on the place of the burial, a ritual widespread in Dacia Romana and not known from the extra-Carpathian regions. But the vessels found in these tombs are to a certain extent similar to those found in Carpic cemeteries in Moldavia and there are 3–4 of them in each tomb, the habit of putting several vessels in a tomb is characteristic of the Cerneachov–Sântana de Mureş culture.[2]

Also the two tombs discovered at Sfântu Gheorghe (cf. above, p. 172) are questionable indications of Daco-Romans: they are of the same type as the cemetery at Bratei from the 4th century.[3] It is also uncertain whether these tombs date from the period after 275.

Objects of the Dacian or Carpic style and Dacian customs are, as shown by the analysis of the settlements as well as of the cemeteries from post-Roman Dacia, widespread. If the Dacians living in the province adopted Roman customs and Roman culture in general, this should be reflected by material remains different from those of the free Dacians, the Carps, and the Goths. However, this is not the case. Regarding the funeral rites, this was stated by Protase:

> Le rite funéraire de l'incinération avec urne, qui existe aussi bien chez les Daces soumis aux Romains que chez Daces libres, ne peut plus servir cette fois à séparer ces deux catégories de populations – la catégorie dace adventice et la catégorie romaine demeuré sur place – de l'espace de l'ancienne province romaine. On l'a vu, le besoin des précisions et des détails que le matériel archéologique peut fournir se fait sentir.[4]

At Soporul de Câmpie,[5] many of the material remains show the provincial Roman style: their fibulae are of this type, in contrast to those found among the

---

[1]Bârzu Cemet 1973, p. 95: "We do not know to what extent the possibility of establishing commercial relations with the towns along the lower Danube existed."

[2]Protase, D., "Considérations sur les rites funéraires des Daces", *Revue d'archéologie et d'histoire ancienne, nouvelle série*, IV, 1962, p. 184.

[3]Protase PCD 1966, p. 128.

[4]Protase Rites Fun 1962, p. 196.

[5]The data about this site were taken mainly from Protase, D., *Un cimitir dacic din epoca romană la Soporu de Cîmpie*, 1976.

material remains of the free Carps, which are of the "barbarian" style. The same may be said about a considerable part of their pottery. A Sarmatian influence, characteristic of the remains of the Carps in Moldavia, was not ascertained at Soporu de Câmpie. In 5 out of 189 tombs, i.e., in 2.6% of all tombs, coins were found and it is assumed that these were used according to the Greco-Roman custom of putting an "obulus of Charon" in the mouth of the deceased.

Of all these, the only sign of adoption of a Roman custom would be the use of coins, if they really were used as assumed. This is one of the largest cemeteries from the age of the Roman domination in this area, in use for more than a century. Even if the coins were put in those 5 tombs in order to follow this Greco-Roman custom, it must be stated that 97.4% of the tombs do not show it. The find is too insignificant to warrant a general conclusion about the adoption by the inhabitants of a Roman custom.

On the other hand, there is ample evidence to indicate that the people at Soporu de Câmpie preserved their old traditions, notwithstanding the fact that they were living in a Roman province. The total number of tombs in this cemetery is 193. Out of these, 189 date from the 2nd and the 3rd centuries and are considered to belong to "Daco-Romans". (Four tombs from the 5th century are not considered Daco-Roman.) A total of 167 tombs contain earthenware and in 62 of these, this is of the Dacian style. The differences as compared to the earthenware of the free Dacians are not essential:

> ...the Dacian pottery of the 2nd to the 4th centuries preserved everywhere – both within the province and outside of it – the powerful traditions from the late La Tène, from which it developed relatively uniformly...[1]

The funeral rites at Soporu de Câmpie continue the Dacian rites from the late La Tène. Although the funeral rituals of the Romans show considerable variation, one must state that in this cemetery, nothing suggests a Roman tradition; there are, for example, no sarcophagi of bricks or tombs of the type *bustum*.

Protase concludes that the people who left these material remains "were able to organically assimilate only minor elements of the rich repertoire of the Roman provincial tradition."[2]

This is true of entire Dacia Traiana: THERE ARE NO INDICATIONS OF A PROCESS OF GRADUAL ADOPTION BY AN INDIGENOUS, NON-ROMAN POPULATION OF ELEMENTS OF ROMAN CULTURE AND CIVILISATION beyond the use of objects and assimilation of Roman style, essentially in the same way as was the case in almost all of contemporary Europe.

(c) The objects of Christian use

Those ten objects presented in 1966 by Protase as indicating the presence of

---

[1] Protase Un cimitir 1976, p. 56.

[2] Ibid., p. 72.

Christians in Transylvania in the 4th century were described above (p. 173–175). Since then, a number of similar discoveries were made, for example crosses and casting moulds for crosses, objects with different Christian symbols, Christian monograms on pottery pieces, etc.[1]

Protase argued in 1966 that these objects were only found on the territory of the former province and there, mostly on the place of former Roman towns or rural settlements. This would prove that the objects were used by a Christian and Daco-Roman population. However, his material was quite unreliable in this respect. (The Christian character of two objects was dubious, in three cases, the place where the objects were found is unknown, possibly even outside the province.) It is possible that there were Christians who used the objects as Christian symbols, but these were not produced in Dacia. The low significance of these objects was admitted, indirectly, also by the authors of IR 1960, when they stated that the Rumanian religious terms of Latin origin are more important:

> More clearly than by the origin of the archaeologiacl objects, is the Latin character of the primitive Christianity of the Daco-Romans shown by the Latin origin of the fundamental terms of the Christian faith, preserved until the present day in the language of the Rumanian people, as for example: *crux* –cruce, *domine deo*–dumnezeu, *christianus*–creştin, [etc.][2]

A fundamental trait of Christianity is its universality. It has been from its early days the religion of the people without regard to their language or ethnicity. The missionaries were forced to speak the language of the people; an example of an early translation of the Bible is that made by bishop Ulfila in the 4th century, in present day Muntenia. This is a proof of Christianity having been propagated north of the lower Danube among the Goths in that period (cf. the record of Auxentius Durostorensis, above, p. 210).

If the ancestors of the Rumanians had adopted Christianity in Transylvania in the 4th century, then they must have moved to Bulgaria in the 10th century. It is namely scarcely possible that they could have been organized in the Bulgarian Orthodox Church, taking over Slavic as the language of the religious services, (and borrowing more than 70 religious terms from Bulgarian), during that century the Bulgarian state ruled over Muntenia and southern Transylvania after 830 AD (cf. above, p.22). – The Rumanian Orthodox Church belonged, until the early 18th century, to the ecclesiastical jurisdiction of the archbishopric of Ochrida.

d) Roman coins

Finds of coins in themselves can be rarely, if ever, sufficient for conclusions about such problems as the language or the ethnicity of a certain population. The

[1] See, for example, the description by K. Horedt, *Siebenbürgen in spätrömischer Zeit*, 1982, pp. 163–171.

[2] IR 1960, pp. 632–633. The religious terminology of Rumanian is discussed above, p. 104.

number of coins found in a certain territory depends to a large extent on chance, as well as on the intensity of archaeological research. If the effects of these factors can be minimized, coins may indicate the intensity of commerce, they may help in determining the period in which a given settlement or burial place was in use, they may contribute to the knowledge about social stratification; they may show the existence of some traditions, such as the Greco-Roman custom of putting an *obulus* in the mouth of the deceased. Significant numbers of hoards of coins suggest war or invasion.

North of the lower Danube, the low number of coins from the period between 271 and 305 AD may be explained by the bad economic situation of the Roman Empire, and the decrease and gradual disappearance of the coins in the 5th century was certainly caused by the severe crisis and final collapse of the Empire.

These factors are recognized also by Protase and Preda, who argued that the coins indicated a Daco-Roman population (cf. above, p. 176–178). However, their reasoning does not take into account other important factors. Roman coins were not only found near former Roman towns or camps and they are by no means restricted to the territory of the former province. Those of a lower value (the bronze coins) were used as money by many European populations in the period in question.[1] Roman coins were discovered as far as in Ukraine (in the territory of the Cerneachov culture) and on the Crimean peninsula. In the most eastern areas, they are rare, but their number increases considerably west of the Dniester.[2] In the territory of present day Rumania, the free Dacians, who migrated to the former province after 275 AD along the Mureş and the superior valley of the Olt, left Roman coins in their settlements and in the Banat, the Sarmatian Iazyges "used extensively, for a long time, Roman coins".[3]

In the case of hoards of coins, drawing conclusions is made difficult also by the uncertainty about basic circumstances connected with the finds. Many of them were found a long time ago and lack proper descriptions of essential data such as their integrity and unity. A number of them might have been imported much later from the territory of the former Roman Empire (cf. the reservations made by Protase, above, p. 177). According to Protase, some of the hoards accumulated entirely in the 4th century may belong to the "autochthonous population". This is not impossible, but this population turns out to have been the free Dacians, who were not Latinized.[4]

---

[1]According to Preda (Circulaţia 1975, p. 445), 2/3 of all coins from the post-Roman period found in Rumania were discovered in the territory of the former province of Dacia, which would suggest a Romanized population there. This difference is not, however, quite certain, because much more research was conducted in Transylvania than in other areas. Moreover, southern Oltenia, the Banat, and southwestern Transylvania were nearest the Roman Empire. Also in other parts of Europe, commerce was most intense in the areas of *barbaricum* which were adjacent to the Empire.

[2]Protase PCD 1966, p. 196.

[3]Ibid., p. 197.

[4]Ibid., p. 198; cf. above, p. 178. – This is an example of the arbitrary use of the term "autochthonous", above, pp. 199–200.

Conclusions regarding the Roman coins

The finds of Roman coins, whether single or in hoards, do not suggest anything about the ethnic situation in the post-Roman period north of the lower Danube. Hoards of coins from different periods may have a certain significance:

Many hoards were buried during the period of Roman domination in Dacia, for example in the 240s, the time of the Carpic incursions. Obviously, the population of the province was attacked and many people were forced to flee, but at least a considerable number of them expected to return in due course. A remarkable contrast to this is shown in the period of the Roman retreat from Dacia. In the 270s, free Dacians, Goths, and Iazyges invaded this territory. Yet, not a single hoard buried between 271 and 305 AD has been found so far.[1] Did people not fear the barbarians in 271 as they did three decades earlier? Or did they not expect to return to their homes?

(e) The Latin inscriptions

The two inscriptions (*Qvartine vivas* and the *ex voto* with the inscription: *Ego Zenovivs votvm posvi*, cf. above, pp. 178–180) do not tell us anything about the ethnic character or the language of the population of Transylvania in the 4th century. Contrary to what Condurachi & Daicoviciu (cf. above, p. 179–180) assert, the *ex voto* was not produced in Dacia. Both inscriptions were imported from the Empire, but it is not even certain if this occurred in the 4th century, later imports cannot be excluded. The finds were isolated, without any distinct archaeological site. The *ex voto* was probably produced in northern Italy; similar objects were found in Aquilea, Bonyhád (Hungary), Ljubljana (Slovenia), etc. Most probably, these pieces reached Transylvania through trade or by plundering soldiers (cf. Latin inscriptions found in other parts of Europe, above, p. 222).

Why not pursue archaeological investigations also south of the Danube?

A serious objection against the concept on which Rumanian archaeologists base their research is that they restrict investigation to the territory of present day Rumania. In view of the fact that it is generally admitted, at least by linguists, that the Rumanian language and people also developed south of the lower Danube (cf. above, p. 140–142), a similar picture of archaeological finds, identical or at least very similar cultures, should exist on both sides of the lower Danube or even at a considerable distance from it towards the south (that is to say, if the material excavated in Rumania really showed the ancestors of the Rumanians.)

[1] Preda Circulaţia monedelor 1975, p. 443; Protase PCD 1966, p. 184.

II. INDICATIONS OF DEMOGRAPHIC DISCONTINUITY

The lack of hoards buried around the time of the abandon of Dacia may be an indication of the abandonment of the province not only by the Roman army and administration but also by the inhabitants. There is also manifest material evidence to indicate that very serious changes of the dwelling places and the cemeteries occurred both at the beginning and at the end of the Roman domination. These do not warrant any conclusions about the ethnical circumstances, but testify to fundamental changes in the society of the province.

a) The towns

In the former Roman towns, archaeological finds show radical changes after the abandonment by the Romans. The Roman handicraft of advanced techniques is no longer produced, no more buildings of stone or of bricks are erected, no monuments and no inscriptions are made. Signs of human activity during the 4th century in the former towns are: changes made in the Roman buildings, for example the erecting of walls of earth, the use of sarcophagi made of bricks (Apulum), the re-use of a sarcophagus, etc. A comparison with the situation in the towns of post-Roman Britain may be of interest: for about half a century after the Romans left, many walled towns not only continued to be inhabited but even new buildings were going up. In at least two towns *(Verulamium* and Wroxeter), archaeological finds show urban communities possessing an elementary internal structure.[1] Nothing of this kind is found in post-Roman Dacia. The presence of burials in the centre of the towns indicates the abandonment of Roman custom. In any case, the remains do not suggest in these few (6 or 7) towns significant numbers of people and these do not behave as Romans. The towns of Dacia Traiana disappeared as such after the abolishment of the Roman domination.[2] At the time of the Hunnish invasion at the end of the 4th century, all signs of life ceased in the former towns.

b) Rural settlements

Protase presented 22 settlements as indicating the continued existence of "Daco-Romans" in post-Roman Dacia Traiana. Out of these, six show the material remains of FREE DACIANS OR CARPS who migrated to the former province towards the end of the 3rd century: Bezid, Cipău, Comolău, Mediaş, Reci (in Transylvania) and Chilia in the region of Argeş. At Sic, a settlement of Dacians during the Roman domination continued possibly until the end of the 3rd century. Seven of these settlements were FOUNDED AFTER 275 AD (the abandonment of the province by the Romans): Archiud, Bratei, Cluj-Mănăştur,

---

[1]Cf., for example, Todd, M., *Roman Britain 55 BC –AD 400*, pp. 241–245.

[2]Protase Autohtonii 1980, p. 252; cf. above, p. 193.

Iernut, Mugeni, Noşlac, and Soporu de Câmpie. Two (Cioroiul Nou and Verbiţa) are situated in Oltenia south of the Furrow of Novac, in an area dominated for some decades during the 4th century by the Roman Empire (cf. above, p. 224).

Thus, six settlements remain north of the Furrow of Novac which were a) inhabited during the Roman domination and with more or less probability also after its end (in several cases only until the end of the 3rd century) and b) in which the material remains do not clearly indicate free Dacians or Carps. This is a very low figure, and even of these, two can scarcely be taken into consideration. At Porumbenii Mici, the existence of the settlement after 271 AD is questionable; at most, it may have existed a few decades at the end of the 3rd century. In Veţel, the only sign assumed to indicate life in the 4th century is a silver fibula.

Villae rusticae

A survey of the data presented by Protase PCD 1966 and Horedt 1973 shows a similar discontinuity of the *villae rusticae* (rural farms) from the time of the province. Only one of these is assumed to have been inhabited after 275 AD (Iernut) and in another (Rahău) is this possible.[1]

c) Cemeteries

Out of those 13 cemeteries or single tombs presented by Protase (cf. above, p. 164) as showing the material remains of Daco-Romans, two (Chilia and Stăneşti) show the material remains of free Dacians who migrated to the area after the Romans had left. The cemetery at Bratei dated to the 4th century was discussed above (pp. 165–169); remains suggesting the Sântana de Mureş culture as well as of free Dacians predominate there. In Mediaş, an urn of cremation from the end of the 3rd century and assumed to belong to the Carpic population was discovered. Of the remaining nine sites, 6 are single tombs and datefrom the end of the 3rd century or (in the case of Cluj) the mid-fifth. Only one cemetery, that found at Iernut, was in continued use after 275 AD; from the mid-third century to about 400 AD. At Moigrad, a cemetery was most probably used during the Roman rule, and its use after 275 is questionable.[2]

---

[1]Protase 1966, p. 135; K. Horedt, in Dacoromania I, 1973, p. 138.

[2]For a detailed presentation of the cemeteries in question see Horedt, *Siebenbürgen in spätrömischer Zeit*, 1982, pp. 88–126.

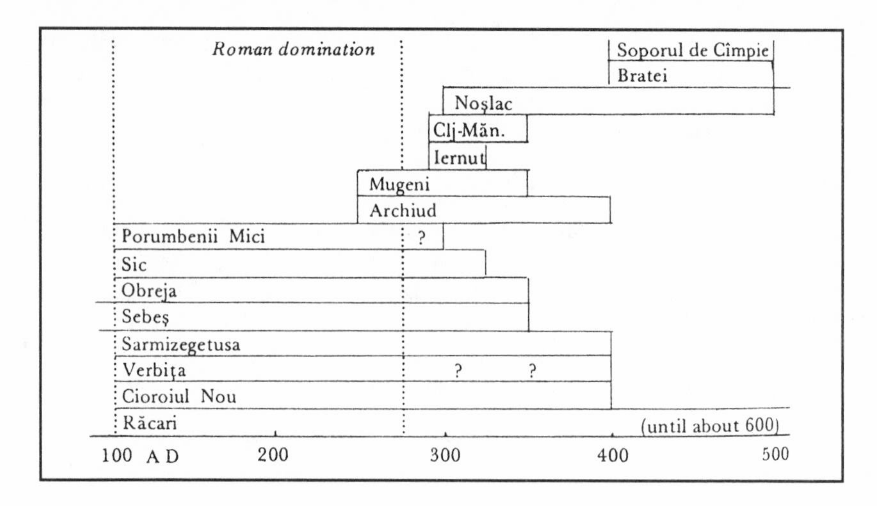

Fig. 2. The time span during which the SETTLEMENTS attributed to a "Daco-Roman" population in post-Roman Dacia Traiana may have been inhabited. Maximal limits of time, earliest start and latest abandonment, are given. (After D. Protase, *Problema continuităţii în Dacia în lumina arheologiei şi numismaticii*, 1966.)

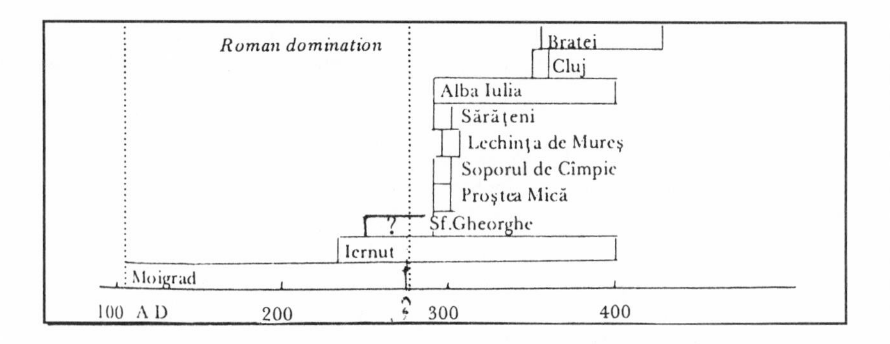

Fig. 3. The time span during which the CEMETERIES attributed to a "Daco-Roman" population may have been in use. (On the basis of D. Protase, *Problema continuităţii în Dacia în lumina arheologiei şi numismaticii,* 1966.)

Conclusions: discontinuity of the settlements and of the cemeteries

At all these sites, the assumption of Daco-Romans is based on objects of Roman style and/or signs of some Roman customs. On the other hand, only one single cemetery and a few settlements show continuity from the Roman period to the 4th century. Without giving any indication regarding the ethnicity of the people who have left these remains, the finds indicate a fundamental discontinuity of the dwelling places (and correspondingly, of the cemeteries) of the population.

III. THE 5th–7th CENTURIES

The archaeological material from the territories north of the lower Danube which dates from the 3rd and the 4th centuries is characterized, as shown above, by a Roman cultural influence. This is true of most other parts of Europe. Latest in the 6th century, the Roman influence decreased sharply, both north of the lower Danube and in Europe in general.

> From the 6th century on, the Roman provincial features in the earthenware do not seem to be as easily distinguishable as before. In spite of the fact that the earthenware became largely uniform, with a general, pre-feudal, "barbarized" character specific to a very large area, a circumstance which makes the exact determination of the autochthonous Daco-Roman elements difficult, until the coming of the Slavs (7th century) when the earthenware shows a qualitative change, some vestiges of the forms and the style of the Roman provincial vessels still may be discerned, although to a lesser extent.[1]

From the 7th century on, the material culture no longer shows any Roman influence:

> Bereits im 6. Jh. besteht in Siebenbürgen eine einheitliche Kultur, die nicht ohne weiteres ethnische Unterschiedungen zulässt und an der Germanen und Romanen teilhaben. Aus der Siedlungsweise und bestimmten kennzeichnenden Einzelfunden und -formen konnten aber doch Hinweise für ethnische Deutungen erschlossen werden. Mit dem Verschwinden der Germanen und dem Auftreten der slawischen Kultur besteht diese Möglichkeit nicht mehr.[2]

The disappearance of Roman provincial traits is another indication of the fact that these traits were not the expression of a new population of a Romance character but of the same cultural influence that may be seen in other parts of Europe.

---

[1] Protase PCD 1966, pp. 137–138.

[2] K. Horedt, in Dacoromania I 1973, p. 147.

Those settlements in which Daco-Romans were assumed (cf. above, pp. 159–164), were abandoned partly already in the first quarter of the 4th century and latest towards its end, obviously attacked by the Huns. Thus, the population of the former province was, less than a century after the abandonment by the Roman Empire, once again exposed to radical changes in its dwelling places.

In spite of the assertion of the presence of Daco-Romans also in this period, the following passage by Condurachi & Daicoviciu (Ancient Civil 1971, p. 179) is rather more an admission of their absence:

> For the 5th and the 6th centuries we have a bronze lamp found at Dej which is clearly Christian, and a pot lid marked with a cross which was found at Tibiscum and undoubtedly belongs to the same period. When western Christianity, using the Latin language, penetrated into this region it not only helped to safeguard the Roman culture and language of the region but also promoted the full development of both culture and language.

a) The theory of the flight to the mountains and the absence of Daco-Romans

It may be assumed, of course, that the Daco-Romans left their places and fled to remote valleys among the mountains. This theory was put forward long ago to explain the absence of placenames and geographical names of Latin origin north of the lower Danube, as well as the lack of an Old Germanic influence on Rumanian:

> The disturbed conditions which prevailed from the 5th century onwards as a result of attacks by the Huns and Avars undoubtedly led the people to seek means of escaping the calamities of the time. [...] The steady disappearance of Daco-Roman farming settlements in the period up to 600 AD was a natural consequence of the repeated harassments of a population which had become accustomed to a settled and peaceable life.[1]

It is also assumed that the new conditions forced the Daco-Roman farmers to become shepherds:

> It is significant also that the Dacians who were required by their new way of life to travel constantly to and fro with their flocks and herds between the Carpathians and the Danube thus inevitably remained in contact with the Roman cities on the right bank of the river and the population living farther to the south, so that the process of romanisation was given fresh impetus in this final stage of a long developemnt which dated back to the 1st century B.C. and reached its term in the 9th and 10th centuries A.D.[2]

---

[1]Condurachi & Daicoviciu Ancient Civil 1971, p. 182.

[2]Ibid.

This assumption would permit the Daco-Romans to escape from the invading barbarians and survive in the summer. But when they travelled to the Danube in the autumn, they would have met exactly those barbarians they had fled from.[1]

Nevertheless, many different explanations have been put forward in the course of time. They often contradict each other. Even the period in which this flight is supposed to have taken place is given vaguely and differently by different authors. Condurachi & Daicoviciu (cf. above, p. 234) state that the attacks of the Huns and of the Avars caused the "steady disappearance of the Daco-Roman farming settlements", which implies that the process started in the second half of the 4th century. According to IR 1960 (p. 627), the Daco-Romans left their old places during the 5th and the 6th centuries. The explanation put forward in IR Compendiu 1969, p. 100, asserts that the Daco-Romans fled to "distant valleys, among hills and mountains, in one word in places better protected from the ceaseless predatory invasions of the migrating troops."
This would be the explanation of the oblivion of ancient placenames. However:

> After a not too long time had passed, the autochthons will return to the open places, mixing with the dominating Slavic population, which they after a symbiosis (*convieţuire*) will assimilate in a short time.

Those who put forward such hypotheses cannot give any material proof. This has been stated by K. Horedt:

> Es gibt aber keine archäologischen Belege dafür, dass die romanischen Elemente vor den Wandervölkern in abgelegene Täler am Fusse der Gebirge ausgewichen wären, da aus diesen Gebieten keine völkerwanderungszeitliche Funde bekannt sind.[2]

As shown above, IR Compendiu 1969 defended the theory of the flight to the mountains. More recently, archaeologists in Rumania deny it. In the 1974 edition of IR Compendiu, the passage about this is omitted, although it is not yet denied: writing about the Gepidae living together with "Daco-Romans", it is asserted that "being different populations, basically inimical, they had few points of contact, which explains the absence of Old Germanic words in the Rumanian language". Eugenia Zaharia disposed of the theory of the flight into the mountains entirely, stating that it belongs to the 19th century, and that the archaeological finds show

---

[1] I. Donat, in Dacoromania I, 1973, p. 79: "Certainement. à ce que l'on affirme habituellement, une pareille économie pastorale n'aurait pas permis à la population daco-romaine de résister au nord du Danube, car nos pâtres n'auraient été en sûreté que pendant les mois d'été, dans les montagnes, tandis que durant leurs longues marches à travers la pleine ils auraient du affronter des périls autrement grands que les agriculteurs établis dans des régions retirées, à l'abri des hauteurs, et des fôrets."

[2] Dacoromania I, 1973, p. 144.

that the Daco-Romans lived in close contact with the migratory populations.[1]

E. The Rumanian language

1. THE THEORY OF ´CORE AREAS´

As shown above, the *Rumanian Lingusitic Atlas* published in the 1930s showed a number of Latin words which were preserved only in certain areas of Rumania, while speakers in other areas used other words, usually loanwords, instead of these. It was then assumed (cf. above, p.181) that in these areas, a Romanized population has been living since the age of Trajan:

> ...the presence of some terms of Latin origin, such as for example *nea*, *pedestru*, and *june*, only in the western parts of Transylvania, from Maramureş and Crişana to the Banat, and absent in the rest of the Carpatho-Danubian region [...] would not be possible if the ancient Rumanians would have come from the Balkan peninsula [and, as asked by Jaberg]:...how could the Latin elements be preserved particularly well in the northwest of Rumania if the Rumanians would have come from Moesia?

If these reasonings are right, then also the following assertion would be correct:

> ...*the presence of some terms of Latin origin, such as for example *ávrî* ´freshness, a light wind´, (< Latin *aura*), *cîprínî* ´goat´s hair´, (< Latin *caprina*, *cîşári* ´sheepfold´ (< Latin *casearia*), *fáuî* ´bean´, (< Latin *faba*), in northern Greece, northwest of Trikkala, and absent in the rest of the Rumanian dialects [...] would not be possible if the ancient Arumanians would have migrated to this territory.*

This is not a quotation, in fact, no scholar of the Rumanian language would even dream of asserting this. The Arumanians living in northern Greece cannot have been living there since their Romanization, but must have migrated there later, since that territory is situated south of the Jireček-line, the frontier between Latin and Greek in the Balkan peninsula. The question put by A. Jaberg is to be answered as follows: The Arumanians migrated, after the period of Common Rumanian, to the region northwest of Trikkala. As a Romance language, their language contained many Latin words, among others, also those mentioned above. The difference as compared to the rest of Rumanian today has nothing to do with the Arumanians. Its explanation is to be sought in the other dialects. Northern Rumanian, for example, has lost *cîşári* and uses only *strungă*, it has

---

[1]Eugenia Zaharia, "Les sources archéologiques de la continuité daco-romaine", *Apulum*, XII, 1974, p. 284: "Cette idée appartient au siècle passé, lorsqu´on ne possédait pas encore de preuves archéologiques..."

replaced Latin *faba* with other words, etc. The explanation of the preserved Latin words in the region of the Munţii Apuseni, in Crişana, Maramureş, and the Banat, is similar. In fact, the impossibility of the argument regarding the ancient Latin core areas appears already in the above quotation from Giurescu & Giurescu. It contains the information that those Latin words appear not only in the region of the Munţii Apuseni, "where the Roman settlements were most dense" (Puşcariu), but also in Crişana and Maramureş, where such settlements were entirely absent, because those areas never belonged to the Roman Empire. Rosetti has pointed out the fact that other Latin words were forgotten or replaced by foreign loan-words in Transylvania but preserved in other areas of Rumania, along the lower Danube, in Moldavia or in Dobrogea:

> [the theory of ′core areas′ *(Kerngebiete)* would be correct if two conditions were fullfilled]: 1. One has to take into account that this geographical distribution may have originated in the course of subsequent linguistic extensions. A series of other Latin terms, which appear in ALR [the *Rumanian Linguistic Atlas*] deny the putative Latin character of Transylvania, by their presence in Ţara Românească and in Moldavia, and prove, by appearing in regions which were not Romanized, that we are dealing with subsequent linguistic expansions. ... 2. The entire lexical stock must be investigated – not only a few words chosen arbitrarily – to be able to decide whether the great majority of the terms confirms the theory (cf. ALR I, vol. I and II, maps 78: *strănut*, 112: *guturai.* 153: *tată vitreg*, 157: *mamă vitreagă*, 208: *colastră*, 20: *cumătru*, 221: *cumătră*, 235 *mîngîia*, 236: *desmierd,* in which the areas of the Latin terms cover Oltenia, Ţara Românească, and Moldavia, while Transylvania or the north-west of Transylvania has terms of foreign origin).[1]

To give an example of how these dialectal differences are to be interpreted, we consider the dialectal distribution of a number of words. The word for ′snow′ is *nea* (< Latin *nivem*) in western Transylvania, Crişana, and the Banat; *zăpadă*, of Slavic origin, in Oltenia, Muntenia, southern Transylvania and Dobrogea; and *omăt*, (cf. Russian *omät,* Ukrainean *omĕt*) in Moldavia and north-eastern Transylvania. For ′abdomen′, there is in the northern part of the country, *pântece (pâncete)* (< Latin *pantex, -ticem*), in the south-west, *foale* (< Latin *follis, -em*), and in the south, *burtă.* The word of Latin origin, *păcurar* (< Latin *pecorarius*) is used by speakers of Rumanian living in the intra-Carpathian territory, with the exception of southern Transylvania, where *cioban* (of Turkish origin but transferred to Rumanian via Bulgarian) is used. It obviously extends from Muntenia and Oltenia, where a homonymic clash occurred between *păcurar* ′shepherd′ and *păcurar* ′merchant of crude oil′ – in those territories, oil was exploited. In the case of the word for ′woman′, it is also possible to follow the

[1] Rosetti ILR 1986, p. 199.

changes. In this case, the original Latin word was preserved in Rumanian spoken today in the Banat, Crişana, and the centre of Transylvania: *muiere* (< Latin *mulier, -erem*). In Muntenia, Moldavia, southern and northern Transylvania, it was replaced, starting with the 17th century, by *femeie*, a word also of Latin origin, but with the sense of ′family′ whose sense changed in the same century to that of ′woman′. Lastly, in Făgăraş, where many Rumanian peasants were ennobled by the Hungarian kings, *boreasă,* from *boier* ′nobleman′, with the suffix *-easă,* replaced the word of Latin origin.

Nea exists also in Arumanian, Meglenorumanian, and Istrorumanian: *neao, nẹuă,* and *nẹ, nẹvu,* respectively. The inherited Latin word *familia* exists also in the south: Arumanian *fumeal′e* , Meglenitic *fămelẹl′ă, fumẹl′ă,* and there with the original sense of ′family′. Also Latin *mulier* is found in the south, and was earlier general in the Rumanian language: Arum. and Meglenitic *mul′ari,* Istrorumanian *mul′ẹre.* [1]

In principle, the explanation of other phenomena put forward as arguments for a "core region" in north-western Transylvania is similar to that of the words. Thus, the habit of putting a *k* between *s* and *l* – *sclab* instead of *slab*, etc., as well as the form *renunculus* (besides *reniculus*) existed in certain areas of Late Latin; also in part of the Balkan peninsula. Given the different forms in the Latin of the Balkan peninsula, it is only natural that they are found also today in the language of the Rumanians – as it is natural that the Rumanian grammar is predominantly Latin, or that there are Latin words in Rumanian.

As regards the geographical names and the placenames put forward by Gamillscheg in favour of the core-region hypothesis, no one of these names is in Rumanian directly inherited from Latin.[2] Consequently, these arguments are also invalid.

The phenomena put forward in favour of the *Kerngebiet* theory are chosen arbitrarily from a vast number of facts of language, such as differences in pronunciation, the preservation or replacement of Latin lexical elements by loanwords in the course of time in the different areas, etc. Some examples of these factors were given above. Although this theory was initially put forward by linguists, present day Rumanian linguists do not accept it. As shown above, Rosetti refuted it definitely and Matilda Caragiu Marioţeanu, in her monograph about the Rumanian dialects, does not even mention it. The same is the case with other publications on Rumanian dialectology as for example the studies by B. Cazacu, collected in one volume (1966). If it has been discussed here in some detail, this is because the theory of core areas seems to be one of the main

---

[1]Cazacu Dialectologie 1966, pp. 161–168, with maps.

[2]In several areas of Transylvania, the majority of the names of the mountains are Rumanian. These names are not, however, older than earliest from the 14th century, when the first Rumanian village names appeared. When the Vlach shepherds started to migrate to Transylvania, in the 13th century, they lived initially in the region of the high mountains, where they took part in defending of the fortresses built by the Hungarian kings. These regions were either uninhabited or populated by a usually sparse Slavic or Hungarian population.

arguments in favour of the theory of continuity accepted also by some western scholars (cf. above, pp. 195–198). E. Illyés, in *Ethnic Continuity in the Carpatho-Danubian Area,* 1992, pp. 272–290, after having given a more detailed review of this theory, also refuted it..

2. OTHER LINGUISTIC ARGUMENTS

a) Rumanian religious terminology

The arguments mentioned in IR Compendiu 1969 (cf. above, p. 182), concerning the Christian terms of Latin origin – namely that in Dacia Romana, Christianity was the bearer of the Latin language – are not acceptable. These terms were inherited by Rumanian in the Balkan peninsula (Albanian concordances, etc, cf. above, p. 115). The theory that the word *biserică* proves that the ancestors of the Rumanians did not live in the Balkans in the 4th century was not mentioned in the 1974 edition of this treatise. As shown above, *basilica* has also been borrowed by Albanian.

b) The sound pattern of the Slavic influence

The theory based on the *difference between the treatment of Common Slavic consonant groups *tj, *dj* , and a number of Common Slavic vowels (cf. above, p. 183) cannot be accepted. The Bulgarian pronunciation reaches far to the southwest to Macedonia. Besides, to refer to the "oldest and most numerous" Slavic elements in Rumanian, as if the oldest elements would also be the most numerous, does not correspond to reality. (The oldest Slavic influence includes about 70 lexical elements, which existed in Common Rumanian. Most numerous Slavic loanwords in Northern Rumanian are those borrowed later, in the 11th–12th centuries (cf. above, p.101).

c) The time span of the Slavic influence on Rumanian

There is significant difference between Rumanian archaeologists and historians on the one side and linguists, on the other, regarding this question. The affirmation in IR 1960 and of Giurescu & Giurescu, that the Slavs living in the territory of present day Rumania were assimilated to the Rumanians in a relatively short time after the 10th century (cf. above, p. 183) cannot be correct. The same applies to the result which Eugenia Zaharia reached on the basis of archaeological finds – the assimilation in the 8th century. This is clearly shown by the analysis of the sound pattern of the South Slavic elements in Rumanian, presented in detail also by Rosetti (ILR 1986, cf. above, pp. 98–101). If IR 1960 would be right, only about 70 South Slavic words were found in the Rumanian language, essentially the same in all dialects. The result reached by Eugenia

Zaharia is an example of the danger of drawing conclusions regarding language from material remains. The disappearance of the Slavic contact already in the 8th century would not even permit this relatively weak Slavic impact. As shown above, p. 101, the South Slavic influence on Northern Rumanian increased after the Common Rumanian period, reaching its peak in the 11th and the 12th centuries.

d) The territory of the Slavo-Rumanian symbiosis

Rumanian historians assert that the Rumanian language was exposed to Slavic (entirely or at least predominantly) north of the Danube. Rosetti presents all the facts but does not draw the logical conclusions. The passage dealing with this in Rosetti ILR 1986 (cf. above, p. 184) may be summarized as follows (with the present author´s comments in brackets): Friedwagner and others, who deny the possiblity of influence in the north, "make a mere assumption because we have no direct information on the connections between the Romanized population and [the migratory peoples]." (The problem is that we have no information about a Romanized population in the period in question north of the Danube.) Rosetti continues the argument by saying that for those who admit that the Rumanian language developed on a large territory of Roman colonization, the existence of contact between such a population and the Slavs also north of the Danube appears to be beyond doubt. (This is not, of course, a linguistic argument and no valid argument at all, because the assumption of a large, both south- and north-Danubian territory in which the Rumanian language developed is not proved. On the contrary, it is denied exactly by the Slavic influence upon Rumanian, which excludes the territory of present day Rumania, cf. below.) The next argument presented is the assumption that "the Romanized population was preserved in Dacia after the Roman domination ceased." (This is not impossible, but it has little relevance for the question discussed; cf. above, p. 209: Latin-speaking populations remained after the Roman retreat in Pannonia, Noricum, Britannia, etc., but they did not survive for many centuries. As regards the statement of Petrovici, it should be made clear that the Roman domination lasted 600 years SOUTH of the lower Danube. Several circumstances indicate that the original areas of the Vlachs were situated much more to the south).

Thus, Rosetti showed in this passage, although indirectly, that there is no LINGUISTIC argument for the assumption of a South Slavic influence upon early Rumanian north of the Danube.

There is, in fact, specific evidence showing a South Slavic influence on Rumanian exerted in the Balkan peninsula. There are words of Latin origin borrowed by South Slavic and then from this language by the Rumanians. Rumanian *sigur, matur,* and *oţet* derive from South Slavic, as shown by the accent on the first syllable in *sígur* and *mátur,* (as opposed to Latin *secúrus* and *matúrus)* and *o* instead of *a* and *ts* instead of *c(e)* in *oţet* (cf. Latin *acetum).*

between the two populations (cf. above, pp. 190). Rosetti stated that there are no Old Germanic elements in the Rumanian language, and that, based upon historical records and archaeological finds, "the permanent habitation of the populations of Germanic language north of the Danube and their symbiosis with the local Romanized populations are well-proved facts." This section in Rosetti´s ILR 1986 does not contain any answer to the question: how can these two facts be reconciled with the theory of continuity? (The affirmation that Old Germanic elements could have been borrowed by the Rumanians also south of the Danube is no sufficient explanation, nor is it valid.) Also ILR 1969 evades to answer this question. Iordan & Manoliu,[1] although criticising the argument presented more than a century ago by Rösler, that the absence of Old Germanic words in Rumanian is not compatible with the theory of Daco-Roman continuity, do not give any explanation of the fact itself.

In order to give a background to the question of Old Germanic elements in Rumanian, the Old Germanic influence on the Neolatin languages will be summarized shortly. During their contacts with Germanic tribes, the Romans borrowed some Old Germanic words as early as the first century AD. Some of these survived in the Romance languages, for example French *jante* < Germanic *ganta* ´goose´, Italian *bandiera* < Germanic *bandum* ´flag´, etc. Most of the Old Germanic words were, however, probably borrowed later, after 600 AD, separately by each Romance language.

The historical data: Most numerous of all Germanic peoples were the Franks, who started to attack Gaul in the 3rd century AD. In 358, they were permitted by Emperor Julian to settle down in what is today Belgium and northern France. From there, they successively extended their domination and, by the end of the 5th century, they ruled over a large territory corresponding to central and northern France.

The Visigoths who lived in most of the 4th century in Transylvania and other parts of present day Rumania (cf. below, p. 261) were forced by the Hunnish invasion to migrate westwards and reached Italy, southern France, and the Iberian peninsula.

The Ostrogoths conquered Italy in 493, in 555, however, the East Roman Empire defeated them.

The Longobards invaded northern Italy in 568 and organized there a state which existed until 774, when Italy was conquered by the Franks.

The Burgundians dominated the eastern part of southern France for about a century until they were defeated by the Franks (532–534 AD).

Gepidae lived in several areas of the Carpathian basin from the end of the 3rd century to the mid-seventh century, cf. below, p. 263.

The Old Germanic influence on the Romance languages was considerable, with hundreds of lexical elements. The largest number (more than 500), of these

---

[1] Iordan, I., Manoliu, Maria, *Introducere în lingvistica romanică*, 1965, p. 275.

Thus, two main conditions were established: (1) The Rumanian lang contains South Slavic elements with a sound pattern from the 7th–8th cent and the most numerous Slavic elements in Northern Rumanian show the sc pattern of Middle Bulgarian (11th–12th centuries). (2) Before the 12th– centuries, only SOUTH Slavic elements were transferred to Rumanian.

Considering the historical situation, these facts indicate that Rumani cannot have been living before that period (a) in central and northwest Transylvania. Archaeological remains excavated there show namely western a eastern Slavic cultures and the placenames of Slavic origin in that area shov western Slavic pattern. (b)The Rumanian language also lacks Ukrainian elemer of a pattern shown before the 12th–13th centuries, which excludes also (at lea northern) Moldavia. (c) But not even the Bulgarian influence upon Rumania could have been exerted north of the lower Danube, because the Bulgaria domination was too short there. The Bulgarian state was founded in 679 sout of the lower Danube and expanded in a southward and southwestward directior In the 9th century, the Bulgarians occupied present day Muntenia and souther Transylvania. However, latest at the beginning of the 10th century, Bulgaria los its power north of the Danube. The Bulgarian domination lasted at most a century in Muntenia and southern Transylvania, obviously too short for the impact of South Slavic on Northern Rumanian. After the Bulgarians, Petchenegs occupied Moldavia and the Valachian plain. The Hlincea I culture in southern Moldavia showed signs of ravages around 930 AD and disappeared some decades later. This, as well as the end of the Dridu culture on the Valachian plain not long after 1000 AD is ascribed to Petcheneg attacks (cf. below, pp. 278–279). The Transylvanian basin and most of the valleys were, beginning with the 10th century, inhabited by Hungarians. From the end of the 11th century, the Cumans dominated the extra-Carpathian territories (cf. below, p. 280). Thus, in the period of the most intense Bulgarian influence on Northern Rumanian, the Bulgarians no longer ruled north of the lower Danube, Slavic archaeological cultures disappeared there, Turk peoples were living in the extra-Carpathian territories and Transylvania was organized into the Hungarian kingdom and was increasingly populated by Hungarians. Neither the absolute amount of the Sout Slavic influence (cf. above, pp. 102–108) nor its increase upon Norther Rumanian after the 10th century can be explained under these circumstances

Consequently, THE SOUTH SLAVIC INFLUENCE ON RUMANIAN BEFORE T 12th–13th CENTURIES WAS EXERTED SOUTH OF THE LOWER DANUBE.

3. THE ABSENCE OF OLD GERMANIC ELEMENTS

Historical records and abundant archaeological finds testify to the pr of Goths and later of Gepidae in most of present day Rumania from the en 3rd to the 7th–8th centuries. Some historians have affirmed that these pop did not have close contacts with the "Daco-Romans", others asserted a sy were left by the Franks, followed by the Longobards, with about 300. Out of words from the language of the Visigoths, about 130, from that of the Ostrogoths, 70, and from Burgundian, about 50 words are still extant in the Romance languages. (These figures are taken from *Întroducere în lingvistica romanică*, by I. Iordan & Maria Manoliu, 1965, p. 276, who quote Gamillscheg, *Romania Germanica*, 1934–1936. According to Iordan & Manoliu, the figures are somewhat exaggerated.)

From the viewpoint of the modern Romance languages, the Gallo-Romance idioms contain most words of Old Germanic origin, followed by the Italian dialects and, lastly, the Ibero-Romance languages. However, the number of personal names of Old Germanic origin in Spanish and in Portuguese is considerable (cf., for instance, Tagliavini Orig Lingu Neolat 1969, p. 305). In Rumanian, as shown above, there are no Old Germanic elements (not even personal names).

In the Balkan peninsula, the role of the Old Germanic peoples was of a very limited importance (cf. above, pp. 13, 16). In contrast, large areas north of the lower Danube were during the 4th to the 7th centuries inhabited and dominated by Old Germanic peoples (Goths and Gepidae). Assuming with Rumanian archaeologists that they were living together, in the same settlements, with Daco-Romans, i.e., the ancestors of the Rumanians (Mugeni, Lechinţa de Mureş, etc.), one would expect to find Old Germanic elements in the Rumanian language. The number of these would not necessarily be as high as it is in the western Romance languages, but the total absence of this influence is very difficult to reconcile with the idea of a symbiosis lasting several centuries. One may assume, as was usually done earlier, that the Daco-Romans fled to the mountains and did not have contacts with the Germanic peoples, who lived in villages in the valleys. But a shepherd population is not entirely independent from peasant groups; and the Vlach shepherds proved, both by their Romanization as well as by their borrowing of a tremendous amount of Slavic elements, contact with surrounding populations. However, there are the Basques living in the Pyrenean mountains whose ancestors were once subdued by Old Germanic peoples and their language lacks, in spite of this, any Old Germanic influence. The absence of Old Germanic elements in Rumanian may thus be considered an argument *ex silentio*, and as such, not decisive in itself, although by no means without significance.

4. PLACENAMES AND GEOGRAPHICAL NAMES

In chapter III, p. 191–193, a number of hypotheses were presented concerning the placenames and names of rivers in present day Rumania.

a) The hypothesis of ancient placenames preserved to our days

Poghirc assumed about five placenames recorded in ancient texts that they may exist even today, because their names are similar and the geographical situation of these settlements is the same as assumed for the settlements mentioned in ancient texts. These are Drencova, Hîrsova, Mehadia, Oltina, and Băroi.

Drencova, in the Banat, is believed to continue *Dric(c)a,* mentioned by Iordanes. It may be a non-identified tributary of the Danube. Another river, a tributary of the Tisza, is Δρέγκων or Δρήκων. There are several places with this and similar names in Rumania. Iordan mentions the following: Dranov, Dranovatul, Drânceni, Drâncova or Drencova (in the Banat), Drencea (in the region of Iaşi), Drincea, and Drinova.[1] It is of course not probable that all these names would derive from ancient *Dric(c)a* or Δρέγκων. Iordan derives these names from Slavic *dren* 'cornel tree *(Cornus mascula)*' (Bulgarian *drěn* 'id.' and *drěnov* 'of cornel tree'). Many Slovakian, Serbian, and Croatian placenames contain this word.

Hîrşova is assumed to continue ancient *Carsium* in Dobrogea. Also in this case, there are several villages with similar names: besides that in the region of Constanţa, there is a village with the same name in Vaslui, and in the region of Craiova, there is *Cruşovul.* This name exists also in Arumanian: *Cruşuva.*[2] Before the 15th century, Hîrşova was written in Slavic documents *Hrušova* or *Hruševa.* Assuming that Hîrşova continues ancient Carsium, the *c* > *h* change must be explained. Poghirc proposes that an "autochthonous" *h* was in Latin written *c,* because *h* did not exist in Latin in that period. However, all places with this name cannot continue ancient Carsium but are evidently of Slavic origin, from Slavic *hruša, kruš(ĭ)ka* 'pear tree'. Many placenames all over the territories populated by Slavs derive from this word. Iordan's conclusion is that Hîrşova in the region of Constanţa may continue, "indirectly and at least formally" ancient Carsium, but it was modified by Slavic *hruš(k)a.*[3]

Mehadia is assumed to derive from Latin *Ad Mediam,* although not from Latin *medius* but "probably from an autochthonous *Mehedia, Mehadia, with intervocalic *h* not recorded by the Romans".[4] This hypothesis cannot be accepted, because, as indicated by the first mentioning in a document (1323: *Myhald, Mihald,* etc.), this name derives from the Hungarian personal name *Mihály,* with the suffix *-d.*[5]

Oltina in Dobrogea is most probably the continuation of ancient *Altina,* with the Slavic *a* > *o* sound change.

Băroi, also in Dobrogea, derives probably from ancient *Bireo, Beroe.*

Thus, out of four placenames and a river name for which "a perfect greographical correspondence" is assumed, two are of Slavic and one is of

[1] Iordan Nume de locuri 1950, p. 45.

[2] Ibid., p. 66.

[3] Ibid., p. 67.

[4] Poghirc, ILR 1969, p. 360.

[5] Suciu, C., *Dicţionar istoric al localităţilor din Transilvania*, 1967, vol. I. p. 389.

Hungarian origin. The rest, two placenames, most probably continue the ancient name, but the settlements in question (as also Hîrşova) are situated in Dobrogea, south of the Danube. They belong to the large number of Roman settlements along the southern shore of the Danube whose names were preserved – in a Slavic sound pattern. These Roman towns, although exposed to the ravages of the barbarians, existed until the end of the 6th century and a Latin-speaking population lived there in the period of Slavic colonization. This explains the fact that these, together with a large number of Latin placenames in the Balkan peninsula, were not forgotten. Many Latin names disappeared also in the Balkans, in those cases in which the settlements were abandoned, and occupied by the Slavs after some time had elapsed. To such settlements, the Slavs gave their own names, for example *Braničevo* ′the tower of the defender′ for *Viminacium* (cf. above, p.20). Of course, one should also take into account that changes may have occurred by chance, reducing the number of preserved names in certain areas. However, north of the lower Danube we find not only a reduced number of inherited placenames but a total absence – not a single name of a Roman town or any other kind of settlement was preserved. The most obvious explanation of this is that the Slavs did not find Latin-speaking inhabitants when they migrated to these territories in the 6th–7th centuries.

b) The problem of the names of the great rivers in Transylvania

It is generally considered that the ancient names of the great rivers were handed down to Rumanian by the Slavs. In the course of time, however, hypotheses were put forward assuming that these names were inherited directly. Poghirc has tried to show that Slavic or Hungarian were not necessary to explain the Rumanian names Mureş, Olt, Someş, Timiş, and Tisa.[1] The argument is based on assumed sound changes which would have occurred in "late Daco-Moesian" between the 3rd and the 6th centuries: *-si-* > *š* and *a* > *o (u)*. Ancient *Marisia* and *Timisia* changed to *Mureş* and *Timiş*, respectively, *Samus* to *Someş* and *Alutus* to *Olt*. A difficulty is *Tisia,* which, according to this hypothesis would have changed to **Tiş*. This may be explained, argues Poghirc, by a different pronunciation by the local population of this name, not corresponding to what was recorded.[2]

The basis of this reasoning is very weak and uncertain, which is, in fact, also pointed out by Poghirc: "We emphasize the hypothetical nature of these phonetical transformations, based upon a scanty and uncertain material."[3] One may add that if Dacia Traiana had had a Latin-speaking population in those times, all these names would have been used by this population IN A LATIN FORM and a sound change in "Daco-Moesian" between the 3rd and the 6th centuries would

[1] C. Poghirc, Dacoromania I 1973, p. 198.

[2] C. Poghirc, ILR 1969, p. 359.

[3] Ibid., p. 317, note 1.

not have affected them.

Another hypothesis is that old Rumanian names were TRANSLATED by the Slavs, and in Transylvania by the Hungarians (cf. above, p. 192). There is, however, no proof that this mechanism was instrumental. It is not known whether the name of a tributary of the Bistriţa, Repede, existed before the Slavic population of the area. It might as well have been given by Vlachs who migrated there much later. ('Fast' is a usual name given to mountain rives and brooks.) It was originally Drăganu[1] who assumed that from Latin *Alutus,* Rumanian *Alt* resulted and this was the name of the river until the Slavs and the Hungarians came to the region and changed it to Olt. The Rumanians then borrowed the Slavic or the Hungarian form: *Olt,* while the Germans, when they in the 13th century settled in Transylvania, borrowed the old Rumanian form Alt.

This is at most a possibility, although very unlikely. It would be justified to formulate such hypotheses in a territory in which most of the geographical names are of Latin or of Rumanian origin. This is, however, not the case here: NOT A SINGLE PLAECNAME OR GEOGRAPHICAL NAME OF PROVED LATIN ORIGIN AND INHERITED DIRECTLY BY RUMANIAN IS FOUND NORTH OF THE LOWER DANUBE. Assumptions that merely permit the possibility of such origin are in these circumstances meaningless. For the most probable explanation of the river names cf. below, p. 272– 273. The example presented by Puşcariu (cf. above, p. 192) of Petra translated by the Slavs into Kamena has no relevance for the territory of former Dacia Traiana. This settlement in Dobrogea belongs, together with Băroi and Oltina, to the Roman settlements along the southern shore of the lower Danube, whose names were preserved (in a Slavic sound pattern) obviously because the Slavs found there a Latin-speaking population.

c) The significance of the absence of inherited Latin names

One has tried to explain the absence of inherited Latin names north of the lower Danube by assuming that the "Daco-Romans" adopted the names given by the Slavs (cf. above, p. 192). These explanations cannot be accepted.

People who migrate to new territories usually borrow the geographical names and the placenames they find there. The numerical circumstances and even the cultural level of the populations in question have a subordinated role in this process. The decisive circumstance is the existence of a name (of a town, of a river, etc.). Thus, for example, the English borrowed very many names of rivers and streams in America, Africa, and elsewhere. This group of nouns is the most easily transferred element of language. In American English, "the numerous names of Indian origin are almost the only loanwords from that source."[2]

In a series of former Roman provinces, the Latin-speaking population was in the course of time replaced by speakers of other languages. In many of these

---

[1]Drăganu, N., *Românii în veacurile IX–XV*, p. 537; quoted by Puşcariu Le rôle de la Transylvanie..., 1938, p. 41.

[2]Weinreich Lang Cont 1964, p. 57.

provinces, placenames of Latin origin are still in use. In England, names ending in *–chester, –caster* (Manchaster, Lancaster, etc.) continue Latin *–castra,* the ending *–coln* (Lincoln, Old English Lindcylne) derives from Latin *colonia.* In Noricum and in Raetia, the Slavs and the Germans borrowed many Latin placenames and names of rivers and streams from the Latin-speaking population they found there in the 6th–7th centuries. About 200 of these are still in use in the territory of the former Roman provinces: Latin *Laureacum* > German *Lorch, Lentia* > *Linz, Bataua (Castra)* > *Passau, Licus* > Lech, *(Ad) Pontes* > *Pfunzen, Celeusus* > *Kelsbach,* etc.[1] In Pannonia, the situation is varying in the different areas, depending on historical circumstances. In the northeast, the changes of population occurred more abruptly and more often, and, consequently, there are no placenames of Latin origin in that part. In the west, however, there are: Latin *Vindobona* > German *Wien, Poetovio* > *Ptuj, Siscia* > *Sisak.* The Hungarians found a number of such names when they, at the end of the 9th century, took possession of Pannonia. They borrowed several river names: Latin *Arrabo* > Hungarian *Rába, Mursella* > *Marcal, Sala* > *Zala,* etc., and *Savaria* was in use (along Hungarian *Szombathely)* until the 19th century.[2]

In the Balkans, the Rumanians have preserved a number of ancient place-names in a sound pattern which shows direct inheritance: *Sărună, Lăsun, Flărina,* etc. This indicates that they have lived in (or were in contact with) those areas continually since the Roman times, which implies Roman-Rumanian continuity.

North of the lower Danube, several toponyms of Scythian, Sarmatian, Petcheneg, and other origin were transferred to Rumanian – and in Transylvania, to Hungarian – via Slavic. The earliest toponyms borrowed directly by the Rumanians from people living north of the Danube were (1) from the Cumans, in the 12th–13th centuries (cf. below, pp. 280–281), and (2) from Slavic, showing the Bulgarian sound pattern in approximately the same period (cf. below, p. 248).

The explanations given (cf. above, pp. 191–192), in themselves more or less valid, can only explain why not ALL Latin toponyms were preserved in the former Roman provinces. They are not sufficient to account for the total absence of inherited Latin placenames and geographical names in Rumanian spoken north of the Danube. The absence of such names is not compatible with the assumption that Rumanian is the continuation of Latin spoken in Dacia Traiana.[3]

d) The significance of the sound pattern of the placenames of Slavic origin

Rumanian placenames of Slavic origin also give some indication regarding the period in which the Rumanians spread over the territories north of the lower

---

[1] Kranzmayer, E., "Frühromanische Mundarten zwischen Donau und Adria in deutschen und slawischen Ortsnamen", *Ztschr. f. Namenforschung,* XV, 1939, p. 195.

[2] Tóth, E., in Köpeczi, B. (ed.), *Erdély története* I, 1986, p. 105.

[3] The conclusion was summarized by E. Petrovici, who stated in 1951 that on the territory of (Northern) Rumanian, the placenames are of non-Romance origin – primarily Slavic, but also Hungarian, Cumanian, and other – which can only be explained by assuming the spread of the Rumanian language in a territory in which mainly Slavic was spoken (cf. above, p. 194.)

Danube. The sound patterns of these names are relatively recent and it has been assumed that this was caused by an adaptation of the pronunciation:

> Notons que les Roumains ont pu employer pour ces toponyms, à une époque plus réculée, des formes à *un, um,* (par ex. *Dumbova, *Glumboaca, etc.). Mais, à mesure que changeait la prononciation de *ǫ* dans la bouche des Slaves, la prononciation de ces toponyms dans la bouche des Roumains s'adaptait à celle des Slaves.[1]

A similar hypothesis was put forward to explain the more recent sound pattern of most Northern Rumanian words of Slavic origin as compared to the Slavic loanwords in Albanian and in Greek:

> In the Danubian provinces, the Slavic elements who immigrated during the first period were constantly renewed by additional Slavic elements, in this way, the pronunciation of the words was during the whole time adapted to the actual pronunciation.[2]

This argument is erroneous. There are several Rumanian words of South Slavic origin with an older sound pattern: *măgură, şchiau, scump, muncă, daltă,* etc. (cf. above, p. 98–99). These words were borrowed early, probably before the 9th–10th centuries, and were not "adapted to the actual pronunciation" (in Slavic). Words borrowed from a foreign language usually develop according to the rules of the borrowing language, not those of the original one. This is true, of course, also regarding placenames and geographical names, which, moreover, are among the most resistant elements of any language. This fact gives them their great significance in historical research.

All the placenames and geographical names north of the Danube borrowed by Rumanian from Slavic are of a much later sound pattern (of the 11th–12th centuries and later) than the above-mentioned words (from the period before the 9th–10th centuries). Since it is known that Slavs were living in the territory also earlier (in the 7th–10th centuries), this circumstance confirms the conclusion above, that Rumanians did not live north of the Danube in those centuries.

e) The theory of the flight to the mountains and the absence of geographical names of Latin origin

The above conclusion applies to all areas north of the lower Danube. However, with regard to the hypothesis that the "Daco-Romans" were, during a certain period, living in far away valleys and high mountains, the situation in these areas should be analysed separately.

---

[1]Petrovici, E., *Studii de dialectologie şi toponimie*, 1970, pp. 197–198.

[2]Rosetti ILR 1986, p. 265.

If the ancestors of the Rumanians had been living, in the period of Slavic colonization, in the region of the high mountains, we may assume that they could possibly have forgotten the names of the towns.[1] They would have preserved, however, at least some names of villages and names of rivers and streams in the territory in which they were living (allegedly the Transylvanian Alps [Munţii Apuseni] and the southern Carpathians). The rivers Arieş, Ampoi, Someş as well as Cerna, Sebeş, Dâmboviţa, flow in this region. The upper course of the Sebeş, a tributary to the Mureş, situated in the area of mountains about 2000 m high, is in the heart of this region; it is called Bistra, a name borrowed from Slavic. Also Târnava (Mare and Mică), Mureş, and Olt should be known by a population living in those mountains. However, not a single of these names was by Rumanian inherited from Latin. As shown below, pp. 271–273, they are either ancient names, or names of Slavic or of Hungarian origin, and ALL WERE BORROWED BY THE RUMANIANS FROM ONE OF THESE TWO LANGUAGES.

The situation in the mountainous region south of Orăştie (Hung. Szászváros) has been investigated by Mircea Homorodean.[2] This author tried to find ancient Dacian names in the region around Sarmizegetusa, once the centre of the Dacian state. The result was negative: not a single geographical name or placename of Dacian or of Latin origin was found.[3] (It may be added that, along with Rumanian names, a considerable amount of Hungarian and also German [Transylvanian Saxon] names were found in the area.)

5. THE TESTIMONY OF THE RUMANIAN DIALECTS

The idea of the development of Rumanian north of the Danube is not compatible with the Rumanian dialects. If the ancestors of the Rumanians lived, during the 4th–6th centuries both south and north of the lower Danube, there would be at least some dialectal differentiation in their language between the territories south and north of the river, as a consequence of the Roman *limes;* even if one would assume more significant contact across this frontier. Such differences in Latin have been caused by the division of the Roman Empire into two halves at the end of the 4th century, and the frontier between the two halves was much less of an obstacle of contact between peoples than was the Danubian *limes.* The dialectal division of Rumanian (presented above, pp. 119–123) shows,

---

[1] Although, as mentioned above, p. 247, in the Balkan peninsula, there are Rumanian names of settlements whose sound pattern indicates inheritance of an ancient name, thus, for example Rum. *Săruna* continues the name of the town Saloniki.

[2] Homorodean. M., *Vechea vatră a Sarmizegetusei în lumina toponimiei*, 1980.

[3] Homorodean Vechea vatră 1980, p. 51 and 78. "In the absence of conclusive historical and particularly linguistic evidence, we were not able to find any toponym from the antique era (in the first place, Dacian) in the region of the former capital of Dacia, Sarmizegetusa."

however, no traces of a division caused by the Roman *limes*. It goes, instead, between Arumanian with Meglenitic in the southern parts of the Balkans on the one hand, and Northern Rumanian with Istro-Rumanian on the other. These two dialects are spoken in Istria, in the Timok valley, and were spoken during the Middle Ages in a large area between Skopje and Prizren up to Niš and Sofia, and also to the west of this territory (cf. above, pp. 26–33 and map No 3).

Northern Rumanian is now spoken mostly north of the lower Danube, where it is the mother tongue of about 20 million people. However, in spite of this, and in spite of the large territory in which its speakers are living, this idiom shows a remarkably weak dialactal differentiation (cf. above, pp. 124–131). Most relevant in this context would be the situation in ancient periods. Unfortunately, data are extant only from the 15th century on. The opinions concerning the dialectal differentiation of the texts written in the 16th century differ. Some authors assume more phonetic differences as compared to the present situation, others, considering mainly the lexical elements, deny the existence of subdialects in that period:

> The linguistic phenomena on which this [the division of the subdialects] is based are not old. The words which give to the maps of vocabulary such a varied picture are relatively recent borrowings of the Rumanian language, words of German (...), Hungarian (...), Serbian (...), (*arghelă 'heghelie'*), Bulgarian (*a ciupi*) origin... It is, consequently, probable that the present day subdialects did not exist before the 15th century.[1]

The phonetic differences are assumed to have been more pronounced earlier among others by Rosetti[2] but it appears from the entire presentation that they were not very great. The low differentiation of Northern Rumanian is thus generally acknowledged. It has been explained by the assumption of lively contact between the population of the different regions, caused by the shepherd way of life:

> The dialectal groupings which we have established are warranted by the contacts between the social groups of northern Transylvania – Maramureş and Moldavia or southern Transylvania and Ţara Românească as well as by the emigration of the population from Transylvania to the adjacent provinces.[3] In the majority of cases, the south of Transylvania is grouped together with Oltenia and Muntenia, while the northeast of this historic province belongs to a common area with Moldavia. This distribution is a consequence of the permanent connections which existed during the centuries among Rumanians living on both sides of the Carpathian mountains.[4]

---

[1] Petrovici, E., "Repartiţia graiurilor dacoromâne pe baza Atlasului lingvistic român", in *Limba română*, III, 5, p. 16; quoted by Mihăilă Studii 1973, p. 53.

[2] Rosetti ILR 1986 p. 540.

[3] Ibid.

[4] Cazacu Studii 1966, p. 169.

Similar connections must have existed, for example, also between the early Albanians – a typically shepherd population – and in spite of this, their language developed, on a much smaller territory than present day Rumania, two distinct dialects (Tosc and Gheg). The Rhetoromance language has a number of dialects. Bulgarian developed marked dialectal differences since its speakers settled, in the 7th century, in the northeast of the Balkans. Intensive contacts are therefore scarcely sufficient to explain the low dialectal differentiation of Northern Rumanian.

If speakers of a certain dialect emigrate to new territories where they find favourable living conditions, their number may rapidly increase so as they spread over large territories. An example from modern times is the populating of the western regions of the United States. In such cases time may not be sufficient for the development of significant dialectal differences, which results in a large area inhabited by speakers of a relatively homogenous language. This mechanism was descibed by J.M. Anderson as follows:

> Observations of the present situation between dialects and geography, however, suggest that if we have a large area only a small part of which is broken up into marked dialect differentiation, the large homogenous area has only recently been settled. For examples one can compare the recently settled and linguistically homogenous western United States with the east coast of the United States (a smaller area with numerous dialects) or the United States and England. In both cases the more recently settled area shows less dialectal differentiation. Deductions based upon these observations may be applied to other linguistic groups such as Eskimo; this inferentially helps to substantiate the notion that the Eskimos settled recently in the north, as their language is fairly uniform from Alaska to Greenland.[1]

These observations may be applied to Northern Rumanian, independently corroborating the conclusion of emigration to the territories north of the lower Danube by groups of Vlachs relatively recently (i.e., starting in the 11th century.) It is hardly possible that a population living in such a large territory as Rumania from the 3rd century AD to the 15th (and the 20th) century i.e., for 1200–1700 years as assumed by the theory of continuity, should not have developed any significant dialectal differences in their language.

The absence of a Transylvanian subdialect in Rumanian

Puşcariu tried to explain this mainly by the following circumstances: (1) The Vlach shepherds followed the ways of transhumance (*les voies de transhumance*) from Transylvania across the Carpathain mountains to adjacent plains: the Banat, the Valachain plain, and Moldavia. (2) In Transylvania proper, there were no

[1]Anderson, J.M., *Structural Aspects of Language Change*, 1973, p. 82.

Rumanian political, cultural, or religious centres around which the Rumanian inhabitants of this province could have aggreagated. The Hungarian and the Saxon towns were for them only market places, administrative and jurisdictional centres. Puşariu affirmed also that "Les cartes de l'Atlas linguistiques nous permettront d'étudier l'expansion des Roumains de Transylvanie dans toutes les directions."[1]

According to this, the Moldavian and the Muntenian sub-dialects would be the continuation of the Transylvanian sub-dialects. This, however, is an interpretation of the information provided by the maps. The maps show only that there is no Transylvanian sub-dialect. Instead, Rumanian spoken in the south of Transylvania is essentially the idiom spoken in adjacent Muntenia and Oltenia, and in the northeast, that of Moldavia. This suggests an opposite direction as compared to that suggested by Puşcariu. Speakers of Rumanian living in Moldavia migrated in the first place to northeastern Transylvania, and those from Muntenia, to southern Transylvania. The main criteria of a Transylvanian dialect transferred to Moldavia and Muntenia by emigrants would be (1) a number of specific traits only found in Transylvania (because even assuming large-scale migrations, it is unlikely that ALL features of a dialect specific to a certain territory would be transferred to other areas) and (2) the presence of at least a number of specific Transylvanian features in both Moldavia and Muntenia.

There are also specific lexical elements whose distribution in Rumania indicates transfer from the extra-Carpathian territories to Transylvania. Thus, for example, the speakers of Rumanian in the Banat, most of the Munţii Apuseni, Crişana, and the region of Satu Mare use the inherited Latin word *nea* (Latin *nevis)* 'snow'. In the northeast of Transylvania, *omăt* is used, as also in Moldavia, a loanword from Ukrainian. In Muntenia and Oltenia, *zăpadă,* (of Slavic origin) is said, and this is the case also in adjacent areas of southern Transylvania.[2] Another word of Turkish origin and transferred to Rumanian spoken in Muntenia and Oltenia via Bulgarian is *cioban* 'chief shepherd'. In that territory, as well as in Moldavia, crude oil, *păcură,* was extracted and those who sold this product were called *păcurar.* A homonymic clash occurred between this and *păcurar* 'chief shepherd', from Latin *pecorarius,* which therefore was replaced by *cioban.* This word penetrated to parts of southern Transylvania (while other areas in that province preserved *păcurar*).[3] The same map by Cazacu shows that *mocan* 'shepherd; simple, uncultivated man' is used in an area in southeastern Moldavia. In roughly the same region, there are many placenames based on *ungurean* 'people from Hungary' or 'Rumanian from Transylvania', which indicates that people from Transylvania did migrate to the territories beyond the Carpathians.

Thus, there is linguistic evidence for migrations of speakers of Rumanian both

---

[1]Puşcariu, S., "Le rôle de la Transylvanie dans la formation et l'évolution de la langue roumaine", *La Transylvanie*, 1938, p. 67.

[2]Cazacu Studii 1966, p. 162, map No. 10.

[3]Ibid., p. 164, map No 12.

to and from Transylvania. However, the overwhelming majority of lexical elements specific to Moldavia are found in adjacent areas of Transylvania, and the same is the case with Muntenia. In the absence of a specific Transylvanian Rumanian (sub)dialect, this can only indicate that northeastern Transylvania was populated mainly by Rumanians coming from Moldavia and southern Transylvania received its Rumanian population mainly from adjacent Muntenia and Oltenia. This is of course incompatible with the thought of Transylvania as an ancient Rumanian province, in which Latin and later Rumanian was spoken continually since the time of Emperor Trajan. It indicates, on the contrary, that this province was the last to be populated by Rumanians.[1]

Chapter V

CONCLUSIONS

Of the linguistic arguments put forward in favour of the development of Rumanian north of the lower Danube, that of the "core regions" is the most important. It is evidently false and is now refuted by authoritative Rumanian linguists. As has also been shown above, the same is the case with other arguments based on elements of the Rumanian language. The absence of any Old Germanic influence in Rumanian makes the theory of continuity less probable, to say the least. The South Slavic influence, in the case of Northern Rumanian, strongest during the 11th–early 13th centuries, cannot have been exerted in the territory of present day Rumania. In contrast to the Balkan peninsula and other

---

[1]Some doubt regarding the assumption of migrations from Transylvania as the explanation of the dialectal situation of Rumania is expressed by Coteanu & Dănăilă: "Beyond doubt, a close connection may be established between the Moldavian dialect and the linguistic situation in Transylvania, in the sense that the Moldavian dialect, particularly its northern part, seems to be a continuation of certain Transylvanian sub-dialects [*graiuri*]. *Less certain is, however, the possibility that the same would have happened in southern Muntenia.* (*Introducere în lingvistica şi filologia românească.. Probleme – biografie,* 1970, p. 244, note 2, referring to the article by Puşcariu, quoted above; emphasis added.) — It should be remembered that in significant parts of Transylvania, the population is not Rumanian but Hungarian (e.g., a large Szekler area in the southeast) or Transylvanian Saxon, and such areas were more extended in the past (cf. tables 3 and 4, above, p. 123–124). In many territories with a mixed population, the Rumanians are newcomers. Historical documents, the placenames, and many other circumstances attest to this. Thus, Rumanian Orthodox churches were started being built about two centuries after the Hungarian Catholic churches. At least five Catholic churches were built in Transylvania in the 11th and the 12th centuries, and another six in the 13th. The first Rumanian church in Transylvania, at Demsuş in the south, was built at the end of the 13th century; and most of these churches were built much later (Cf. Á. Kosztin, *A dákorumán legenda. Keresztény kultuszhelyek Erdélyben.*) For a more detailed presentation of the population of Transylvania, see Illyés, *Ethnic Continuity in the Carpatho-Danubian Area,* 2nd edition, 1992, chapter IV, pp. 291–336.

former Roman provinces, not a single Roman placename has been preserved north of the lower Danube. The ancient names of the great rivers are continued, but were transferred to Rumanian via Slavic or Hungarian. But if the territory north of the Danube was not included in the early territories of the Vlachs, where did they live during most of the Middle Ages?

In the following, the elements of the Rumanian language will be summarized which, considered in the context of history, testify to the region in which the ancestors of the Rumanians lived.

1. The Late Latin developments, Balkan Latin, and concordances with Italian dialects

As shown above, in chapter II, the Rumanian language contains vestiges of the Late Latin changes, as well as the characteristic features of Balkan Latin (approximately the 4th–7th centuries AD). There are concordances with a number of Italian dialects, which testify to close, everyday contacts with the Latin-speaking population of the Italian peninsula during the early Middle Ages. In this period, the northeastern frontier *(limes)* of the Empire was the lower Danube. The *limes* was defended and strongly supervised by the Roman army. Later, in the 5th and 6th centuries, the Byzantine Empire defended the frontiers against recurrent attacks from the barbarian populations. During all this time, no everyday contact was possible across the Danube. Therefore, after the end of the 3rd century, the language of a Latin-speaking population north of the river could not have developed in the same way as did Rumanian. Consequently, in the period of Late Latin, the ancestors of the Rumanians were living in the Roman Empire, i.e., in the Balkan peninsula and in close contact with Italy.

2. The correspondences between Rumanian and Albanian

Also concerning this problem, the opinions of Rumanian historians and linguists are different. Historians speak about "a few words" shared by Rumanian and Albanian, (IR 1960, cf. above, p. 185) and affirm that these derive from an "ancient Indo-European, Carpatho-Balkanic word stock". The opinion of Rosetti (above, p. 186) is more cautious: "the ancestors of the Albanians were neighbours of our ancestors".

That it is not the question of only "a few words" appears from any treatise on the history of the Rumanian language, not least from that of Rosetti. The question is then: what is the relation of Rumanian and of Albanian to the ancient language from which these correspondences derive? And: Where did the speakers of this language live?

The languages spoken in antiquity in southeastern Europe and particularly in the Balkan peninsula are little known. Before discussing them, it must be stated that the assumption of a "Carpatho-Balkanic word stock" implies that the same language was spoken from Macedonia through parts of present day Serbia and Bulgaria and farther away towards the north, as far as Transylvania and

Moldavia.[1] For a long period of time, the hypothesis that the ancient populations of the Balkan peninsula north of Greece spoke Thracian (in the eastern half) and Illyrian (in the west) was generally accepted ..“si bien que nous employons souvent le terme ′thraco-illyrien′”[2] as stated by V. I. Georgiev. This view was made possible by the paucity of information from these languages, which disappeared more than a thousand years ago. The Greek authors did not give obejctive and exhaustive information about the barbarian peoples. They wrote not only about Thracian and Illyrian as if these woud have been uniform languages, but affirmed, for example, that the Dacians and the Phrygians were Thracian tribes and spoke the Thracian language. Similarly erroneous was the assertion made by Tyrannion de Amisos and Varro that Latin was an Aeolian dialect of Greek.

Modern science has shown that in primitive societies without any higher political organization, large areas do not contain one uniform language. Instead, there is a diversity of idioms, often showing considerable differences even within relatively small areas. As formulated by Georgiev, regarding the situation in the period in question in southeastern Europe:

> Il est peu vraisemblable, qu′il ait eu une langue commune dans une région aussi vaste fortement entrecoupé de grandes montagnes et dans une societé primitive alors que les rapports économiques entre les differentes tribus etaient insignifiants et qu′un État commun n′existait pas.[3]

According to this principle, the differentiation of languages spoken in the Balkans in the period in question must have been even greater than it is today. But there is also some concrete, albeit limited evidence for a considerable differentiation. That Thracian and Dacian were different is indicated by the placenames and personal names preserved. The placenames and personal names from Thracia, i.e., from the eastern half of the Balkan peninsula, are completely different from those recorded from Dacia, north of the lower Danube. In Thracia, there are about 50 placenames ending in *–para* (Bendipara, Bessapara, Skaptopara, etc.), about 20 ending in *–bria* (Mesembria, Poltymbria, Skelabrie, etc.) and 10 which end in *–diza* or *–dizos* (Beodizos, Orudiza, Tarpadizos, etc.). None of these endings is known north of the Danube. There are also certain lexical differences: ′town′ in Thracian: *bria,* in Dacian: *dava.* A consonant change *(Lautverschiebung)* occurred in Thracian but not in Dacian.

The ending *–dava, –deva,* mostly known from ancient placenames in Dacia, occurs also in the northern part of Moesia Inferior. According to Georgiev, out

---

[1]Given the correspondences between Rumanian and Albanian, with elements of morphology concerning even details and lexical elements which are often identic, it is not sufficient to assume only related languages.

[2]V. I. Georgiev, “La thracologie: état actuel”, *Études balkaniques*, 3, 1972, (Sofia), p. 14.

[3]Ibid.

of a total of 47 (or 45) such names known at present, 9 (or 10) were found in northern Bulgaria and in Dobrogea, and 7 (or 8) in the region of Niš, Kjustendil, and Sofia[1]. On this basis, the term "Daco-Moesian language" was created, as stated, for instance, by Poghirc: "We call the language of the population in this territory Daco-Moesian or, for the sake of conciseness, Dacian." (ILR 1969, p. 313, note 6). This is, however, an hypothesis based on a questionable basis, which is also mentioned by Poghirc: "We emphasize the hypothetical character of these phonetical transformations based upon a scanty and uncertain material" (ILR 1969, p. 317, note 1).

The underlying assumption, that before the Roman period, essentially the same language was spoken from northern Bulgaria to Transylvania, is particularly difficult to accept if one considers that Dacian and Getian were also different:

> The affirmation of Strabo that the Dacians talked the same language as the Getae (VII, 3, 10), and that the language of the Getae was the same as that of the Thracians (VII, 3, 13), is of no greater value than the assertion made by Italian travellers in the Rumanian countries *[Ţările Române]* in the 16th century that Rumanian was a dialect of Italian.[2]

The material extant is not sufficient to permit more detailed description of the linguistic situation in question, but it is most probable that the terms Thracian, Illyrian, and also Dacian, and Getian, give us only rough information. There were certainly languages totally unknown by the Greek authors or, in any case, about which no record has been preserved. This is suggested by the fact that not a single Rumanian word assumed to derive from the substratum of the language appears among the lexical elements preserved in Greek and Latin texts (cf. above, p. 55). Because of the scarcity of data, there is no absolute proof; the number of words, including placenames preserved from Thracian and Illyrian is small. But it is very probable that records on the ancient Balkan language, Proto-Albanian, which is the substratum of Rumanian, were either lost or never made, or that this language was simply not known by the Greek and Roman authors, since it was spoken by a population of shepherds living in the mountains in small villages with little interest for the chroniclers.

3. The territory of the ancient Albanians

The Albanians, an ancient population of shepherds of the Balkan peninsula, lived in the region of Mati and adjacent areas, Dukagjin and Merdita, as well as in parts of Dardania and old Serbia before the Roman colonization in the Balkans and to a large extent also after (cf. above, pp. 17–18). Thus, the fact that the substratum of the Rumanian language was Proto-Albanian indicates that

---

[1] Georgiev, V., "Raporturile dintre limbile dacă, tracă şi frigiană", *Studii clasice,* 1960, pp. 39–57.

[2] C. Poghirc, ILR 1969, p. 318, note 2.

the ancestors of the Rumanians essentially lived in the same region, mainly south of Niš (the northernmost area of the Albanians).

The many correspondences between Albanian and Rumanian also regarding the Latin elements (cf. above, pp. 56, 60–63) indicate that the two populations lived together during many centuries of Roman domination. The territory they occupied in these centuries must have been adjacent to the territory where Greek was spoken. Considering the territory of the Albanians and that of the Greeks, the Vlachs must have been living in this period in parts of Macedonia, in the region of present day Prizren and Skopje, and towards the north possibly as far as the region of Niš (Naissus).

4. The significance of the Balkan Linguistic Union

Before their Romanization, the ancestors of the Vlachs spoke the same language as the Proto-Albanians, and the two populations lived together during many centuries of Roman domination in the Balkan peninsula. The most important difference between them was that while the Vlachs were entirely Latinized, the Albanians kept their language, although strongly influenced by Latin. Both populations were for centuries exposed to a strong Greek influence and, after the Slavic migrations to the Balkans in the 6th–7th centuries, the Vlachs lived in very close contact also with the Slavs.

These circumstances resulted in an impact on the language of the Vlachs which is still discernible today, perhaps nine centuries after these close contacts ceased. Among the Balkan languages, two groups may be distinguished (cf. above, p. 86): there is a CORE AREA, with languages that show most of the typical Balkan features (Balkan languages of the first grade) and another, *Randzone,* (Balkan languages of the second grade). Bulgarian belongs to those of the first grade, and, within this idiom, the Macedonian dialects are most "typical". Thus, the core area was Macedonia, adjacent to the territories of speakers of Greek as well as of Albanian, both Balkan languages of the first grade. Dalmatian, once spoken in the northwest of the Balkan peninsula, is not considered to belong to the Balkan Linguistic Union. One would believe that Serbian belongs to the most typical Balkan languages. Its speakers came to the Balkan peninsula in the same era as the ancestors of the Bulgarians, in the 6th century AD, and have been living there since that time, for about one and a half millennium. In spite of these facts, Serbian, spoken north of Macedonia, shows the features of the *Randzone,* it is a Balkan language of the second grade.

Regarding *Rumanian,* the situation in the first millennium AD must have been very different from that of today. Considering the present situation, one would not assume many Balkan features in Northern Rumanian. But this would be the case also given the theory that Rumanian was formed "on a large territory, both north and south of the Danube," – one would, in any case, expect fewer Balkanisms in Rumanian than in Serbian. Moreover, there should be regional differences in the number of typical Balkanisms, for example, such as found in

Bulgarian, with most of the Balkanisms in the Macedonian dialects and less towards the northeast. The corresponding situation in Northern Rumanian would be that the southern dialects show more or less pronounced Balkanisms, while Rumanian spoken farther to the north and the northeast, particularly north of the Danube, would contain fewer, if any, of such elements.

Such is not the case, however. Instead, in its entire present-day territory from the Timok valley in the south-west to Moldavia in the north-east, Northern Rumanian is uniform regarding its Balkan traits. Moreover, the RUMANIAN LANGUAGE BELONGS TO THE BALKAN LANGUAGES OF THE FIRST GRADE, TO THOSE IN THE CORE AREA, MACEDONIA. IT WAS CONSEQUENTLY FORMED IN (PARTS OF) MACEDONIA AND ADJACENT AREAS, in close contact with the speakers of Albanian, Greek, and Bulgarian. How exact their areas can be traced is a question for future resarch. The ancient Vlachs were a mobile population, and the picture of their territories as shown by the numerous Northen Rumanian placenames and geographical names preserved in the Serbian and Bulgarian toponymy (cf. above, pp. 29–33) in the central and northern parts of the Balkan peninsula is the result of early migrations.

Chapter VI

THE POPULATIONS NORTH OF THE LOWER DANUBE IN THE 4-th TO THE 13-th CENTURIES

1. THE DACIANS, CARPS, SARMATIANS, GOTHS, HUNS, GEPIDAE, AND AVARS

a) The free Dacians and the Carps

In the 3rd century, i.e., in the time of Roman Dacia, Carps inhabited the territory of what today is Moldavia; free Dacians lived north and northwest of Transylvania, in parts of the Banat and Muntenia.

The material culture of the Carps is mainly known from the cemeteries of the type *Poienești,* after the name of a village in the region of Vaslui. Cemeteries of this type were also found at Vârtişcoi, near Focşani, as well as in the surroundings of Roman, Bacău, etc. Isolated finds were reported from the entire Moldavia, which is said to indicate that this culture was widespread and that the Carps were numerous.[1] The predominant rite in these cemeteries is cremation.

[1] IR 1960, p. 638.

There are urns made by hand and decorated by alveolar streaks in relief, of a form characteristic of the Geto-Dacian tradition. This culture shows very powerful influences also from the Romans and particularly from the Sarmatians. The Roman influence is most noticeable in the pottery, in which new types of vases appear (e.g. amphorae), and superior techniques are used (a clay of better quality, more uniform burning, etc.). The Sarmatian influence is more intense: new forms of pottery pieces appear (e.g., vases with characteristic Alanian features), as well as new kinds of jewels (a large number of pearls made of corals from the region of the Persian Gulf). There is also a metal mirror, made after the model of Greek mirrors, highly characteristic of the Alanian remains. In some places also the funeral rites changed.

The Carps probably lived in tribal unions. Their main trade was agriculture and animal breeding. Many Roman coins as well as products from the Empire from the 3rd century were discovered in Moldavia, indicating that the Carps had economic contacts with the Romans.[1]

In the mid-third century, the Carps made several incursions into the Roman Empire. Ten hoards of coins from this period were found in Transylvania and in Oltenia, suggesting invasions. In connection with these incursions, the Romans left the *limes Transalutanus* (245 AD). Archaeological finds show that the area between the *limes* and the Olt as well as eastern Transylvania were, in the mid-third century, populated by free Dacians and Carps.[2] In the years 295–297, the Carps were defeated by the Roman army and, according to Roman historians, the whole nation was settled within the frontiers of the Empire. There are, however, records on Carps from the mid-fourth century: during the period of Constantine the Great, Carps were recorded to have attacked the East Roman Empire and according to Zosimos (IV, 34, 6; in Fontes II, p. 312):

> Theodosius repulsed the Scirs and the Carpodacians who were mixed with the Huns, and conquering them in a battle, forced them to cross the Danube and return to their places.

Most of the territories of the Carps were, towards the end of the 3rd century, occupied by the Goths, and no traces of the Poieneşti culture were found from the 4th century.

Vestiges of free Dacians who migrated to the former province were found in southern Oltenia, and at Cipău (Hung. Csapó), "punctul Gârla", in Transylvania. A cemetery of cremation dated to the second half of the 3rd century discovered there probably belonged to the western Dacians, as judged by the funeral rite and the urns. Some elements of this material culture were powerfully influenced by the Sarmatian Iazyges. The last mention of Dacians is from the 4th century, and

---

[1] Ibid., p. 639.

[2] Protase PCD 1966, p. 139; cf. above, table 9, p. 170.

their language disappeared probably in the 6th-7th centuries.[1]

b) The Sarmatians

The Sarmatians belonged to the western Iranian populations. In the 5th century BC, they lived east of the river Don and their western neighbours were the Scythians. They started to migrate westwards probably during the 3rd century BC. They were nomadic shepherds and equestrian warriors living on the steppes.

> West of the Dniester, they came into contact with the Geto-Dacian populations whose history will be influenced, for several centuries to come, by the complex and varying contacts with the newcomers. The Sarmatians infiltrated and settled in certain regions of the Carpatho–Danubian area of the Geto-Dacian tribes.[2]

The Roman poet Ovide, living in exile in Tomis (present day Constanţa) in the years 9 to 17 AD, mentioned Sarmatians crossing the Danube in a southern direction. Tacitus *(Annales,* XII, 29 and 30) reported them living in the first century AD between the Danube and the Tisza. Their presence in present day Crişana and the western parts of the Banat is proved by archaeological finds which date from the 2nd and 3rd centuries. The earliest find is from about 100 AD, left by the Sarmatian Iazyges. After the retreat of the Romans, they occupied also the central parts of the Banat. In 332, they were attacked by the Goths, but received help from Constantine the Great, who defeated the Goths. In the course of this war, the ruling class, called Sarmati Argaragantes, gave arms to their slaves (the Sarmati Limigantes). These then revolted against their outnumbered ruling class and finally succeeded in driving them out of the country.[3]

The *Roxolani,* another group of Sarmatian peoples, populated Moldavia and Muntenia starting with the first decades of the 2nd century AD. Towards the end of the 2nd century and during the first half of the 3rd, they were living in these areas in considerable numbers. They disappeared at the end of the third century, probably migrating to the present day Hungarian plain. A small number of Roaxolani tombs were found also in the Banat and in Crişana.

The *Alani,* the last wave of the Sarmatian peoples in southeastern Europe, started to migrate westwards of the Don in the first half of the 3rd century AD and reached the territories of the present day Republic of Moldavia and the province of Moldavia (Rum. Moldova) in Rumania, as well as Muntenia during the second half of that century.

In Transylvania and in Oltenia no remains of the Sarmatians were found. In other areas of present day Rumania, they are numerous: Sarmatian tombs were

---

[1]Pippidi Dict ist veche 1976, p. 218.

[2]IR 1960, pp. 671–672.

[3]Ammianus Marcellianus, XVII, 12, 19; cf. Pippidi Dict ist veche 1976, p. 522.

discovered at 134 different sites.[1] The funeral rite was inhumation. The tombs contain remains of men, women and children. In the tombs of women, jewels were often laid down and in those of children, bells of bronze. Of weapons, there are short swords and daggers. Their pottery, besides typically Sarmatian forms, contain also pieces of the Dacian and of the provincial Roman style. Very characteristic of these tombs is the circular or fronto-occipital deformation of the cranium by a bandage applied in childhood. This was regarded a sign of beauty and distinction. This rite was not practized by the Iazyges.

The cultural influence of the Sarmatian peoples on what is considered the material culture of the Dacians and the Carps was quite powerful. The two populations intermingled to such a high extent that sometimes "objects specific only of the Carps or only of the Sarmatians become cultural assets shared by both peoples."[2]

The Sarmatians left a considerable number of placenames, handed down to the Rumanians by Slavs. One group of these peoples, the Alanians, still live in the Caucasus; the present day *Osset*-s.

c) The Goths

The Goths belonged to the eastern branch of the Old Germanic populations. They migrated from the area around the estuary of the Vistula in a southern and southeastern direction; from the second half of the second century AD, they were living north and east of Dacia Traiana.

The first battle between the Goths and the Roman army took place during the reign of Emperor Caracalla, probably in 213–214 AD, and was followed by many attacks led by the Goths during the 3rd century. From the end of that century, the Goths were divided into two branches: Ostrogoths and Visigoths (eastern and western Goths, respectively). The Visigoths migrated in large numbers into the areas west of the Pruth and their material remains, from the end of the third and from the 4th century were found in Moldavia, Muntenia, Oltenia, and Transylvania. The occupation of these territories by the Goths created a new ethnic configuration. The settlements and the cemeteries of the type Poieneşti in Moldavia, attributed to the Carps, as well as those of the type Bucureşti-Militari in Muntenia were abandoned at the end of the 3rd century. The country was populated and dominated by the Goths and was, accordingly, called *Gothia.*

In southwestern Russia, the material culture left by the Goths is known as the *Cerneachov-culture*, after a cemetery at the river Dnieper. In Rumania, it is named, after a cemetery in the valley of the Mureş, *Sântana de Mureş culture*. It covers a large territory, from the Dnieper to central Transylvania and from the region of the rivers Pripet and Bug to the lower Danube. This territory was dominated by the Goths.

---

[1]Pippidi Dict ist veche 1976, p. 520.

[2]Ibid., p. 522.

A large number of settlements and cemeteries left by the Goths were discovered and studied after the second World War. In Moldavia, 150 settlements are known and in Muntenia, 100.[1] They are also numerous in the regions of the upper Olt, the Târnava Mare and Târnava Mică (Hung. Nagyküküllő and Kisküküllő) and the Mureş, in Transylvania. The settlements were often built on the sun-lit shores of the rivers and were not fortified.

About 1500 tombs of the type Cerneachov-Sântana de Mureş are known. In the vicinity of the village Sântana de Mureş (Hung. Marosszentanna), 74 were excavated. The predominant funeral rite was inhumation, and the tombs were arranged in a north-south direction. Such tombs are attributed to the Goths and the Sarmatians, while those of cremation (the type found at Târgşor–Olteni) probably belonged to the Taifals. In certain places, also earthenware of the Dacian style was found (in the tombs of the type Târgşor–Gherăseni).[2] No weapons were put in the tombs but often food, for example, eggs.

Most of what remained from this culture is earthenware. Very characteristic are the complex reverberating kilns in which earthenware of high quality, both red and grey, was produced. The wheel driven by foot was used in the making of pottery pieces. As shown by finds of coulters and sickles, the inhabitants also pursued agriculture and the raising of animals, as well as handicraft.

In the territory of Rumania, this culture ended at the end of the 4th century, when the Huns conquered large parts of eastern Europe.

d) The Huns

In the 3rd century BC, the Huns lived in parts of northern China, in the present day provinces Sansi, Sensi, and Hopei. After having been attacked by the Chinese, they migrated westwards and were living for a long period of time in the region of the Volga. In 375 AD, they attacked the Goths in Moldavia and Muntenia and occupied in a short time all the territory formerly dominated by the Goths.

The Huns are recorded [3] to have been living in Dacia and in Pannonia, together with other populations subjugated by them. Thus, Iordanes wrote in Getica, 226: ..."the provinces of Dacia and Pannonia, in which in that period the Huns lived with several subjugated populations."[4] There is a record of their mixing with the Carps (Zosimos, cf. above, p. 259).

Archaeological finds of Hunnish material remains (jewels, kettles, etc.) are known from the valleys of the Pruth, the Buzău, and the Danube, from the surroundings of the towns Braşov (Hung. Brassó), and Roman, etc. No Hunnish

---

[1]Pippidi Dict Ist Veche 1976, p. 542.

[2]Ibid., p. 543.

[3]An eye-witness' report from the Hunnish Empire and from the court of Attila, the Hunnish king in the mid-fifth century, is found among the writings of Priscus Panites (The History of the Goths); cf. Fontes II, pp. 246–299.

[4]Cf. Fontes II, p. 428.

cemeteries, only isolated tombs were found in the territory of Rumania.

The power of the Huns was at its height in the mid-fifth century. In 451, the West Roman Empire defeated them in the battle at Catalaunum (near Troyes in France). Attila died in 453. In the following year, a coalition led by the Gepidae defeated the Huns at the river Nedao in Pannonia, which marks the end of the Hunnish power in Europe.

e) The Gepidae

The Gepidae, a branch of the Old Germanic peoples who at the beginning of the first millennium AD were living along the shores of the Baltic Sea, started to migrate southward in the mid-third century. They settled in the region of the upper course of the Tisza (Rum. Tisa). Most of them remained in their places during the Hunnish domination and regained their independence in 453. In 471, they occupied the town Sirmium at the shore of the Sava and made it the residence of their kings. In the following century, they ruled over a large territory from the Sava to the eastern Carpathian mountains. In 567, the Avars, in coalition with the Longobards, defeated the Gepidae and abolished their kingdom. Gepidae are, however, mentioned in historical records even later. Theophylaktos Simokattes related that Priskos, the Byzantine general, when fighting the Avars in the Banat in 601 AD, found three Gepidic villages there.[1] According to Theophanes,[2] Priskos defeated the Avars and collected 9.000 prizoners, of whom 3000 were Avars, 800 Slavs, 3.200 Gepidae, and 2.000 "barbarians". Archaeological excavations revealed material remains of the Gepidae which date as late as from the mid-seventh century.

Gepidia extended, according to Iordanes, from the plains between the Danube and the Tisza to the east, as far as to the river "Flutausis" (probably the Olt).[3] This record was confirmed by archaeological finds. Two periods may be distinguished: the first is that of the Gepidic kingdom (475–567 AD). Characteristic are the settlements with large dwelling places with cottages around (Moreşti–Malomfalva, Şeica Mică –Kissejk, Porumbenii Mici–Kisgalambfalva) and the cemeteries of inhumation, with rows of tombs (Cluj–Cardoş, Lechinţa de Mureş–Maroslekence, Moreşti–Malomfalva, Someşeni–Szamosfalva, etc.). There are many objects typical of the Gepidic settlements, such as combs, fibulae with 3 or 5 buttons, clasps, sometimes decorated by the pattern of an eagle-head, arms, sickles, *fusaiol*-s (cf. above, p. 168, note 3), earthenware made on a wheel or by hand, etc. Weapons are rare in the tombs. The orientation of the tombs in a west to east direction and certain Christian symbols, for example on a breast-plate found at Cluj–Someşeni suggest the presence of Christianity at the end of the 5th century and in the 6th. The first period ended in 567 AD, when the Gepidic

---

[1]Theophylaktos Simokattes, *Historiae*, VIII, 3; *Fontes* II, p. 548.

[2]II, 282, 1 (ed. Boor); quoted by Tamás, L., *Rómaiak, románok és oláhok Dácia Trajánában,* 1935, p. 83.

[3]Iordanes, *Getica*, 33 and 74; *Fontes* II, pp. 410–412 and 418.

kingdom was defeated by the Avars. In the following, second period, the Gepidic material remains show a different character. This period is characterized by large cemeteries with hundreds of tombs (Band–Mezőbánd, Bratei–Baráthely, Noşlac – Nagylak). The fibulae disappear, there are sets of belts, more lances and bows; inlay of iron with silver *(Tauschierung)* was used; among earthenware pieces, pear-formed vases dominate. New funeral rites appear: horses are being put into the tombs. In this period, the Gepidae were ruled by the Avars and a part of the new material culture was probably induced by Avar influence.

The Gepidae pursued agriculture and raised cattle; workrooms of silversmiths and of weaving were discovered at Band and at Moreşti, respectively.[1]

f) The Avars

Probably coming from Mongolia, the Avars occupied the steppes of southern Russia some time before the 6th century. In 558, they sent an envoy to Byzantium, offering their services in exchange for certain territories and for money. In 567, the Avars attacked the Gepidae, defeated them and occupied their country. During the second half of the 6th century and the first three decades of the 7th, Byzantium suffered many invasions from the Avars, who reduced Sirmium after a siege of three years. In alliance with the Persians, the Avars laid siege to Constnatinople but were driven back.

At the height of their power, the Avars reigned over a vast territory between the Alps, the Adriatic Sea and the Black Sea. The main sources concerning the ethnic composition of the Avar Empire are the writings of Byzantine authors, who recorded Avars, Gepidae, and Slavs. Several successfull uprisings of Slavic tribes are recorded, for example the revolt of the Vends in 623.

A large number of Avar settlements and cemeteries were found, particularly in Hungary. Fortifications are described in historical records. Best known are the cemeteries: more than 30.000 tombs were excavated. Characteristic of the material in this tombs is, among other things, that the waist-belt replaces the fibula of earlier periods. This is explained by the fact that the Avars were equestrians and a waist-belt is more effective in holding the clothes together when riding. The men were laid down in the tombs with their horses, arms and horse-trappings. Up to the end of the 7th century, the art reflected by these objects was being characterized by geometrical ornaments pressed upon a print. It shows a certain degree of Byzantine influence. After a transition period of about 40 years, i.e., after 720 AD, the motives changed. Figures of plants and of animals were used more frequently and they were cast and decorated. This new art shows Asian features. The cause of this change is probably that a new population coming from the east took the place of the earlier one.[2]

---

[1] Cf., for instance, Pippidi Dict Ist Veche 1976, pp. 79, 294–295, 415.

[2] Cf., for instance, IR 1960, p. 720. According to Gy. László, this new population may have been Hungarian: László, Gy., *Vértesszöllőstől Pusztaszerig. Élet a Kárpát-medencében a magyar államalapításig,* 1974, p. 214.

Their centre of power being in the Great Hungarian Plain, the Avars penetrated into Transylvania along the valleys of the great rivers. Archaeological remains were described from Dumbrăveni (Erzsébetváros), Corund (Korond), Tg. Secuiesc (Kézdivásárhely), etc., as well as from the Banat and from Crişana. Specific Avar objects from around 700 AD were also found along the Mureş and some of its tributaries at Aiud (Nagyenyed), Gâmbaş (Marosgombás), Teiuş (Tövis), and Câmpia Turzii (Aranyosgyéres), mostly in tombs. These tombs also contain objects of the Byzantine style, particularly fibulae and ear-rings.

Thus, according to archaeological evidence, the Avars populated the Banat, Crişana, and parts of Transylvania. Their number in Transylvania does not seem to have been very high, but this is difficult to estimate. As in other territories, they probably lived together with Slavic tribes.

The power of the Avars was broken in 795–796, when the Franks destroyed the residence of the *kaganat* (the *hring)*. The chronicle of Nestor affirms that all Avars died, but it is known that part of them retired to the territories east of the Tisza whence the Franks did not follow them. The last reliable mention of Avars in Central Europe is from the year 822, and from 873 there is a record of uncertain character. However,

> ...elements of Avar material culture continue to exist in the course of the 9th century AD but it is not known whether these indicate the real existence of Avars or only the preservation of some cultural influence.[1]

2. THE SLAVS.

A number of Avars were still living in the eastern parts of the Carpathian basin when the Hungarians occupied the territory. The most important population, however, who lived there immediately before and also at the beginning of the Hungarian presence were the Slavs. The same applies to the Rumanians in the extra-Carpathian areas and in south-western Transylvania and parts of the Banat. The material culture of the Slavs in their original areas is quite well known (the *Praga–Penkovka,* respectively the *Praga–Korčak* culture). Differences between them – western, eastern and southern Slavic features, different material remains and variations in language – appeared successively during the centuries following their southward migration. Written records about them are scanty and also the archaeological finds are often difficult to interpret.

a) The Slavs in the extra-Carpathian regions of Rumania

From their territories north and northeast of the Carpathian mountains, Slavic tribes started to migrate southward during the 5th century. The defence system

[1] IR 1960, p. 717.

of the Gepidic kingdom is considered to have impeded their penetration in masses into Transylvania during most of the 6th century.

According to Procopios, the regions along the lower Danube were in the 6th and 7th centuries inhabited by Sclavinae, Antes, and Huns (probably Bulgarians). Moldavia and northeastern Muntenia were populated by the Slavic tribe of the Antes. The frontiers between the different tribes were, however, not stable and many battles were fought.

The Slavs undertook a series of incursions across the Danube into the East Roman Empire, reaching as far as to the suburbs of Byzantium. After 562, when the Avars occupied the area of what is today the Great Hungarian Plain, they extended their sphere of influence also over Oltenia and Muntenia. In 579, Emperor Tiberius Constantine succeeded to incite the Avars against the Sclavines in Muntenia and Baian's great army of 60.000 equestrian warriors was transported with the help of Byzantium along the shores of the Danube to Dobrogea and from there on Byzantine ships to the northern shore, where it attacked the Slavs. These hid in the mountains and in the forests and the Avars had to retire. Apart from episodes of this kind, the Avars and the Slavs were most of the time allies in attacking the Byzantine Empire.

In the course of time, many Slavs migrated to the Empire; for example there are records about nine tribes who settled there in the early 7th century. As a consequence of this, their number north of the lower Danube decreased.[1]

The oldest archaeological remains left behind by Slavs in the extra-Carpathian regions of present day Rumania were discovered at Suceava–Şipot in Modavia.[2] These are rectangular huts with hearths marked out by stones. The earthenware was handmade and shows features of the earthenware from the Zhitomir area. As judged by a "fingered" fibula, the oldest stratum is from the second half of the 6th century.

The most important of this type of finds is the large cemetery of cremation discovered at Sărata–Monteoru, with more than 1500 tombs. Characteristic of this culture is the "fingered" fibula with 5 buttons. The earthenware is primitive, hand-made, but from a later date, also pieces made with the help of a primitive wheel are found. No weapons were laid down in these tombs. These material remains belong to the eastern Slavic culture named Zhitomir–Korčak, known from the regions along the middle course of the Dnieper.[3] The inhabitants were probably the Antes. Finds of the same type were made in Muntenia and Oltenia.

Many complexes of settlemens without fortifications (called *silişti)* from the 7th century were found in Moldavia, at Dorobanţi (near Iaşi), Hlincea, and Suceava. Two or three huts are grouped together. They contain kilns of stone or of clay and earthenware made by hand or with some instrument. Vases of a similar type were found near Bucharest and at Lişcoţeanca (near Galaţi). This

---

[1]Pippidi Dict Ist Veche 1976, p. 546.

[2]IR 1960, p. 733.

[3]Ibid., p. 734.

culture is probably a continuation of the Zhitomir-Korčak culture of the 6th century. It is called the *Hlincea-Luka Raikoveţ kaia* culture. It extended from the Dnieper to the Forestrian Carpathians. In the course of time it developed into a new phase, with a new type of hearths and pottery made by a primitive wheel and decorated by horizontal lines and wave-lines, alongside with the pottery made by hand. This culture was considerably uniform:

> The identity of the complexes in Moldavia [...] with those in the regions west of the Dnieper proves that in the 8th and 9th centuries, the Slavic tribes in central and northern Moldavia developed in close contact with the eastern Slavic tribes who lived between the Dnieper and the Forestrian Carpathians.[1]

On the plains of Muntenia, another Slavic culture was identified, which dates from the 6th–7th centuries. In this Ipoteşti–Cândeşti–Ciurel culture, the participation of a Dacian element is assumed.[2]

The period of the 9th and 10th centuries is dominated by the Balkan–Danube culture, which extended over a large territory from the Balkan mountains across the Danube over a broad strip of territory through the southern halves of Muntenia and Moldavia and towards the northeast north of the Black Sea. In Oltenia it is weakly represented. This culture is divided into four phases, with local variations. It is correlated to the expansion of the Bulgarian state north of the lower Danube during the 9th century.

b) The Slavs in Transylvania

What is known about the Slavs in Transylvania derives mostly from archaeology. Slavic tribes came to this territory probably as early as during the period of the Gepidae, in the 5th century; a number of them were apparently settled there by the Avars in the 6th century. The first specific Slavic object, a *klebec* (a kind of baking-plate) was found in the Avar cemetery found at Band (Hung. Mezőbánd). It dates from the period between 600–630 AD.[3] These Slavs came probably from their original homeland at the beginning of the 7th century to the upper course of the Mureş. Approximately in the same period migrated other Slavic tribes to the territory of present day Covasna county, where an unusually high number of placenames and river names of Slavic origin are still found in the Hungarian (Szekler) toponymy (such as *Csernáton,* cf. Slavic *černa* ′black′, or the river name Feketeügy, translated from Slavic *černa voda,* etc.). In the 7th century, the Slavs populated also the valleys of the rivers Târnava (Hungarian Küküllő), and the name of these rivers was transferred to Rumanian

---

[1]Ibid., p. 741.

[2]According to C. Daicoviciu, this is a "mixed, Slavo-Dacian (not Slavo-Daco-Roman) culture" (Dacica 1969, p. 551).

[3]István Bóna in Köpeczi, B. (red.), *Erdély története* I, 1986, p. 179.

and Transylvanian Saxon (Kokel); the Hungarians translated it. Slavic cemeteries with the rite of cremation appeared in Transylvania during the 7th century. The largest of these is that found at Bratei, cemetery No 2, which started to be used in the early 8th century. There, 210 tombs of cremation were found. Avar remains include 34 tombs of inhumation, 2 tombs with horses, as well as objects typical of the Avars (stirrups, bridles, decorations of girdles of cast bronze, vases, etc.) are found together with material remains of the Slavs. Most of the Slavic cemeteries in Transylvania show the rite of cremation, but a small number of the tombs contain bones. The rite of cremation was used also in the large cemeteries found at Nuşfalău (Szilágynagyfalu) and Someşeni (Szamosfalva). As shown by the style of some metal objects, these cemeteries date from the period between the early 8th century and the end of the 9th century. A number of objects show analogies in tombs found in present day northern Hungary and southern Slovakia (Érsekújvár, Slovakian Nové Zámky), Győr, Komárom, etc. According to István Bóna (in *Erdély története* I p. 187–188), the Slavs living here came from the northeast. IR 1960 considered, on the basis of metal objects of the type Keszthely (western Hungary), wooden buckets of the same type as those found in Hungary and in Moravia, pottery decorations (bands of horizontal and wave-lines) typical of the Slavs who lived along the middle course of the Danube, that the population here belonged to western Slavic groups.[1]

c) The Bulgarian domination in southern Transylvania

The Bulgarian state, founded in 679 AD, increased its power in the 8th century. Khan Krum (802–814) defetated the Avars and extended the frontiers of Bulgaria in the north of the Balkan peninsula, to the frontiers of the Frankish Empire, which then ruled over Pannonia. Khan Omurtag (827–831) occupied Sirmium and eastern Slavonia, some areas along the Tisza and in southern Transylvania. The Bulgarians controlled then the exploitation of salt in Transylvania, as indicated by the record in *Annales Fuldenses* a. 892: King Arnulf sent envoys to Vladimir, the Bulgarian chief, asking him not to permit the sending of salt to the Moravians.[2]

Archaeological remains of Bulgarians from the 9th–10th centuries were found in the region of the middle course of the Mureş in southern Transylvania. In the cemetery found at Blândiana (Hung. Maroskarna), pottery pieces of the type the Bulgarians produced along the lower Danube were found. Material remains left by a Bulgarian population were found in a territory 30–40 km long on both shores along the middle course of the Mureş.[3] Another Bulgarian cemetery found at Ciumbrud (Hung. Csombord) dates from the 9th–10th

---

[1] IR 1960, p. 744.

[2] István Bóna, in Erdély története I, 1986, p. 190.

[3] Ibid., p. 192.

centuries. These settlements were most probably created after 830 AD, when the Bulgarians, under Omurtag, conquered several territories north of the Danube. In this area, there were a number of salt-mines, exploited by the Bulgarians. The name of former Apulum: *Belgrad,* was most probably given by this population. The Rumanians borrowed it *(Bălgrad)*, while the Hungarians translated its sense *(Fehérvár* 'white castle'). In the 9th century, the differentiation of the Slavs was at a level which permits to state that most of Transylvania was, in that period, inhabited by eastern and western Slavs. Bulgarians lived in the south. It must be stated, however, that Slavs migrated to Transylvania also later (from Russia, Slovakia, the Ukraine, Bulgaria, etc). These later settlements received also Slavic names or were named after the respective population *(Orosz, Tót, Cseh,* etc.)

The Bulgarian state reached its largest territorial expansion during the reign of Czar Simeon the Great (893–927). During the reign of his son, Peter (927–969), the power of Bulgaria declined. The Bulgarian rule over the territories north of the lower Danube ended during the first decades of the 10th century.

d) The question of non-Slavic remains from the Slavic period

"Daco-Romans" were assumed to participate in several Slavic cultures. However, it can easily be shown that these hypotheses do not stand up to critical examination. C. Daicoviciu refuted, in an article published in 1967,[1] several such claims. Thus, Panaitescu assumed (1964) Daco-Romans during the 6th–9th centuries among the Slavic cultures of Muntenia and Moldavia. Daicoviciu pointed out that this assumption was based on a wrong translation of the text Panaitescu referred to. The Ipoteşti–Cândeşti–Ciurel culture is, according to Daicoviciu, Slavo-Dacian, NOT Slavo-Daco-Rumanian, and Daicoviciu questioned also the participation of Daco-Romans in the Moreşti-Bandu-Noşlac culture. About the Dridu culture, Daicoviciu showed that it is of Bulgarian origin, whith considerable influence from Byzantium, from Moesia (provincial Roman traits) as well as from the territories north of the Black Sea.

The idea that the Ipoteşti–Cândeşti–Ciurel culture shows "a powerful Daco-Roman component" has been put forward again.[2] The pottery shows Slavic forms, but a certain form made by hand "reminds of the Dacian forms and reflects the indigenous tradition" and the earthenware made by a wheel shows the features of the Roman–Byzantine earthenware.[3] This is an example of the ambiguous use of the terms "Daco-Roman" and "autochthonous" ("indigenous"), cf. above, p. 199–200. Dacian style and influence from Byzantium do not, of course, indicate a Latin-speaking population.

IR Compendiu 1974 (p. 84), asserts that the Balkan–Danube culture (called

---

[1] Daicoviciu, C., "Der Ursprung des rumänischen Volkes im Lichte der neuesten Forschungen und Ausgrabungen", *Forschungen zur Volks- und Landeskunde*, Hermannstadt (Sibiu), 1967, 2, pp. 5–19; in Dacica 1970, pp. 544–558.

[2] IR Compendiu 1974, p. 77.

[3] Pippidi Dict Ist Veche 1976, p. 348.

"Carpatho–Balkan") may have belonged to several peoples, Bulgarians as well as Proto-Rumanians:

> The Carpatho–Balkan culture, extending over both shores of the Danube, may be attributed, consequently, south of the river, to the Slavo–Bulgarians, because there, the Slavo–Bulgarian ethnic component dominated, while in the north, between the Danube and the Carpathians, it may be considered Proto-Rumanian, because here, the predominant element was Romance. In any case, it constitutes the stage directly before the really Rumanian culture (*verigă imediat anterioară culturii româneşti propriu-zise*).

This change of opinion as compared to the 1969 edition, where this culture was stated to have been Slavo-Bulgarian (p. 106), is not, as seen from the above passage, warranted by new discoveries but is motivated by the assumption that the "dominating element" north of the Danube was Romance. (In the preceeding passage, the record of Anonymus about Vlachs in Transylvania is mentioned.) A more adequate method would be to draw conclusions concerning the "dominating element" from the archaeological remains, not inversely.

e) The Slavs and the placenames of Rumania
Placenames of Slavic origin

Slavs were living in the territory of present day Rumania from the 6th century until the 12th–13th centuries. In Byzantine chronicles, the territories north of the lower Danube were, after the 5th century, designated *Sclavinia* (Σκλαβηνια). The early Slavic migrants found most probably Gepidae, Avars (many Slavic tribes were brought to the territory by the Avars), and possibly Dacians in several places. All these peoples disappeared in the course of time in the masses of the Slavs.

A placename or geographical name based on a Slavic word does not automatically imply a Slavic namegiving. In case the word in question exists (or existed once) in the Rumanian language, the placename or geographical name may have been given by Rumanians. The number of names of Slavic origin, given by Slavs and borrowed by the Rumanians is very high in the entire country. According to the Slavic language they derive from, these names are divided into four groups: (1) an eastern Slavic (Ukrainian) in the northeast, (2) a small area of western South Slavic in the southwest, (3) an eastern South Slavic (Bulgarian) area in the south (the largest of the Slavic areas), and (4) a northwestern area with special features.[1]

The sound pattern of these names is of a more recent date as compared to the placenames of Slavic origin in Greece. They show:

---

[1] Petrovici, E., *Studii de dialectologie şi toponimie*, 1970, pp. 77–78; Rosetti ILR 1968, p. 328 (omitted in the 1986 edition).

(1) Metathesis of the groups *tart, talt* – Bălgrad, Predeal, etc.

(2) The *y* > *i* change – *Bistra* (older form in Slavic: *bystrь).*

(3) The disappearance of the semi-vowels: *Crasna* (older form in Slavic: *krasьna), Ocna* (*okьno*).

(4) Slavic *ǫ* corresponds always to Rumanian *în, îm.*

Since these sound patterns appeared in Slavic in or after the 9th century, the Slavic placenames and names of rivers and streams in Rumania cannot have been borrowed by the Rumanian language earlier than that century. In reality, the borrowings occurred much later – that Slavic *ǫ* always corresponds to Rumanian *în, îm* indicates that names containing this sound were borrowed EARLIEST during the 12th century (cf. above, p. 100).

Examples of placenames and geographical names of Slavic origin in Rumania

Bălgrad (at present Alba Iulia) – Old Slavic *bělŭ* + *gradŭ* ′white′ + ′castle′, translated by the Hungarians: Fehérvár. The town (on the place of former Roman Apulum) was the residence of the Hungarian chief Gyula and is in Hungarian called Gyulafehérvár. The modern Rumanian name is modelled after this.

Bistreţ, Bistriţa, in many areas – Old Slavic *bystrĭcu* ′fast′.

Cerna, Cernişoara, in many areas – Old Slavic *čьrna* ′black′.

Craiova, in several areas, also the central town of Oltenia – Old Slavic *kralĭ* ′king′+ the Slavic suffix *-ova.*

Crasna, in many areas – Old Slavic *krasĭna* (*rěka*) ′beautifull′.

Dâmboviţa, Dâmbova – Slavic *dǫbъ* ′oak′.

Ialomiţa – Old Slavic *jalovica, jalov* ′unfertile, barren′.

Ilfov – Bulgarian *elhov.*

Moldova (ancient forms: Moldua, Mulduva, the name of the province Moldavia in the east of Rumania) – Slavic *mold-* (*molid* + the Slavic suffix *-ov, -ova*).

Novac, in many areas – Old Slavic *novaku.*

Ocna, in many areas – Old Slavic *okno* ′pit′.

Prahova – Old Slavic *praxu,* Serbo-Croatian Praxovo (*praxъ* ′dust′).

Predeal – Old Slavic *prědělŭ,* Bulgarian *predel* ′mountain pass′.

Snagov – Old Slavic *sněgŭ,* Bulgarian Snegovo.

Târnava – Old Slavic *trŭnŭ* ′spine, thorn′.

Zlatna – Old Slavic *zlata,* Bulgarian *zlatna* ′gold′.

As pointed out by Popović,[1] it is characteristic of the density of the Slavic placenames in Rumania that the same name often appears in many different areas throughout the country: e.g., Crasna in the counties of Craiova, Ploieşti, Bacău, Suceava, and Iaşi, Ocna in Piteşti, Bucureşti, Ploieşti, and Bacău, etc. Moreover, in many cases, there are several derivations from the same Slavic root: from *čern* ′black′, there are Rumanian Cerna, Cernaia, Cernat, Cernădia, Cernica, Cernofca, and Cernişoara; from *dǫ bъ* ′oak′, Dâmbul, Dâmboiul, Dâmboviţa,

[1]Popović GSKS 1960, pp. 117–118.

Dâmbovicioara, and Dâmboviceanul, etc.

Another very important aspect is that the Slavic placenames and names of rivers and streams occur all over the country:

> ... the placenames of Slavic origin which we meet everywhere, regardless of the geographical situation of the Rumanian provinces and of the physical nature of the place in question.[1]

f) Ancient names of rivers

In contrast to the Balkan peninsula, where ancient placenames, borrowed by Latin and later from Latin by Slavic are still in use, north of the lower Danube, only the names of the more important rivers were preserved. While their etymology is still debated, the sound pattern of most of these names indicates that they were transferred to Rumanian via Slavic and, in Transylvania, via Hungarian or Slavic.

> Among the old names of streams in the territory north of the Danube, some are considered Thracian; the sound pattern of the Rumanian form of some of these names indicates, however, that they were handed down to the Rumanian-speaking populations by the Slavs who, in their turn, borrowed them from the ancient populations of the territories north of the Danube.[2]

A difficulty in explaning these names is that they were recorded by Greek and Roman authors often in different forms and the original forms used by the local populations may have been distorted in this process.

Mureş (Hungarian *Maros,* Serbian *Morišь).* In Greek texts, it is written Μαρις, Μαρισος, Μορησης; Iordanes used the form *Marisia.* It may be of Thracian origin, with the sense of ´swampy, boggy´. The transition of *a* to *o* may have taken place in Slavic or in Hungarian and the Rumanians may have borrowed the form *Moreš.*

Olt (Greek Αλουτας; Latin *Alutas, Alutus, Aittus, Alutum;* Hungarian *Olt,* Transylvanian Saxon *Alt).* A river named *Alutus* (probably of Iranian origin) which flows into the Caspian Sea was described by Ptolemaios. Initial *a* appears in all ancient forms and must be considered as certain; its change to *o* occurred most probably in Slavic (cf. ancient *Altina* in Dobrogea, now *Oltina).* Rumanian *Olt* was thus most probably borrowed from Slavic.

Someş (not recorded in ancient documents; *Samus* is mentioned as the name of a settlement, and also *regio Ansamensium;*[3] Hungarian *Szamos).* If the original form contained *a* , the *a* > *o* change is tyipcal of Slavic and the Rumanian form was borrowed from Slavic.

---

[1] Iordan Nume de locuri 1952, p. VII.

[2] Rosetti ILR 1986, p. 210.

[3] ILR 1969, p. 358.

Ompoi, Ampoi, Hungarian *Ompoly*. Ancient attestation uncertain *(Ampellum?* ILR 1969 p. 356 refers to Dacian *Ampee*, CIL III, 14507, 1308, 1293.) The Rumanian sound pattern suggests that this name was borrowed by the Rumanian language from Hungarian, which borrowed it from the Slavs.

Timiş (In the texts of Ptolemaios and Herodotos Τίβισις, Τιβίσκος; Hungarian *Temes*, Serbian *Tamiš)* derives from Slavic or from Hungarian.

Dunăre, with the stress on the first syllable, (German *Donau*, Hungarian *Duna*, Serbocroatian *Dunav*, Bulgarian *Dunava*, 'Danube'.) The name may be connected with Avestic *danu* 'fluid, mist, dew', but also Iranian, Celtic, Thracian, Dacian and Cuman origin has been assumed. In Greek texts, it is written 'Λανούβιος, Λανούϊος, Λάνουβις, Λάνουσις; in Latin, *Danubius, Danuuius*. A different ancient name of the Danube (east of the Iron Gate) is *Istros* (Ιστρος). The first part of the Rumanian name *(Dună-)* was handed down to the Rumanians by Slavs, as shown by certain sound changes characteristic of Slavic.[1] In its entirety, however, *Dunăre* cannot be explained from any of the known names of the river.[2] Assumed Dacian etymologies are as uncertain as other attempts at explaining Rumanian words from Dacian lexical elements.[3] *Dunăre* does not continue ancient *Danubius* or *Istros*. The ancestors of the Rumanians had apparently no name for this river before they borrowed its Slavic form, which confirms the conclusion drawn also from other circumstances, namely, that they did not live in the valley of the Danube.

Pruth (in the Middle Ages, *Alanus Fluvius*). The Avestic word *peretav* means 'shallow place, ford; bridge'. The Rumanian form derives from Slavic.

Iaşi (placename). Besides being the name of the central town of Moldavia, this name appears also in several other parts of the country: *Gura Iaşului, Valea Iaşului, Iaşi* (a village in the county of Gorj). It reproduces the name given after the 9th century to the Alanians, *As*. Avestic *asav* 'fast, rapid'. Also this name was borrowed by Rumanian from Slavic.

3.THE HUNGARIANS IN TRANSYLVANIA AND IN THE BANAT

a) History

The Hungarian occupation of Transylvania started in the early 10th century. Constantinus Porphyrogenitus (905–959), the erudite scholar and historian, whose works possess a special documentary value,[4] recorded in his *De*

---

[1]Rosetti 1986, pp. 217–218.

[2]ILR 1969, p. 357.

[3]A Dacian **Donaris* has been proposed to explain *Dunăre*, sometimes presented as if it really did appear in ancient records, which makes it necessary to point out that such a name is not attested. For details, cf. G. Schramm, "Der rumänische Name der Donau", in *Dacoromania* I, 1973, pp. 228–236; cf. also Vékony, *Dákok, rómaiak, románok*, 1989, pp. 237-238.

[4]Cf. Fontes II, p. 657.

administrando Imperio, written about 945, that in the eastern part of the present day Hungarian Plain and in the Banat, Hungarians were living in the 10th century:

> The Turks (=Hungarians) were driven away by the Petchenegs, they moved and settled in the country which they inhabit even now. In those places, there are some old vestiges: the first is the bridge of Trajan, at the gate of Turcia (=Hungary), then there is Belgrade, at a distance of three days′ journey from this bridge; in Belgrade there is also a tower of the sacred Emperor Constantine the Great; farther on the river, there is Sirmium, at two days′ journey from Belgrade, and farther away, there is great Moravia, not Christianized, which was devastated by the Turks (=Hungarians) and was earlier ruled by Svatopluk.
>
> (40, 35–44): These are the places worthy of mentioning [...] along the river Istros. Those inside of these, where there are Turk (=Hungarian) settlements all over, were named after the rivers which flow there. These rivers are: *Timisis* (Τιμήσης), *Tutis* (Τούτης) , *Morisis* (Μορήσης), *Krisos* (Κρίσος), and the *Tisza* (Τίτζα). The eastern neighbours of the Turks (=Hungarians) are the Bulgarians, separated from them by the river Istros (῎Ιστρος) also called Danubios (Λανούβιος). To the west, there are the Franks, and to the south, the Croatians.[1]

The only name in this text which was not identifed is the Tutis.

b) Archaeology

The Hungarians′ tombs are typical: the warriors were laid down with their weapons and their horse, often only its head and leg bones. From the entire Carpathian basin, such cemeteries were excavated at 550 sites.[2] Also the tombs of the ′common people′ (Hungarian *köznép*) show characteristic Oriental features. Such cemeteries, which date from the 10th century, are very numerous in the eastern Hungarian plain and in the Banat; in Transylvania, they were found in the valley of the *Kisszamos* (Rum. *Someşul Mic),* the rivers *Küküllő* (Rum. *Târnava)* and *Maros (Mureş),* as well as in the south-eastern corner of the Szekler territory (mainly present day Covasna county).[3] IR vol. II p. 47 listed *Biharea-Oradea, Şiclău, Cluj, Gâmbaş* and *Lopadea.*[4] The Hungarian tombs in *Kolozsvár (Cluj), Zápolya-utca* (Rum. *Str. Dostoievski*), were excavated long ago, but not far from that site, another Hungarian cemetery from the 10th century was

---

[1]Constantinus Porphyrogenitus, *De administrando Imperio,* 40, 25–44; in Fontes II, p. 666.

[2]István Bóna, in Köpeczi, B., (red.) *Erdély rövid története*, 1989, pp. 117–119.

[3]A map showing these sites, as well as settlements named after ancient Hungarian tribes, Hungarian fortresses etc. in Transylvania in the 10th century is found in *Erdély rövid története*, 1989, p. 108.

[4]Four of these Rumanian placenames were borrowed from Hungarian: Marosgombás, Siklód, Várad, Magyarlapád; see below. The name of Cluj, German Klausenburg, Hungarian Kolozsvár derives most probably from Slavic.

discovered in the 1980s during excavations conducted with the aim of exploring a Roman cemetery from the 2nd–3rd centuries. According to *Erdély rövid története*, p. 123, about 30 tombs were unearthed at this site, of which about 5 contained the remains of a horse. A third ancient Hungarian cemetery was probably situated about 600 m from this site.

c) Placenames

The archaeological remains give only a vague picture of the situation in those times. The finds are often made by chance and planned excavations are and have been for many decades aimed mainly at finding material remains of a Roman population. A large number of ancient Hungarian placenames give a better picture of the areas where Hungarians were living in the 10th, 11th, and 12th centuries. Of these, we present here only one special group, those formed with the suffix *–d*. Originally a suffix forming diminutives, *–d* in Ancient Hungarian was often used to form placenames:

> The study of the distribution in space of the Hungarian placenames with the archaic suffix *–d* [...] indicates what parts of Transylvania were conquered and organized in the Hungarian feudal system until the 12th century, the last century in which this suffix was used.[1]

These areas are shown on map No. 10, p. 277. As indicated by these ancient placenames, a large part of the area within the northwestern and southern Carpathian mountains – the valleys of all major rivers, and the Transylvanian basin – was inhabited by Hungarians in the 11th and 12th centuries. These data complete the picture given by archaeology.

(It should be pointed out that the total number of Hungarian placenames formed with the suffix *–d* is higher than the figures given on this map, which only reflect those listed by Popescu, and that the total number of ancient Hungarian placenames in Transylvania is much higher than the number of those containing the suffix *–d*.)

Most of these placenames formed with the suffix *–d* were borrowed by Rumanian. Some examples (modern forms):

Buzád (from Hungarian *búza* ′wheat′) > Rumanian *Buzad.*

Élesd (*éles* ′sharp′) > Rum. *Aleşd.*

Erősd (*erős* ′strong′) > *Ariuşd.*

Fejérd (*fejér, fehér* ′white′) > Rum. *Feiurd;* (later changed to *Feiurdeni).*

Fenyőd (*fenyő* ′fir, pine′) > Rum. *Fenied;* recently translated: *Brădeşti* (*brad* ′fir, pine′).

Galambod (*galamb* ′pigeon′) > Rum. *Galambod;* recently translated: *Porumbeni* (*porumbel* ′pigeon′).

---

[1] Popescu, R.S. "Note de toponimie transilvăneană", *Limba română*, XXIV, 3, 1975, p. 266.

Komlód (*komló* ′hop′) > Rum. *Comlod.*
Kövesd (old forms: *Kuesd, Kewesd*) (*kő* ′stone′) > *Cuied, Cuieşd, Chieşd.*
Siklód (*sikló* ′slide′) > Rum. *Şiclod.*
Telegd (*telek* ′piece of ground, plot, parcel′) > Rum. *Tileagd.*

Out of those 59 Hungarian placenames ending in *–d,* 54 are based upon Hungarian appellatives and adjectives:

Hung.	sense	**Hung.**	sense	**Hung.**	sense
búza	wheat	kapu	gate, door	nyires	birch grove
erdő	forest	komló	hop	örvény	whirlpool
fenyő	fir, pine	korom*	soot	sár*	mud
galamb	pigeon	kő*	stone	telek	piece of ground
holló	raven	kovács	smith	vessző	twig, rod
ikló	part of a cart	fejér	white	nagy	great, big
éles	sharp	jó	good	sikló	slide
erős	strong				

* Words marked with an asterisk occur in more than one placename.

Four of these placenames ending in *–d* derive from Slavic appellatives:

(1) Vezend (1268: "Wezend") < Slavic *vezen,* from *vezъ* ′ash (Fraxinus)′ + suffix *–d.*

(2) Calmand (1335: "Keethkamar") < Hungarian *kámán* + *–d* < Slavic *kamen* ′stone′. Kaman > Calman by popular etymology.

(3) Vecerd (1337: Wecherd") < Old Slavic *večerŭ* ′evening′ + *–d.*

(4) Suhard, probably from Bulgarian *suhar* + *–d.*

There is no unequivocally Rumanian word on the basis of these placenames, although one of them has been assumed to be of Rumanian origin. This is Oşand (1213: "villa Vosian", or Vărşand (1214: "villa Vosian"), Hungarian Varsánd. I. Kniezsa considered that this is based on the Hungarian personal name Varsány, while Popescu connected it, on the basis of its first documentary mentionings (Vosian), with Rumanian *oşan* or *oşean* ′person originating from Ţara Oaşului′. (The name of this territory in the northwestern corner of present day Rumania was borrowed, much later than the 10th century, from Hungarian: Avas > Rum. Oaş.)

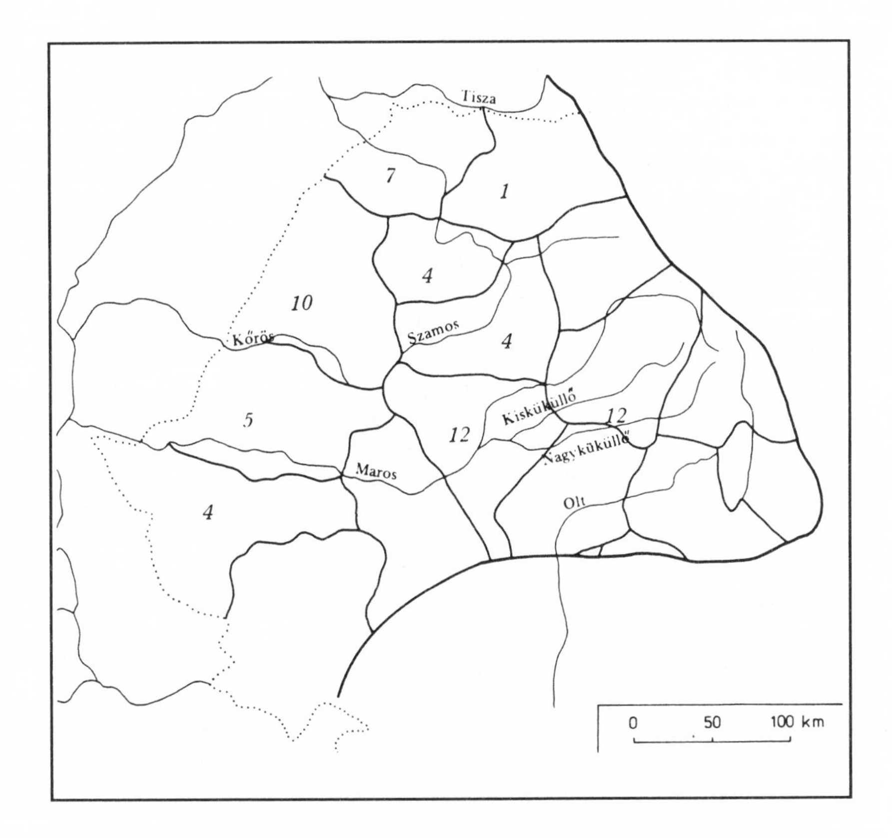

Map 10. The distribution of 59 ancient Hungarian placenames formed with the suffix –d in the area of the eastern and southern Carpathian mountains (Transylvania, the Banat, Crişana, and Maramureş). The numbers of these names are given for each county; an additional 12 are found in the valley of the Mureş (Maros) and another 12 in the valley of the rivers Târnava Mare and Târnava Mică (Nagyküküllő and Kisküküllő, respectively). — Since the suffix –d was no longer used in constructing placenames after the 12th century, the existence of such names in an area indicates the presence of Hungarians in the 10th, 11th, or, latest, in the 12th century. (The data were compiled from R.S. Popescu: "Note de toponimie transilvăneană," *Limba română*, XXIV, 3, 1975, pp. 263–266 and "Mărturii toponimice privind istoria Transilvaniei medievale," by the same author, in *Limba română*, XXII, 4, 1973, pp. 309–314.)

(The total number of Hungarian placenames formed with the suffix –d is higher than the figures given here, which only reflect those given by Popescu. The number of ancient Hungarian placenames in Transylvania is, of course, much higher than those containing the suffix –d. This type was only taken as an example of ancient Hungarian placenames in Transylvania.)

In the above-mentioned article, Popescu[1] asserted that "many of these Hungarian names are translations of older Rumanian names." He presented four examples, none of which is based upon a Rumanian appellative or adjective but only on personal names: *Bogdand, Ivand, Peterd,* and *Petrind.* None of them contains, however, any specific element to be decisive in this question. Bogdan, Ivan, and Peter are found equally in Slavic, Hungarian, and Rumanian: Bogdan is an old name of Slavic origin and its sense is ′given by God′ (*Bog* ′God′). It is probably a semantic loan from Greek (Theodoros). It is mentioned in Serbo-Croatian documents from the 11th–12th centuries. Hungarian as well as Rumanian borrowed it from Slavic. Ivan is the Russian form of a very frequent European name, originating from Hebrew: Johanan. The main Rumanian form is Ion, although there are very many variants. Ivan is specific to the Slavs and frequently used by the Russians, Ukrainians, and Bulgarians. The form specific to Serbian is Iovan. Peter was created from the Greek word signifying ′stone′, from which Latin *petra,* in the early Christian era. The form used in Western Europe is based on the Latin variant, while the Slavs and the Rumanians continue the Greek form. In documents, the Rumanian form appeared in the 14th century. The modern Rumanian forms are Petru, Petruc, Petraş, Petre, etc. In Bulgarian, there are Petar, Petre, Petra, in Serbian, Petar, and in Hungarian, Péter, Pető, Petur.

In summary, the placenames Bogdand, Ivand, Peterd and Petrind may have been based on Slavic, Hungarian, or Rumanian personal names. Since all other placenames with the ending *–d* were based on Hungarian words (appellatives or adjectives), it is most likely that also these four placenames derive from Hungarian. (The data used in this section were taken from C. Ionescu, *Mică enciclopedie onomastică,* 1975.)

4. THE EXTRA-CARPATHIAN AREAS IN THE 10th–13th CENTURIES

a) The Petchenegs (Patzinaks)

Towards the end of the 9th century, a Turk people, the Petchenegs appeared in the region of the lower Danube. In 896 they devastated, in alliance with the Bulgarians, the Hungarian settlements in *Atelkozu* (Hung. *Etelköz,* between the Dniester and the Pruth) which forced the Hungarians to migrate westwards.

The earliest Petcheneg archaeological remains in present day Rumania date from around 930 AD. In the same period, in the southern part of the region between the Dniester and the Pruth, the Hlincea I culture shows signs of ravages

---

[1]Popescu, RR. S., "Note de toponimie transilvăneană", *Limba română,* XXIV, 3, 1875, p. 313.

and ends some decades later. These changes may have been caused by the occupation of the area by the Petchenegs.

The first incursion of this population into the Balkan peninsula (933–934) was described by the Arab historians Al Masudi and Ibn-al-Ahtir. Together with the Petchenegs were several other peoples, also Hungarians.

The Valachian plain was, according to Diaconu,[1] occupied by the Petchenegs in the same period when northeastern Bulgaria and southern Dobrogea were occupied by the Byzantine Empire, i.e., about the year 1000. The Dridu culture there ended latest in the mid-eleventh century.

During the 11th century, the Petchenegs made a series of incursions into the Balkan peninsula until they, in 1091, were finally defeated by Byzantium. In this battle, the large Byzantine army was reinforced by "Bulgars from the valleys of the Struma and the Vardar as well as by Vlachs from Thessaly."[2] The Cumans were also the allies of Byzantium in this battle.

The Petchenegs made incursions also into Transylvania fighting with the Hungarians (e.g., king Ladislas the Saint, 1077–1095). Groups of this Turk people were, however, also settled by the Hungarian kings in several parts of Transylvania, for example in the region of present day Barót (Rum. Baraolt), in the southeast. Petchenegs were still mentioned living there in the 13th century. From 1213, Petcheneg soldiers are mentioned in the army of the Hungarian king and a document from 1224 tells us about the *silva Blachorum et Bissenorum* in southeastern Transylvania.

Archaeological remains of Petchenegs were found, for example, in the above-mentioned area (a vessel in the river Vargyas [Rum. Vârghiş]) and in a settlement near Bratei from the 12th–13th centuries (cf. above, p. 166, the fourth level of settlement No. 2). Material remains characteristic of this population were also found in the tower of Doboka (Dăbâca), north of Cluj.

According to historical records, the language of the Petchenegs belonged to the Turk languages and was similar to that of the Cumans. No remains of this language are known, however, and one cannot determine its influence on the placenames of Rumania, except those which are based upon the ethnic name of this population. These are Slavic *pečeněžĭskŭ* (adjective), Serbian *Pečenoge* (placename), Hungarian *besenyő*, and Rumanian *peceneg*. Of these names, Iordan mentions the following:[3]

Placenames based on the ethnic name of the Petchenegs in the extra-Carpathian territories

Peceneaga (reg. Buzău, raion Beceni; reg. Galaţi, raion Călmăţui, county Teleorman), Pecineaga (reg. Constanţa), Picineaga (reg. Galaţi, raion Măcin), Picineagul (county Muscel), Picinoaga (reg. Galaţi, raion Călmăţui), Pecenevca and Pecenişca or Pecenicica (county of Severin).

[1] Diaconu, P., *Les Petchénègues au Bas-Danube*, 1970, p.38.

[2] Ibid., p. 133.

[3] Iordan Nume de locuri 1952, p. 237.

Placenames based on the ethnic name of the Petchenegs in Transylvania

Beşeneu or Beşineu (in the counties Alba [Hung. Fehér], Năsăud [Naszód], Târnava Mică [Kisküküllő], Trei Scaune (today Covasna) [Háromszék, today Kovászna], Beşimbac (from Hungarian Besinbák, transferred to Hungarian from Transylvanian Saxon Beschenbach, in the county of Făgăraş [Fogaras]), Beşenova and Beşenova Nouă (county of Timiş-Torontal [Temes-Torontál]), Dealul Beşinoului (county of Sibiu [Szeben]). Peceneagul (county of Făgăraş); Pişineaga (county of Hunedoara [Hunyad]). (Beşeneu in the county of Năsăud is also called Beşimbav; cf. Beşimbac, above).

The geographical distribution of these placenames in Rumania is significant: IN THE EXTRA-CARPATHIAN TERRITORIES, all of them (a total of 9) are based on the Slavic or Rumanian forms. IN TRANSYLVANIA, two names of this type appear, both along the southern frontier, in the counties Făgăraş and Hunedoara. Except these frontier areas, all placenames (a total of 8) based on the ethnic name of the Petchenegs were derived from the Hungarian form *Besenyő.* The present day Rumanian forms *(Beşeneu,* etc.) were borrowed from Hungarian.

b) The Cumans

The place of the Petchenegs was, towards the end of the 11th century, taken by the Cumans, another Turk population.They dominated Moldavia and the Valachian plain until the beginning of the 13th century; contemporary writers called these territories *Black Cumania.* Like the Petchenegs, the Cumans conducted several incursions into the Balkan peninsula, waging wars against Byzantium and Bulgaria. They were, however, often allies of the Bulgarians in attacking Byzantium. The founders of the Vlacho-Bulgarian Empire, the brothers Ivan and Peter were, in 1187, helped by the Cumans (cf.above, p. 25).

The Cumans conducted also incursions towards the north, into Transylvania, fighting against the Hungarians. Groups of them settled in the Hungarian kingdom, mostly between the Danube and the Tisza.

The Cumans were Christianized and adopted the Roman Catholic faith at the beginning of the 13th century and in 1227, a diocese was organized for them in the valley of the Milcov.

Vestiges of the Cuman language in Rumania

The Cuman language is partly known from some texts and from a Latin–Persian–Cuman dictionary, written in 1303 by Italian and German missionaries and given by Petrarch to St. Mark's Library in Venice.[1] Because the language spoken by the Cumans was closely related to Turkish, it is difficult to distinguish this influence from later borrowings of Turkish words. On the basis of certain criteria, Denusianu considered that the following Rumanian words were of

[1]Densusianu HLR (1975), p. 352.

Cuman origin: *beci* 'cellar', *toi* 'climax', *scrum* 'ash'.[1]

Placenames of Cuman origin in Rumania are for example: Bărăgan, Burnaz (steppes in Muntenia), Caracal (from Cuman *kara* 'black', and *kala* 'fortification, castle'), Caraiman, Teleorman (from Cuman *teli* 'wild', and *orman* 'forest'); probably also Caraba, Călmăţui, Covorlui, Dăsnăţui, Tâncabă, Toxabă, and Vaslui.[2] Originally, Teleorman probably was the name of a much larger territory than later (the county of Teleorman). It is mentioned by Cinnamos in the context of a Byzantine attack conducted against the Cumans in 1148.[3]

The ethnic name of the Cumans is preserved in many Rumanian placenames: Comana, Comanca, Comăniţa, Comanul, Comăneanca, Comăneşti, etc. More than 40 such places are listed by Iordan (*Nume de locuri* 1952, pp. 227–228), most of them in the extra-Carpathian territories.

The Cuman lexical elements, as well as the placenames were transferred to the Rumanian language directly, without the mediation of the Slavs. This indicates that Vlachs lived together with Cumans, which proves the presence of Vlachs north of the lower Danube in the 12th–3th centuries. This presence is also recorded in historical texts. (The Cumans disappeared from the territories north of the lower Danube during the 13th century.)

5. THE FIRST RECORDS ON VLACHS NORTH OF THE LOWER DANUBE

The first known mention of Vlachs north of the lower Danube was writtern by the Polish chronicler Jan Dlugosz (1415–1480). It relates that Ruthenians, Petchenegs, and Vlachs were in 1070 AD fighting in Moldavia in the army of prince (*cnez*) Wiaczeslav against Boleslaw, who later became the king of Poland (Boleslaw II. Smialy).[4] Vardan, an Armenian historian, who wrote his *Geographia* in the mid-thirteenth century, mentioned that Vlachs were found north of the lower Danube in the second half of the 11th century.[5] Niketas Akominatos reported that Andronikos, who fled to Halič, was in 1164 captured by some Vlachs serving the Byzantine Empire. Kinnamos reported Vlachs north of the lower Danube from 1166. Thus, from the second half of the 12th century onwards, Vlachs were mentioned north of the lower Danube by several chroniclers, but for more than 100 years there was no indication of Vlach settlements. From 1213 it is reported that Germans (Transylvanian Saxons),

---

[1]Ibid., p. 354, cf. Hungarian *korom* 'soot'. A series of other Rumanian words may derive from the language of the Cumans.

[2]Giurescu & Giurescu Istoria Rom 1975, p. 190.

[3]Densusianu HLR (1975), p. 355. *Teli orman* probably included all the mountainous regions of Moldavia and Muntenia.

[4]IRD 1971, p. 61.

[5]Ibid.

Szeklers, Vlachs, and Petchenegs were fighting in the army of the Hungarian king Andreas II (1205–1235), but it is not stated where these Vlachs came from. A document from 1222 describes the "*terra Blachorum*" along the southeastern frontiers of Transylvania (in present day Făgăraş).[1] The *Diploma of Pope Gregeory IX* from 1234 mentions Vlachs living in the Diocese of the Cumans in the region of present day Focşani in southern Moldavia.

This population, migrating from the region of the high mountains in the central and northern parts of the Balkan peninsula, found their niche – areas suitable for shepherding – in the Southern Carpathians, the mountainous parts of Moldavia, and later also in the Transylvanian Alps (Munţii Apuseni). The bulk of the Vlachs came to these areas, which in that time were sparsely populated and partly uninhabited, because the Slavs and the Hungarians (as also the Cumans and other Turk populations) pursued agriculture and the raising of animals and were mainly living on the plains, in the valleys and in the region of lower mountains. In their new habitat, the Vlachs were exposed to the invading armies (for example the Tartars in the 13th century) in a much lesser degree than the surrounding populations in the valleys. These and a number of other circumstances explain the relatively rapid increase of this population in the centuries after the Tartar invasion, which almost extinguished Hungary. As shown by the Rumanian influence on several Slavic languages spoken in the northern Carpathains and also beyond them (cf. above, pp. 133–137), groups of Vlachs reached also these territories, but these groups were not sufficiently strong to resist assimilation into the surrounding Slavs.

These are of course only the main outlines of a protracted process, which, however, is not the topic of the present monograph.

The first Vlach principalities

The first Vlach political organizations are mentioned in a document written in 1247. In the first state-buildings of the Vlachs north of the lower Danube, the Cumans were of great importance: by their alliance with the Rumanians particularly in the mountainous regions of Argeş and Muscel, the Cumans gave the Vlachs an impulse to organize a state, which passed from Borciu the Cuman to Băsărabă.[2] Stadtmüller stated that they even helped the Vlachs in their migrations to the areas north of the lower Danube:

> Die grosse Ausbreitung des rumänischen Volkes in das damals noch unerschlossene Urwaldgebiet der Karpaten ging aber nicht von den sesshaften Romanen des Paristrion, sondern von den "wlachischen" Wanderhirten der innerbalkanischen Berglandschaften aus. Auch ihre Führer nördlich der

---

[1] Ibid., p. 65; Tamás, *Rómaiak, románok és oláhok Dácia Trajánában*, 1935, p. 191.

[2] Ştefănescu, Ş., "Les premières formations étatiques sur le territoire de la Roumanie", *Dacoromania* 1, 1973, p. 106, referring to N. Iorga, "Imperiul cumanilor şi Domnia lui Băsărabă. Un capitol din colaboraţia româno-barbară în evul mediu", in *Analele Academiei Române, Memoriile Secţiunii istorice*, III, VIII (1927–1928), p. 101.

> Donau tragen zu einem guten Teile kumanische Namen. Die Kumanen scheinen also an dieser grossen Walachischen Nordwanderung einen beträchtlichen Anteil gehabt zu haben.[1]

The *Diploma of the Ioanites* from 1247, written by king Béla IV of Hungary and the chief of the Order of the Ioanites, mentions the following political organizations of the Vlachs: *Țara Severinului* in the western part of Oltenia and the southern part of the Banat; two small principalities (*cnezat*-s) in Oltenia with Ioan and Farcaş, respectively, as chiefs; the voivodate of Litovoi between the rivers Jiu and Olt, which included also Haţeg (< Hungarian Hátszeg), a small area north of the peaks of the southern Carpathians. There was a *ț ară* also in the region of Argeş whose chief was Seneslav.[2] The names *Vlaşca* and *Codrul Vlăsiei* ('the forest of Vlach country') given by a Slavic population are vestiges from such voivodates.[3] .

These small principalities had their own army. In the first half of the 14th century, those to the west and to the east of the Olt were united by Basarab I (around 1310–1352). Somewhat later, also Moldavia emerged as a united principality.

[1] Stadtmüller GS 1950, pp. 207–208.

[2] IR Compendiu 1969, p. 127.

[3] Iordan Nume de locuri 1952, p. 262.

BIBLIOGRAPHY

ANDERSON, J.M. *Structural Aspects of Language Change,* Longman Linguistic Library, Title 13, London, Longman group Ltd., 1973.

ANONYMI (P. Magistri), *Gesta Hungarorum*, ed. by József Deér, in: Scriptores Rerum Hungaricarum ducum ergumque stirpis Arpadianae gestarum, Budapest, 1973. *Anonymus, Gesta Hungarorum*, translated by Dezső Pais, Budapest, 1975.

BÂRZU, Ligia, *Continuitatea populaţiei autohtone în Transilvania în secolele IV – V (cimitirul 1 de la Bratei)* [The Continued Existence of the Autochthonous Population in Transylvania in the 4th – 5th Centuries (Cemetery No 1 at Bratei)], Edit. Acad. RSR, Bucharest, 1973

Abbreviation: Bârzu Cemet 1973

BOLIN, S., *Fynden av romerska mynt i det fria Germanien. Studier i romersk och äldre germansk historia* [Finds of Roman Coins in Free Germany. Studies of Roman and ancient German history], Dissertation, Lund, 1926.

BOURCIEZ, E., *Éléments de linguistique romane* (5th edition), Paris, Librairie C. Klincksieck, 1967.

Abbreviation: Bourciez Éléments 1967

BRÂNCUŞ, G., "Albano-romanica III. Vocala ă în română şi albaneză" [Albanian and Roman Studies III. The Vowel ă in Rumanian and Albanian], *Studii şi cercetări lingvistice*, XXIV, 3, 1973, pp. 291–296; Edit. Acad. RSR, Bucharest.

Abbreviation: Brâncuş Albano-romanica 1973

ÇABEJ, E., "Unele probleme ale istoriei limbii albaneze" [Problems of the History of the Albanian Language], *Studii şi cercetări lingvistice*, X, 4, 1959, pp. 528–560.

CAPIDAN, T., "Raporturile lingvistice slavo-române" [The Relations between Slavic and Rumanian], *Dacoromania* III, 1922–1923, pp. 129–238, Cluj.

CARAGIU MARIOŢEANU, Matilda, *Compendiu de dialectologie română (nord- şi sud-dunăreană)* [Compendium of Rumanian Dialectology (North and South of the Danube)], Edit. ştiinţifică şi enciclopedică, Bucharest, 1975.

Abbreviation: Caragiu Marioţeanu Dialectologie 1975.

CAZACU, B., Studii de dialectologie română [Studies of Rumanian Dialectology], Edit. Ştiinţifică, Bucharest, 1966.

Abbreviation: Cazacu Studii 1966.

CONDURACHI, E., & DAICOVICIU, C., *The Ancient Civilizations of Romania,* Nagel Publishers, Geneva1971. First published in Great Britain by Barrie & Jenkins, London. Translated from the French by James Hoghart.

CONSTANTINESCU, M., DAICOVICIU, C., & PASCU, Ş., *Istoria României. Compendiu* [The History of Romania. Compendium], Edit. Didactică şi Pedagogică, Bucharest, 1969 (first edition),
(3rd edition, 1974, red. PASCU, Ş,).
Abbreviation: IR Compendiu 1969 and 1974, respectively.

COTEANU, I., *Morfologia numelui în protoromână (română comună)* [The Morphology of the noun in Common Rumanian], Edit. Acad. RSR, Bucharest, 1969.
Abbreviation: Coteanu Morfologia 1969.

COTEANU, I., & DĂNĂILĂ, I., *Introducere în lingvistica şi filologia românească. Probleme – bibliografie* [Introduction to Rumanian Linguistics and Philology], Edit. Acad. RSR, Bucharest, 1970.
Abbreviation: Coteanu Dănăilă Introd lingv 1970.

DACOROMANIA 1, 1973 — see MIRON

DAICOVICIU, C., *Dacica,* Bibliotheca Musei Napocensis, Cluj, 1969.
Abbreviation: Daicoviciu Dacica 1969.

DAICOVICIU, C., (red.) *Istoria Romîniei* [The History of Rumania], Edit. Acad. RPR, Bucharest, 1960.
Abbreviation: IR 1960

DAICOVICIU, C., & CONSTANTINESCU, M., *Brève histoire de la Transylvanie*, Bucharest, 1965.

DAICOVICIU, C., PETROVICI, E., & ŞTEFAN, G., *La formation du peuple Roumain et de sa langue*, Edit. Acad. RPR, Bucharest, 1963.

DAMI, A., "La controverse de la continuité daco-roumaine," *Humanitas Ethnica, Ethnos* 5. Menschenwürde, Recht und Gemeinschaft. Festschrift für Theodor Veiter. Dargeboten zum 60. Lebensjahre im Auftrag eines Freundkreises von Franz Hieronymus Riedl. W. Braumüller, Wien – Stuttgart, 1967.

DENSUSIANU, O., *Opere II. Lingvistica. Histoire de la langue roumaine,* I. Les origines. II., Le seizième siècle. Edited by Cazacu, B., Rusu, V., & Şerb, I, Edit. Minerva, Bucharest, 1975.
Abbreviation: Densusianu HLR (1975)

DIACONU, P., *Les Petchénègues au Bas-Danube.* Bibliotheca Historica Romaniae, Edit. Acad. RSR, 1970.
Abbreviation: Diaconu Petchénègues 1970

DIMITRESCU, Florica, *Contribuţii la istoria limbii române vechi* [Contributions to the History of Old Rumanian], Edit. Didactică şi Pedagogică, Bucharest, 1973.

DRAGOMIR, S., *Vlahii din nordul peninsulei Balcanice în evul mediu* [The Vlachs in the North of the Balkan Peninsula in the Middle Ages], Comisia pentru studiul formării limbii şi poporului romîn, 2, Edit. Acad. RPR, Bucharest, 1959.
Abbreviation: Dragomir Vlahii 1959

FRIEDWAGNER, M., "Über die Sprache und Heimat der Rumänen in ihrer Frühzeit," *Zeitschrift für romanische Philologie*, Halle, LIV, 1934, pp. 641–715.

GAMILLSCHEG, E., "Über die Herkunft der Rumänen," *Preuss. Akademie der Wissenschaften, Sitzungsberichte, Philos.-hist. Klasse*, Berlin, 1940.

GEORGIEV, V., "Zur dakischen Hydronymie," *Linguistique Balkanique*, II, 1960, pp. 115–117.

GEORGIEV, V., "Raporturile dintre limbile dacă, tracă şi frigiană" [The Relations between the Dacian, Thracian, and Phrygian languages], *Studii clasice*, Bucharest, 1960.

GEORGEV, V., "La thracologie: état actuel," *Études balkaniques*, Académie Bulgare des Sciences, Institut d'études balkaniques, 3, 1972, pp. 5–15, Sofia.

GIURESCU, C.C. (red.), *Istoria României în date* [The Chronological History of Rumania], Edit. Enciclopedică Română, Bucharest, 1971.
Abbreviation: Giurescu IRD 1971

GIURESCU, C.C., & GIURESCU, D.C., *Istoria românilor din cele mai vechi timpuri pînă astăzi* [The History of the Rumanians from Ancient Times to the Present], Edit. Albatros, Bucharest, 1975 (2nd edition).
Abbreviation: Giurescu & Giurescu Istoria Rom 1975

GRAUR, A., *Gramatica limbii române*, Vol. I – II, Edit. Acad. RSR, Bucharest, 1966.

GRECU, V., *Şcoala ardeleană şi unitatea limbii române literare* [The Transylvanian School and the Unity of the Rumanian Literary Language], Edit. Facla, Timişoara, 1973.

GYŐRFFY, Gy., "Anonymus Gesta Hungarorumának kora és hitelessége" [The Age and the Reliability of Anonymus′ *Gesta Hungarorum*], *Irodalomtörténeti Közlemények*, 7, 1970, pp. 1–13, Budapest.
Abbreviation: Győrffy Anonymus 1970

HADLICH, R.L., *The Phonological History of Vegliote,* University of North Carolina, Studies in the Romance Languages, 52, 1963.

HALL, R. A., Jr., "The Roumanian definite article and noun-phrase," in *Wortbildung, Syntax und Morphologie, Festschrift zum 60. Geburtstag von H. Marchand*, Mouton, 1968, pp. 109–114.

HALL, R. A., Jr., *External History of the Romance Languages*, Foundation of Linguistic Series, Edit. C.F. Hockett, Comparative Romance Grammar, Vol. I, American Elsevier Publishing Company Inc., New York – London – Amsterdam, 1974.

HOMORODEAN, M., *Vechea vatră a Sarmizegetusei în lumina toponimiei* [The Ancient Dwelling Place of Sarmizegetusa in the Light of Toponymy], Edit. Dacia, Cluj, 1980.
Abbreviation: Homorodean Vechea vatră 1980

HOREDT, K., *Siebenbürgen in spätrömischer Zeit*, Edit. Kriterion, Bucharest, 1982.

ILLYÉS, E., *Ethnic Continuity in the Carpatho–Danubian Area*, East European Monographs, No. CCXLIX, Boulder, Columbia University Press, New York, 1988; second revised edition: Hunyadi Öcs.Mk., Hamilton, On., [Canada] Struktura Press, 1992.
Abbreviation: Illyés Ethnic Cont 1992.

IORDAN, I., *Nume de locuri românești în Republica Populară Română* [Rumanian placenames in the People′s Republic of Rumania], vol. 1, Edit. Acad. RPR, Bucharest, 1952.
Abbreviation: Iordan Nume de locuri 1952.

IORDAN, I., *Alexandru Philippide*, Editura Ştiinţifică, Bucharest, 1969.

IORDAN, I. (red.), *Istoria ştiinţelor în România. Lingvistica* [The History of Sciences in Rumania. Linguistics] Comitetul român de istoria şi filizofia ştiinţei, Edit. Acad. RSR, Bucharest, 1975.

IORDAN, I., & MANOLIU, Maria, *Introducere în lingvistica romanică* [Introduction to Romance Lingustics], Edit. Didactică şi pedagogică, Bucharest, 1965.

IZZO, H., "On the History of Romanian," in *The Twelfth Lacus Forum 1985*, pp. 139–147; edited by M.C. Marino & Language. A. Pérez, Linguistic Association of Canada and the United States, Lake Bluff, Illinois, USA.

JIREČEK, G., *Geschichte der Serben* (Geschichte der Europäischen Staaten, 38. Werk), Gothia, Friedrich Andreas Perthes A.-G., 1911.
Abbreviation: Jireček GS 1911

KARSAI, G., "Ki volt Anonymus?" [Who Was Anonymus? Critical discussion of Anonymus′ Gesta, problems concerning its contents and its language, especially regarding the phototechnical problems of the palimpsest-texts], in *Középkori kútfőink kritikus kérdései* [Critical problems of our historical sources from the Middle Ages], red. by J. Horváth & Gy. Székely, Akadémiai Kiadó, Budapest, 1974.
Abbreviation: Karsai Középkori kútfőink 1974

KAZÁR, L., *Facts against Fiction: Transylvania – Wallachian/Rumanian Homeland since 70 B.C.?* Forum of History, Sidney, 1993.

KOSZTIN, Á., *A dákorómán legenda. Keresztény kultuszhelyek Erdélyben* [The Daco-Roman Myth. Christian Cult-places in Transylvania], Népszava, Budapest, 1989.

KRANZMAYER, E., "Frühromanische Mundarten zwischen Donau und Adria in deutschen und slawischen Ortsnamen," *Zeitschrift für Namenforschung,* München, XV, pp. 193–224, 1939.

LÁSZLÓ, Gy., *Vértersszöllőstől Pusztaszerig. Élet a Kárpát-medencében a magyar államalapításig* [From Vértesszöllős to Pusztaszer. Life in the Carpathian Basin up to the Foundation of the Hungarian State], Gondolat, Budapest, 1974.

LOMBARD, A., *Le verbe roumain. Étude morphologique*, I–II, Lund, 1954–55.
Abbreviation: Lombard Verbe 1955

LOMBARD, A., *Latinets öden i Öster* [The Destinies of Latin in the East], Filologiskt arkiv 12, Lund, 1967. (Translated to Rumanian: "Destinele latinităţii orientale", *Ramuri*, 1976, 3, p. 16.)

LOMBARD, A., *La langue Roumaine. Une présentation.* (Biblothèque francaise et romane publiée par le Centre de Philologie et de Littératurs romanes de l′Université des Sciences humaines de Strasbourg, sous la direction de Georges Straka. Série A: Manuels et études linguistiques, No. 29.) Edit. Klincksieck, Paris, 1974.
Abbreviation: Lombard Langue Roum 1974.

LÖFSTEDT, E., "Syntactica. Studien und Beiträge zur historischen Syntax des Lateins. II: Syntaktisch-stilistische Gesichtspunkte und Probleme," *Acta reg. societatis humanorium litterarum lundensis*, X, 1–2, Lund, 1933.
Abbreviation: Löfstedt Synt 1933

LÖFSTEDT, E., *Late Latin.* Instituttet for sammenlignende kulturforskning, serie A: Forelesninger, XXV, Oslo, H. Aschehoug & Co. (W. Nygaard), 1959.
Abbreviation: Löfstedt Late Latin 1959

MACREA, D., *Studii de lingvistică română* [Studies of Rumanian Linguistics], Edit. didactică şi pedagogică, 1970, Bucharest.
Abbreviation: Macrea Studii 1970

MACREA, D., "Despre dialectele limbii romîne" [On the Dialects of the Rumanian Language], *Limba romînă* V, 1, pp. 5–24, 1956.
Abbreviation: Macrea Dial 1956

MACREA, D., *Limbă şi lingvistică română* [Rumanian Language and Linguistics], Edit. didactică şi pedagogică, Bucharest, 1973.

MAIOR, P., *Istoria pentru începutul românilor în Dacia* [The History of the Origins of the Rumanians in Dacia], Editură critică şi studiu asupra limbii de Floarea Fugariu. Edit. Albatros, Bucharest, 1970.

MIHĂESCU, H., *Limba latină în provinciile dunărene ale imperiului roman* [The Latin Language in the Danubian Provinces of the Roman Empire], Acad. RPR, Comisia pentru studiul formării limbii şi poporului romîn, vol. III, Bucharest, 1960.
Abbreviation: Mihăescu Limba lat 1960

MIHĂESCU, H., *Influenţa grecească asupra limbii române pînă în secolul al XV-lea* [The Greek influence on the Rumanian Language into the 15th Century], Edit. Acad. RSR, Bucharest, 1966.

MIHĂESCU, H., & ŞTEFAN, G., (red.), *Fontes Historiae Dacoromanae* II. Ab anno CCC usque ad annum M. Edit. Acad. RSR, Bucharest, 1970.
Abbreviation: Fontes II 1970

MIHĂILĂ, G., "Împrumuturi vechi sud-slave în limba română" [Old South Slavic borrowings in the Rumanian Language], *Materiale şi cercetări lingvistice,* VII, Edit. Acad. RPR, 1960.
Abbreviation: Mihăilă Imprum Slav 1960.

MIRON, P., (red.), *Dacoromania. Jahrbuch für östliche Latinität*, Freiburg-München, Edit. Karl Alber; vol. I, 1973; (vol. II, 1974).
Abbreviation: Dacoromania I 1973.

MÓCSY, A., *Gesellschaft und Romanisation in der römischen Provinz Moesia Superior*, Akadémiai Kiadó, Budapest, 1970.

MOÓR, E., *A nyelvtudomány mint az ős- és néptörténet forrástudománya* [Linguistics: the Source of the Ancient History of Peoples], Akad. kiadó, Budapest, 1963.

PÂRVAN, V., *Dacia. Civilizaţiile antice din ţările Carpato-Danubiene* [Dacia. The Ancient Civilizations in the Carpatho-Danubian Countries], 5th edition, translated from the French original by R. Vulpe, Edit. Ştiinţifică, Bucharest, 1972.

PĂTRUŢ, I., *Studii de limba română şi slavistică* [Studies of the Rumanian Language and Slavistics], Edit. Dacia, Cluj, 1974.
Abbreviation: Pătruţ Studii 1974.

PEI, M., *The Story of Latin and the Romance Languages,* Harper & Row, New York – San Francisco – London, 1976.

PETROVICI, E., "Repartiţia graiurilor dacoromîne pe baza atlasului lingvistic romîn" [The geographical distribution of the Daco-Roman subdialects on the basis of the *Rumanian Linguistic Atlas*], *Limba romînă,* III, 5, pp. 5–17, 1954.
Abbreviation: Petrovici Repartizarea graiurilor 1954

PETROVICI, E., *Studii de dialectologie şi toponimie* [Studies of Dialectology and Toponymy], (volum îngrijit de I. Pătruţ, B. Kelemen şi I. Mării), Edit Acad. RSR, Bucharest, 1970.
Abbreviation: Petrovici Studii 1970

PHILIPPIDE, A., *Originea romînilor* [The Origin of the Rumanians], I, 1923, II, 1927, Iaşi.

PIPPIDI, D.M. (red.), *Dicţionar de istorie veche a României (Paleolitic - sec. X)* [Dictionary of the Ancient History of Rumania. Paleolithic - 10th Century] Edit. Ştiinţifică şi enciclopedică, Bucharest, 1976.
Abbreviation: Pippidi Dict ist veche 1976.

PÓLAY, E., *A dáciai viaszostáblák szerződései* [The contracts found on the vax-tablets from Dacia], Közgadasági és jogi Kiadó, Budapest, 1972.

POPESCU, R., "Mărturii toponimice privind istoria Transilvaniei medievale," [Toponyms as evidence regarding the History of Transylvania in the Middle Ages], *Limba română*, XXII, 4, pp. 309–314, 1973.

POPOVIĆ, I., *Geschichte der serbokroatischen Sprache*, Wiesbaden, 1960.
Abbreviation: Popović GSKS 1960

PREDA, C., "Circulaţia monedelor romane postaureliene în Dacia" [The circulation of the Roman coins from the period after Aurelian in Dacia], *Studii şi cercetări de istorie veche şi de arheologie*, 26, 4, 1975, pp. 441–485.
Abbreviation: Preda Circulaţia 1975

PROTASE, D., "Considérations sur les rites funéraires des Daces," *Revue d'archéologie et d'histoire ancienne*, nouvelle série, IV, Bucharest, 1962.
Abbreviation: Protase Rites Fun 1962.

PROTASE, D., *Problema continuităţii în Dacia în lumina arheologiei şi numismaticii* [The Problem of Continuity in Dacia in the Light of Archaeology and Numismatics], Edit. Acad. RSR, Bucharest, 1966.
Abbreviation: Protase PCD 1966

PROTASE, D., *Un cimitir dacic din epoca romană la Soporu de Cîmpie. Contribuţia la problema continuităţii în Dacia* [A Dacian Cemetery from the Roman Period at Soporu de Cîmpie. Contribution to the Problem of Continuity in Dacia], Edit. Acad. RSR, Bucharest, 1976.
Abbreviation: Protase Soporu 1976

PROTASE, D., Autohtonii în Dacia [The Autochthonous /People/ in Dacia], vol. 1, Edit. Ştiinţifică şi enciclopedică, Bucharest, 1980.
Abbreviation: Protase Autohtonii 1980

PUŞCARIU, S., "Le rôle de la Transylvanie dans la formation et l'évolution de la langue roumaine," *La Transylvanie*, Académie Roumaine, Bucharest, 1938, pp. 37–69.

ROSENKRANZ, B., *Historische Laut- und Formenlehre des Altbulgarischen (Altkirchenslavischen)*, Carl Winter Universitätsverlag, Heidelberg, in Verbindung mit Mouton & Co. N.V. S.-Gravenhage, 1955.

ROSETTI, A., *Istoria limbii române de la origini pînă în secolul al XVII-lea* [The History of the Rumanian Language from its Origins into the 17th Century] Editura pentru literatură, Bucharest, 1968; Definitive edition, 1986.
Abbreviation: Rosetti ILR 1986 (or 1968, respectively)

ROSETTI, A., *La linguistique balkanique suivi par le nouveau en linguistique dans l'oevre de l'auteur*, Editura Univers, Bucharest, 1985.

ROSETTI, A., CAZACU, B., & COTEANU, I. (red.), *Istoria limbii române.* [The History of the Rumanian Language], Vol. II, Edit. Acad. RSR, Bucharest, 1969 (Vol. I, 1965).
Abbreviation: ILR 1969 (or vol. I, 1965, respectively)

RÖSLER, R., *Romanische Studien. Untersuchungen zur älteren Geschichte Rumäniens,* Leipzig, 1871.

RUNCIMAN, S., *A History of the First Bulgarian Empire,* Edit. G. Bell & Sons Ltd., London, 1930.

RUSSU, I.I., *Limba traco-dacilor* [The Language of the Thraco-Dacians], Edit. Ştiinţifică, Bucharest, 1967.
Abbreviation: Russu LTD 1967.

RUSSU, I.I., *Illirii. Istoria – limba şi onomastica – romanizarea* [The Illyrians. History, Language, and Onomastics, and Romanization], Biblioteca Istorică, XVII, Edit. Acad. RSR, Bucharest, 1969.
Abbreviation: Russu Illirii 1969.

RUSSU, I.I., *Elemente autohtone în limba română. Substratul comun româno-albanez* [Autochthonous Elements in the Rumanian Language. The Substratum Shared by Rumanian and Albanian], Bucharest, 1970.
Abbreviation: Russu Elemente autohtone 1970

RUSSU, I.I., *Etnogeneza românilor. Fondul autohton traco-dacic şi componenta latino-romanică,* [The Ethnogenesis of the Rumanians. The Autochthonous Thraco-Dacian Basis and its Latino-Romance Component], Edit. Ştiinţifică şi enciclopedică, Bucharest, 1981.
Abbreviation: Russu Etnogeneza 1981

SALA, M., "Evoluţia grupurilor latineşti ct şi cs în română" [The development of the Latin /Consonant/ Groups ct and cs in Rumanian], Studii şi cercetări lingvistice, XXIV, 4, pp. 343–355, Bucharest, 1973.
Abbreviation: Sala Evoluţia 1973

SANDFELD, K., *Linguistique balkanique. Problèmes et résultats.* Libraire ancienne Honoré Champion, éditeur Édouard Champion, Paris, 1930.
Abbreviation: Sandfeld LB 1930

SLATARSKI, W.N., *Geschichte der Bulgaren.* Teil I–II. Bulgarische Bibliothek, V- VI, Edit. Dr. Iwan Parlapanoff, Leipzig, 1918.
Abbreviation: Slatarski Gesch Bulg 1918

SOLTA, G. R., *Einführung in die Balkanlinguistik mit besonderer Berücksichtigung des Substrats und des Balkanlateinischen*, Wissenschaftliche Buchgesellschaft, Darmstadt, 1980.

STADTMÜLLER, G., *Grundfragen der europäischen Geschichte.* R. Oldenbourg, München – Wien, 1965.

STADTMÜLLER, G., *Forschungen zur albanischen Frühgeschichte.* Albanische Forschungen, 2, (2nd edition), Edit. Otto Harrasowitz, Wiesbaden, 1966.
Abbreviation: Stadtmüller FAF 1966

STADTMÜLLER, G., *Geschichte Südosteuropas*, Edit. R. Oldenbourg, München, 1950.
Abbreviation: Stadtmüller GS 1950

STENBERGER, M., *Det forntida Sverige* [Ancient Sweden], (2nd edition), Almqvist & Wiksell, Stockholm, 1971.

STOICESCU, N., *Continuitatea românilor. Privire istoriografică, istoricul problemei, dovezile continuităţii* [The Continuity of the Rumanians. An Historiographic Survey, the History of the Problem, the Proofs of Continuity.] Edit. Ştiinţifică şi enciclopedică, Bucharest, 1980.

STRAKA, G., *Revue linguistique romane*, XXIV, Paris, 1960. (Livres, Compte rendues sommaires, pp. 405–406.)

SUCIU, C., *Dicţionar istoric al localităţilor din Transilvania* [Historical Dictionary of the Localities in Transylvania], vol. I 1967, vol. II 1968, Edit. Academiei Republicii Socialiste România, Bucharest.
Abbreviation: Suciu Dicţionar istoric (vol I; vol II)

ŞTEFAN, G. (red.), *Fontes ad historiam Dacoromaniae pertinentes* I. Ab Hesiodo usque ad Itinerarium Antonini. Edit. Acad. RPR, Bucharest, 1964.
Abbreviation: Fontes I 1964

TAGLIAVINI, C., *Le origini delle lingue neolatine. Introduzione alla filologia romanza* (5th edition), Casa editrice prof. Ricardo Patron, Bologna, 1969.
Abbreviation: Tagliavini Orig Lingu Neolat 1969

TAMÁS, L., *Romains, Romans et Roumains dans l'histoire de Dacie Trajane.* Études sur l'Europe Centre-Orientale I, Budapest, 1936. (In Hungarian: *Rómaiak, románok és oláhok Dácia Trajánában*, Edit. Magyar Tudományos Akadémia, 1935.)

TODD, M., *Roman Britain 55 BC – AD 400. The Province beyond Ocean.* Fontana History of England, edited by G.R. Elton, 1981.

TODORAN, R., "Cu privire la repartiţia graiurilor dacoromîne," *Limba română*, V, 2, pp. 38–50, 1956.

TÖRÖK, S., *Településtörténeti tanulmányok és határproblémák a Kárpát-medencében* [Studies on Settlement History and Frontier Problems in the Carpathian Basin], American Hungarian Literary Guild, Astor Park, Florida, 1973.

TREIMER, C., "Albanisch und Rumänisch," *Zeitschrift für Romanische Philologie*, XXXVIII, pp. 385–411, Halle, 1912.

TUDOR, D., *Oraşe şi sate în Dacia Romană* [Towns and villages in Roman Dacia], Edit. Ştiiţifică, Bucharest, 1968.
Abbreviation: Tudor Oraşe 1968

ULLMANN, S., *Semantics. An Introduction to the Science of Meaning*, Basil Blackwell, Oxford, 1970.
Abbreviation: Ullmann Semantics 1970

VÉKONY, G., *Dákok, rómaiak, románok* [Dacians, Romans, Rumanians], Akadémiai Kiadó, Budapest, 1989.

VIDOS, B.E., *Handbuch der romanischen Sprachwissenschaft,* München, 1975.
Abbreviation: Vidos Handbuch 1975

VRACIU, A., *Studii de lingvistică generală*, Edit, Junimea, Iaşi, 1972.

WEINREICH, U., *Languages in Contact. Findings and Problems.* Mouton & Co., London – The Hague – Paris, 1964.
Abbreviation: Weinreich Lang Cont 1964

WINKLER, Iudita, "Procesul romanizării în lumină monumentelor epigrafice şi sculpturale din aşezările rurale ale provinciei Dacia" [The Process of Romanization in the light of epigraphy and the sculptural monuments of the Province Dacia], *Studii şi cercetări de istorie veche şi de arheologie*, 25, 4, 1974, pp. 497–515, Bucharest.

ZAHARIA, Eugenia, "Les sources archélogiques de la continuité daco-romaine," *Apulum,* XII, 1974, pp. 279–294.

Abbreviations begin usually with the name of the author. Where this is not the case, complete bibliographic data are found under the name of the relevant author/editor, as indicated in the following list:

Fontes I 1964	ŞTEFAN
Fontes II 1970	MIHĂESCU & ŞTEFAN
ILR 1969	ROSETTI
IR 1960	DAICOVICIU
IR Compendiu 1969 IR Compendiu 1974	CONSTANTINESCU et al.
IRD 1971	GIURESCU

English translations of quotations in French and German.

Introduction, p. 6

This childrens´ disease of autochthonomany is characteristic of the early periods of modern historiography in Eastern Europe, where many different peoples live, and it is felt still today in different shapes, although less conspicuously, when problems of ancient history are discussed. (Stadtmüller)

Chapter I

p. 11:
The most glorious period of the Illyrian army units was the 3rd century. Numerous emperors originated from this military frontier area. (Jireček)

p. 16:
Those small groups of Germans left, i.e., of Goths, who remained in some mountainous areas, adopted in the following generations Latin or Greek and were thus assimilated to the local populations. (Stadtmüller)

All these constructions for defence had little success. There was a shortage of people for defence. The troops along the *limes* had financial difficulties and consequently degenerated, and the mobile army, which according to Agathias numbered 150,000 men, was dispersed in garrisons from southern Spain to Armenia and upper Egypt. The degenerated population of the towns were more interested in religious problems than in the defence of the country. (Jireček)

pp. 16–17:
In this area, Roman life was possible as late as in the 6th century, in which in the east, the storms of the Peoples´ Migration blew more intensely, because this area was mountainous and the barbarians attacked mainly Constantinople. The Roman population was STRENGTHENED by migrations from the north. Dardania was, as the country of origin, certainly particularly loved by the great emperors Constantine (originating from Naissus – Niš) and Justinian (from the area of Scupi – Skopje, in Turkish earlier Üsküb). Thus, after having been destroyed, this last-mentioned town was re-built not far from the destroyed one and made

in 535 AD the seat of the Metropolitan Bishop Catellianus. This became the centre of the entire united Diocese (Dacia Ripensis and Mediterranea, Moesia Superior, Praevalis and Macedonia secunda, as well as the eastern part of Pannonia Inferior). (Friedwagner)

pp. 19–20:
When this happened at the same time as the occupation of the country, the old name of the town was preserved with some small changes. This explains why earlier Roman towns reappear as the centre of their province when dioceses are organized. The ancient names were changed either according to certain phonetic rules, or with a Slavic word of a similar sound pattern. In those cases in which the towns of Roman origin received a totally new name in the Slavic period, for example the "white castle" Beograd (*Singidunum*) or the castle of the "defender" (*branič*) Braničevo (*Viminacium*), a longer period of time had elapsed between the perishing of the ancient town and its re-population. (Jireček)

p. 33:
M. Malecki, About the Balkan Linguistic Union, Proceedings of the 3rd International Congress of Linguists, Firenze, 1935, p. 75. "Such is the case in all the regions of Serbia, along the Morava, around Valjevo and along the Drina. Eighty to one hundred percent of the inhabitants there are immigrants who came mainly in the last three centuries... The documents of the archives... give no idea about the great significance of the migrations." (Quoted by Rosetti)

Originally, both were situated near each other, e.g. in the document from Žiča (around 1220) the summer grazing place on the mountain Kotlenik, the winter grazing place in the nearby valley of the Ibar. (Jireček)

Chapter II.

p. 41:
In Rhaetia, the diphthongues *ie, uo* seem to have appeared, and spread through Friuli and Istria along the Dalmatian coasts, even in the case of entrave (Istrian *mierlo, kuorno, puorta*, Vegliote *fiasta, puarta*). In the Balkan peninsula proper, where only ę comes into question, (for ǫ, see § 153), diphthongation occurred also before the Latin entrave: there is not only Rum. *ierĭ (hĕri)* but also *piept (pĕctus)*. (Bourciez)

It would be difficult to admit that *hora* became the synonym of *vices* in Rumanian independently from Venetian. This is a too subtle change, too surprising for its occurance in two languages with no contact with each other. This is why we don´t hesitate to see in this a vestige of the period of time when Rumanian was not yet isolated from Italian. There is another circumstance which gives special significance to the word in question. This is that *hora* appears with the same sense also in the Albanian *herε,* which also means ′time′. Albanian *herε,* Rumanian *oară* and Venetian *ora* form thus a common family and throw some light on one of the most obscure chapters of the history of Balkan Latin. (Densusianu)

p. 42:
...confirms strikingly what we have said about the development of Balkan Latin; it shows, by its origin and its wide dispersion, that this Latin did not cease to be in contact with that of Italy until quite late in the Middle Ages. (Densusianu)

p. 45:
It leaves the Adriatic Sea at Lissus, stretches across the mountains of the Miredites and the Dibra to northern Macedonia between Scupi and Stobi, proceeds then south of Naissus and Remesiana with their Latin inhabitants, while Pautalia (Küstendil) and Serdica (Sofia) and the region of Pirot belong to the Greek territory; and finally, the frontier continues along the northern slopes of the Haemus mountains to the coast of the Black Sea. (Jireček)

p. 66:
The Albanian words are treated as inherited words in Rumanian; they are thus as old as the latter′s Roman elements. Fom another point of view, they are even older, since they are indigenous. (Treimer)

pp. 77–78:
We believe that Vegliote must be regarded an intermediary dialect between Roman spoken in Italy and in the Balkan peninsula. By its sound pattern and lexical elements, it is sometimes like one, sometimes like the other. Also its geographical position justifies seeing in it the transition from Italian to Rumanian. (Densusianu)

p. 80:
In linguistics to replace the notion of origin with that of "affinity," as one wants to do now, means to attribute to phonetics and vocabulary and to syntax more importance than to morphology, and consequently, to substitute the superficial for the essential. (Graur)

p. 97:
On the other hand, the borrowing of Slavic words pertaining to the intellectual and the moral aspects of life shows how intimate the mixing of the populations has been. Besides Latin *tempus* (Rum. *timp*), one has Old Slavic *vremę* (Rum. *vreme*), and here are some other loans: Rum. *slovă* Old Slavic *slovo* ′writing′, *războiu* = *razboj* ′war′, *rană* = *rana* ′wound′, *ciudă* = *ciudo* ′miracle′, *groază* = *groza* ′horror′, *nădejde* = *nadežda* ′hope′, *noroc* = *naroku* ′luck′, etc. The same is the case with the words pertaining to social life: (Rum. *jupîn* = Old Slavic

županu ´lord´, *slugă* = *sluga* ´servant´), and with a large number of frequently used adjectives: Rum. *drag* = Old Slavic *dragŭ* ´dear, beloved´, *bogat* = *bogatŭ* ´rich´, *mîndru* = *madrŭ* ´proud´, *gol* = *golŭ* ´naked´. Lastly, many verbs were borrowed, such as Old Slavic *saditi* ´to plant´, *izbaviti* ´to save´, (Rum. *sădi, izbăvi*), *darovati* (Rum. *dărui*), along Latin *dare,* and it is characteristic to see a word such as *amare* disappear for Old Slavic *ljubiti* (Rum. *iubi*). The impersonal word which expresses necessity, Rum. *trebuie* ´to be necessary, to need´, originates also from Old Slavic *trěbovati.* (Bourciez)

p. 102, note 1:
"It is evident that such a fatal outcome for the Roman character of the Rumanians could only occur in a firmly established Slavic–Rumanian symbiosis." (Popović)

p. 122:
When examining the maps (of the Rumanian Linguistic Atlas)... one is primarily impressed by their relative uniformity, which is sometimes near poverty; we are most of the time far away from the exuberant richness presented by other linguistic atlases, particularly those of Gilliéron. (Boutière)

p. 123:
Only a people for whom shepherding has played an essential role may say: *mă paşte un gînd* lit. ´a thought grazes me´; on the basis of this expression, there is the image of a flock of sheep which grazes eveything to the last stalk of grass, until nothing is left. (Puşcariu)

Chapter III

p. 130:
The meaning and the value of this opinion consists in its political aim, which is to serve as a theoretical basis for concrete activity in order to re-unite the "Romano–Moldo–Vlachs" from Moldavia, Valachia and Transylvania in one uniform Rumanian state. (Armbruster)

p. 132:
The Slavic toponymy of Rumania, particularly in the Banat, in Transylvania, in Oltenia and Muntenia, shows the same phonetic features as the Slavic elements in the Rumanian vocabulary. Consequently, the original homeland of the Rumanian language must be sought north of the peaks of the Haemus mountains, and in territories to which Romanization expanded – thus [also] IN DACIA, and east of the present day frontier between Yugoslavia and Bulgaria.

During the early Middle Ages (approximately in the 7th–9th centuries, thus after the coming of the Bulgarians), Roman shepherds wandered from these Danubian–Moesian territories not only to the south, southwest and west, (the ancestors of the present day Arumanians, Megleno-Rumanians, and, on the Istrian peninsula, of the Istro-Rumanians), but also to the north, to mountainous Dacia (C. Daicoviciu)

pp. 145–146:
The continued presence, of long duration, of the Roman domination over a large part of southern Dacia also after the official abandonment of the province by Aurelian constitutes a highly significant documentary material for the discussion of historical problems debated so intensely as the continuity of Roman-ness north of the Danube, the development of the Rumanian language and people, the spread of Christianity in ancient Dacia Traiana, etc. If one wants to reach definitive solutions regarding these problems, historians, archaeologists, and linguists must necessarily depart from this archaeological reality. (Tudor)

p. 154:
Remains of dwelling places are very few and they could be demarcated only in strata whose age is known with certainty. They should be discovered at excavations in the centre of towns, which, however, were made only under special circumstances in connection with constructions and had so far not given results... (Horedt)

p. 168:
...if we consider the map of ancient Dacia Traiana ... we find that the region in which the Roman establishments were more dense, and consequently, Romanization more intense, coincide with the region in which the words of Latin origin are best preserved. (Puşcariu)

Now, if *sklab(ŭ)* is said here instead of general Rumanian *slab,* in this pronunciation, the ancient Latin sound system breaks through with the same strength as in the 5th century in the territory of southern France or northern Italy. (Gamillscheg)

p. 173:
... make out a common goods which both have inherited from the ancient Indo-European linguistic material (Thracian, respectively Thraco–Illyrian), indigenous in the Carpatho–Balcanic space.

In fact, the elements shared by Rumanian and Albanian are perfectly explained by common origin, by their proximity and possibility of influencing each other in the Antique Age, with Illyrian or Thracian as ancestors of Albanian, and with Daco-Moesian as the substratum of Rumanian. (Poghirc)

p. 179:
The case of the river *Bistriţa* is instructive. Its name is of Slavic origin and it

means ′fast′, in Rumanian, *′repede′*. But *Repede* is today the name of one of the tributaries of this river, in the mountainous region of its course, and this name was translated by the Slavs who settled along its shores by corresponding *Bistryca.* In this way, something has occurred which one may observe quite often in our country as well as in other countries: the ancient population accepts the new, official name given by the conquerors. (Puşcariu.)

Similarly, the name of a village in Dobrogea, *Camena,* is a Slavic translation, handed down to the language of the Rumanians, of ancient *Petra,* which appears in a Latin inscription found there (C.T. Sauciuc: *A Latin inscription* in ′Annals of Dobrogea′, XV (1934), pp. 93–112). (Puşcariu.)

Chapter IV

(M. Friedwagner: *About the Language and the Dwelling Places of the Rumanians in their Ancient Period.*)
p. 181:
Generally, however, one must maintain the idea of A UNITARY AND COHERENT LIVING SPACE also because of compelling linguistical grounds (pp. 713–714).

Linguists no longer doubt that the CENTRE of the ancient Rumanian people *(centrul vieţii române)* [= the centre of Rumanian life] was once situated in the region of the Danube, and south of the river (p. 713).

... it is Illyrian territory, in the Antique Age comprising Dardania, according to a newer definition, the country east of Montenegro: old- and southern Serbia (in its earlier frontiers) and western Bulgaria (p. 714).

North of the Danube, Roman remains may be thought to have existed in southeastern Banat; it is possible that such remains may have persisted also in the southwestern mountains of Transylvania and in northern Oltenia (Little Valachia). It needs to be shown whether this may be verified in the speech of those areas (p. 715).

...that lingustic [...] unity was possible with the people living in such a large territory in ancient times (p. 715).

(I. Popović: *History of the Serbo-Croatian Language.*)
pp. 181–182:
It can scarcely be doubted that the Rumanians lived south of the Danube (p. 62). The first Slavic elements were transferred to Rumanian in the "ancient Rumanian" period, i.e., in the era when the Rumanian language [...] yet constituted a geographical and linguistic unity (somewhere in the centre of the Balkans) (p. 200.)

If we accept the dominating assumption today, namely that the ancient home of the Rumanians was situated both north and south of the Danube, then this is based more on a general conviction rather than upon verified linguistic facts. Concrete linguistic arguments must be presented by future research because those extant today are not sufficient (p. 63).

(G. Stadtmüller: *Basic Problems of European History.)*
p. 182:
Regarding Transylvania, it is probable that the Bulgarians were there first, followed by the Hungarians and later the Rumanians. After the Linguistic Atlas by Puşcariu and research by Ernst Gamillscheg and Günter Reichenkron, however, one has to consider the possibility of small groups of provincial Romans remaining in Transylvania also after the Romans abandoned the province Dacia Traiana (271), and that they were, after the 12th century, strengthened by a massive immigration of Rumanians from the central parts of the Balkans. Such an immigration has doubtless taken place: it has been shown convincingly by non-Rumanian as well as Rumanian scholars on the basis of documents and records (p. 91)

(É. Bourciez: *Basic Concepts of Romance Linguistics.)*
p. 183:
Nevertheless, during a number of centuries, the main territory of the populations who spoke East Latin must have been south of this river: they were living in Moesia, Dalmatia, and had close contact with Italy, whose prolongation they were... (p. 135).

(B.E. Vidos: *Handbook of Romance Linguistics.*)
pp. 183–184:
On the basis of this linguistic and historical consideration, it is assumed that the Roman population retired after the abandonment of Dacia south of the Danube, and that the Rumanian language was formed there, in the Balkan peninsula. However, since almost the entire Daco-Rumanian territory is situated north of the Danube, it is assumed that the Rumanians wandered during the Middle Ages from the Balkan peninsula to the left shore of the Danube and colonized again present day Rumania (pp. 360–361).

p.184:
The great majority of the people, peasants, shepherds, and poor people, who constitute even today the largest part of the Rumanian population, have not moved to the right shore of the Danube (p. 361).

p. 196:
On the frontiers of the empire, along the Danube, as well as on the Persian frontier and on the edge of the deserts in Africa, circulation was strictly

supervised and permitted only on certain days and in certain localities, under the control of the army. Exports of weapons, iron, gold, cereals and salt were not allowed (p. 43).

pp. 198–199:
One cannot find any evidence of the continuation of linguistic contact between Dacia and the Romanized territories south of the Danube from 271 and the end of the 6th century; the assumption of H. Mihăescu on this topic is thus not based upon objective facts. Lastly, regarding the contact between the Balkans and western *Romania* by the mediation of Byzantium and Christianity (contact with which, moreover, Dacia seems to have been excluded), only the influence of the language of the state or the Church is possible, and this is something quite different from direct contact with everyday western Latin which the Balkan territories have had earlier, before their separation from the Roman empire. Under these circumstances, and contrary to what Rosetti believes (*The History of the Rumanian Language*, vol. I, 3rd edition, 1960, pp. 49–50), there is no reason to alter the opinion of Bourciez *(Éléments,* § 50, 4) nor our opinion (RLR, 71, p. 276, and RLiR, 20, p. 253 and 258; see also Väänenen, op. cit., p. 27) about the linguistic isolation of the eastern provinces following their abandonment by the Romans. Nothing in the work of H. Mihăescu seems to invalidate the theory that after 271, i.e., from the time when no more colonists came to Dacia, the linguistic changes of the West no longer spread to the Romance idiom of this ancient province, which therefore after the last quarter of the 3rd century, no longer participated in the linguistic evolution of the other parts of *Romania* and started to develop an independent language (p. 405–406).

p. 209
The funeral rite of cremation and the use of the urn, which is found among the Dacians under Roman rule as well as among the free Dacians, cannot be used to distinguish these two populations of the ancient Roman province – the newly immigrated Dacians and those who stayed in their places. The archaeological material lacks details and accuracy. (Protase)

p. 216:
In the 6th century, a uniform [material] culture dominates in Transylvania, which makes impossible to discover ethnic differences and in which both Germans and Romans take part. On the basis of the features of the settlements and of certain typical single finds and forms, it was possible to discern indications useful in the interpretation of the ethnic situation. With the disappearance of the Germans and the appearance of the Slavic culture, this possibility no longer exists. (Horedt)

p. 218:
However, there is no archaeological evidence to show that the Roman element evaded the migrating peoples by moving to far away valleys at the feet of high

mountains, because there are no finds in these areas which date from the period of the Peoples´ Migrations. (Horedt, in *Dacoromania* I, 1973, p. 144)

p. 229:
The Rumanians could, in an ancient period, use the forms with *un, um* of these toponyms (e.g., **Dumbova, *Glumboaca,* etc.). But, when the pronunciation of *ǫ* changed in Slavic, the pronunciation by the Rumanians of these toponyms was adapted to that of the Slavs. (Petrovici)

Chapter V

p. 236:
It is hardly probable that a common language existed in such a large territory, which was divided by high mountains, and in a primitive society, with insignificant economic contact between the different tribes and without a common state. (Georgiev)

Chapter VI

p. 263:
However, the massive migration of the Rumanian people to the primeval forests of the Carpathians, which in that epoch were not yet populated, did not depart from the sedentary Romans of Paristrion, but from the "Vlach" wandering shepherds of the mountainous areas of the central parts of the Balkans. Their leaders north of the Danube have largely Cuman names. Thus, the Cumans seem to have taken a considerable part in this great Vlach migration towards the north. (Stadtmüller)

SUBJECT INDEX

NAME INDEX

ERRATA

page:	line: (– *from below*)	reads:	should read:
VI	32 *and* 33	b) *and* c)	c) *and* d)
IX	3	134–136	135–136
IX	–4	pp. 299–307.	pp. 296–304.
XII	–6	Declararation	Declaration
1	–7	prolems	problems
4	9	**inerpret**	**interpret**
10	*add* after line –1: Illyrian pirates ravaging the west coast of the Peloponnesos.		
19	–6 and –12	Slavis	Slavic
25	1	(118–1185),	1184–1185),
27	1	cf. above, p. 5).	cf. above, p. 3).
28	–4	we must to go back	we must go back
37	note 2	pp. 122–127.	pp. 133–137.
41	–9	pp. 106–111).	pp. 115–119).
48	2	Latin *inuxorare*) *ammessarum*	Latin *inuxorare*); *ammessarum*
71	11	p. 39).	pp. 37-38).
84	–9	Dalmtian	Dalmatian
87	17	"relstionshipes	"relationships
88	note 2	andfeld	Sandfeld
90	–7	areras	areas
95	18	mentined	mentioned
96	11	as	ask
96	note 1	anguages	languages
106	note 4	Macre	Macrea
110	–1	p. 20).	p. 21)..
110	note 3	(emphasize	(emphasis
121	map 7	*add:* frontier of the Bulgarian language – – –	
120	–1	*add*: Miklosich recorded 2953 Istro-Rumanians. The most recent figure from the	
129	Table 5	palatailazation	palatalization
130	Table 6	condiitonal	conditional
133	6	pp. 36-37,	pp. 35-37
134	5	lagginbg	lagging
137	–11	(*cnezi*,	(*cneji*,
142	–10	Sèveres	Sévères
144	note 3	(1-13)	(1-14)
162	–6	roman	Roman

176	18	p. 155).	p. 154).
185	note 1	limba albaneza	limba albaneză
206	–3	manifesttions	manifestations
227	note 2	p. 104.	pp. 111-115.
230	note 2	cf. above, p. 193.	cf. above, p. 208.
231	5	datefrom	date from
236	7	A. Jaberg	K. Jaberg
239	11	above, p. 115).	above, p. 111-115).
239	18	p. 183)	pp. 182-183)
243	16	pp. 13, 16).	p. 16).
255	4 *and* note 2	V.I. Georgiev	V. Georgiev
278	note 1	Popescu, RR. S., *and* 1875	Popescu, R. S., *and* 1975,
288	2	Marino & Language. A. Pérez,	Marino & L. A. Pérez,

Unfortunately, most of the page numbers of the quotations in French and German are wrong in the list of their English translation (pp. 296–304). Here are the correct page numbers (in Italics):

page 296: 6 (wrong)—*5-6* (*correct*), 11—*11 n2*, 16-17—*17*
– 297: 19-20—*20*, 33—*35 n2*, *add after line 21*: *n3*, 41—*44-45*
– 298: 42—*46*, 45—*49*, 66—*72*, 77-78—*85*, 80—*87*, 97—*105*
– 299: 102 nl—*110 n4*, 122—*131*, 123—*132*, 130—*139*, 132—*141*
– 300: 145-146—*155-156*, 154—*165*, 168—*180*, *add after line 23*: *181*, 173—*186*, 179—*192*
– 301: *add after line 6*: *192*, 181—*195*, 181-182—*196*
– 302: 182—*196*, 183—*197*, 183-184—*198*, 184—*198*, 196—*211* *add*: (Jireček)
– 303: 198-199–*214* add: (Straka), 209—*225*, 216—*233*, 218—*235*
– 304: 229—*248*, 236—*255*, 263—*282*

Add to the list of English translations of quotations in French and German:

p. 9 nl — (quoted by Russu):
"The notion ´Illyrian´ is, from the very beginning, quite vague..."

p. 12 — (Stadtmüller):
"The change of language was essentially completed at the end of the 3rd century."

pp. 12–13 — (Jireček):
"In the 5th and 6th centuries, the Latin-speaking inhabitants of the Danube-area were often on the side of the Roman Church against the Emperor of Constantinople, particularly against Anastas and Justinian."

p. 18 n4 — (Sandfeld):
"This theory is entirely unacceptable and leaves many things unexplained."

p. 25 — (Slatarski):
"God has decided to give back the Bulgarians and the Vlachs their freedom and to relieve them from the yoke [under which they have lived] in many years..."

p. 43 n2 — (Coteanu):
"The history of the Rumanian language shows that the Rumanian [definite] article evolved in a similar way as did the Romance article, the change from the sense of pronoun of *ille* to that of article presented approximately the same phases in the entire Romania."

p. 44 — (Löfstedt):
"Thus, the definitive restriction and specialization of the sense occurred late and gradually."

p. 48 n1— (Densusianu):
"The conclusion to which we have arrived here is similar to that stated for thirty or so years ago by Gaston Paris in the article published first in the first volume of Romania, 11: 'Rumanian ... was in contact with the rest of the Roman territory until the Slavic invasion and was therefore exposed in the 5th and even in the 6th century to the influences which affected the rest of this territory'."

p. 104, n2 — (Puşcariu, quoted by Popović):
"If *nevastă*, 'young woman, wife', is of Slavic origin, it was most probably borrowed by the Rumanians in a period in which they started to marry Slavic women. Thus, the sense of *mi-am luat o nevastă* [I have taken a *nevastă*] was initially not 'I have taken [married] a woman' but 'I have married ... a Slavic woman'".

p. 106 — (Popović):
"...in a list of 5764 words, 1165 are of Latin origin while the number of words of Slavic origin is as high as 2361 (the rest are of Turkish, New-Greek, Hungarian, and Thracian origin), thus, 2/5 of the words are Slavic..." ... "Regarding the lexical elements, Rumanian is not a Romance but a Slavic language..."

("Basic elements", "if only the basic words are taken into consideration, from which the derivations are formed") (I.I. Russu)

p. 110 — (Schuchardt):
"it is not yet proved that Rumanian is a Romance language."

p. 142 — (Besnier, quoted by Rosetti):
[the evacuation of Dacia] "was not complete... The masses of peasants did not move... In this way is the tenacious persistence of the Latin race and language in the territory conquered by Trajan explained."

p. 184 n2 — (Popović):
..."however, the loanwords cannot be used in this case, because **the problem of the so called original Rumanian homeland (south or north of the Danube) is not yet decided** (see Chapter II, § 22) and we cannot know whether a loanword reached the Rumanian language north or south of the Danube..."

p. 190 — (IR 1960, p. 782):
The way in which the Germanic peoples dominated Dacia, their restricted numbers, the lack of any symbiosis of long duration with the Daco-Romans...

p. 213 n2 — (Popescu):
"In the 4th and 6th centuries, the Roman-Byzantine domination north of the Danube was relatively of short duration and affected only a restricted area of former Dacia."

p. 235 n1 — (Donat):
"Certainly, in contrast to what is often affirmed, such a shepherd economy would not have made possible for the Daco-Roman population to persist north of the Danube, because our shepherds would have been in security only during the summer, in the mountains, while under their long wanderings through the plains, they would have to face greater perils than the peasants living in faraway regions, in the protection of the hills and the forests."

p. 236 n1 — (Eugenia Zaharia):
"This idea belongs to the last century, when no archaeological proofs were yet available..."

p. 252 — (Puşcariu):
The maps of the *Linguistic Atlas* make for us possible to study the expansion of the Rumanians from Transylvania to all directions."